The Age
of Reason

THE AGE OF REASON

From the Wars of Religion
to the French Revolution, 1570–1789

MEIC PEARSE

The Monarch History of the Church, Vol. 5

John D. Woodbridge and David F. Wright,
Consulting Editors

MONARCH
BOOKS

Originally published in the United States of America by Baker Books in 2006. Reproduced from the original setting by agreement.

First published in the UK by Monarch Books
an imprint of
Lion Hudson plc
Wilkinson House, Jordan Hill Road,
Oxford OX2 8DR, England
Email: monarch@lionhudson.com
www.lionhudson.com/monarch

ISBN: 978-1-85424-771-1

Acknowledgments
Unless otherwise stated, Scripture quotations are taken from the Holy Bible, New International Version, © 1973, 1978, 1984 by the International Bible Society. Used by permission of Hodder & Stoughton Ltd. All rights reserved.

A catalogue record for this book is available from the British Library.

To Barrie White, best of church historians, wisest of tutors,
and to his wife, Margaret,
with grateful thanks

CONTENTS

Maps and Illustrations

PREFACE

Of the various books that I have perpetrated over the years, only one has taken longer to produce than this. The period of gestation has spanned two jobs as well as sojourns in a variety of countries; other projects have been started and finished while work on this was—theoretically, if not always actually—in progress. I am reminded of the wonderful exchange between those stars of the 1960s, Peter Cook and Dudley Moore, in which both men are reclining in deck chairs. One remarks to the other, "I'm writing a book." After a long silence, the other replies, "Neither am I."

But here it is at last, blinking in the light of destiny. Like the human race, it is doubtless insufficiently appreciative of its creator; unlike the human race, it has good cause.

In a work of this kind, which is intended to be global in its scope, it is the nature of the case that some readers will feel a little cheated. Norwegians and Icelanders, Ndebele and Ibo, Nepalese and Irian Jayans: none feature on the pages of this work (except, obviously, on this one). It was impossible to give coverage of literally every country and people group. I have sought instead to do three things. In the first place, I have tried to give *representative* treatment of developments within Christianity during the period with which this book is concerned; not all Catholic (nor all Protestant, nor all Orthodox) lands are covered, and of those that are, some are treated more fully than others. But I have attempted to tell those aspects of the story that delineate and exemplify the general pattern. In the second place, I have been concerned to focus upon *strategic* aspects, such as significant growth, contraction, or important internal development within churches. Finally, I have paid particular attention to those people, places, and activities that have had greatest effect upon the *future*—by which is included, obviously, the present. It should be added that Britain and America receive more than their fair share of coverage, partly for this last reason and partly because the book is intended especially for British and American readerships.

Of those readers whose churches and countries are covered, it is to be hoped that all will feel they have been dealt with fairly. Or, if that is too much to hope, that they have at least been dealt with no more harshly than the wretched schismatics who dare to adhere to churches rival to their own, or than the *Untermenschen* who infest the territory adjacent to the readers' beloved homelands.

My debts are far too numerous to mention. So that's enough about that. Those concerned know who they are—from the colleagues who incrementally (and entirely momentarily) depleted the ocean of my ignorance about, say, the Baltic Orthodox Church of Molvania; to the kind of friendship that can make my heart skip like a wallaby from a distance of thousands of miles; to the wonderful people of the Evangelical Church in Skopje, Macedonia, who included me in their communal life during the summer of 2003 as I struggled to write (and, some days, even succeeded); to Gary Baxter and Dr. Judy Congdon, who saved me from at least some errors concerning, respectively, art history and church music; to Dr. Tim Dowley, the long-suffering (and we do mean long!) series editor who cajoled and nurtured this volume through to the impressive artifact you hold in your hands; and last, but certainly not least, to my wife, Ann, who single-handedly packed and unpacked several houses, and baked about a thousand delicious cakes, while her feckless husband was writing a book. Or, sometimes, wasn't. I can never repay any of you (though that is information you will have been expecting), but you are, at least, hereby absolved from guilt for all of the many contestable statements that doubtless remain in the following pages.

This book treats subject matter that significantly affects the lives of each of us today. We live in the era of the "global church," in which the effects of our forebears' actions redound in ways they may hardly have dared hope for—and in some cases, could never have had reason to fear. The corruptions of the link between state and church and the bitter Protestant-Catholic conflicts of the so-called "Age of Reason" contributed toward the religious disillusion and secularization that have come to characterize most of Europe since compulsion was removed in recent centuries. Conversely, the eastward and southern expansion of Christianity in the period covered by this book has been magnified many times over. As Professor Philip Jenkins has lately argued persuasively, the twenty-first century will be dominated in no small part by the consequences of these two developments alone.[1] It is to be hoped, therefore, that the longer-term causes of such critical present realities have been covered here with at least some analytical rigor, with due proportionate weight, and, above everything, with all due seriousness.

Meic Pearse
Houghton, New York
September 2005

INTRODUCTION

The reader stands (or, more probably, sits) removed at a distance of rather more than two centuries from the French Revolution. Both the world and the position of Christianity within it have changed unimaginably since the storming of the Bastille unveiled that first appearance of aggressive secularism and its dizzying assault upon the alliance of throne and altar. The Revolution was the doorway into the modern world; its repercussions and the ideas contended for—and against—are with us still. This book, however, is concerned with an epoch beginning at the same distance in time from that event as ourselves, only in the opposite direction (that is to say, with the period beginning 1570), and traces developments down to the moment when the small tradesmen of St. Antoine, Paris, seized the Bastille prison, killed its governor, and released its handful of bewildered captives, blinking, into the light of day.

When our book opens, Pope Pius V was issuing a bull declaring Queen Elizabeth I of England deposed—and with at least some hope that it might be carried out. Though the Reformation had fractured Western Christendom, churches were still clinging to their traditional power to make and unmake secular governments. By the close of our period, that power had long since passed away. By the eighteenth century, the state churches—Catholic, Protestant, and Orthodox—were the tools, not the masters, of kings and princes. They were useful allies in governing their territories and keeping their populations in submission; that was why the rising generation of intellectuals—democrat, nationalist, and republican—was determined to break the power of the churches. It was why the muskets of the revolutionaries would be turned not just on the aristocrats but on the priests.

Massacre of French priests in 1792.

This should not be taken to imply a decline in the influence of Christianity during the two centuries under review. At the start of the era, Western Christendom was inward-looking, riven with religious strife, and obsessed with its own quarrels; at its end, the Western churches were on the threshold of an unprecedented period of missionary expansion that would see the "faith once delivered to the saints" (or, at any rate, the competing varieties of the faith developed by Europeans) spread to the uttermost parts of the earth.

Nevertheless, this is still not the whole picture, for the West is not the whole world—even if it continues to suffer under delusions to the contrary. The Christian churches of the East, living mostly under Muslim rule in Egypt, Palestine, Syria, and Persia, were, for most of our period, withering slowly under the inevitable disadvantages, both legal and social, of their circumstance. Yet they maintained their existence and perpetuated their life. Their brethren to the north and west, the Christians of Greece and the Balkans, lived under similar conditions yet had suffered somewhat less attrition because they had more recently come under the Muslim yoke. By the time our story closes, however, some of them had been reincorporated into Christendom in the form of the expanding Russian and Austrian Empires, and the day was not far distant when others, first in Serbia and Greece, then later in Romania and Bulgaria, would establish states of their own.

In Russia, the opening of our epoch saw Christian Muscovy increasingly confident of its ability to hold its own against its erstwhile infidel rulers from the east. By 1570 the Mongol hordes who had devastated the east of Europe and terrified its center in the thirteenth century had long since dissipated into small khanates and princedoms. The seventeenth and eighteenth centuries would witness the decisive reversal of the tide, with Russia putting its eastern neighbors under pressure and beginning a long period of expansion that would eventually take in vast territories to the east, beyond the Ural Mountains, and also to the south, leaving the descendants of Genghis Khan the subjects of those very Orthodox Christians whom their ancestors had conquered.

Further afield, the Americas were thinly populated in 1570. Indeed, the areas under Spanish rule were a lot more thinly populated than they had been sixty years previously, for European diseases had carried off more than three-quarters of their indigenous population. It was already clear in both North and South America, as well as in the isthmus that connected them, that the future belonged to the Europeans and their religion. Yet by the late eighteenth century, Catholicism in the lands colonized by Iberians had taken on a distinctive life of its own. In North America, by contrast, no official church had been able to impose itself, and sectarians were firmly in the saddle—a possibility that would have horrified the age of Pius and Elizabeth.

And the rest of the world? Roman Catholic—especially Jesuit—missions had proceeded apace in many parts of Asia. An underground community of their converts kept a troglodyte existence in Japan, awaiting the *parousia* of Commodore Perry. In India, the Mar Thoma Christians maintained their distinctive culture in spite of Portuguese "help." Nevertheless, many millions of people in the world beyond western Eurasia and the Americas remained in 1789, for the most part, strangers to any variety of Christianity. All of that was about to change. And, although we cannot pursue that change within these pages, we can at least attempt to discern the developments within Christianity that made it possible. For the late eighteenth century was the starting point of the worldwide expansion of Christian faith that has characterized the past two hundred years. The launching of the evangelical missionary movement, as much as the fall of the Bastille, was the threshold of the modern age.

1

CHRISTENDOM UNRAVELING

THE SCENE IN 1570 AND A GLANCE BACKWARD

Christendom in 1570 did not present an edifying spectacle. The hopes entertained by a constellation of Renaissance scholars from the early part of the century had been dashed in the fires of the Reformation and its attendant Catholic reaction. They had dreamed of a renewed, educated, enlightened Europe that would be both tolerant and united. Instead, they had witnessed growing intolerance—religious diversity leading directly to persecution and religiously motivated warfare—and disunity as the fabric of Western Christendom was torn asunder, at first over papal authority and then over a host of related issues.

Erasmus of Rotterdam, by common consent the greatest of that venerable tribe of scholars, had died in 1536, an unhappy and deeply worried man. Cardinal Contarini, the Catholic evangelical and humanist scholar, had been fortunate to die in 1542, the year that the Roman Inquisition came into existence. He was under suspicion for his attempts to achieve reconciliation with the Lutherans at Regensburg the previous year, and his writings were already proscribed by the church authorities. Philip

Melanchthon, an irenic scholar who had as a young man attached himself to the Protestant cause, was similarly unable to stem the ascendancy of the most truculent elements on his own side of the new divide. On his deathbed in 1560, he thanked God that he would soon "be freed from care, and from the fury of theologians."[1]

Tolerant and united: the very phrase, so obviously self-contradictory and yet still embraced with passion by the denizens of our universities, sums up the imperviousness of the liberal mind-set to mere facts, evidence, and experience. Tolerance can only be exercised if there is real, hard, intractable difference upon which to exercise it; conversely, unity can be achieved only by intolerance of separatism and of the opinions that make for it.

And the princes, emperors, kings, and worshipful councillors of 1570 had opted decisively for unity. To be sure, they could not agree upon the form that unity should take—so they imposed their own versions at local levels. These impositions were legitimized in the largest, most powerful, and yet most variegated part of Europe, namely the Holy Roman Empire, by the Peace of Augsburg of 1555. This treaty put an end to the latest bout of ostensibly godly fighting between the German princes with an arrangement that would come to be described by the formula *cuius regio, eius religio* (according to the prince, so the religion). Already the pattern of the future was evident: a state's confession would depend upon the decision of its ruler.

The reality, of course, was more complicated. Few popular fallacies about the past are more enduring—or more absurdly wide of the mark—than the "Queen of Hearts theory" of monarchy: the monarch as petulant child and sole decision maker, shrieking "off with his head!" at the first murmur of dissent. In point of fact, almost all rulers in early-modern Europe were heavily constrained by the wishes of their subjects. Not by all of their subjects, of course; the views of the half-starved majority counted for little in the grand scheme of things—though even they were capable of revolt if their sensitivities were outraged too deeply. But the ruler who failed to take into account the beliefs and interests of the principal noble families and wealthier burghers (who were in turn influenced by the smaller fry) was headed for trouble. The most successful were those who knew just what they could get away with and who were possessed of consciences sufficiently pliable to match the new political conditions. The name of Elizabeth Tudor comes to mind.

The Christendom of 1570 was fragmented as never before. Of course, the old fissures were still there. The Nestorian and Monophysite schisms were the most ancient of these, dating from the two centuries after the Council of Chalcedon (A.D. 451) had attempted to define the nature of Christ in terms that propelled the churches of the East—the Egyptian and Ethiopian Copts, the Armenians, and the Syrian Orthodox from Mesopotamia to Malabar—into irreconcilable dissent. Then, during the Middle Ages, the churches of Byzantium and Rome had drifted into mutual anathemas over the *filioque* and the extent of papal authority.[2] The year 1054 is often cited as the occasion of the divorce, but for most practical purposes the churches had been living apart for centuries before—and, indeed, continued to have at least some sense of communal feeling afterward. The Greek patriarch held the loyalty of the eastern and southern Slavs, while the Roman pontiff's church encompassed the Latin West as well as central and northern Europe.

Now the unity of this last ecclesiastical empire was shattered also. Martin Luther had dealt the first, and decisive, hammer blow in the years after 1517 and had incited many of the states of Germany, whether principalities or self-governing cities, to form separate churches governed from within their own frontiers. Several of the Swiss cantons had followed suit. So, too, had the Scandinavian kingdoms and many areas of the southern and eastern Baltic. In the 1530s the English king, Henry VIII, had led his country into schism from Rome. Though the Church of England remained a half-cooked form of Protestantism perpetually contested between competing factions, it was nevertheless lost to the papacy (apart from a brief attempt at recovery under Mary I from 1553 to 1558). By the 1560s Protestantism was rampant everywhere in the erstwhile papal realms except in the Mediterranean south: Calvinist Huguenots were infiltrating France, proselytizing rapidly and preparing to challenge for power; Calvinists in the Netherlands had allied themselves with local grievances against Spanish rule and raised much of the country to revolt; Scotland was fiercely contested between the old religion and the new, with the latter somewhat uncertainly in the saddle; Lutherans and Calvinists were gaining strength in Hungary and Transylvania; Protestants of several kinds were taking root in Poland. The German emperors found themselves confronted in strength by Protestantism even in their own heartlands of Austria and Bohemia.[3]

Nor was this all. The Reformation had triggered a number of radical breakaway movements, with a wide assortment of agendas—doctrinal, ecclesiological, and political. Though their enemies lumped them all together under the name of "Anabaptists," this did not begin to describe the full range of their concerns. In number and variety, they far outweighed the incidences of pre-Reformation dissent and "heresy." Although in 1570 their numbers remained modest and they found themselves persecuted everywhere, they were the true harbingers of the future, presaging the religious pluralism that would make necessary the rise of the secular state.

The Protagonists for the Soul of the West

The Catholic Church was—and is—a hierarchical institution whose structure had mirrored the hierarchy of feudal Europe during the Middle Ages. To that extent, it was eminently suited to the society that it both shaped and reflected. Like all organizations in which human beings have any hand in affairs, however, it was open to corruption, both institutional and in the personal faults of its priests, bishops, and, indeed, popes.

Although premodern social changes were incremental rather than sudden, by the early sixteenth century there had been a significant cumulative shift in the social, political, and economic structures of western Europe. In consequence, the age-hallowed structures of the Roman Catholic Church were no longer unquestionably fit-for-purpose. The newfound strength of secular governments—kings, princes, city councils—made the authority of a church governed from outside of the ruler's frontiers seem irksome. For town dwellers living in the more egalitarian atmosphere of the world of trade, the rigid hierarchy of the Roman Church spoke all too eloquently of the feudal countryside from which they had escaped; its suspicion of commerce and condemnation of usury (the lending of money at interest) hampered business. Furthermore, its central devotional activity, the Mass, was a visual spectacle and a purported miracle—just the thing for holding illiterate peasants in awe but less certain to hold the allegiance of townspeople, who might be more open to the word-centered appeal and abstract doctrines of Protestantism and its printed text, the Bible.

As for the famed clerical abuses—nepotism, sexual immorality, pluralism (the holding of more than one benefice), simony (the selling of clerical positions for money), clerical ignorance, and illiteracy—these were little worse in the early sixteenth century than they had been before. However, a rising tide of popular piety from the late fourteenth century onward meant that tolerance levels for abuses were falling as people learned to "condemn a little more, understand a little less." This, combined with an increasingly literate population's declining tolerance for clerical ignorance, was bound to spell trouble.

Lutheranism

From 1517 Martin Luther, a professor of theology at Wittenberg in Saxony, had protested about a range of issues that quickly gravitated to the core question of papal authority. After a brief demur, Luther had insisted that scriptural authority must take precedence over that of the pope. He was relieved to find a growing number of German princes inclined to agree with him and to offer him military protection from papal threats of impending incineration. Within the mostly quite conservative constraints they permitted, he was enabled to reform the churches inside their boundaries in line with his doctrinal views.[4]

This soon raised the question, of course, of what was to happen when competing exegetes understood Scripture in a different sense from Luther himself. The answer was not long in coming. During the 1520s those competitors who could find the backing of civic or princely authorities elsewhere did so, thereby producing states that championed other, non-Lutheran forms of Protestantism. Most of these are now designated as Reformed. Would-be reformers who could find no backing of this kind—and these included all of the most radical—found themselves obliged to retreat into silence or else suffer persecution if they persisted.

The Reformed

One Reformer who found civic authorities to back him was Ulrich Zwingli (1484–1531). He persuaded the leaders of Zürich, Switzerland, to permit him to reform the church within their borders. His Protestantism was more austere than Luther's, his preferred form of service simpler, his didacticism more matter-of-fact and less attentive to paradox. In essentials, however, Zwingli and Luther were at one: sinners are justified by faith and not by good works; God has predestined from before all eternity which individuals are to be saved, a choice that is as inscrutable in its results as in its causes; Scripture, not tradition or the pope, is the preeminent authority and reference point for belief and practice; the church is subject to secular government, which in turn has a duty to uphold the church and enforce adherence to it upon its subjects.[5]

Martin Bucer (1491–1551) introduced similar reforms in the somewhat more shaky political environment of Strasbourg. From 1536 to 1538 and again from 1541 onward, John Calvin (1509–1564) did likewise in Geneva. His theological systematizing, especially as reflected in his book *Institutes of the Christian Religion*, made him the preeminent force in Protestant theology in the long term, and the expressions *Reformed* and *Calvinist* are often used synonymously—as they will be, for the most part, in this book. Reformed Protestantism was on the advance almost everywhere in Europe in 1570. Its strength was in its intellectual robustness and, by virtue of its uncluttered approach, its modernity. It was also, in general, very well organized. For these reasons, it had an overwhelming appeal to the urban middle classes than did Lutheranism. For the same reasons, it was generally repugnant to peasant populations.[6]

The Radicals

Those who belonged to the second group (that is, those radicals who found no support among secular rulers) were of an infinite variety. The most noteworthy, both for their personal merits and for their future significance, were those usually described as evangelical Anabaptists. Beginning in 1525 as a breakaway from Zwingli's Reformation, they spread rapidly in Switzerland, southern Germany, Austria, and Bohemia. They did not seek the endorsement of governments (though they stood less than no chance of receiving it in any case) because they sought to establish believers' churches, that is, congregations consisting only of the personally converted. By the same token, they rejected any possibility of a Christian state. To emphasize this, they taught and practiced believers' baptism, the decisive marker between their own ecclesiology, on the one hand, and that of the Protestants and Catholics (and Eastern Orthodox as well, for that matter) on the other. These latter concurred with this judgment by uniting to persecute Anabaptists wherever they found them.

Protestant and Catholic governments were fortified in their determination by the lamentable fact that many radicals were far from peaceable. Thomas Müntzer (ca.1490–1525) was a crazed megalomaniac who saw himself as a new Daniel, preaching social revolution and the extermination of the godless—by which he meant, of course, all who disagreed with him. His emphases were sufficiently distant from those of the Sermon on the Mount as to enable the twentieth-century government of Communist East Germany to elevate him to hero status and to name streets and squares after him. Müntzer was executed for his part in the German Peasants' War of 1524–1525, but other prophets of violence appeared. From 1534 to 1535 the city of Münster, in the Rhineland, was turned into a messianic kingdom by deviant Anabaptists led by their "king," Jan Beuckels of Leyden. Predictably, it ended in a bloodbath at the hands of the authorities, though not before the Münsterites had spilt a good deal of blood on their own account.

Radicalism did not escape the stain of Münster for centuries to come. It was a handy tool for dismissing all sectarian religion—or even opinions consistent with a state church that were nevertheless more radical than the person speaking happened to like. "It will lead to another Münster." That was enough.

Later sectarianism encompassed a huge range of beliefs and practices: mysticism, secret messiahs, spiritualizing of Scripture, unitarian heresy. In general, though, it was the varieties of evangelical Anabaptism that were most successful and enduring. But all suffered persecution. After Münster, "Anabaptism" had become a catchall phrase, as mindless and wildly inexact in its usage as "fundamentalism" today, to denote opinions of which the speaker disapproved and with whose nature he or she had, ninety-nine times out of a hundred, failed to acquaint himself or herself. It had become a bogeyman.[7]

Roman Catholicism

And what of the Catholic Church itself? Had it simply stood idly by while it was robbed of such a large portion of its traditional adherents? Astonishingly, the answer, for almost the first thirty years of the Reformation, is "yes." The popes and cardinals wrung their hands, fretted and fussed, resolved that reform was necessary—and did little. Even before the Reformation broke out in 1517, many scholars and divines had been calling for the church to set its house in order by convening a general council. But there were always equally good reasons for not calling one. Those who wished to evade reform could point to the Fifth Lateran Council of 1512–1517, which had proved (from the papal viewpoint) a gratifyingly toothless, tame dog. But it was that very toothlessness that fueled demands for another, more rigorous affair. There were those in the Catholic world of the 1520s and 1530s who suspected that the papacy's failure to convene a truly reforming council was caused by a wish to remain unreformed. The popes feared that a future gathering might follow its predecessor, the Council of Constance of 1414–1418, which had put an end to a protracted schism by deposing all of the rival claimants to the papacy and appointing someone else, thereby making itself the decision maker of last resort. Pope Clement VII (1523–1534) feared that his illegitimate birth and the simony that had attended his election might cause any future council to depose him as well. And all sixteenth-century popes wished to emphasize that final authority inhered with the papal office, not with church councils.

The Holy Roman emperor, Charles V, was desperate for a council to be called in order to heal the Protestant schism and restore unity to his empire. His bitterest enemy, Francis I, the Most Christian King of France, was equally determined, for the same reason, to head off any such possibility. The weakness of the Protestant challenge in his own kingdom during the first half of the sixteenth century meant that Francis could afford domestic complacency; for Charles to have worries at home suited him very well. Vested interests at every level of the Catholic Church put a brake on reform. Although Clement's virtual imprisonment, for a while after 1525, at the hands of Charles V made it difficult for him to refuse anything the emperor might ask of him, yet he managed to eke out the delays and prevarications until the crisis had passed—and, indeed, until his death in 1534.

Yet slowly, with an air of appalled inevitability, the church crept unwillingly toward the awesome task of reforming itself. The more painless measures came first, while the patient nerved herself for the surgery to come. To begin with, several new monastic orders were created. These provided an outlet for zeal and charity, without any danger of inflicting curative pain on existing, sickly institutions.

The most successful by far of the new orders was that founded by the Spaniard Ignatius Loyola (1491–1556), the Society of Jesus (or Jesuits), which obtained papal endorsement in 1540. It was to achieve spectacular results. The Jesuits were to be the most highly educated of all the Catholic orders—or at least on a par with the long-established Dominicans, whose rivals they were. Jesuits were at the forefront of pioneering missions to Asia and missions of reclamation in Europe. More than any other body, they helped to change the Catholic Church's image of itself and to restore morale.

Cardinal Alessandro Farnese had assured the German cardinals that, if elected pope, he would convene a council at once. Instead, his first acts as Pope Paul III (1534–1549) included appointing two of his grandsons to the cardinalate. (Popes, it will be remembered, were not generally supposed to have grandchildren to appoint.) These essentials over with, however, Paul proceeded to further the cause of reform by every means at his disposal save that of personal example. So all things considered, it is perhaps less remarkable than might appear at first sight that in May 1542 he duly (or perhaps overduly) issued a bull summoning a council to convene the following November. In July he issued another bull, empowering Cardinal Pietro Carafa to establish a Roman Inquisition modeled on that of the Spanish. While the council was delayed for a further three years by a fresh outbreak of warfare between France and the Holy Roman Empire, the Inquisition began work immediately. From his modest private funds, the devoted Carafa bought property, which he fitted out as prison cells. "Even if my own father were a heretic," he said, touchingly, "I myself would gather the wood to burn him."

From December 1545 onward, however, the longed-for Council of Trent met in fits and starts over two decades and four pontificates—though it should be mentioned that when Carafa himself acceded to the papal throne as Paul IV (1555–1559) no sessions were convened, since he disapproved of councils as an affront to papal dignity and a threat to pontifical authority. Despite their mutual antipathy, both Carafa and the council represented the triumph of reform in the church. Carafa was a tenacious, determined tyrant, who slashed the papal budget and bureaucracy, closed down the whorehouses in Rome, burned any heretics he or his officials could lay their hands upon, and exerted severe discipline upon the clergy.

The Council of Trent was a little less murderous than Carafa but equally determined to cleanse the church of the corruptions that had plagued it for so long. It defined Catholic doctrine in a way that excluded the central Protestant teachings and reaffirmed many of the tenets to which the Reformers had objected. Sacraments conferred grace *ex opere operato*, actually containing the grace they signified. The church had sole right to interpret the Bible, of which the authoritative text was Jerome's Vulgate. Thomas Aquinas, the thirteenth-century Dominican theologian and mainstay of arid, late-medieval scholasticism, was reinstated as *doctor communis*. This last point was a move that bucked the trend of the previous three-quarters of a century and reversed the initial inclinations of the council itself, which had generally been in favor of critical and historical study of the biblical texts, improving clerical and lay education upon humanist lines, and seizing the intellectual high ground from the Protestants. But the council as a whole witnessed the eclipse of the Erasmian, irenic party and redefined Roman Catholicism in harsh, traditionalist, and polemical terms. It also set in motion a number of structural and educational reforms that, though they took a while to take effect, transformed the character and effectiveness of the Roman Catholic Church during the latter part of the century.[8]

The External Threat

At the start of our period, Western Christendom found itself in the midst of a prolonged internal crisis. But it was also threatened externally.

The Turkish tide was rising ever higher, and it seemed easily thinkable that the Christian culture of Europe might be swept away entirely by it. Never since the eve of the Battle of Poitiers (or Châlons) in A.D. 732, when Charles Martel had sent the Arab armies reeling back south of the Pyrenees, had the prospect of an Islamic Europe seemed so likely.

By the time Constantinople finally fell to the Turks in 1453, it had long been reduced to a mere island of Christendom in an Ottoman Muslim sea. Beginning in 1345, the Turks had advanced far into Europe. Famously, they had defeated the Serbs at Kosovo Polje in 1389. The following two generations saw all of the southern Balkans pass into Turkish hands.

The Turks did not stop there. Most of Croatia and the Dalmatian coast fell to the Ottoman forces in the early sixteenth century and Belgrade was captured in 1521. For a while the Turks were held along the Danube, but in 1526 they moved north again and crushed the Hungarian army at the Battle of Mohács. Transylvania and Moldavia fell into their hands.

No one knew it at the time, but the Turks were almost at the high-water mark of their success. Though they made dangerous forays yet further to the north and west, and would twice besiege Vienna, their territorial expansion was at an end. But it had brought them very far indeed. Hungary and Croatia were reduced to mere vestiges of their former territory; the Turks shared a common border with Poland.

The sense of anxiety about the possibility of Christian collapse had been building for over a century. To the Christians' south, Islam had long dominated North Africa. To their east were the Tartars, still hemming in Muscovy and still bearing the folk-memory of Genghis Khan. To the north was frozen ice, and to the west was the limitless ocean. The Christians were trapped between the infidels and the elements. And from the southeast, the Muslims were advancing!

It has often been suggested that the fifteenth-century explorers were motivated, in part, by the desire to escape this growing Islamic encirclement of Christendom and to make contact with non-Muslims in the distant parts of Asia. Might it not be possible to sail down the west coast of Africa and perhaps find the fabled Christian priest-king, Prester John? Failing that, there might at least be potential allies to the south of the Islamic world who could aid them against the Muslims. The Portuguese Prince Henry the Navigator seems to have thought so. The reality was nearly as good as the hope. Africa had a southern tip, and one could sail around it to reach India. Columbus, famously, had tried in 1492 to reach the East by sailing west, with consequences for the spread of Christianity, which we shall notice briefly in chapter 3 and at much greater length in chapters 11, 12, and 13. But part of Columbus's reason for undertaking his enterprise was to establish a route to India that would be free of Muslim control.

No account of European Christendom at this period makes any sense, and no empathy with the state of mind of sixteenth-century Christians is possible without a clear recognition of the slow, gnawing, gut-wrenching anxiety experienced by millions of people—and especially by the inhabitants of central and Germanic Europe—that their entire culture was about to be extinguished beneath an utterly alien Muslim tide.

It was this gnawing fear that injected the debates of the Reformation with such venom. God was judging Christendom for its sins by sending the Turks against them. The meaning of this judgment could cut several ways. In Protestant eyes, it was the moral and doctrinal corruptions of the Catholic Church that had caused this outpouring of divine wrath; the Reformation would put the Christians' house in order and appease an angry God. So Catholics who refused to see the truth and join the Reformation were, whether they recognized it or not, agents of Satan. In Catholic eyes, however, it was the Protestants who were making the situation a hundred times worse; if Christendom were deserving of judgment before 1517, how much more so after the sins of heresy and schism had become so rampant? And by dividing Christian forces and diverting Christian energies, the Protestants were making the Turks' task all the easier. Both Catholics and Protestants agreed, though, that the various radicals were the most dangerous of all agents of the devil, and that to suffer them to exist was positively inviting a Turkish invasion.

In 1571, however, Christian spirits were suddenly raised when combined Christian forces, led by the Spanish, inflicted a crushing defeat on the Turkish navy at the Battle of Lepanto. The event was unprecedented, but the European anxiety was not lifted overnight. In retrospect it can be seen that Lepanto marked something of a watershed, that the Christians' military technology had finally caught up with that of the Ottomans at the very moment when the latter were about to enter a period of internal decline and, as future centuries would show, decadence. None of this was obvious at the time. (Indeed, the Turkish assaults upon Vienna still lay in the future.) The Europeans knew only too well that they had occasionally bested the Turks in battle before but that, for every time they had done so, they had lost on many more occasions. However gratifyingly spectacular, Lepanto might prove to be just a flash in the pan.

Only on the easternmost fringes of Christendom, so remote from the centers of power as scarcely to matter to them, were those fundamentals beginning to shift. For centuries the Slavic inhabitants of central Russia had been subject to the Tartars—at first to their overlordship and then, even after the rise of Muscovy as a powerful state, at least to their continuing raids and depredations. The conversion of Berke, Khan of the Golden Horde, to Islam in the thirteenth century had set the pattern for the Tartars on the Volga River; Russian Orthodox Christians continued to feel Islam as a threatening presence.

The tide began to turn in 1552 when the young Grand Duke of Muscovy, Ivan IV, who had recently had himself designated first Tsar of all the Russias, led an expedition that devastated the city of Kazan, capital of the principal Muslim khanate, slaughtered most of its inhabitants, forcibly converted the survivors, and resettled the city with Russian Christians. The governor, Yedigar-Mohammed, was one of few survivors. He was taken back in triumph to Moscow, where he submitted to baptism by immersion the following February (a hole was dug specially in the ice of the Moscow River), insisting in response to Metropolitan Macarius's interrogations, and with no obvious attempt at irony, that he was not taking this step in response to any outside pressure.

In the countryside around Kazan, the conversions of humbler folk from Islam to Christianity followed similar patterns of enlightenment; rebellious tribesmen were killed by the thousands during the winter of 1553–1554, a slaughter that induced many of the survivors to embrace the faith of their conquerors. The Church of the Intercession of the Holy Virgin (later called the Cathedral of Basil the Blessed) was built in the central square of Kazan; other churches were dotted around the city. In 1555 the area was established as a diocese. The khanate of Astrakhan swiftly followed, leaving the Christians in possession of the entire course of the Volga and access to the Caspian Sea.

In the northeast, the tide of Islam had—for the next four hundred years, at least—been stemmed decisively. During the later part of the century, Russian expeditions pressed relentlessly eastward, across the Urals and into Siberia. Amid the snowy wastelands, Christendom was expanding.[9]

Under Infidel Rule

The Christians of the Balkans were not the only churches subject to the rule of unbelievers. The churches of Africa and Asia had for centuries held the status of minorities, surviving on the sufferance of rulers who were animists, polytheists, Hindus, Zoroastrians, Buddhists, or Confucians.

Overwhelmingly, however, the churches of the south and east found themselves adrift in Muslim societies. As such, they were *dhimmi,* "protected people," because of their adherence to the Scriptures and to the God of Ibrahim, or Abraham. (Jews under Muslim rule held the same status.) But they suffered all manner of legal disadvantages as well as the long, slow cultural attrition with Islam. Furthermore, any inter-communal frictions or violence could have only one possible outcome—at least until European bossiness began to exert itself against Muslim governments during the eighteenth and nineteenth centuries, thereby re-tilting the scales.

The rise and rapid military spread of Islam in the seventh century had overwhelmed the churches of North Africa and of the Near East. They had survived, but they continued to diminish during the course of the following centuries. Though their disaffiliation with Rome allowed their Muslim rulers to treat them relatively kindly, as posing no potential fifth column for foreign enemies, they were, by the same token, isolated and at the mercy of their domestic lords. Furthermore, they lacked unity among themselves; it was possible to perceive them as relatively local faiths. As such, they possessed the strength of stubbornness that goes naturally enough with enshrining venerable historic cultures. But they were mostly bereft of the universalizing drive that could alone give them expansionist vigor.[10]

The Copts, in theory, championed the Monophysite theology—that Christ was possessed of only one nature, which was divine—a theory that sixth-century Byzantium had rejected. In practice, as the name "Copt" suggested, they enshrined the religious culture of pre-Islamic, non-Hellenic Egypt. By the thirteenth century, their numbers had been whittled down to 7 percent of the population, a figure more or less maintained since—though such statistics are notoriously debatable and subject to distortion. (A French observer in the nineteenth century estimated that Christians were 8 percent of the population; current levels may be as low as 6 percent, as claimed by the Egyptian government, or as high as 20 percent, as claimed by some Christians.)[11]

By the start of our period, Egypt was a loosely attached province of the Ottoman Empire, having been seized in 1517. It was ruinously taxed and inefficiently overgoverned. But, thanks to the invasion, the tendency of the late medieval Mameluk rulers to display their Muslim piety by persecuting Christians had been thwarted. Indeed, under the Ottomans, Copts were particularly prominent government officials, enforcers of overtaxation, and instruments of overadministration.

The historic churches of Sudan-Nubia and Ethiopia were also Coptic, though the former had been pushed toward the edge of extinction by Muslim incursions before the start of our period, surviving only in outlying villages. The Ethiopians, too, had faced severe Muslim pressure during the 1530s and 1540s. Whereas the Sudanese had been overcome by Arab raiders, the Ethiopians faced the might of the Turks. Though they suffered the loss of churches and the systematic destruction of many of their ancient manuscripts, the guerrilla warfare of their young king, Claudius, was vindicated in 1542 with a crushing defeat of the Turkish general, Ahmad Grañ.

The Syrian Orthodox (often known as Jacobites after an early bishop, Jacob Baradaeus) espoused the same theology as the Copts. But in reality it had been, as with their coreligionists of the Nile delta, a cultural expression of the faith; its adherents came from those eastern borderlands of the Byzantine Empire where the Greek language gave way to Syriac and Aramaic. Sixth- and seventh-century chroniclers of ecclesiastical matters in Asia Minor had recognized this quite frankly; in their terminology, *Greek* and *Chalcedonian* were synonymous terms. So too were *Syrian* and *Monophysite*. During the Middle Ages, the Syrian church had suffered badly from persecution, massacre, isolation, internal splits, and conversions to Islam. By the sixteenth century it numbered, at most, a few hundred thousand people, though the centuries of Ottoman rule, beginning with the conquests in western Asia by Selim I (1512–1520) and Suleiman the Magnificent (1520–1566), saw a period of surprising growth in Iraq, Syria, Lebanon, and Palestine.[12]

One other area of historic Syrian Orthodox strength, Kerala in southern India, was home to about 100,000 Christians. The main threat to them came, not from the surrounding Hindus, but from the Portuguese who had come to offer them "help" of a kind and a degree that were to prove nearly fatal.

The Nestorian church had long held the allegiance of the Indian Christians, who claimed to have originated from the evangelism of the apostle Thomas in the first century. Certainly, Christianity was in existence there by around A.D. 200. From the fourth and fifth centuries onward, the Indian churches had been heavily dependent upon those of Mesopotamia and Persia, and there is strong evidence that many of their members were, in fact, Persian immigrants, who brought their Nestorian form of Christianity with them. For centuries the Indians had looked to their brethren in western Asia for a supply of bishops—a reliance that was often disappointed and repaid with neglect.

A document dating from the turn of the fifteenth and sixteenth centuries, one of very few from the period to survive, records a delegation from the Indian Christians to the catholicos (or primate) of Seleucia-Ctesiphon requesting that a new metropolitan be appointed for their long-vacant see of Malabar. Two monks, Mar Thomas and Mar John, were duly consecrated and sent to southern India, where they were received joyfully. Further appointees followed shortly afterward.

The Indian Christians could not know it at this moment of jubilation, but their nemesis was already at the door. In 1498 Vasco da Gama reached Calicut, interested primarily in wresting the monopoly of the spice and pepper trade between India and Europe from the Egyptians. Yet the meeting of original sellers and final buyers portended much more than merely cutting out the middleman; immediately, the relationship began to have religious effects.

The Christian leaders of Cochin, perceiving the potential in the Europeans' superior weaponry, approached da Gama on his second voyage in 1502, asking for protection by their fellow Christians against their Muslim and Hindu rivals. The Indian Christians complained that they had quite recently had self-rule as a Christian kingdom of Diamper but that, when the royal house died out, power had been seized by the Raja of Cochin.

The Portuguese were just embarking upon sending an endless flow of soldier-adventurers to establish an empire in the East. Many of the soldiers settled in India and married, bequeathing a variety of Lusophone surnames, which persist to this day. They were accompanied by a variety of Catholic missionaries: Franciscans, Dominicans, Augustinians, Carmelites, and others. But it was the Jesuits who would leave the most indelible mark upon the *Padroado*: the Portuguese dominance over and transformation of the ancient Christianity of southern India.

As the two sides got to know each other better, mutual delight gave way to irritation and worse. The Indian Christians would not venerate images, considering such behavior to be as idolatrous as that of their Hindu neighbors. Nor would they reverence Mary as "Mother of God," but only as "mother of Christ"—reflecting their Nestorian heritage. Their clergy wore no distinctive dress and, without the dubious benefit of Augustine's identification of sexual procreation with the passing on of original sin, were allowed to marry and have families.

The Portuguese were appalled. But the Indians found the low standard of moral life among the rough soldiery to be no less scandalous. A whole host of ceremonial differences and cultural misunderstandings exacerbated the tensions. While Mar Jacob, a long-lived bishop sent by the patriarch of Babylon, kept relations between the two sides on a frosty but stable basis during his lifetime, things degenerated after his death around the middle of the sixteenth century, eventually leading to catastrophe for the Indian Christian tradition within a few decades.[13]

The subcontinent was not the only land upon which European Christians were beginning to make an impression by the start of our period. Missions had already commenced in many of the African coastlands around which the Portuguese had passed on their way to India, with effects we shall consider in chapter 3. The real impact of Christianity upon North America still lay in the future, but its mark further south, in the Caribbean and in Central and South America, was already deep and permanent.

Much of that permanence was a result of the savage destruction and catastrophic epidemics that followed in the wake of the Spanish and Portuguese conquests from 1492 onward. The surviving population was so gravely weakened and demoralized, as well as so powerless, that it could do little but accept, whether merely outwardly or with inner conviction, the God of their conquerors. That those conquerors had established themselves as a numerically significant portion of the population only made that process easier. Again, this is a process the ramifications of which we shall examine in more detail in chapter 3. In the meantime, it should be noted that the role of the church was more than merely that of an aider and abettor in conquest and massacre. The Christianization was compulsory, but the clergy frequently took the side of the natives in seeking to protect them from continuing mistreatment at the hands of the conquerors—a fact that lends their record a moral ambiguity that continues to be debated.

In summary, the Christian world of 1570 was one in which authentic Christianity had been subverted by the power of the sword. Too many of its adherents appeared to have taken too much to heart—and misinterpreted—Christ's dictum that "the kingdom of heaven suffereth violence, and the violent take it by force" (Matt. 11:12 KJV). Europe had already entered a period of chronic religious warfare; it was a process that would continue for another three quarters of a century. In the Americas, Christianity was being promoted at the point of a sword—or at least was coming in closely behind swords that had been wielded in the hunt for gold, slaves, and empire. Only in Asia were attempts at Christianization mostly peaceful—and that because the Europeans could not feel the thrill of mastery in force of arms that was already theirs in the Americas. Or not yet.

If the global picture of Christianity from a moral perspective was unedifying, the picture in terms of changing strengths and weaknesses was more mixed. In Europe, Christianity was besieged and in danger of being eclipsed by Islam. In North Africa, the Middle East, and western Asia, Christian minorities were declining and under threat. In the Americas, parts of Asia, and sub-Saharan Africa, a period of expansion was underway. It is a pattern so remarkably similar to the present (no matter how different the numbers and proportions) as to give any thoughtful person pause for reflection.

2

CONTESTED TERRITORY

THE AREAS OF CONFLICT BETWEEN
PROTESTANTISM AND CATHOLICISM
(1570—1609)

In principle, Protestantism and Catholicism were in conflict every-where in the lands of Latin Christendom in the last third of the sixteenth century. But in practice, certain areas were "safe" for one side or the other. Catholicism never really seemed likely to recover Scandinavia, for example—or at least not unless and until all of the other Protestant lands had fallen to re-Catholicization first. Conversely, there were a few brave Protestant souls in the states of Italy and the Iberian Peninsula, but they faced stiff persecution, and few pragmatists were expecting a Reformation there anytime soon. In England, Queen Elizabeth I faced the plausible threat of assassination by those who wished to replace her with a Catholic relative (such as Mary Queen of Scots). But most of her Catholic subjects wanted nothing more than a quiet life; they preferred to keep their heads down (or rather, on) and leave the plotting to zeal-ots who were willing to deal treasonably with foreign powers. Short of invasion from outside (a possibility we shall have cause to notice later in this chapter), the Reformation in England was assured, at least by the century's end, even if Protestant paranoia continued to fear otherwise. This left large areas of the European continent in hot dispute. The Netherlands and France both suffered ferocious warfare in the late sixteenth century, in which the conflict over religious identity was a primary ingredient. If the Dutch and French wars represented Catholic struggles to contain Protestant growth, wars in Germany and central Europe were aimed at reversing Protestant gains and regaining people and places that had been lost by the papacy. These areas avoided actual fighting, for the most part, but the battle between the new confessions and the old continued by other means, in a "cold war" that proved to be merely an extended prelude to the violent cataclysm of 1618–1648. Spain and England also found themselves locked in asymmetrical struggle with one another until the early seventeenth century. During some periods the confrontation between them was direct; sometimes, however, each played the part of meddling and malicious neutral in conflicts in which the other was engaged elsewhere. On all occasions, the motivating force that gave the contest its venom was religious.

The Netherlands

Until 1555 the territories broadly comprising the modern Netherlands and Belgium formed part of the huge empire of Charles V. But in old age he divided his realms between his son, Philip (the Netherlands, Spain, and parts of Italy), and his brother, Ferdinand (the Holy Roman Empire, i.e., Germany, Austria, Bohemia, and Moravia). From this time onward the Dutch provinces were essentially an appendage of the Spanish Crown. Along with northern Italy, this region was the most economically developed part of Europe, with Antwerp (population 90,000) its greatest and busiest port.

It was perhaps surprising that the Netherlands had been touched but little by the growth of Lutheranism during the 1520s to 1540s. The various Dutch provinces shared a common language—"Base Almayne" as the English called it—with those regions of north Germany most welcoming to Protestantism, as well as many elements of the same culture. They also had a relatively high density of towns and cities, and a commercial economy—both good predictors of susceptibility to Protestant ideas. But the piety of the general population tended to be Erasmian, tolerant, and easygoing; the two hundred or so *rederijkerkamers* encouraged an atmosphere of free discussion that would be as ill-disposed to the new, Protestant rigidities as to harsh reassertions of the old orthodoxies.

If Luther's Reformation made little impression in the Netherlands, the fact was perhaps not unconnected with the strength of homegrown alternatives to Catholicism, which had developed at about the same time. Cornelis Hoen and Hinne Rode were the most prominent leaders of Dutch sacramentarianism, a fast-growing movement during the 1520s and early 1530s, which encouraged lay participation, denied Catholic doctrines of transubstantiation, and fostered biblicism. Sacramentarian doctrines went much further than Luther had gone and taught that the communion elements were a memorial of Christ's death, not a physical manifestation of his body. Luther's implacable hostility to such rationalist notions, expressed in his famous preference for "drinking pure blood with the Pope rather than pure wine with Zwingli," served to distance sacramentarians from early German Protestantism.[1]

In the early 1530s, most of this sacramentarian movement had moved over to Anabaptism under the apocalyptic preaching of Melchior Hofmann. Unfortunately, however, Hofmann's ideas included a heterodox Christology (he taught that Christ did not take his humanity from Mary but brought it with him from heaven) and introduced much instability, including a tendency to violence. The Melchiorites fragmented into factions soon enough, with the largest group realizing the potential for violent revolt (by seizing the city of Münster) and being massacred for their pains.

From the mid-1530s onward, the leaders of a pacifist-biblicist faction worked tirelessly to reconstitute the shattered remains of Dutch Anabaptism into an evangelical movement. Though still vulnerable to its own internally divisive tendencies, the anarchic atmosphere of the early 1530s gave way slowly to the more organized structures built by outstanding leaders such as Menno Simons and Dirk Philips. Such structures were better equipped to bear the heat of the persecution that continued to hound them and kept numbers low: we know of only forty-four Anabaptist cells in Flanders in the 1550s and early 1560s, most of them small (the largest, at Ghent, numbering only seventy people).

By this time, however, a new form of Protestantism was making its presence felt in the Netherlands. As with the evangelical Anabaptists, organization was the key to the survival and progress of the Reformed, or Calvinist, churches. Most of their early growth was in the French-speaking (or Walloon) areas. Just twelve such churches had been established by 1561, when a confession of faith was tossed over the wall of Tournai Castle at night with a letter to King Philip II attached. Guy de Bray, the pastor of the Tournai congregation, was its author, convinced that "the king will see that the Reformers are neither schismatics, nor rebels, nor heretics, but believers in Jesus Christ and in his Church, as it was before it was corrupted by human inventions, and in Holy Scripture."

Philip, of course, saw nothing of the kind. He was unimpressed by this extraordinary postal delivery and, in any case, was rather partial to the corruptions and human inventions to which his correspondent referred. Equally unsurprisingly, the writer's coreligionists were more impressed with the document's orthodoxy and adopted it as their standard of belief—the Belgic Confession of Faith—from 1565, following which it was read aloud at each Reformed synod and had to be signed by each new elder or deacon upon accepting office.

It was this desire for organizational unity and cohesion that assisted the Calvinist advance and prevented morale from crumpling under the weight of persecution. A tight cell system of church government and a hierarchy of consistories and synods also contributed to the same end.

The growth was further augmented by an inrush into the southern Netherlands of French Protestants fleeing the massacres of their co-religionists in the early 1560s. By 1566 there were approximately three hundred Reformed communities or cells in the country. In the city of Ghent the Calvinists constituted an eighth of the population, and they were well established in most of the other main towns and cities. In Antwerp, they had separate churches for Walloons and Dutch-speakers. Being the cosmopolitan place that it was, Antwerp also had a significant number of *marranos*, Spanish and Portuguese Jews who had nominally become Christian under extreme pressure. These were inclined to favor the Protestants, and some of them gave advice on strategies for avoiding detection or for gaining toleration. The authorities found it all quite unnerving.

The year 1566 saw the first outbreak of that series of hostilities known collectively as "the Dutch revolt." With occasional pauses for breath, it was to last until 1609, when an intermission was declared for twelve years, that is until 1621. When that period had elapsed, each side was as good as its word and resumed the violence (to little territorial effect) for a further twenty-seven years.

The rebellion had three main causes. In the first place, the nobility resented the centralizing policies of the Crown and its regent, Philip II's half-sister Margaret of Parma. All of the European monarchies were attempting to assert greater central control over their territories during the sixteenth and seventeenth centuries, and everywhere the process generated conflict. Philip was less sensitive in his approach than was wise.

In the second place, economic woes unfolded over the Netherlands during the mid-1560s: the English queen had transferred her country's cloth exports from Antwerp to Emden, creating unemployment in the former; war in the Baltic had cut off the grain imports from those regions on which the Dutch urban-dwellers depended; poor weather created harvest failure at home. In consequence, the price of wheat in Flanders rose by 200 percent during 1565.

But the third cause of the revolt was the resentment stirred up by religious persecution. Anticlericalism ran far wider among the Dutch population than simply among those inclined to embrace Protestantism. The Catholic clergy, as yet unimproved by the reforms envisaged at the Council of Trent, received little respect in the Netherlands. Clerical absenteeism reached 40 percent in some areas, and those who actually served were not, in general, famed for their learning and sanctity. The laity in some rural areas had long required their priests to marry—however unofficially and whatever the church authorities might try to insist upon—as the surest way of keeping their own wives unmolested. It was this splendid pragmatism and clear-eyed contempt for high-mindedness that were outraged by the official policy of renewed, vigorous persecution of the Protestants in their midst. Executions of Protestants at Valenciennes in 1562 and at Antwerp in 1564 provoked riots. When the government of Margaret recruited a special militia from the craft guilds in the summer of 1566, the enlisted men, while declaring themselves ready to defend the royal authority, were not prepared to defend the clergy from attack.

The first and third causes mentioned here (that is, resentment at centralizing policies and anger at persecution) tended to merge into one another. The reorganization and expansion of the Inquisition from the late 1540s gave the inquisitors powers to encroach upon the jurisdictions of local authorities. This was most acutely felt when heresy was redefined as a species of treason, thereby allowing central government to withdraw such cases—which were now very numerous—from local officials. Some towns tried to exclude the inquisitors, and the city of Bruges even found a pretext to arrest two of them. In much of Brabant the Inquisition was reduced to making arrests only in rural areas where local authorities were too weak to resist. After 1549 the government claimed the property of condemned heretics and this, too, was alienated from the town if the heretic was tried elsewhere. Angry citizens responded to all of this by refusing to denounce their neighbors—a reticence that naturally hindered the inquisitors in their work. Philip wondered, in a letter of October 1565 to Margaret of Parma, "whether [the heretics] ought not to be executed in secret in some way or other (though it is true that a public execution also serves to set an example)." By that time Peter Titelman, one of the provincial inquisitors, had been reduced to making his arrests at night or during thunderstorms, the inclemency of the elements being far preferable to that of the citizenry.

The following month a group of nobles, including the Prince of Orange and his younger brother, Louis of Nassau, the Calvinist brothers Jean and Philippe de Marnix, and the Count of Brederode, sent an open letter to the king demanding a change in religious policy. They spent the winter canvassing support, so that in April a group of two hundred nobles rode into Brussels to bully Margaret of Parma into submission. Crisis loomed. Although one of her ministers told her not to fear *ces gueux*, "these beggars," Margaret found herself intimidated anyway. She gave her assent to their principal demand enshrined in the so-called Compromise, according to which persecution of Protestants would be suspended pending fresh instructions from Madrid.

Despite the celebrations that ensued upon this agreement, famine now intervened to remove any threat of tranquility. The food shortage had been increasing since the winter of 1564–1565, and by the summer of 1566 it had reached a critical point. Popular receptivity to Calvinist propaganda increased sharply in the climate of hysteria and desperation. In August iconoclastic rioting broke out, despite the advice of the more sober heads among the Reformed ministers.

Forced to act, Margaret raised troops to suppress the disorder, whereupon several Protestant nobles joined the rebels. The revolt had begun. From the outset, the issues involved in the conflict were far wider than just religious dissent, but the Protestants were the irreducible core of the rebel forces and were to remain so during the eighty years of conflict that ensued. Philip shared this perception. He told his ambassador in Rome that "I have preferred to expose myself to the hazards of war . . . rather than allow the slightest derogation from the Catholic faith and the authority of the Holy See."

The brief opening phase ended in the spring of 1567 with the comprehensive defeat of the insurgents. The respite from trouble was temporary, however. The ostensible peace that followed saw all kinds of political and religious maneuvering, including the Prince of Orange's firm alignment with the Protestant cause (as opposed to his previous mere pleading to abate the persecution). In June the Duke of Alva, Margaret's son and Philip's most feared military commander, led a force of 9,000 north from

Milan along the so-called "Spanish Road" that wound its way between French and imperial territory. In doing so he passed by the city of Geneva, Calvin's erstwhile home, which Pope Pius V had implored Philip to conquer. Philip, however, permitted himself at least some derogation from the authority of the Holy See and declined to attack a target that had been hastily reinforced by its terrified inhabitants and that, despite its symbolic value, could only distract him from the task at hand.

To say that the Duke's arrival in Brussels was greeted by a show of maternal affection would be an exaggeration: Margaret was appalled at this display of force and what it signified. Having put down the initial outburst of Protestant defiance, her son's arrival at the head of a new, foreign army could only portend a harsh military crackdown.

She was right: it did. During the following months a special tribunal was established for the trial and execution of rebels and Calvinist ministers. The processes of government were further centralized. Alva was anxious that the new, strident, earnest, Tridentine (i.e., emanating from the Council of Trent) Catholicism should replace the easygoing, Erasmian variety that had predominated hitherto.

His immoderation provoked a second outburst of the revolt, which a more pacific policy would have allowed to subside. Spanish rule, which Protestants had found tyrannous for religious reasons, was now perceived by a wider public as tyrannous for its vindictiveness and for economic reasons.

The second act of the drama commenced in Brill on (appropriately enough) April Fool's Day, 1572. The beginning was not auspicious. The little port was captured by bands of brigands styling themselves the "Sea Beggars," in ironic reference to the *gueux* of 1566, but they were pitifully few in number, a mixture of run-of-the-mill bandits and refugees from the official fury. They also insisted that they were Calvinists.

Alva famously responded, when told of the landings, *No es nada*—"It's nothing." To describe this assessment as flawed would not, on the whole, be unjust; the pinprick raids, as the Sea Beggars took one tiny coastal strip after another, marked the beginning of a military comeback that would cause half of the Netherlands to be lost to Spanish rule forever.

A week after taking Brill, the rebels captured Flushing from its token garrison. This port was the key to Zeeland and commanded the entrance to the Scheldt. Once there, the rebels were rapidly joined by a motley assortment of English and Huguenot adventurers. Louis of Nassau saw the possibilities in the new situation and opened a new front the following month by returning, at the head of a force of French Huguenots, to Mons in the south of the country. Alva concentrated his forces on this latter threat, leaving the Sea Beggars a free hand to spend the summer capturing small, watery towns across Zeeland and Holland.

Spanish brutalities that autumn (Zutphen was sacked and Naarden was burned down, its inhabitants massacred) made surrender an even less attractive option for those who continued to hold out; they stiffened their resistance. The pattern was emerging that would characterize the rest of the revolt: the inability of the Spanish elephant to trample all of the pygmies at once; the counterproductivity of attempting to rule by terror; the willingness of moderate Catholics (and most Dutch Catholics were moderate) to help their Protestant fellow citizens against a cruel, foreign ruler; the tendency for Protestantism to be pushed by events—and to push itself—into the central role in the rebellion.

Many—perhaps most—pitched battles were won by the Spanish. But always their enemies were able to regroup, to flee over the border into German Protestant principalities, or to sail away to sea. The Sea Beggars themselves seldom lost control of the coast and so had the advantage of cutting off military supplies and reinforcements from their enemy; for Alva, the only sure source of help was from the long, slow, vulnerable Spanish Road snaking its way up from northern Italy.

The most notorious incident in the long, protracted conflict was the "Spanish Fury" in Antwerp in 1576. For eleven days the mutinous, unpaid troops ran wild in the commercial, heavily Protestantized center of trade and wealth. By the end of it, 7,000 of its citizens were dead. The effects were shattering. Seven years later, when the Duke D'Alençon's French troops attempted to rally Catholics in the same city with cries of "Long live the mass!" the citizens, Catholic and Protestant alike, united to rout them. Protestantism, or at least a toleration of it, had become a key element of the common cause.

The commercial dominance of the city of Antwerp failed to survive the shattering blow of 1576 and the continued violence of the rest of the century. Those with most to fear, such as Protestants, or most to lose, such as traders and printers (and they were often the same people), fled north into territory that was more securely in rebel hands. The city of Amsterdam grew rapidly and proved even more variegated in its population than the metropolis from which so many of the new arrivals had fled. Almost one in six of all bridegrooms in Amsterdam during 1586–1601 were southern immigrants, half of those from Antwerp alone. Most of the 320 largest depositors in the city's Exchange Bank were likewise from the south. So were two-thirds of the known teachers in the schools and University of Leiden during 1575–1630 and just over two-thirds of all of the publishers and booksellers known to have been active in the United Provinces

"Spanish Fury": sack of Antwerp.

during the same period. The cloth trade in Leiden grew from practically nothing in 1570 to 100,000 pieces per annum by the 1620s, as industry and population moved northward to a climate of religious toleration. Ironically the northern part of the Netherlands, because it was the center of revolt, became most solidly Protestantized by these changes while the south, where the Reformed had made so much initial progress, was deserted by the new converts and remained in Spanish hands—and so, in the long run, Catholic.

Distressing though it is for academic theologians, the development of doctrine has had a habit, throughout the long history of the church, of following practice at least as regularly (indeed, more regularly) than practice following precept. And, after two decades of resisting Catholic governments by force, the Calvinists were developing a theology to justify armed rebellion. The Reformed had always approved the use of lethal force against misbelievers. But such coercion was to be used only by government, once the secular authorities had themselves been persuaded to adopt the Reformation. This left the issue of what was to be done when they had not been so persuaded and were persecuting the Protestants. Under such circumstances, Calvin had mostly urged that it was the lot of the godly to suffer until such time as the magistrates were converted; only then would wrath be brought to bear upon their opponents.

In 1579, however, Philippe du Plessis-Mornay produced his *Vindiciae contra Tyrannos* (Protection against Tyrants) to justify insurrection against an ungodly (that is, a Catholic) ruler who was, ipso facto, a tyrant. It was "not only lawful for Israel to resist a king who overturns the Law and the Church of God, but if they do not do so, they are guilty of the same crime and are subject to the same penalty."[2] Du Plessis-Mornay's conflation of Israel with "the Church" was hardly accidental; in Calvin's own thought, every Christian kingdom was hypothesized to have entered a "covenant" with God at some stage (usually unspecified, but presumed to be the point of first Christianization in the early Middle Ages, in kingdoms that had little or no continuity with those existing in the sixteenth century). Du Plessis-Mornay went on to argue that the people as a whole and the junior officials of the kingdom, collectively and individually, "gravely sin against the covenant with God if they do not use force against a king who corrupts God's law or prevents its restoration." So military rebellion against idolatrous, papist rulers was not merely permissible but positively obligatory.

By that year in any case, those Dutch provinces where the rebels were in control signed the Union of Utrecht to become the United Provinces, thereby making the Calvinists the legitimate magistracy. Since the new federation was ostensibly Reformed in worship, Catholicism was officially forbidden and violence could be used against it, with or without du Plessis-Mornay's theories. In fact, however, this viciousness was no more than a pious aspiration, for Catholics formed the bulk of the population; there was no question of persecuting those moderate Catholics on whose support the revolt against Spanish rule depended. Dutch pragmatism was to reign supreme after the Reformation as well as before it. The ghost of Erasmus was simply too hard to shake off.

In consequence, the Netherlands was to become the first truly pluralist society in Europe. One Swiss observer in the 1570s thought that the Dutch population was 33 percent Calvinist, 33 percent Catholic and 33 percent Anabaptist. Apart from being too neat, however, this greatly overstates Anabaptist strength and understates that of the Catholics. But it does indicate the fact that the unique Dutch circumstances both created pluralism and acted as a magnet to those who feared persecution elsewhere. The Spanish connection worked well, for Spain had a ready supply of Jews and *conversos* who wished to escape intolerable pressure at home. They came especially to Amsterdam. An observer of Rotterdam in 1622 said that there were ten different religions in the city, and some people who adhered to none, thereby vindicating the common accusation against religious pluralism, namely that it was tantamount to atheism. One early seventeenth-century English writer managed to smuggle a sneaky curse into his sentence, even as he was claiming the religious high ground of opposition to a pluralist polity, which would, he claimed, leave England "Amsterdamnified."

But religious dissenters are, of course, often intelligent, creative people; those who make independent decisions about this, the most important aspect of life, are likely to make independent decisions about a good many lesser things also. They are also more than likely to be frugal, serious-minded, hard-working, and honest. Those rulers who chased such people out of their own lands and into the Netherlands (or into other countries that, later, granted religious toleration) found that they had made a present of their most useful and industrious people to rival states. In the atmosphere of the Netherlands, business thrived. The majority of all the printed books made anywhere in the world (and in any language) during

Protestantism in the Netherlands in 1648.

the seventeenth century were printed there. The Netherlands entered into its period of greatness during the seventeenth century in trade and sea power, in art, and in culture.

The fighting with Spain continued to 1609 when, exhausted, the two sides agreed to a twelve-year truce. It resumed again, pointlessly, from 1621 to 1648. But the die was already cast: the north would be broadly Protestant and accidentally pluralist; the south would remain under Spanish rule and solidly Catholic.[3]

France

By 1570 France had already suffered three wars of religion in less than a decade; there were to be six more before compromise was reached.

Protestantism had been present in France from an early stage of the Reformation, but it had remained fairly disorganized until the Calvinists came along in the 1550s. Persecution had become fierce during the 1530s, causing the newly converted Calvin, a native of Noyon and student in Paris, to flee to Switzerland, where he made his glittering career. Back in France, however, persecution had continued, including a horrifying massacre of Waldensians (Vaudois) in 1545 and constant pressure thereafter.

But the years after 1555 saw a very rapid Calvinist growth as French-speaking Geneva turned out pastors and missionaries, many of whom, like Calvin himself, had originally fled from France to the safety of the Swiss *Eid* (or *Bund*, or Federation). Once there, they were trained and educated in the Reformed doctrines and then returned, *Helveticized*, to their native land. The French term for these Calvinists, *Huguenots*, seems possibly to have originated in a very bad Francophone attempt to pronounce *Eidgenossen*, or "comrades of the *Eid*."

By 1562 there were about 1,750 Huguenot churches inside France; at its height, Calvinism would have the allegiance of perhaps 10 percent of the population. These included half of the nobility, with the rest overwhelmingly middle-class and urban in composition. The only area of peasant strength was the Cévennes, where many worked part-time in industries connected with the local towns. Apart from this, the Huguenots had almost no support among the peasantry, whose elemental life everywhere predisposed them toward the more magical, incantatory religion that Catholicism represented. This was a serious deficiency, since peasants, obviously, constituted the vast majority of the total population.

The explanation for this social imbalance lies in the nature of Geneva's other principal export to its chief pastor's native land: books. In addition to the secret presses operating inside France itself, Geneva had thirty-four printing houses, kept at full throttle in the production of Bibles, catechisms, Calvin's own writings, and other Protestant literature—all aimed at converting the French to the Reformed faith. And all of it would have gone over the heads of the illiterate rural population. Indeed, it was the extreme bookishness of Calvinism and its reliance on abstract doctrinal formulations that was to make it a domain of the literate, educated, middle class. The proportion of those coming to study in Geneva who already had legal training was an even more marked feature. Perhaps the Calvinist emphasis upon imputed sin, ascribed righteousness, corporate headships (all men in Adam, all believers in Christ), and other parallels to legal fiction and contract law had a particular appeal to the legal mindset. But it found no landing strip in the peasant mind—and perhaps there was none to find.

In 1559 the French king, Henry II, had drawn to an end a long bout of warfare with the German emperor, Charles V, at the Peace of Cateau-Cambrésis, when both monarchs had vowed for the future to vent their violence, not upon one another, but upon the Protestant heretics within their own realms. Henry celebrated by getting himself accidentally skewered in the jousting contest that followed, and power passed to his widow, Catherine de' Medici, while their three young sons grew to maturity. Francis II, the eldest, sickly offspring, was married at the age of fifteen to Mary Queen of Scots, but he died two years later. His younger brother then became Charles IX at the age of ten, and his mother was faced with the prospect of having to shoulder the burden of a protracted regency.

Factions anxious to help share this burden battled for power around Catherine. Jeanne, niece of Francis I and next in line to the French throne after Henry II's children, was queen of Navarre, a small Pyrenean state between France and Spain. She was strongly Protestant, as was her husband, Antoine de Bourbon, and his influential brother, Louis, Prince of Condé. Despite Huguenot weakness among the peasantry, strength among the senior nobility was a potentially decisive factor in attaining to power.

The Catholic nobles thought so too, and there existed a counterbalancing, strongly Catholic party determined to make the suppression of heresy a government priority. This group was headed by the Guise family, of whom Mary Queen of Scots was herself a member on her mother's side. The fact that she had been married to Francis II indicates clearly the influence of the house of Guise over the royal family.

The Peace of Cateau-Cambrésis inadvertently accelerated the rapid spread of Protestantism, however. The disbanding of the army sent home many men who had picked up reforming ideas from their time as prisoners of war at the hands of German princes or from other fraternization with the enemy.

Both the outbreak and the continuation of the French civil wars were a compound of two elements: religious strife, in which frequent massacres of the Protestants provoked rebellion, and the struggle for control over the throne—and finally for the throne itself—between the houses of Guise and Bourbon.

The first war was fought from 1562 to 1563, precipitated by a massacre of unarmed Huguenots at Vassy, an event that Louis, Prince of Condé, then used to wrest the leadership of the Protestants from the pastors (who mostly counseled nonresistance at this stage) to the leading Huguenot aristocrats, particularly himself. The fighting ended indecisively, with a limited toleration and various restrictions on Protestant worship. A failed Protestant attempt to seize the young king provoked the second war from 1567 to 1568, which ended with a very similar outcome to that of its predecessor. A few months later a third war broke out when the Cardinal de Lorraine (a member of the House of Guise and a key adviser to Catherine) attempted—and failed—to seize the Protestant leaders. This war was more protracted and saw the death of Condé at the Battle of Jarnac.

Although the Huguenots had a presence in all regions, their bastion was overwhelmingly in the south of France. The third war saw fighting spread into the countryside of the south and center. Despite Protestant defeats, the peace was a little more generous to them than after the previous conflicts, guaranteeing them some equality before the law.

By this stage, however, the Huguenot battle to defeat the Catholic forces in France had effectively been lost. During the 1560s the rate of conversions to Calvinism had slowed considerably. The climate of fear and hostility prevented much further growth. Already Calvinist hopes rested on a combination with the forces of Catholic moderation against the power of the Guises. Although this was not impossible, and Catherine de' Medici could occasionally be accommodating of Protestants in her desperation to escape domination by the house of Guise, the French situation was fundamentally unlike the Dutch, for the Catholic hard-liners were not a foreign occupier offending newly awakened national sensibilities but an integral part of native society reflecting majority opinion. On this rock, the Huguenot ship was to founder.

In 1572 one of the most notorious incidents of the Counter-Reformation occurred: the St. Bartholomew's Day Massacre. Catherine and the young king, who was now twenty-two, were persuaded to perform yet another *volte-face* (about-face) and encourage a plot that would kill all of the Huguenot leaders at one blow, thereby saving the kingdom for the Catholic faith and from further violence. In the event, neither purpose was achieved.

At 4:00 a.m. on Sunday, the twenty-third of August, Catholic Parisians in the know began breaking into Huguenot homes and killing all they found within. The Duke of Guise, in the company of other Catholic noblemen, entered the house of Admiral de Montmorency, one of the most senior Protestant nobles, finding him in bed. The Duke dispatched him with a pistol shot to the head, whereupon the naked corpse was thrown from the balcony.

Maximilien de Béthune, Duke of Sully, recalled in old age his experience as a thirteen-year-old Huguenot during the massacre. Trying to reach the Collège de Bourgogne, where he was a student, he was stopped several times by soldiers and other assassins but was able to bluff his way out of the situation because he was carrying a Catholic breviary. Upon reaching the college and bribing his way past the porter, he found that his arrival had been preempted by two priests, to whom his identity was known, and who pleaded with the principal, "talked of Sicilian Vespers and tried to get me out of his hands, saying that the order was to kill every one down to babies at the breast." The principal overruled them and hid the young de Béthune for three days in a cupboard in an obscure part of the building.

The bloodletting continued for forty-eight hours. At the end of it, at least 3,000 had been killed in Paris; a similar number were to perish in the provinces during the following weeks. On that Tuesday, Charles IX, Most Christian King of France, went to the Parliament to justify his complicity in the killing and to insist that he had agreed to the peace terms with the heretics of two years before only because he had been left with no choice. Now, he implied, the evidence of his more unfettered inclinations lay strewn around the streets of the city. The limited toleration for Protestantism was emphatically withdrawn. On Thursday the leading Huguenot nobles tremblingly did as they were bidden and accompanied their monarch to Mass; as they would have said, they were left with no choice.

This was perhaps one of the darkest incidents of the period. The St. Bartholomew's Day Massacre, the Spanish Fury of Antwerp, the Marian persecution of English Protestants, the Inquisition: the so-called "Black Legend" of Catholicism, which Protestants would recite so lovingly over centuries, was a compound of all these. It was a picture of Counter-Reformation Catholicism as persecuting, devious, murderous, and unbending, with a preference for killing those whom it could not rule and for torturing those whom it could not persuade. It was an image that endured in the Protestant consciousness for at least three centuries, and when it was beginning to fade, Pius IX foolishly revived. In the darker corners of Northern Ireland, it endures still.

As the dust settled and the bodies were being taken away for burial, many Huguenots recanted in fear. Others fled to the south, where they were more numerous, thereby strengthening the regional aspect of Protestantism. Although not as yet confined to the "Huguenot crescent" from La Rochelle to Lyon, the demarcation was made more pronounced. Still more fled to the Netherlands, England, and Geneva. But the autumn brought new courage, and a brief fourth war was fought around the port

Horribles crüautez des Huguenotz en France.

Cet tyrans infenſez n'eſtants iamais contents,
Inuentent tous les iours autres nouueaux torments;
A leur ardant courroux ne ſuffit nulle paine:
Ilz s'eſgaient à voir ſouffrir cruelle mort.
Aux pauures innocents, qu'ilz font mourir à tort,
Montrant par tel tourments leur tant mortelle haine.

Catholic depiction of outrages perpetrated by (not against) Huguenots. Engraving from Richard Vestegen, *Théâtre des Cruautez des Hérétiques de notre temps*, Antwerp, 1607.

of La Rochelle, a Protestant stronghold then and for long afterward. The siege ended the following May, when foreign policy moved higher up the government's agenda, and peace brought the usual compromise and concessions, though far fewer than after the previous bouts of fighting.

But the struggle was not even nearly over. In 1574 Charles IX died, and his younger brother Henry III succeeded him. The Protestant nobles raised troops in Germany; the king of Navarre escaped from Paris and returned home to raise new forces, and Montmorency, the Catholic lord of mostly Huguenot Languedoc, entered into alliance with him. The Duc d'Alençon, younger brother of Henry III, made overtures to them also, putting himself forward as an alternative king who would pursue a more tolerant policy—though in fact he was unhampered by principle of any kind. In 1576, 20,000 troops invaded from Germany and, in alliance with the various armies raised elsewhere, Henry III was forced to make large concessions to his various enemies, including the Protestants. The Duke of Guise (also named Henry), appalled at the concessions and determined to curtail the power of the Protestant house of Navarre, was the leading spirit behind the formation of the Catholic League that year—an alliance of nobles determined to resist the Huguenots' rising influence.

Just as the terms of the fourth war were so unfavorable to the Protestants as to make further fighting inevitable as soon as they recovered their strength, so the Edict of Beaulieu of May 1576 was so humiliating for the Catholics as to leave them smarting for revenge and a fresh opportunity to tilt the scales in their favor. The sixth and seventh wars (of 1577 and 1580 respectively) were brief attempts to achieve this, and they made limited headway.

However, when Henry III's younger brother died in 1584, the position of heir to the throne passed to the nearest relative, Henry of Navarre—the

Henry of Guise.
Illustration from Château de
Beauregard, France.

Protestant leader. Given that
the king himself seemed set
to remain childless, Navarre's
new status as heir presumptive was more than theoretical; it portended a Protestant
future for France.

The Duke of Guise was particularly appalled at the new
turn of events. Swiftly manufacturing a pedigree that
went back to Charlemagne,
he began to push his own
position as an alternative
monarch, to avert the disastrous prospect of a heretic on
the throne. Many senior magnates across the country were prepared to
back his Catholic hard-line if not his candidacy for the throne. So, too,
was much of the population of Paris. Denouncing the king as unprincipled and too soft on Protestantism, the Duke of Guise and the Catholic
League rose in revolt. The period 1584–1589 witnessed the so-called War
of the Three Henries: Henry III, Henry of Navarre, and Henry of Guise.
It was the bloodiest conflict so far.

Spain poured money into the Catholic League; the Protestants sought
what help they could from the German principalities, from the Dutch,
and from England. On Christmas Eve 1588, King Henry III called the
Duke of Guise to a meeting in his apartments at Blois for consultations.
When the latter was unwise enough to appear, the doors were bolted
behind him and he was cut to pieces. His brother, the Cardinal de Guise,
was similarly dispatched. What goes around comes around, and the
king himself died the following July by a knife hidden in the habit of
a monkish assassin. Catholic League tracts had been urging just such
action for months.

The mutual elimination of their principals by the two Catholic factions could hardly fail to pass the initiative to Henry of Navarre and the
Huguenots, but it did not create a Protestant majority in France. Indeed,
their numbers were down, depressed remorselessly by massacre and persecution, by terrified recantation, by exile, and by sheer disheartenment.

Henry IV of France.
Illustration from Château de
Beauregard, France.

Navarre himself, even as he basked in his new position as legitimate (though not unchallenged) king, could not help but be aware of Protestant unpopularity and particularly of the overwhelming concentration of Huguenot support in the south and west. If he wanted to be accepted as king of all France, something needed to be done.

The desire of magisterial Protestants being to create a religious monopoly that would displace that of Catholicism, their hopes necessarily had to rest upon their adoption by government or by a party that was capable of capturing government. This basic fact of political life left sixteenth-century Protestant causes in something of the nature of a client relationship with secular political interests, and this relationship now backfired badly in the case of the Huguenots when the secular partner, Henry of Navarre, finally concluded that power was more surely to be attained by switching religious allegiances at the crucial moment.

In July 1593, Henry of Navarre declared himself converted to Catholicism. "Paris," he reputedly said, "is worth a mass." The wars continued as the new King Henry IV tried to garner moderate Catholic support from the Catholic League without alienating too many of his core Protestant adherents—even if the latter had nowhere else to go. The Catholic League had plenty of life left in it, a continuing leadership in the new Duke of Guise, and plenty of money and political support from the Spanish. But the future clearly lay with the former-Protestant-turned-Catholic, who had hereditary law on his side and had been named as successor by the dying Henry III. In 1598 the wars came to an end leaving Henry IV as the first Bourbon king.

Under the Edict of Nantes, issued that year, the Huguenots received guarantees of toleration in most of the country, with worship permitted only in stipulated places. These did not include Paris. This measure spelled the long-term doom of the Huguenots, ensuring that they remained

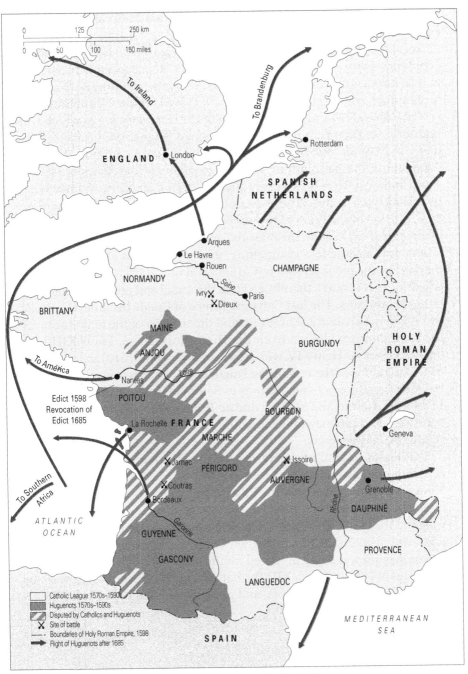

French Protestantism 1560–1685.

stagnant (unable to spread beyond their existing base) and provincial (banned from the capital).

Regulations spelled out what each side could and could not do; Catholics could proselytize but Protestants could not. The Huguenots were permitted to hold over a hundred fortified villages and towns, including La Rochelle, Montauban, and Montpellier, and nine hundred temples (churches).

The peace allowed a fragmentation of the Huguenot party, which war had to some extent prevented. At this stage, Huguenot numbers were down to between one million and one and a quarter million (i.e., 6 to 7 percent of the population); of these, perhaps 80 percent were in the south and west. Numbers were reduced further over the next thirty years by a variety of factors. There was official harassment and constant de facto erosion of the Edict of Nantes by the government. With the coming of a political settlement, the reasons for the Huguenot nobility to remain Huguenot became less compelling, and the decades after 1598 were marked by the reconversion to Catholicism of the aristocracy (as a way of getting on at court), thereby eroding the social and political leadership of the Protestants. The last Calvinist Prince of Condé became a Catholic in 1599 at the serious age of seven, and the support of the major nobility for Protestantism slipped from the Huguenots' grasp. Louis XIII (son and successor to Henry IV, who was assassinated in 1610) succeeded in provoking some of the remaining Huguenots into hopeless revolt in 1621 by extending the edict's restrictions to Béarn, in the Huguenot heartland. Led by the heroic and sincere duc de Rohan, the revolt unfortunately justified—and the inevitable outcome enabled—government in further tightening of the screw.

This was not a uniform picture, of course. The ban on Huguenot proselytizing notwithstanding, there were 450 conversions to Calvinism in Nîmes during the years after the Edict of Nantes, years that saw a number of erstwhile monks becoming Huguenots. But in general the losses outweighed the gains. Protestant piety in France was declining into aridity and formalism just at the time when Catholic piety was being renewed.

The ground was being prepared for the formal Revocation of the Edict of Nantes in 1685 by Louis XIV. By that time numbers were down to fewer than half a million Huguenots, and persecution then began in earnest.[4]

Germany

The Peace of Augsburg of 1555 had brought an uneasy end to religious warfare in Germany. Although the peace held, with the passing of the years it increasingly bore the nature of an armed truce. The religious wars in France during the later sixteenth century helped to keep the peace within the Holy Roman Empire. On the one hand, the emperor had the reassurance that the French kings were temporarily disabled from meddling in German affairs by trouble closer to home, and on the other the German Protestant princes knew that the French could not be used as a counterweight to Vienna. But the erosion of imperial authority inside Germany, along with that of the diet and imperial courts, left few peaceful means for resolving conflicting claims to land and titles. The empire being the crazy patchwork of territories that it was, such conflicts could arise quite frequently, and the religious competition inside the empire both caused and exacerbated them.

Peace and diplomacy, of course, are simply the continuation of warfare by other means, and the mere cessation of hostilities did not stop the continuing proselytization by Protestants in southern Germany and Austria, nor the missions by Jesuits and the opening of new Catholic schools in marginal areas to attempt to reclaim for Rome those territories that had already fallen into schism. Each side feared erosion by the other and did everything in its power—usually short of an actual breach of the Peace of Augsburg—to forestall it.

During the period from the mid-1560s to the mid-1580s, the initiative passed from the Protestants to the Catholics. At the start of the period probably a majority of the population of Austria was inclined to Protestantism, and many Catholic churches there and in southern Germany were giving communion in both kinds and urging the papacy to grant the regularization of priests' domestic lives by converting their concubines into wives. But the sheer determination and truculence of several rulers, such as Albert of Bavaria and the bishops of Bamberg and of Paderborn, to resist such moves and withstand the apparent flow of events allowed a recovery in Catholic fortunes. So, too, did a flagging in Protestant morale as the early enthusiasm of the Reformation subsided into formalism and new rigidities replaced the old. The Lutherans were divided among themselves and even more divided from the Calvinists; the Catholic Church, on the other hand, was in the throes of reforming itself in the wake of the Council of Trent.

The Lutheran-Calvinist split did serious harm to the Protestants in 1582, when the archbishop of Cologne wished to convert from Catholicism to the Reformed faith. When Spanish and Bavarian soldiers were sent to evict him and replace him with the decidedly unreformed (but Catholic) Duke Ernest of Bavaria, the Lutheran states stood by and watched rather than help a Calvinist.

The Jesuit schools and the Jesuit University of Ingolstadt did much to imbue a rising generation with the certainties of Counter-Reformation Catholicism. The establishment of a Jesuit college was one of the first recourses of the bishop of Paderborn in the closing years of the century when offering his subjects the choice of reconversion to Rome or exile from his lands. Archduke Charles went one better in the mid-1580s: he raised the status of the Jesuit college there to a university as part of the process of forcibly re-Catholicizing the overwhelmingly Protestant city of Graz.

Neither did the temporary paralysis of France end the problem of foreign involvement in German domestic woes. Spain was determined to reconquer the United Provinces and needed the Spanish Road through Germany to supply its troops. The presence of hostile German principalities in the Rhineland threatened to cut that tenuous lifeline. That being so, the king of Spain could be relied upon to fortify the resolve of his Hapsburg cousins in Vienna to deal decisively with the heretics in Germany. For the same reasons, the Dutch were fearful of Catholic advances within the empire, whether achieved by peaceful conversion or by military means. Most European powers feared close cooperation between the Hapsburg emperor and the Hapsburg king of Spain, but France had most cause to do so, fearing Hapsburg encirclement, as it always had done. An active anti-Hapsburg (and so tacitly pro-German-Protestant) policy was renewed under the governance of Cardinal Richelieu.

Furthermore, some foreign monarchs were also princes of the empire by virtue of the fact that they held territories within Germany. Such was the situation of the kings of Denmark, who were also dukes of Holstein, and who both had claims on secularized bishoprics in northern Germany and aimed to control the Baltic coast.

Finally, the peace settlement had recognized the Roman and Augsburg (that is, Lutheran) faiths only, but much second-generation Protestantism in Germany was Calvinist. This situation left those states embracing the Reformed religion in something of a legal limbo.

Nowhere was this more painfully apparent than in the case of the Palatinate, which was a key Protestant principality, both because of its geographical centrality and the fact that its prince, Frederick V, was the head of the Protestant Union. His foreign policy, however, was run for him by Prince Christian von Anhalt, an aggressive, scheming politician and strategist for the Protestant cause in Germany.

Anhalt was quite clear in his mind that a confessional war was inevitable, sooner or later, and so political wisdom consisted in the practice of brinkmanship and gaining the most advantageous position possible in order to fight the war successfully when it came. To this end, his diplomatic efforts on behalf of his ostensible masters (or, more realistically, clients) the Palatine electors were indefatigable.

In 1605 Anhalt concluded a private agreement with Brandenburg and the Dutch to finance the occupation of Cleves-Jülich on the death of its Catholic and childless duke, John William, by Dutch troops on behalf of John Sigismund, elector of Brandenburg. Anhalt's invitation to Henry IV of France to participate in this little arrangement fell foul of the uncomfortable circumstance that the Palatinate was currently sheltering a truculent Huguenot duke from the wrath of his sovereign.

An attempt in 1603 to persuade James VI and I (of Scotland and England respectively) to become the head of a Protestant alliance had also been declined, but Anhalt's diplomacy within Germany bore more fruit in 1607 when a treaty was concluded between the Palatinate, the city of Nuremberg, and the margravates of Ansbach and Kulmbach (both margraves were Anhalt's nephews) to protect the Upper Palatinate against any threat of Bavarian attack. This broadened, the following year, when the coerced re-Catholicization of Donauwörth frightened the previously rival, Lutheran alliance of Pfalz-Neuburg, Württemberg, and Baden-Durlach into a joining of the two alliances into a Protestant Union. Although the institution was to prove somewhat rickety during the years that followed, its very existence, especially when considered alongside that of the Catholic League, established the following year under the leadership of Bavaria, helped to convey the impression that the empire was dividing itself into two armed camps.

Anhalt's analysis was largely a self-fulfilling prophecy; men who believed that the future held religious war acted as Anhalt did to secure their positions and, in doing so, raised tensions further. Maurice, Landgrave of Hesse-Kassel, wrote to Louis XIII in 1615 that "I am very much afraid that the states of the Empire . . . may start a fatal conflagration embracing not only themselves . . . but also all those countries that are in one way or another connected with Germany. All this will undoubtedly produce . . . the total collapse and unavoidable alteration in the present state of Germany." He had clearly held this view for a while, for in 1600 he had set up a new militia of 9,000 men. In 1601 he had written a moderate-sized book giving directions for its use. After converting to Calvinism in 1603, Maurice had used his forces the following year to invade the neighboring state of Hesse-Marburg after the extinction of its ruling house. Travelers in Germany commented on the prevalence of local militias and the building of fortresses and defenses.

The predictions of doom were not entirely self-fulfilling, however, although the tensions of the first two decades of the seventeenth century contributed to the explosion that followed. The pressures for Counter-Reformation sponsored by the emperor, by Bavaria, and by the German ecclesiastical authorities were such that Protestants were bound to defend themselves in those areas—Bohemia, Tyrol, Donauwörth—where they were under attack and to feel threatened, and so to adopt a defensive posture, in the rest of the empire.

Imperial strategies for Counter-Reformation were facilitated by disarray in the Protestant camp. Lutheran mistrust of Calvinism ran deep, and the Protestant Union proved a difficult little club to keep together. The potential for conflict between Pfalz-Neuburg and Brandenburg over the Cleves-Jülich succession was present from the start, and in 1613 Wolfgang William, heir to the duchy of Pfalz-Neuburg, made a judicious conversion to Catholicism, consolidating this move that November with a marriage to Maximilian of Bavaria's sister, Anna Magdalena. The same year, however, Frederick V of the Palatinate achieved an equivalent diplomatic coup by marrying Elizabeth, daughter of James VI and I.

During the last three decades of the sixteenth century and the first two of the seventeenth, Germany increasingly resembled a powder keg awaiting a fatal spark. This was a feature upon which Catholic and Protestant observers alike ceaselessly commented. All the features that were to be played out again in the decades before 1914 were present: the shifting alliances, the mortal fears, the arms buildup, the string of local crises and petty triumphs bringing the larger players teetering to the brink of war. So too was its sequel: a gargantuan and apocalyptic bloodletting in the years after 1618.

Central Europe

Central Europe might be seen as the borderland (albeit rather a large one) of Western Christendom, where the lands that had adhered to Rome adjoin and mingle with those that had preferred loyalty to Byzantium. By the late sixteenth century, the Christian empire of the east was already a distant memory. The frontier that mattered now was that with the Muslim world—a frontier that seemed none too stable and which, if it buckled at all, could only erode Christendom further. Obviously, this menace loomed larger in Hungary and Transylvania than in, for example, Bohemia—but it was never far from anybody's mind.

Bohemia and Moravia

Bohemia had been Christianized from the ninth century onward, an early dalliance with Byzantium swiftly yielding to a more realistic orientation toward the papal allegiance shared by the Germans. In the early fifteenth century, the Prague professor Jan Hus had initiated a religious reformation, just over a century in advance of the main European event, by denouncing transubstantiation, affirming the centrality of Scripture and of preaching, and teaching justification by grace rather than works. The resultant disturbances led to two decades of violence, to which the outcome, from the 1430s onward, was a begrudging toleration of the most moderate Hussite faction, the so-called Utraquists, who insisted upon no more than giving the laity communion *sub utraque specie* (in both kinds—bread and wine) and at least some freedom for biblical preaching.

Bohemia had lived ever since with an official, limited religious pluralism—mostly German-speaking Catholics and mostly Czech-speaking Utraquist-Hussites. It had been accompanied by a wider pluralism in practice, since more radical, dissident Hussite groups continued to eke out a shadowy existence. During the 1520s and 1530s many of the German speakers in Bohemia had turned to Lutheranism; Wittenberg was, after all, only just over the border in territories that were part of the same empire. This presented a dilemma for the Utraquists, who saw the affinity with their own doctrines quite clearly yet experienced a certain queasiness at finding themselves in danger of being on the same side with their erstwhile enemies—to say nothing of the destabilizing effects that rampant Protestantism would bring to the uneasy, hard-won toleration afforded the Hussite faith. Meanwhile, the illegal radicals continued to proliferate and, under the impact of spreading varieties of Anabaptism, to diversify.

The mid-sixteenth century witnessed a period of attempted suppression of the new "heresies" by the government, but this was singularly ineffective. Beyond the establishment of a Jesuit college, the reestablishment of a Catholic archbishopric in Prague, and the exile of some of the Bohemian Brethren to Poland, the Counter-Reformation gains were limited. The accession to the Bohemian Crown in 1562 of a man disposed toward tolerance, Maximilian II (1527–1576; he acceded to the imperial title in 1564), slowed the pace of the Catholic offensive yet further. When the various streams of Hussites ("old" Utraquists, Lutheran-influenced, "new" Utraquists, and remaining Bohemian Brethren) presented him with a unified *Confessio Bohemica* in 1575, he professed himself ready to tolerate and accept it—though the pressures upon him from his Spanish wife Maria and his wider family were such that he remained unwilling to commit such assurances to writing.

This situation was inherited by Maximilian II's son and successor, Rudolf II (emperor 1576–1612). Though, unlike his father, he was not suspected of Protestant sympathies, he was nevertheless torn between, on the one hand, his own desires for coexistence with subjects who were both numerous and powerful and, on the other, the Counter-Reformation zealotry of his mother, relatives, and advisers.

The first consideration was clearly the more prudent: according to some estimates, only 10 to 15 percent of the population of Bohemia remained Catholic by the early seventeenth century. The Protestant Estates used this strength as a powerful negotiating tool in the rivalry between Rudolf and his brother, Matthias, during the years after 1600. They were rewarded with the so-called Letter of Majesty of 1609, according to which Protestantism was accorded legal recognition in Bohemia. However, the key political appointees remained ardent Catholics, opposed to the letter's provisions and able, with imperial connivance, to thwart in practice much that had been granted in theory. This was a circumstance that the more intransigent among the Protestants were able to exploit in favor of a policy of confrontation. The mutual disgruntlements continued to fester in the long, slow slide toward the catastrophe of 1618.

Hungary and Transylvania

To the southeast of these territories, Hungary had been dismembered in consequence of the overwhelming Turkish victory at the Battle of Mohács in 1526. The religious situation developed a little differently in each of the three main fragments.

In Upper Hungary (effectively Slovakia and such westernmost vestiges of Hungary and Croatia as remained beyond the Ottoman tide), Austrian rule had already begun to extend itself eastward—as it was to continue to do down to the early twentieth century. The Hapsburgs were naturally anxious to reverse Protestant growth here, as in all regions, but the progress of re-Catholicization was hampered by the fact that they were obliged, until the early seventeenth century, to pay tribute for the territory to the Turks. And the Ottomans saw no merit in promoting, let alone enforcing, the favored religion of their principal rival.

A little to the east, Transylvania had emerged as a separate kingdom, albeit officially a vassal of the sultan. It practiced a more principled religious pluralism than that which prevailed in the Hapsburg lands.

Second edition of Gáspár Kàrolyi's Bible.
Illustration from Hanover, 1608.

The estates of 1557, and again in the early 1560s, declared toleration for both the Lutheran Confession of Hermannstadt (Sibiu) and the Calvinist Confession of Koloszvár (Cluj).

It was the Transylvanian Saxons who had first brought Protestantism to the region (the German name for the whole region, Siebenbürgen, reflects the fact that the seven principal towns had for long been German-speaking settlements), and these naturally inclined to Lutheranism. It was a propensity relatively unhindered by pressures from the ecclesiastical hierarchy for, back in the mid-twelfth century, the Transylvanian Germans had been granted the right to elect their own priests. The new faith spread from this base to embrace many Hungarian speakers also. However, in the disputes that rent the Lutheran churches in the mid-sixteenth century, it was the Philippist (or Crypto-Calvinist) party that had gained the greater support. During the 1550s many of the Magyar Lutheran leaders moved beyond this position to explicit Calvinism—though it always remained a Calvinism tempered by the Renaissance humanism that flowed from the tradition of Melanchthon.

This did not mean that Hungarian Calvinism was as unremittingly bookish as its Western counterparts. Literacy rates were lower, and it was not until 1590 that the Reformed pastor Gáspár Kàrolyi produced the first complete Bible in Hungarian.

In the south and center of the country, the Turks ruled Lower Hungary, including both Slavonia and Bačka, directly. They also practiced religious toleration, subject to all of the usual caveats that attended Ottoman rule everywhere. They permitted Mihály Sztárai, for example, to extend his Calvinist evangelism from Baranja across the Drava River into Slavonia. There, with the aid of mostly Magyar but also some Slavic co-workers, he succeeded in establishing 120 congregations by the time of his death in 1575. In giving free rein to Protestant preachers, the Ottomans impeded any Austrian attempt to "liberate" Hungary from Muslim rule in the name of a Catholic crusade because Catholic intolerance would win the Hapsburgs the enmity of those about to be liberated; pluralism undermined a central plank of Vienna's polity.

This point was amply illustrated in the 1590s and early 1600s, when Emperor Rudolf II's armies trampled their way into Transylvania to promote the cause of just such a crusade. For about a decade the country was devastated by competing armies. If Hapsburg rule and reincorporation within Christendom were seen as synonymous by the invaders, then the battles against Islam and against Protestant heresy were seen as one and the same also. The excesses of the imperial troops provoked inevitable reaction; when the Ottomans offered István Bocskai the position of prince of Transylvania in 1604, he found widespread support among his compatriots. He was also the first holder of that office actually to adhere to the Reformed confession. His military campaign was so successful that Protestants were given full recognition and toleration, not only in Transylvania but also in Upper Hungary. The entire episode illustrated the reality that pluralism was inevitable in such unstable border zones.

If late-sixteenth-century Hapsburg attempts at re-Catholicizing the lands already under their control lacked some of the vigor they were later to possess, that did not stop them from trying in the meantime. This was most successful (or perhaps least unsuccessful) in Hungarian Croatia. There, Juraj Drašković, bishop of Zagreb and, from 1567 to 1578, Ban (or viceroy), introduced measures depriving converts to Protestantism of their inheritance and debarring them from public office. The career of Luther's assistant, Matthias Flacius Illyricus (Matija Vlačić, 1520–1575), was illustrious, but it was conducted almost entirely in Germany, having little repercussion in his homeland.[5]

The work of the Slovene Reformer Primož Trubar (1508–1586) in translating the Lutheran catechism and the Scriptures into his native tongue was of sufficient long-term importance that even today he is considered one of the founders of the modern Slovene language.[6] But his aspirations to repeat the feat for dialects further south and to print them in the Glagolitic and Cyrillic alphabets came to nothing. And though translations of the New Testament and some of the key Old Testament books were achieved by others, it was not enough to compensate for weaknesses of Protestantism among the population as a whole.

Toward the end of the century, General Lenković, commander of the Military Frontier (*Vojna Krajina*) with the Turks, drove all Protestant pastors out of the zone and excluded their followers from the ranks of his officers. Early in the following century, the *sabor* (Parliament) issued a decree of banishment for all Protestants in Hungarian Croatia, a measure that necessitated the disbanding of Varaždin's entire town council. Like most policies of premodern states, however, it was less than entirely effective; Protestants were still found in Karlovac as late as 1658.

Given the relative failure, at least until the early seventeenth century, of repression in the Hapsburg-controlled territories, some recent historians have emphasized the de facto similarity of religious conditions in all three parts of Hungary. In the meantime—and, indeed, until the late seventeenth century—the overwhelming majority of the population of Hungary adhered to one or another variety of Protestantism. By 1600 at least 80 percent of the five thousand or so parishes were Protestant, most of these being Reformed. Re-Catholicization took place in earnest only after the Turkish defeats of the 1680s and 1690s; in the meantime, the fact of living under the threat of the Turks meant that all rulers had to treat at least the more prominent of their subjects with leniency.

Nowhere was this more pronounced than in Transylvania, where a significant antitrinitarian movement took root. Perhaps its emblematic figure is Francis Dávid (ca. 1510–1579), who served as superintendent respectively of the Magyar Lutheran synod in 1557, of the Reformed synod in 1564, and of the Unitarian synod in 1576. In 1572 Prince István Báthory (reigned 1571–1586), though himself a Catholic, issued a decree recognizing all of these faiths, plus his own, as the four "accepted" religions; mere "toleration" was granted also to Jews, Armenians, and Orthodox. Everywhere, it was local decisions that determined religious affiliation. To that extent, toleration was a symptom not of higher civilization or of liberalism but simply of the weakness of central government in socially and politically fragmented border zones. That said, the religious divisions tended, as so often, to follow ethnic or linguistic lines: the Germans remained mostly Lutheran, the Magyars were Calvinist or Catholic, the Székelys were largely Unitarian, while the Romanians followed the Greek rite.

Poland

Central government weakness was also a factor in the religious pluralism that prevailed in Poland for much of the sixteenth century. There the *szlachta*, or nobility, were numerous (10 percent of the population) and enjoyed a high degree of independence. Furthermore, they entertained the touching and consoling belief that, unlike the peasants whom they governed, they were not Slavs at all but descendants of the Sarmatians, a tribe of warriors from the steppes who had swept through eastern Europe in the sixth century. Under the influence of this bizarre idea, the sixteenth and seventeenth centuries saw the adoption of supposedly Sarmatian styles of dress—though they were in fact gathered mostly from the Ottomans, who inhabited the regions immediately beyond Poland's southern borders.

In addition to their sartorial and pseudoethnic idiosyncrasies, the Polish *szlachta* cherished a fond tradition of anticlericalism. This was fostered in part by Hussite influences from nearby Bohemia but even more by resentment and jealousy of church landownership, which in some regions ran as high as 25 percent. The irksomeness of clerical celibacy (which was nowhere a negligible consideration in prompting some clergy to support the Reformation) was made all the sharper in Poland by proximity to the Eastern Orthodox Ukrainians, Ruthenes, and Russians, whose priests were permitted to marry.

Although Lutheranism had established an early preponderance among the largely German-speaking populations of the northern and western towns, it was Calvinism that, from the 1540s onward, made deeper inroads among the Polish upper classes. It had several advantages. In the first place, it was untainted by Germanic origins. In the second place, Calvinism tended to favor an aristocratic, rather than a strictly monarchical, form of government—a predilection admirably congenial to aristocrats. Finally, the Reformed faith proclaimed a bare, plain—and therefore cheap—form of worship as well as lay involvement in congregational government via a system of elders.[7]

By the late sixteenth century, perhaps one in ten of the *szlachta* were Reformed, although the Calvinist representation in the *sejm* (Parliament) and the Senate far exceeded this. But other new movements made a showing in the country. Mennonites established a colony on the Lower Vistula in the 1550s. More significantly, Arianism enjoyed its greatest flourishing in Poland, with up to 40,000 followers and 200 churches as well as an academy at Raków. As in Hungary, many Arians were erstwhile Calvinists; the intellectual austerity of Calvinism and its overwhelming emphasis upon divine transcendence over immanence was perhaps conducive to making the transition seem natural. Their greatest luminary was the Italian, Fausto Sozzini (1539–1604), who lived in Poland from 1579 and whose uncle Laelio (1525–1562) had pioneered the revival of the ancient heresy. Leading lights among the natives included Marcin Czechowicz and Szymon Budny, the latter translating the Bible into Polish and doing much to create an alliance with the Jews.

Jews constituted about a tenth of the population of Poland. Few settlements of any size lacked a synagogue, while many towns and villages in the south and east of the country were almost entirely Jewish. Arianism (or Socinianism—named for Fausto Sozzini—as it is usually denominated in this period), had some affinities with Judaism, at least insofar as it abolished at a stroke the greatest single barrier (for Jews—or, indeed, for Muslims) to Christian belief: the apparently compromised monotheism represented by the doctrines of the Trinity and of the deity of Christ. In consequence, many Polish Jews turned to Socinianism, while a number of Socinians and Calvinists traveled in the opposite direction and converted to Judaism. But that nontrinitarian heresies should find their greatest flourishing in two areas—Poland and Hungary-Transylvania—immediately abutting Muslim territory is, perhaps, hardly coincidental.

In 1569 the Union of Lublin occurred—a long overdue marriage of the kingdom of Poland with the Grand Duchy of Lithuania, states that had been living in a state of betrothal for so long (personal union of the crowns, i.e. sharing the same ruler, since 1386) that it might have been occasioning some gossip. In any case, the mere accident of a shared ruler was about to become insufficient to keep the partners together; the reigning king, Zygmunt Augustus, was clearly destined to be the last of the Jagiellonian dynasty, since his mother had poisoned his first two wives before they could provide him with sons, and the unfortunate monarch was so revolted by his third spouse that he could not bring himself to approach her bed.

The constitutional regularization represented by the Union of Lublin provided for the election of any future monarch by the entire *szlachta* and prompted the various Protestant leaders to form a united front in the interests of gaining recognition under the new commonwealth. Accordingly, in 1570 the Confession of Sandomiersz achieved a reconciliation between the various trinitarian Protestants: Czech Brethren, Lutherans, and Reformed. The Warsaw Confederation of 1573 gave them the desired toleration, though in language that was at once emphatic ("We will not, for the sake of our various faith and difference of church, either shed blood or confiscate property, deny favour, imprison or banish, and that furthermore we will not aid or abet any power or office which strives to this in any way whatsoever") and vague as to specific rights.

Even so, Polish forbearance in religious matters was, for a while, proverbial. Catholic voters regularly returned Protestant deputies to the *sejm*. And when a Calvinist martyrologist of the mid-seventeenth century came to write a history of his coreligionists, he could discover no more than twelve victims in Poland during the preceding hundred years—and that included the odd sectarian killing, alongside actual executions. If one bears in mind that when the Calvinist Marcin Kreza in 1580 seized the host from a Catholic priest, spat on it, trod it underfoot, and fed it to a dog, he received no more than a royal reprimand and an admonition to sin no more, one wonders what the twelve victims did to get themselves killed.

Bishop Drohojowski of Kujavia graciously allowed Catholics and Lutherans to share parish churches in his diocese and gave over the Church of St. John in Gdansk wholly to the Lutherans, since most parishioners had transferred their allegiance to that faith. More pragmatic still was Bishop Andrzej Zebrzydowski of Kraków, who told parishioners who were hesitating between the old faith and the new: "I don't care if you worship a goat, as long as you keep paying your tithes!"[8]

It was spirituality of this sort, of course, that had led many Poles to reject the old church in the first place. Fortunately, other Catholics were made of sterner stuff. But few extended that sternness as far as a taste for persecution. Most admirable was Cardinal Stanislaw Hosius, whose doctrinal work *Confessio* was a much-reprinted classic of the Counter-Reformation. He introduced the Jesuits to Poland, with a view to reclaiming those who had lapsed to Protestantism and to educating future generations as good Catholics. Yet Cardinal Hosius saw the English Queen Mary's failed attempt at re-Catholicization as due to her reliance on persecution, a failure he saw as an awful warning for the Poles: "Let Poland never become like England," he admonished. And the astonishing thing, given the generality of events in Europe at the time, is that the advice was heeded.

There were perhaps a thousand Protestant churches in Poland during the 1570s, half of them Calvinist. By the early 1590s, a sixth of all parishes had abandoned Catholicism. Lithuania, Malopolska, western Galicia, and Volhynia were the areas of particular strength for the Reformed. Wielkopolska and the north saw the greatest Lutheran strength. Yet for all this, Protestantism hardly touched the peasantry and made only limited inroads into the towns. Once the heyday of *szlachta* autonomy had spent its force, the social base for the Reformation would be undermined.

Already, in the very period of greatest Protestant strength in Poland, Catholic forces were regrouping, organizing, educating, and reforming their institutions. Meanwhile the Protestants were divided (the Consensus Sandomiriensis [Confession of Sandomiersz] notwithstanding) and would, in due course, become moribund. The Socinians could never count as part of the Protestants' base of support, for they were deemed heretical by everyone and counted as a liability and an embarrassment, not as an asset. The seventeenth century was to see a decisive reversal of the Protestant tide.

Spain versus England

Katherine of Aragon proved to be the last genuinely popular Spaniard in England until the advent of Julio Iglesias. She was the Spanish wife whom King Henry VIII had set aside in order to marry Ann Boleyn, separating the Church of England from that of Rome to do so. When their daughter, Mary, finally ascended to the throne in 1553, she had been determined to reverse not only the Reformation, but also the rift with Spain. Half-Spanish herself, she married King Philip II of Spain in order to reassert England's ties with that country. It provoked more resistance than her attempt at Counter-Reformation.

National consciousness was coming to birth in the more economically developed parts of northern and western Europe and was already quite strong in southeast England. The marriage to the Spanish king was resented as part of a foreign design to include the kingdom of England within an Iberian-dominated empire. A Kentish rebellion directed against the match came within an ace of succeeding. And when Philip and his retinue spent some months in London, nationalist sentiment in the capital ran so high that the Spaniards were blackballed; not one of his retainers succeeded in finding an English bride, so complete was their social isolation from the populace.

When Elizabeth came to the throne on her sister's death in November 1558, therefore, Protestant factional enthusiasm for the rescue from re-Catholicization was mingled with a more widely felt nationalist relief at the delivery from Spanish power. Alas, the new queen was diplomatically and militarily so weak at her accession that when Philip gallantly suggested that she replace her half-sister in his marriage bed, she did not have the courage to make an outright refusal. Instead, she gave the diplomatic equivalent of fluttering her eyelashes and promising to give the matter due consideration.

In reality, the future pattern of hostility between England and Spain was already sealed. In the following decades, Elizabeth came to represent everything that Philip was determined to crush: a Protestant monarch, of dubious legitimacy, repressing Catholic subjects in Ireland, encouraging piratical attacks upon his ships, and assisting Protestant rebels against him in the Netherlands. As a sort of mirror image, Spain stood for everything that the Protestant English most detested and feared: a dominant and persecuting Catholic Leviathan, whose hand was to be found behind every plot by papist traitors at home, in league with Irish rebels over the water, threatening to crush fellow Protestants over the channel in the Netherlands and then use that country as a springboard for the invasion of England.

All circumstances conspired to bring the two kingdoms into conflict. And religion underpinned—or, at any rate, rationalized—every aspect of it. Certainly for generations of English Protestants, Spain epitomized the Catholic threat to their faith and to England's independence—and the link helped forge the fusion between nascent nationalism and Protestantism.

Elizabeth was unmarried and childless; the heir to the throne was her nearest relative, her first cousin once removed, Mary Queen of Scots (1542–1587)—a devout Catholic. The Protestant ascendancy in England, therefore, hung by the single thread of the queen's life—a circumstance that gave some Catholics every cause to hope (and Protestants cause to fear) that that life might be snuffed out by, say, a little external encouragement.

The upheavals north of the border had the effect of bringing England's actual ruler and her putative successor into close conjunction. Mary fled for her life from the Protestant lords of Scotland, who vowed justice upon her for her part in the murder of her second husband, Lord Darnley, and she crossed into northern England in 1568. After brief sisterly formalities, Elizabeth had her would-be replacement imprisoned for safe keeping. Despite various plots during the following years and the constant urging of her advisers, Elizabeth maintained a nice squeamishness about executing fellow monarchs, perhaps uncertain where such practices, once precedent had been established, might lead.

An early attempt to bring Mary to trial in England for her alleged misdemeanors in Scotland foundered, and the investigating commission concluded in January 1569 that "nothing has been sufficiently proved, whereby the Queen of England should conceive an evil opinion of her sister."[9] But her troubles were only just beginning. A number of Catholic (or, at any rate, deeply conservative) lords in England tried to obtain an annulment of Mary's third marriage (to the Scottish Lord Bothwell) so that she could be married off to the Duke of Norfolk. Mary herself appealed to the Spanish ambassador for his king's assistance to make her queen and to re-Catholicize England.

In mid-November 1569, Catholics in the North rose in revolt, under the leadership of the Earls of Northumberland and Westmorland, assisted by papal money and promises of Spanish aid. The leadership was poor, the funds insufficient, and the Spanish help did not materialize. Before Christmas the rebellion had been squelched, with bloody reprisals.

Pope Pius V, unaware that the uprising had even begun, let alone already sunk, issued the bull *Regnans in excelsis* in February 1570, declaring

Elizabeth deposed and excommunicated and her subjects released from their vows of loyalty and obedience to her. A chaplain to the Spanish embassy secretly brought a copy to London.

Even after the rising, the machinations to marry the Duke of Norfolk to Mary Queen of Scots continued. For this, the would-be bridegroom was beheaded in June 1572. Plots continued to surround Mary during the following years of her imprisonment, and the degree of her complicity in them continues to be debated. But Spain remained the likeliest instigator and beneficiary of any sudden change of regime in England and was feared accordingly.

Secret services, then as now, entailed all manner of double agents, idealistic heroes mingling freely with fellow conspirators possessed of more mundane motives, *agents provocateurs*, and others who wished to find weapons of mass disinformation in order to strengthen the ideological stance of the existing government. Certainly, many in Elizabeth's Privy Council (that is to say, her government) were determined upon an anti-Spanish policy and wished to secure England's Protestant future by having the Catholic heiress presumptive executed.

In 1586 their chance came. A complex plot against Elizabeth was revealed, the correspondence of which indicated a plan to release Mary and "dispatch the usurper," meaning Elizabeth. What the conspirators did not know was that every letter was being read and copied by a network of agents under Lord Walsingham, Elizabeth's secretary of state. When the evidence was damning enough, they swooped. The conspirators were tried and executed—bar one. Mary protested "that she had not procured or encouraged any hurt against her Majesty"[10]—and Elizabeth, whether she believed such pleas or not, remained unwilling to have her cousin put to death, the entreaties of her councillors notwithstanding. In February 1587, in a moment of weakness, Elizabeth finally yielded and signed the warrant for Mary's execution. Then, after another change of mind, she tried to withdraw it—but too late. Her ministers knew her mind better than she herself did, and the document had been rushed to Fotheringay, where Mary was imprisoned, and it was enacted forthwith. When the Spanish Armada sailed the following year, the Spaniards' most credible replacement for Elizabeth was already dead.

The naval war between England and Spain had long been underway, however. On the English side, this operated on strictly commercial lines. The Spaniards were possessed of a vast empire in the Americas, from which they were extracting gold and silver on a scale that has been blamed for European price inflation throughout the sixteenth century. Determined to relieve the Spanish of the burden of some of this wealth,

English privateers, funded by Puritan merchant companies in London, attacked the *flota* (the Spanish bullion fleet) at every opportunity, sometimes extending their depredations to the Spanish colonies themselves or even, in the run-up to the Armada, to Cadiz harbor in mainland Spain. Elizabeth, as frugal as her father had been spendthrift, was glad to take her share of the pickings.

Furthermore, occasional help was given to the Dutch Protestants who were in rebellion against Spanish rule. This was seldom militarily significant, but the denial of the English coast to Spanish forces meant effective denial of the sea approaches to the Netherlands, for the Dutch rebels themselves controlled the coasts on their side of the English Channel. This meant that Spanish forces in the Netherlands, flanked on the south by their old enemy, France, were forced to rely upon the Spanish Road.

In a somewhat symmetrical relationship, Spanish help was frequently forthcoming for Catholic Irish rebels against English rule. In conquering Ireland in the late Middle Ages, the English monarchs had bitten off far more than they could chew. But, her ancestors having done so, Elizabeth was precommitted to repression, since an unrepressed Catholic Ireland would be a natural staging post for amassing large Spanish forces for the invasion of England. When the Irish province of Munster revolted in 1579, a force of Spaniards and Italians landed at Smerwick the following year to assist the papist rebels. Survivors from the wrecked Armada sought—and were given—shelter in Irish coastal settlements, though the English inflicted punishment on those who did so. Nevertheless, a number of Spanish survivors helped train Irish rebels in the use of firearms against the English during the 1590s.

The combination of forced Protestantization with dispossession of Catholic lands was a recipe for continuing resistance and, in 1593, many of the Ulster lords rose in revolt, to be joined and led by Hugh O'Neill from 1595. O'Neill was characterized by the English as a would-be deputy, not only of the pope, but of the Spanish king. In late 1601 Spanish forces did indeed arrive in Kinsale, where they were promptly besieged by the English. The attempts of their Irish allies to rescue them met with disaster and delivered the war into English hands in 1603. But the mutual characterization of each party by the others had been confirmed.

In its conflict with Catholic Spain, England was punching way above its weight in European affairs, and everyone concerned knew it. Spain was at the zenith of its power in the late sixteenth century, with wealth and population far greater than that of England. The heretical kingdom got away with its audacity by virtue of the fact that Spain's position of greatness encumbered it with equally great responsibilities, and it was never able to attend to all of them at once. The servicing and holding down of an empire in the New World, the holding at bay the menace of the Turks in the Mediterranean, the war against the Dutch rebels—all of these were more important than the troublesome English. For the long-term development of England as a Protestant country (which was at its most crucial and decisive stage during precisely the period of conflict with Spain), it was as well that the Spanish had too many other fish to fry.

3

LIFE ON THE FRONTIERS (1570–CA. 1610)

▼

The boundaries of Christendom during our period were already long. And they were getting longer. But they presented a mixed picture. The extended, awkward, fragile border with the Muslim world saw change and development in the late sixteenth century. The frontiers in sub-Saharan Africa, the Americas, and Asia were just opening up and saw Christian expansion—modest, rather than dramatic—with almost every passing year. The ancient churches of the Middle East and western Asia, however, found themselves locked in a process of long-term decline.

The Union of Brest and Its Causes

Before the rise of Muscovy as a powerful state, and even before the Mongol invasions of the lands to the west of the Urals during the thirteenth century, the heartland of the Rus' had been the country that today we call the Ukraine, centered in Kiev. It was there that Orthodoxy had been brought to the Slavs by the decision, in A.D. 988, of Prince Volodymyr to accept the religion of the Byzantines. Christianization of such a large, primitive country had been a long, slow process. But during the four centuries that followed, the Orthodox liturgy, celebrated in the language known as Church Slavonic, had gradually become deeply embedded in the psyche of the population.

By the late Middle Ages, however, the original Ukrainian lands had come under the rule of Poland and Lithuania, whose power extended to the Black Sea. The Union of Lublin in 1569 united the Polish and Lithuanian states, and Ukraine within them.

What made all of this religiously problematic was that Poland and Lithuania were (and still are) Roman Catholic, and their rulers naturally desired subjects who would share the same confession. Late in 1594 the bishops of the Kievan metropolitanate began to put out feelers for an agreement with Rome. If the Ukrainian church were not to remain adrift as a minority church in a large kingdom, it needed anchoring in an external authority somewhere—and the Polish-Lithuanian rulers would never tolerate their subjects giving religious fealty to Moscow.

It is possible that the overtures to Rome stemmed also, in part, from a desire to fend off the encroachments of Protestantism, which had started to put up a strong showing in Poland. The bishops bewailed "these miserable times when heresies have become widespread among the people and so many abandon our Orthodox faith." Given that they were making overtures to Rome, Catholicism can hardly have been among the "heresies" to which they were referring. Following the fall of distant Byzantium to the Turks in 1453, nothing further was to be looked for from its patriarchs, and "our hope in them weakens with time, as they find themselves in pagan bondage, and can do nothing, even if they wished to."

The Jesuits arrived in Poland in 1564 and in Lithuania five years later. They quickly made themselves busy, founding colleges and schools, many of them in the Ukrainian lands. These were aimed at converting the offspring of Protestants and Orthodox to the One True Church.[1] Their publications called loudly for church union, along the lines that had been negotiated, abortively, at the Council of Florence a century and a half earlier. They also called for the adoption by all Christians of the new Gregorian calendar, introduced by Pope Gregory XIII to compensate for the maddening tendency of the sun to get ahead of itself.

These admonitions counted for little among the Orthodox, however. Yet a substantial proportion of them did indeed seek unity with Rome, though for reasons that owed little to Jesuit courtship and nothing at all to the shortcomings of the Julian calendar.

During the 1580s the patriarch of Constantinople, Jeremiah II, had started to interfere in the affairs of the Orthodox Church in Polish Ukraine in ways that irked the senior clergy. In 1589 he recognized the autocephaly of the church in Muscovy while insisting that church affairs in Poland-Lithuania were to remain under his own jurisdiction. He had already delegated wide-ranging powers to the Stauropegial Brotherhood in Lviv, thereby infuriating the bishop of that city, Gedeon Balaban. Bishop Balaban then approached the Polish Roman Catholic Archbishop of Lviv, asking him "to liberate [our] bishops from the slavery of the patriarchs of Constantinople."[2]

It was in 1596 that, in order to ease all of this tension, a device was hit upon that would decisively affect Ukraine's religious (and in more recent times, also its political) future. The Union of Brest united the Ukrainian Orthodox Church with the see of Rome, yet in such a way as to leave the sacred liturgy, the Church Slavonic language, and the rites and ceremonies more or less unscathed by the transfer. The agreement recorded "that no changes be initiated in our churches, but that all remain true to the tradition of the Holy Greek Fathers for ages unto ages." The Ukrainian bishops were required only to "make a profession of our faith at the assembled Sobor, and pronounce our obedience to the Roman See of St. Peter, to Pope Clement VIII and his successors." The resultant Ukrainian Catholic (or Uniate) Church was a sort of semidetached arrangement, exhibiting a flexibility of which many Western Protestants (who live in ignorance, for the most part, of Eastern affairs) have long erroneously supposed the papacy incapable. It is not that the prejudice about papal intransigence is entirely misplaced but that necessity has a habit of making pragmatists of us all—or of all of us, at least, who survive.

The agreement was resisted by some, not on the Catholic side but on the Orthodox. Prince Ostrozky furiously declaimed against the bishops, "the damned ones," who have "secretly agreed among themselves, like Judas the betrayer of Christ had done with the Jews, to break off the pious Christians of this region." These episcopal sons of iniquity had "become wolves, and have renounced the one true faith of the Holy Eastern Church . . . and have gone over to the West."[3] Truth and error, it seems, were determined by points of the compass. We should hardly be surprised when such propositions, with only a little more logical finesse, are still defended down to the present.

A schism loomed between those who would make their peace with Rome and those who held out for "the region." In 1620 a new Orthodox metropolitan was established in Kiev with the support of armed Cossacks. Ukraine has been religiously divided ever since.

In the second half of the seventeenth century, Ukraine was partitioned between Poland and the newly emergent Russia, and those Uniates who now found themselves in Russian territory soon discovered that they were, by the same token, politically unacceptable to their new rulers. In 1685–1686 the Kievan Orthodox metropolitan was moved from the jurisdiction of Constantinople to that of the patriarch of Moscow. The Orthodox Church in Ukraine was made thoroughly Russian in character and government, and the Uniate church itself was liquidated during the eighteenth and nineteenth centuries.

In western Ukraine, however, the Uniates continued to thrive under Polish rule, while it was the Orthodox who were out of favor. This situation continued when the area came under Austrian (and therefore still Catholic) government from the late eighteenth century.

The Uniate church, then, started life as a political ploy by (part of) an Orthodox minority in a Catholic state. It has been a political football ever since. It ensures that Ukraine is a "cleft" country, straddling two of Samuel Huntington's "civilisation blocs," namely the Eastern and Western Christendoms.[4] The presence of the Uniates also created a situation in which at least three religious confessions (four, if one includes the significant number of Jews) coexisted. This was a circumstance that made entry by later movements seem less like an unnatural intrusion into, or dissipation of, a culture—there being relatively large numbers of people with fractured ethnic and religious identities and parentages. It helped to make Ukraine a natural and easy growth point for evangelicalism in recent centuries.

The Conflict with Islam in the Mediterranean and Southeast and Central Europe

The various parties to the agreement—and disagreement—around the Union of Brest did not have the luxury of complete security for their part of Christendom within which to debate. For seventy years, since the Battle of Mohács, Poland had been bordering a vast, hostile, Muslim empire whose ultimate ambitions clearly entailed the unraveling of Christendom. It was not unthinkable that the Turkish juggernaut might begin to roll north again at any time. The urgency of agreement between the largest possible numbers of Christians is an idea that saturates the language of the Kievan bishops in their various missives leading up to the Union in 1596.

The Turks already occupied Moldavia, immediately to the south and west, and held territory along the northern coast of the Black Sea east of the Dniestr River. Goaded by Cossack raiding from Polish territory into the Ottoman lands, raiding which sometimes approached Constantinople itself, the Turks combined with the Tartars of the Crimean Khanate to field an army of over 100,000 against Poland in 1620. This army defeated the Poles at Cecora, near Iaşi, and continued to march north. Invasion threatened, but the Catholic kingdom was saved with the help of 40,000 Orthodox Cossacks at the Battle of Khotyn, where the Muslim tide was stemmed.

Despite this reprieve, Christians of the steppe continued to live in constant fear of abduction and enslavement by roving Muslim bands, usually Tartars operating for Ottoman purchasers. The incredibly rich lands of southern Ukraine remained thinly populated, the economic advantages of habitation outbalanced by the terror of living on the vast, indefensible plains. Epic poetry of the period consists frequently of laments for those captured:

> On the holy day of Sunday, it wasn't the grey eagles screaming,
> But the poor captives weeping in bitter slavery, . . .
> Liberate, O Lord, all the poor captives
> From bitter Turkish slavery,
> From infidel captivity!
> Let them reach the quiet waters,
> The bright stars,
> The merry homeland,
> The Christian people,
> The Christian cities![5]

During this period Ukraine was indeed what its name reflects: a borderland—in this case, between the *dar al Islam* (Ottoman Empire and Crimean Tartars) and Christendom (Poland and Muscovy).

The frontier with Islam extended south and west from the Ukraine, passing through Hungary and down to the eastern shores of the Adriatic Sea. This left almost the whole of the Balkans within the Ottoman grasp; the Venetians held only the Istrian Peninsula, the Croatian islands, and a strip of the coast from Zadar (Zara) to Split (Spalato), while the Ragusan Republic (Dubrovnik) maintained a precarious independence from the Muslims, not by military might but by economic usefulness to its would-be invaders. But the Dalmatian cities as a whole, cut off from their natural hinterland in Bosnia and the central Balkans, entered upon a period of economic decline. The eastern Mediterranean, and the entirety of that sea's southern shore (both east and west), was in Muslim hands.

The frontier between Christendom and the Muslim world, then, was characterized by frequent small-scale raids and skirmishes and by more occasional large battles. These were both on land, along the frontier zone between the Adriatic Sea and the steppes, and at sea. In the western Mediterranean, the Barbary corsairs kept up constant attacks, not only upon the coasts of southern Europe but also upon England and Ireland and even, though more infrequently, upon Madeira and Iceland.

The Muslim corsairs were based largely in Tunis, Algiers, and Tripoli and were, in effect, privateers who had the blessing of the sultan. Renegade Christians (the very word *renegade* was originally coined to describe them) had helped to establish them and taught them their skills. During the early 1610s an average of fifty-eight ships and other vessels were being captured by them annually in English and Irish waters alone. (Even in the late 1670s the number was still running at an average of forty ships, or 2,000 people, a year.) And this does not take into account those inhabitants of coastal villages who found themselves attacked and captured during the night. All were taken to "the Barbary Coast" and enslaved.

In 1577 over 260 Christian slaves, of many nationalities, made a dramatic escape from Alexandria, rowing one of the very galleys in which many of them had served; one man had been a prisoner for over thirty years. They eventually fetched up in Naples, "where they departed asunder, each man taking him to his next way home." The note of Christian solidarity in this tale is striking: along the way, they had received help from Orthodox monks; one of the fugitives' leaders, an Englishman, was given a reward for his deed by the pope, along with letters of commendation to the king of Spain, who helped him on his way to Protestant England![6]

Six years later, the company of the English ship *Jesus* were fortunate to be rescued from captivity in Tripoli by the diplomatic intervention of Queen Elizabeth I with the sultan. Even so, one of their number had already been executed, despite "turning Turk" (i.e., converting to Islam) in a failed attempt to save his life, while the others had served time, alongside Italians and Spaniards, as galley slaves. In yet another case, ten survivors of the *Toby*, shipwrecked on the Moroccan coast in 1593, were eventually ransomed from the Muslims for £70 per man, but not before they had endured forced marches, the loss of all their property, the deaths of two fellow survivors from harsh treatment, and several months of slavery.[7]

But the Christians were not the only victims. Corsairs based in Christian Malta inflicted similar depredations, if on a smaller scale, upon the Muslims of the southern shores.

Occasionally, the raiding would give way to a serious sea battle, such as that of Lepanto, in the Gulf of Corinth in October 1571. This marked a watershed in several ways. It was the last time that galley ships, manned and rowed by crowded ranks of slaves, were used in a major battle. It also demonstrated that the Turks were not, after all, invincible. Yet it required the combined forces of the Holy League—Spain, Venice, the pope, and the knights of Malta—to accomplish it. The destruction was appalling, with pieces of ships and corpses covering the sea for eight miles around. The Turks lost 30,000 men (of whom many, of course, were Christian galley slaves on Ottoman ships), while the Holy League lost perhaps a quarter of that number. In addition, about 15,000 Christian captives were liberated and 5,000 Turks captured, along with 150 of their ships (50 more had been sunk).

Decisive victories on land still lay far in the future. In the meantime, there were continuing small-scale losses. The Muslims had captured the fortress of Klis in 1537, placing the port of Split, over which it towers, in a precarious position and cutting it off from its hinterland. (Apart from a brief interlude in 1596, the stranglehold was maintained until 1648.) Throughout the 1540s, the Muslim tide crept forward through western Slavonia. During the later sixteenth century, one area of northwestern Bosnia after another fell, culminating in the disastrous loss of Bihać in 1592, in which the town was burned and the surviving inhabitants fled.

The Christian resistance produced a variety of interesting arrangements. The Hapsburg emperor established a string of forts as bastions of Christendom, the most important of which was the new town of Karlstadt (Karlovac) in 1581. But he found that he could not then be too fussy as to what kind of Christians did the defending. All comers were invited to the marshy, dangerous border zone—and many who accepted were Slavs and Vlachs who adhered to Eastern Orthodoxy. Early military commanders of the Military Frontier (*Vojna Krajina*), as it was known, were Protestants; so were many of the inhabitants of the new—or renewed—border towns, notably Karlovac and Koprivnica. The local senior Catholic clergy were nervous of the encroaching religious pluralism. Furthermore, the peasants on the Military Frontier were free, unlike their counterparts in Croatia and Hungary, who were serfs. The nobles were anxious about the bad example of freedom set by the newcomers. But the emperor, though theoretically sympathetic on both religious and secular counts, was driven by financial weakness and military desperation to take help and settlers wherever he could get them.

The same financial crisis pressed on the peasantry around Zagreb and in Slovenia as the perpetual warfare turned much of the countryside into an armed camp, raised taxes, disrupted agriculture and trade, and caused landowners to tighten belts and raise charges. When many serfs rose in revolt in 1573, the bishop of Zagreb, Juraj Drašković, endeared himself to the defenders of feudalism by taking a leading role in crushing the rebellion. At his order, Matija Gubec, the captured peasant leader, was crowned *rex rusticorum* (king of the peasants) in Zagreb cathedral—with a rod of molten iron.[8]

In fact, however, the loss of Bihać proved to be the last major loss on that frontier. The following year, 1593, saw a heavy defeat of the Turks at Sisak and, when peace was eventually made in 1606, it was a treaty between equals, in which the Christians were no longer required to pay tribute to the sultan.

The Christianization of the Americas

By the late sixteenth century, the Christianization of the Americas was more or less coterminous with the extent of advance into those continents by Europeans. This advance was far greater in the south and center as well as in the Caribbean, where the Spanish and Portuguese had been active, than in the great northern land mass, where Spaniards, French, Dutch, and English were making cautious inroads.

Inroads into the south and center had been hardly cautious at all. Columbus's four voyages had made the initial contact with the Caribbean islands, the third and fourth, in 1498 and 1502, proceeding to the mainland of Mexico. The following two decades witnessed a bloodbath of apocalyptic proportions as the Aztec Empire of Mexico was shattered and replaced by New Spain and the Inca Empire of Peru was similarly ransacked in the quest for precious metals. The Indians[9] simply had no weapons that could withstand the power and ferocity of the invaders. Guns, steel blades, wheels, even horses: all were unknown to them until they found themselves on the receiving end of their military potential.

Many who survived the Iberians' military onslaught were often enslaved in the *encomiendas* (properties allocated to European soldier-settlers), especially in the gold, silver, and mercury mines, as the conquerors frantically sought for easy riches. Those who eluded both massacre and enslavement succumbed, for the most part, to imported diseases to which they had no resistance: smallpox, diphtheria, and measles in the sixteenth century; malaria and yellow fever from Africa in the seventeenth century, brought over with the slaves whom the Europeans imported. That the principal disease passing in the other direction—from America to Europe—was syphilis tells its own story about the utter subjection of the natives to their conquerors. Estimates of the scale of indigenous demographic decline during the century after Columbus have varied; the figure of 90 percent has been questioned lately, but an estimated population collapse on the order of 75 percent would be safely within the extant evidence.

Conversion of the survivors to the faith of their conquerors was never likely to be a matter of warmed hearts and aroused consciences. Yet however repulsive the manner of the conquests—and their participants—the fact remained that the Indians' gods had failed them. It was this, rather than the love of Jesus, that impressed itself forcibly upon the minds of many who remained. Furthermore, the atrocious treatment at the hands of the conquistadores often gave way, within a generation, to the more solicitous care of the Spanish and Portuguese kings, for whom their new subjects were a resource to be protected and husbanded, and of churchmen, for whom they represented souls to be saved.

This last point did not go quite uncontested at first. The conquerors had noted with disgust the practice of human sacrifice in Mexico and of cannibalism both there and in Brazil and some of the Caribbean islands. The theological question arose as to whether people who could do such things were truly *human* at all. (That the same question might have been posed in respect of Cortés, Pizarro, and their soldiers was, of course, too absurd to occur to anyone.) Then as now, the chief purpose in denying the humanity of certain people is to justify the deniers in treating them as mere objects that can be used or disposed of at will. Nazis; abortionists; slaveholders: all have followed the path of the early conquistadores in denying the full humanity of their victims, thereby reducing opponents to the frustration of defending the blindingly obvious as if it were somehow a contentious point of view.

It took a papal bull in 1537 to settle the question. According to *Sublimis Deus*, it was a lie sponsored by "the enemy of the human race," the devil, to suggest that the Indians "should be treated as dumb brutes created for our service." On the contrary, they were "truly men," who were "not only capable of understanding the Catholic Faith but, according to our information, . . . desire exceedingly to receive it." The Catholic Church's interest in promoting the One True Faith both hallowed the conquest of infidels and served as some protection for them once that conquest had been achieved. Within those morally dubious parameters, however, the church's record was a good one. The same papal bull attempted, albeit unsuccessfully, to prohibit the enslavement of Indians and the theft of their property.

As early as 1511 Father Antonio Montesinos had thunderously denounced, in a sermon, the "cruel and horrible slavery" visited upon the Indians and the "detestable wars" that had "consumed infinite numbers of them with unheard-of murders and desolations." But it was the Dominican Bartolomé de las Casas (1474–1566) who made the campaign for protection of the Indians the central cause of his life. He knew whereof he spoke. He had witnessed the depopulation of Hispaniola and the other Caribbean islands firsthand; he had himself been a conquistador and *encomendero*. His writings, describing the horrors of Spanish conquest and rule, were important in persuading the Spanish king to promulgate the famous New Laws of 1542. These threatened to undermine the power of the *encomenderos* and to give better protection to the natives.

Alas, the New Laws were difficult to enforce and, in any case, much of the damage was already done. Unwittingly, Las Casas's writings had also given ammunition to Protestants in their formulation of "the Black Legend"—the catalog of Spanish-Catholic cruelties and sinister deeds in the Netherlands, in the Armada scheme, and via the Inquisition—that persisted, albeit in greatly weakened form, until recent times in the English-speaking world. (One need only think of the difference in public image between Portugal and Spain. Yet the deeds and methods of the Portuguese in Brazil were similar in every important respect, and the death rate among the natives was just as catastrophic. The Portuguese, however, had no Las Casas to denounce them.)

The Indians, insisted Las Casas, should be converted peacefully to the Christian faith, without the use of force. It was a fine ideal—though, on the whole, not one for which the Counter-Reformation is much remembered back in Hapsburg Europe. Inevitably, the conversion process in the Americas entailed a mixture of persuasion and coercion. But all of the advantages lay with the newcomers. The clergy could augment their numbers easily enough. They had literacy and the prestige that attended it. They could fall back upon secular force for protection if threatened. The idolaters were a subject people, frightened and declining in numbers, needing all of the help they could get—which, upon conditions, the priests and friars offered them.

By 1559 there were eight hundred friars in Mexico alone. As with the Christianization of barbarian Europe in the early Middle Ages, they concentrated their efforts upon chieftains, who would exert pressure upon their underlings to follow suit. Again as with that earlier Christianization, churches were frequently established on the sites of old pagan shrines in order to make the transfer from the old faith to the new as painless as possible. And, as with medieval Europe, the results were in many ways similar: syncretism abounded; pagan practices continued in new guises; Christian purists were horrified, while pragmatists shrugged and got on with it. Polygamy and, in Brazil, nudity were particularly hard habits to shake.

Many of the missionaries were excellent linguists and sought to instruct the Indians in their native tongues: Nahuatl (the principal Aztec language of Mexico), Quechua and Aymara (spoken in Peru), and Tupí (in Brazil). They did this despite the wish of the secular authorities that the converts should learn the language of their conquerors. This disobedience, along with the founding of new villages by the friars for the Indians, stemmed from the missionaries' desire to protect the neophytes from too much contact with Europeans, whom the friars—who should know—believed to be a corrupting influence.

Even so, the process of conversion was patchy. It advanced much more quickly in Mexico than in Peru. Of the destruction of the two great indigenous empires, that of the Aztecs was more immediate and complete. The capital, Tenochtitlán, was demolished and replaced by Mexico City. The political and religious sites were eradicated early on, and so Christianization proceeded swiftly, alongside political subjection. By the end of the century a Catholic university and two theological seminaries had been established.

In Peru, by contrast, Catholicization was slowed by civil war among the conquerors, by a poorer quality of missionary, and by resistance from the natives. The Spanish chose to establish a new capital on the coast at Lima, a decision that inadvertently allowed the Inca tradition, especially its religion, to continue at the old capital of Cuzco. Moreover, Manco, one of the half-brothers of the executed Inca emperor, Atahualpa, eluded early attempts to co-opt him into the structure of Spanish rule and instead set up a new Inca state centered in the mountainous region of Vilcabamba, including the sacred site of Machu Picchu. A pagan revival movement in the Andes during the 1560s was founded upon the claim that the old gods had sent the disease epidemics as a punishment for turning to the Catholic faith. Manco and his successors claimed that the Spaniards' deeds had not shown them to be sons of God but sons of the devil. This was what one recent commentator on Latin American church history has called "the overt irony of Christian teachings of love versus Christian brutish behaviour."[10]

It was a dichotomy seen starkly in 1572 when the new viceroy, Francisco de Toledo, after having overrun the remnant Inca state, had the captured Inca leader, Tupac Amaru, beheaded in the main square of Cuzco before a horrified crowd and in contravention of the pleas of the church. Though the rebellion had been squelched, the perceptions that underlay it were less easily dispelled.

The commander of Toledo's men who had captured Tupac Amaru was Martin Garcia de Loyola, the nephew of the sainted founder of the Society of Jesus. Six years after the execution, in 1578, Loyola married the dead Inca's niece. Her name, Beatriz Ñusta, conveys clearly enough that the price of Christianization included cultural assimilation to the conquerors. The wedding of two such prominently connected people was celebrated with all due pomp, for it seemed to symbolize the marriage of Inca aristocracy with Counter-Reformation spirituality. Yet the pagans were not utterly vanquished: in 1598 Loyola was captured by Indians, beheaded as Tupac Amaru had been, and his head displayed on a spear.[11]

The Jesuits reached Brazil in 1549, Peru in 1568, and Mexico in 1572. As in Europe, they provided first-class education in the cities for the elite. Unlike Europe, they established new villages for their putative converts in Brazil and, calling upon the secular muscle of the military to persuade recalcitrants, more or less forced the pacified Indians to reside in them and to adopt European ways, including patterns of agriculture, crafts, and music. By 1600 almost all Indians in the region of Baía were living under Jesuit tutelage of this kind. During the opening decades of the seventeenth century, the Jesuits were turning their attention to Paraguay, where they established a string of thirty mission villages which, by 1707, contained 100,000 Guaraní Indians.

These methods seem, to postmodern Western eyes, outrageously patriarchal, prescriptive, and culturally imperialistic. And so they were. Yet the Jesuits and Dominicans were the Indians' best (indeed, their only) defenders against the much more brutal exploitation that the colonists had in mind for them. The Indians in the mission villages were working (albeit using imported methods) for themselves; the colonists wished to use them for forced labor. When slavers from São Paulo moved inland to capture Indians, the Jesuits did not scruple to arm the intended victims against the Jesuits' own compatriots. This incident and related frictions led to the expulsion of the Society of Jesus from some districts of Brazil and Paraguay in 1661. The long-term dynamic portrayed to such stunning effect in the 1980s film *The Mission* was already in place.

The Franciscans, Dominicans, and Jesuits made impressive gains for the church in the New World. Partly for this reason and partly because the parish and diocesan structure was only in the process of being created around them (rather than, as in Europe, inherited from a dim and distant past), relations between the various orders, on the one hand,

and the secular clergy, on the other, were sometimes strained by mutual jealousy and the conviction that the seculars were men of lesser ability and spiritual commitment (which—on average, at least—was probably true). Sometimes the tension could degenerate into actual violence. In 1559 secular clergy attacked a Dominican convent in Puebla, Mexico, trashed the buildings, took away all valuables, and, for good measure, broke the prior's teeth. In Toluca, a group of Franciscans armed six hundred Indians and led them in an attack on a church with whose clergy the friars had quarreled; the building was destroyed.[12]

The Spanish did not confine their activities to South and Central America. From Florida and Mexico they pushed north into the center and southwest of the lands that would later become the United States. Their penetration of these areas was led by missionary priests, two of whom were martyred in 1542 in territory that would later become Kansas. By 1630 perhaps 35,000 Christian Indians were living around mission stations in New Mexico.

The English, French, and Dutch settlers of the North American continent, as yet blissfully unaware of Hollywood or Las Vegas, were nevertheless progressing up the St. Lawrence (the French) and Hudson (the Dutch) rivers around the turn of the century. The English had made some fitful attempts during the 1580s to establish themselves in the new colony of Virginia (named for Elizabeth I), the better to prey upon the Spanish fleets sailing to or from their own settlements in Florida and the Caribbean. By 1607 they had attained a permanent settlement at Jamestown.

Although early Virginia has the reputation of being less "godly" in inspiration than the later, Puritan settlements in New England, the distinction is relative rather than absolute. The Virginia colony was indeed the child of a trading company in London, which existed, like all companies, in order to make a profit. But this did not mean that religious concerns were of no account; indeed, its royal charter included among its objectives the spreading of the Christian faith. The first act of the colonists as they disembarked was to celebrate communion, led by their chaplain, Rev. Robert Hunt, in order to give thanks for their safe arrival. The colony's legal code provided for firm punishments, not only for the usual moral lapses, but also for breaking the Sabbath and even for extravagant dress—the last stricture being a sure sign of Puritan influence.

Pocahontas, whom the fortunate John Rolfe secured as his bride, was the most notable of the Indians to convert to Christianity. Rev. Alexander Whitaker counted evangelistic work among the indigenous peoples as being at least as important a part of his work as his care for the souls of the colonists.

The Portuguese in Africa

The wave of global exploration in which Europeans had indulged from the fifteenth century onward had been started by the Portuguese. Their first steps on the way to India had been down the west coast of Africa and then up the eastern shore. By 1497 the Cape of Good Hope had been rounded by Vasco da Gama on his way to Goa, in India. But more than mere geographical curiosity had been at stake; slave trading and Catholic evangelism followed in the wake of the explorers.

The mouth of the Congo River had been reached as early as the 1470s. In 1491 several key Kongolese leaders converted to Christianity, and the king, Nzinga Nkuvu, ordered the destruction of all idols. He took the baptismal name of João, while his son, Mvemba Nzinga, was baptized as Afonso.

The son went on to establish schools for both boys and girls. In 1509 he sent his own son, Henry, to Portugal, where he learned Latin and Portuguese and was consecrated suffragan bishop. By the time of Mvemba's death in 1543, about two million people, or half of the population of his kingdom, had been baptized. But tensions had arisen. The church in Kongo had not been allowed its own archbishop, and in 1534 it had been placed instead under the bishopric of São Tomé, a slave-trading island off the West African coast. Worse, the Portuguese, the source of his country's Christianization, were depopulating parts of Mvemba's dominions with their insistent slave-trading. Furthermore, the Portuguese freedom to do this was underpinned by papal authority, by which Africa had been assigned to Portuguese control.[13]

Perhaps fortunately for the Kongolese, with the passing of time Rome began to find its own division of the world into Spanish and Portuguese spheres irksome. This was especially so after 1580, when Portugal itself was absorbed into the Spanish kingdom, in theory subjecting all of the newly discovered lands to King Philip II of Spain. The papacy began to search for creative ways out of the situation and in 1596 named the Kongolese capital, São Salvador, as an episcopal see. Kongo seemed to be making progress toward becoming a Christian kingdom on a tolerably equal footing with those of Europe.

But the appalling behavior of the Europeans kept getting in the way. The Kongolese envoy to the papacy in 1604 was captured by Dutch pirates, thereby arriving in the Vatican four years late, in health so broken that he died a few hours before he was due to meet the pope. In the midcentury, Kongolese chafing at the activities of the slave traders provoked a Portuguese army to invade from Angola, its colony to the south. These troops smashed the Kongolese army, beheaded their king and his relative (the first black Capuchin monk), and destroyed the capital city with its cathedral and eight churches.

It was no way to convert anyone. Yet, strangely, the conversions continued. Kongo saw wild fluctuations in the level of Christian adherence during the period from the first contacts with the Portuguese until the eighteenth century. Yet many of these fluctuations owed as much to the vagaries of the Europeans' missionary efforts and their extreme reluctance to allow a native clergy on anything other than an occasional basis than to disloyalty by the Africans.

The Capuchin monks succeeded, a generation after the disastrous war and the destruction of São Salvador, in baptizing over a third of a million natives. Yet the teaching needed constantly to be mediated through interpreters, who were high-status members of noble families—for the missionaries seldom gained competence in the local language. And the instruction given was minimal; generally, the monks contented themselves with teaching the natives the sign of the cross and the names of the persons of the Trinity, as well as to venerate images of the Virgin.

Unsurprisingly, traditional beliefs continued under this veneer of Christianity. Christian concepts, where they were explained, were generally closely related to preexisting terminology—a procedure which, in the abstract, might be thought admirable but which, in the absence of any thorough teaching, could often lead to mere syncretism.

Further north, the Portuguese made gentle progress throughout the sixteenth century in bringing Catholicism to Benin, whose king, called the Oba, made a point of avoiding foreigners. The religious courting of the monarch—a courtship that never quite reached the final nuptials— became an entrenched feature of life in the region, while the Portuguese got on with the business of slave-trading.

Unknown to the Spanish Capuchin monks, who provided religious instruction wherever they could, the Oba had a nasty secret of his own. In 1665 the missionaries discovered it when several of them secreted themselves into the crowd in the royal palace in order to get a glimpse of the native religious ceremonies. When the horrified missionaries realized they were about to witness the ritual decapitation of five men, they betrayed their presence by protesting loudly that the natives were in a "state of perdition" and that "the devil whom they served was deceiving them." Furiously ejected from the proceedings, the brave Capuchins were perhaps fortunate to escape with their own lives.[14]

However appalling the practice of human sacrifice or courageous the Capuchin protests against it, in most other respects it was the inability of the Portuguese to work with others or to treat non-Europeans as anything other than their inferiors that constantly led either to the frustration of their efforts or to the suppression of all who were unfortunate enough to be "discovered" by them. In the 1540s they had helped the desperate Ethiopian Christians defeat the Turkish forces led by Ahmad Grañ, forces which had been bent upon the Islamization of the country. Yet the Europeans' assumption that this help entitled them to Catholicize the Coptic church there led to bitter conflict and ultimate rejection. The Catholic bishops sent by the Portuguese behaved with an arrogance that led, in two cases, to their swift exile from the kingdom. A third emissary, Pero Paez, a Spanish Jesuit who arrived in 1603, behaved more circumspectly and respectfully, winning in turn the respect of his hosts and eventually, after a number of years, persuading King Susinyos that the Monophysite doctrine was a mistake. In the year of Paez's death, 1622, the Ethiopian king professed a willingness to embrace the Roman Church.

But the king changed his mind when Paez's successor, Afonso Mendez, swept in and insisted that the "heretic" population of Copts must be rebaptized, the clergy reordained, and the distinctive Ethiopian ceremonies and festivals abolished. A brief civil war ensued, but the result was not in doubt. In 1632 King Susinyos was able to declare to his people: "We restore to you the faith of your forefathers. Let the former clergy return to the churches; . . . let them say their own liturgy." The Jesuits were banished from the kingdom.[15]

After establishing friendly contact with the Malindi people in East Africa, the Portuguese set up "Fort Jesus" in 1593 and a monastery at nearby Mombasa four years later. The colony soon boasted 4,000 Christians. In 1597, the seven-year-old son of the local king was taken over the Indian Ocean to Portuguese Goa, where he was baptized, changing his name from the Muslim Yusuf ibn Hasan to the Christian Dom Jeronimo Chingulia, and later taking a Portuguese wife. But in 1631, five years after his return home, he led a rebellion against the overbearing manner of his European overlords, stabbed the commandant, and reverted to Islam.[16] The rioting that followed led to the martyrdom of 250 of the local Christians, Portuguese and Africans alike, while another 400 were sent as slaves to Mecca. The Omanis from across the Arabian Sea came to the defense of their fellow Muslims in fending off future Portuguese attacks.

Jesuit Missions in Asia

Of all the new devices and organizations produced by the efforts of the Roman Catholic Church to reinvigorate itself—efforts to which we refer collectively as the Counter-Reformation—the Society of Jesus was by far the most successful. And of all the many and varied contributions made by those same Jesuits to the church's life, it was the foreign missions to Asia that have done most to capture the popular imagination, both at the time and ever since. It is those missions that have also left the deepest mark. European penetration of the world's largest continent would have looked very different—and, in all probability, would have been far less effective—without the Jesuits. Asian Christian history would have been almost unrecognizable without their contribution, for it was they who introduced Christianity in some fields, reintroduced it after a period of absence in others, and strengthened the Christian presence where it already existed.

India

Of the early missionaries, Francis Xavier (1506–1552) is, by common consent, deemed the greatest. His work in India began in Goa in 1542, where the long-established Thomas Christians were getting into difficulties with the Portuguese. But he rounded Cape Comorin in order to work during 1544–1545 among the Paravas, a group of some 20,000 people who had made a mass profession of Christianity and embraced baptism in 1537 in order to obtain Portuguese military protection from their Hindu and Muslim neighbors. The Portuguese had been only too willing to oblige because of the control it gave them over the Paravas' pearl fishing. Xavier and his companions embarked on the more arduous task of converting a nominal loyalty into at least a modicum of knowledge.

From 1606 the Jesuit Roberto de Nobili began his extraordinary career in Madurai, where he extended his learning of the local high culture to the point of turning himself into a Christian Brahman. He succeeded in converting and baptizing over sixty high-caste Hindus during the following three or four years. He went on to adopt an Indian name and to deny that he was a *farangi*—the catch-all, derogatory term for "foreigner," which had become tantamount, thanks to European behavior, to "barbarian." Nobili created a significant corpus of Christian-Indian writing and literature during the fifty years prior to his death in 1656. It was a legacy that was continued and taken to, if anything, an even greater length by another Jesuit, Constanzo Giuseppe Beschi (1680–1747), who continued Nobili's tradition of prodigious scholarship in the milieu of the local culture and added the further Brahman characteristic of living in sumptuous style. This last was made easier when the local Nawab (Mughal provincial governor) appointed him as a senior government minister and showered gifts and income upon him.

Beyond this, several missionaries made contact with the Mughal court in north India, most notably during the reign of Akbar (1556–1605). The Muslim emperor showed polite interest in the Jesuits' theological arguments, but he was more concerned to obtain information about the European technologies that provided telescopes and firearms. Jerome Xavier, great-nephew of Francis, was the only one of the Christians to engage the emperor in more than superficial discussion; he accomplished this feat by the simple though arduous technique of mastering enough of the court language to hold a conversation. Even so, Christian influence in the Mughal Empire remained merely at the level of diplomacy. It was an achievement even to have progressed so far.

Japan

Portuguese traders made their first contacts with Japan in 1543. The following year, one of their ships sailed away with a local man fleeing arrest for manslaughter. This fugitive, Yajiro, converted to Christianity and took the baptismal name Paul. Thus it was that when, in 1549, Francis Xavier and his Jesuit companions arrived in Satsuma, western Japan, they were accompanied by a native Christian translator and guide.

Xavier remained in the country only until 1551, but his fellow Jesuits continued their work with remarkable success, directing much of their effort at the local elites. Contact with the Japanese seems to have taken the wind out of the sails of the Europeans; these were a people whom even the habitually racist Europeans could not count as any whit inferior to themselves. The intelligence of the Japanese and their reticence about speaking their minds were constantly remarked upon in the journals and letters of the missionaries. So too were their fearful and frequent resort to lethal violence and their predilection for homosexuality. The Europeans also became acutely aware that Japanese cleanliness in both cooking and bodily hygiene contrasted so strongly with their own habits that they seemed to their hosts like unpleasant, smelly animals. Some made attempts to amend themselves.

The Jesuits, as always, were the fastest to adapt. From 1569 they succeeded in cultivating the friendship of Oda Nobunaga (1534–1582), the shogun, or principal military ruler. The first two decades of the missionaries' activity had coincided with the later phases of a period of chronic instability and civil war in Japan, in which both the fairly recent encroachments of Buddhism upon the underlying Shinto religion and the usual conflict between local autonomy and centralized rule were implicated. Since a number of Buddhist groups had opposed Nobunaga's rise to power, he was inclined to lend an interested ear to the beliefs and teachings of the exotic newcomers, "despising both Shinto and Buddhist deities and all other forms of idolatry and superstition." However, he himself, as the Jesuit Luis Frois noted after the initial meeting, "openly proclaims that there are no such things as a Creator of the Universe nor immortality of the soul, nor any life after death."[17]

Notwithstanding the failure to see eye-to-eye on such theological nuances, the relationship got off to a good start, and Nobunaga issued the padre a letter granting freedom from molestation and immunity from assisting the military. Freedom to preach was not explicitly stated, but it was undoubtedly implied.

Certainly Frois and his Jesuit companions needed all of the immunities they could get, for shortly afterward Buddhist zealots persuaded Emperor Ogimachi Tenno to issue an edict of death against Frois and to outlaw the preaching of Christianity. Fortunately for the Jesuit, however, the emperor was far less powerful than the shogun, who put the ostensible monarch firmly in his place.

The following years were good ones for Christians in Japan. Under Jesuit leadership and the protection of the shoguns, their numbers grew. Nobunaga's successor, Toyotomi Hideyoshi (1536–1598), took an equally benign view of the Christians during the early part of his tenure, giving them land in Osaka to build a church.

The number of converts during these early decades is variously estimated. Certainly they numbered in the hundreds within two years of Xavier's first arrival. One of the Jesuit missionaries, Gaspar Vilela (1525–1572), thought that there were 30,000 Japanese Christians by 1571; another, Alexander Valignano (1539–1606), estimated 150,000 by 1583. It is possible that the 1570s witnessed the explosion in Christian strength that these two figures imply, but it is likelier that the former estimate is a little pessimistic and the latter too optimistic. The turn of the century saw further advance, with the first two Japanese Jesuits ordained as priests—a development that Valignano had long urged as a necessity, on the straightforward ground that the local language was so complex that no foreigner could hope to master it to the level of educated natives, leaving the mission at a perpetual disadvantage in its campaign to win intellectual respect. By the early years of the seventeenth century,

Christian numbers had grown to 300,000, or a little more than 1 percent of the population.

But trouble was looming. The Jesuits had benefited from their position as exclusive bearers of the Christian faith, but the arrival of Spanish Franciscans in 1596 created the conditions for competition and conflict. Since the Jesuits had emphasized mission to the powerful and (following a reversal in 1579 of initial Jesuit policy on cultural matters) the virtues of accommodation to Japanese mores, dress, and customs, so the Franciscans did the reverse. Franciscan evangelism targeted the poor and challenged Japanese cultural norms.

The shoguns were alarmed, partly by the trends themselves and partly by the prospect of European quarrels being fought out on their shores. As early as 1587, Hideyoshi had shown signs of reversing his earlier policy by issuing some anti-Christian edicts. But these had not been well enforced and were limited in scope, designed as much for domestic consumption and to placate outraged Buddhists as for actual implementation. Christian growth continued during both the later part of Hideyoshi's shogunate and, after his death in 1598, the early years of his successor, Tokugawa Ieyasu (1542–1616). Unfortunately, Ieyasu's accession was marred by a rebellion in which one of the Christian nobles, Konishi Yukinaga, was a leading participant. Neither was the Christian reputation helped by Franciscan accusations that the Jesuits had urged Konishi on. It hardly mattered that Ieyasu decided, for the moment, to give the foreigners the benefit of the doubt; intra-Christian rivalries had surfaced again. The arrival in Japan, during the early years of the century, of Dutch and English merchants—Protestants whom the Portuguese and Spaniards decried as heretics—made internal Christian rivalries appear worse still. It was becoming apparent to the Japanese rulers that the advantages for trade and political relations with Europeans created by tolerating their faith might be outweighed by the rivalries and instabilities into which such a dalliance might drag Japan.

Perhaps the most important factor in the impending reversal of fortunes for Christianity was the changing situation inside Japan itself. During the early years of the mission, the faith of the Christians had seemed like a handy ally against the various Buddhist sects that stood in the way of powerful military leaders like Nobunaga. But with the country united under Hideyoshi, the utility of promoting a foreign religion seemed less compelling. The coming of the Franciscans and Dominicans, with their appeal to the poor and their insistence upon foreign ways, made Christianity seem subversive.

In 1606 decrees were issued declaring Christianity to be illegal. Persecution began in earnest from 1613, when a group of martyrs was burned in Arima. Two years later a Portuguese priest reported that the census taken in Nagasaki showed the local population to have fallen by 20,000 since the executions began, almost certainly as a result of internal migration of Christians. It seems that many of the local Christians moved to other areas of Japan in the aftermath of this event, thereby spreading the foreign contagion from its heartland in the southwest of the country to the north and east. As with the dispersal of the Jerusalem church in the mid-30s of the first century, new areas were evangelized as a result of persecution.

This did not stop the killing, however. A minimum of 434 Christians are recorded as having been put to death during the period 1614–1622. Tokugawa Ieyasu's successor, Tokugawa Hidetada (1579–1632), was even more committed to persecution, while his son, Tokugawa Iemitsu (1603–1651), was a sadist who positively delighted in the cruelties he contrived to inflict upon the Christians.

As the forcible suppression proceeded, it became apparent that the samurai and daimyo (noble) converts of the Jesuits stood less firm in their new faith than did the peasants and humble artisans converted by the Franciscans and Dominicans. For the nobility, the claims of feudal loyalty to their masters ranked even higher than the hope of heaven. Indeed, the perception that this was necessarily the case was the very linchpin of feudal order in Japan. By denying it and setting up a set of religious claims that trumped even those of fealty, Christianity stood revealed as a subversive religion; it was exactly what might have been expected of unwashed, garrulous Europeans.

But the undaunted faith of so many Christians among the common people of Japan was all the more irksome because of that subversiveness. Many of them attended the early executions to encourage the faithful martyrs in their hour of extremest need and to add their voices to the prayers and invocations cried out from the burning pyres. Many of the deaths were by crucifixion, rather than burning. As the authorities came to realize that the gruesome deaths encouraged, rather than daunted, the believers, measures were taken to curtail the victims' opportunities to bear witness: bits were placed in mouths; heads were held backward so they could look in no direction but upward.

The winter of 1637–1638 saw a peasant revolt in Shimabara and Amakusa of which the Christians were the principal protagonists. Many, perhaps most, of them had outwardly recanted their Christian faith already, though continuing to hold to it inwardly. In rebelling rather than suffering passively, they were also disregarding their missionary instructors' warnings about the requirements for a martyr's crown. So the rebellion should be seen as a measure of desperation. Indeed, the motives were not entirely religious, for the local magnates' methods of tax collection had extended to confiscating and torturing the wives and daughters of peasants until the required money had been extracted. It was an incident of this sort that sparked the revolt. But once it was underway, it quickly assumed a religious character.

The rebels seized Hara castle, where they were promptly besieged by a much larger force of samurai and professional soldiers. Even so, they repulsed them several times, inflicting serious casualties. The Dutch, who had lately replaced the Portuguese as Japan's principal European trading partner, obligingly sent a ship, the *De Ryp*, to bombard their fellow Christians from the sea. But that also was of little effect.

Starvation of the defenders and the exhaustion of their ammunition eventually did the work that the early assaults had failed to achieve. In April the enfeebled defenders were finally overrun. All, women and children included, were massacred. It is estimated that 37,000 Christians were killed in the revolt, though they had taken 10,000 of their vaunted enemies with them. The Dutch intervention may have been militarily ineffectual, but it had its commercial reward. From 1639, Portuguese trade with Japan was brought to a definitive halt. And what was a measly chink in Christian solidarity compared to a prize like that?

Japan was entering upon its two centuries of self-imposed isolation from the outside world. Yet the authorities continued to fear that the foreigners' religion might spread and pave the way for European domination of the country. Accordingly, suspect populations were often required to trample upon pictures of Christ and the Virgin in order to demonstrate their rejection of the Christian faith. That such grotesque ceremonies continued to be enforced until 1857 is ample testimony to the authorities' failure to be convinced that Christian beliefs did not linger on. And concerning that, at least, they were right. For some 60,000 secret Christians, their beliefs and practices handed down through generations, would later emerge into the light of day to astonish the age of Commodore Perry.

China

That the Jesuit mission in China was not commenced by the indefatigable and ubiquitous Francis Xavier was a circumstance prevented only by the death of the rugged pioneer in 1552, while he was on the way there, situated on an island just off the coast. The Portuguese had arrived as early as 1514 and had managed to antagonize the natives straight away by their behavior, which "was such that their status as barbarians was only too definitely confirmed."[18] Expelled from the country in the 1520s, they were reluctantly readmitted in the following decade, as further reflection persuaded the Chinese authorities that the monetary advantages outweighed, marginally, the distasteful necessity of containing the Europeans. From 1557, this awkward circle was finally squared when the Portuguese were given the use of Macao, an uninhabited island close to Canton (Guangzhou), which could easily be reoccupied by the Chinese at any time and from which the obnoxious foreigners were only occasionally permitted to venture forth to the mainland.

It was not the most auspicious start nor the greatest of recommendations for the Europeans' religion. The Jesuits did not finally succeed in gaining entrance to the country until 1583, when Matteo Ricci (1552–1610) and Michele Ruggieri (1543–1607) arrived in Zhaoqing, near Canton. But the two Italians had spent the previous years in Macao, imbibing principles that, under the guiding hand of Alessandro Valignano, the superior for all Jesuits in the Far East, were becoming central to the missionary thrust of their order. These dictated that maximum cultural adaptation and profound interaction with indigenous scholarship were to be top priorities, with a view to gaining influence over the learned and, ultimately, the endorsement of the monarch. Accordingly, Ruggieri and Ricci had been instructed to abandon reliance on interpreters and to learn Chinese.

The two men spent the next years establishing other missions in central China, including Nanjing and Nanchang. Adopting the dress and hairstyle of Confucian scholars, they insinuated themselves into their circles and engaged in quiet, tactful pre-evangelism, the purpose of which was to gain credibility and win a hearing for the Catholic faith as well as to defuse the Chinese prejudice that all Westerners were barbarians. A further large obstacle to Christianization presented itself in the mid-1590s when the Japanese invaded Korea and thereby came into conflict with China; the Japanese army included a Christian general, Konishi Yukinaga, and more than 15,000 Christian soldiers.[19]

Although Ruggieri returned to Europe in the 1590s, Ricci spent the final years of his life in China, from 1601 in Beijing, where by 1608 he was able to claim that there were "more than two thousand Christians." In the same year one of his most important converts, Xu Guangqi, and the Italian Jesuit Lazzaro Cattaneo had established a group of over two hundred Christians in Xu's native city of Shanghai—a number that would

Matteo Ricci.
Illustration from Emmanuel
Pereira (Yu wen-huit), 1610.

multiply to between 18,000 and 20,000 by the mid-seventeenth century.[20] Back in Beijing, Ricci continued, until his death in 1610, to use his expertise in astronomy, geography, and mathematics to gain a respectful audience for his specifically religious teachings.

That audience never included the Ming emperor, however. For a foreigner to remain in the imperial capital unmolested was triumph enough. But several key scholar-officials did make the leap and become Christians. During those years Ricci produced his *T'ien Chu Shih-i*, on the true idea of God, a book that achieved posthumous fame when, in 1692, the Manchu emperor K'ang Hsi issued a formal edict of toleration for Christianity after reading it.[21]

In his book, Ricci had tried to infuse Chinese ideas with Christian content. It was a methodology that became more controversial when it came to the vexing subject of ancestor veneration. How far was this practice idolatrous? How far was it merely compatible with biblical injunctions to "honor your father and mother"? Wherever possible, the Jesuits inclined to a generous view.

Despite a bout of localized persecution of Christian missionaries and their converts in 1615, the missionary work in China continued to proceed smoothly for several decades after Ricci's death. He was succeeded by likeminded and similarly brilliant Jesuit advocates of Catholicism who, like him, could intrigue their Chinese hosts with a knowledge of scientific and technological subjects, even as they plied them with their alien religion. Such was the Rhineland Jesuit, Johann Adam Schall (1592–1666), who came to China in the early 1620s; others included two friends and colleagues of Galileo and Kepler.[22] The discovery of the Sigan-Fu stone in 1625 and of a cross cut in stone at Fukien in 1638 allowed the Jesuits to disprove the claim that Christianity was something entirely foreign to China. The artifacts showed that Nestorian Christianity (the same variety, of course, that the Jesuits had tried so hard to dismantle as heretical in India) had been present for many centuries.

As elsewhere, the Jesuits were keen that the faith be indigenized by translating the liturgy and the Scriptures into classical Chinese and by appointing Chinese clergy. The translation was managed early on, though with some difficulty; Cardinal Robert Bellarmine argued back in Italy for this necessary derogation from the Church's predilection for Latin. However, it was not until 1656 that Gregory Lopez, a Chinese Dominican, was ordained priest; a Chinese Jesuit followed suit eight years later. But the Jesuits had to wait almost another generation, until 1688, before three more Chinese were ordained. In the meantime, Lopez had been appointed bishop in 1673.

During the midcentury a series of disruptions had broken out over the mission—one on the side of the Chinese and one on the side of the missionaries. The first of these disruptions stemmed from upheaval inside China itself. During 1644 the Ming dynasty came under serious—and, as it turned out, terminal—threat. Rebels captured Beijing, provoking Emperor Zhu Yiujian to commit suicide. The members of his government, in desperation, asked the Manchus, nomadic warriors from beyond the Great Wall, to expel the rebels from the city. They did so, but felt disinclined to leave so rich a spoil to its original possessors, and concluded by conquering the whole of China and establishing a dynasty that was to endure until 1911.

The very fragility of Manchu rule inclined them to leave all possible stones undisturbed, and this included, fortunately for the missionaries, a willingness to overlook the fact that some of them remained with the fleeing (and then exiled) Ming court. Accordingly, Johann Schall was retained as royal astronomer. In the mid-1660s, the Confucian thinker Yang Guangxian briefly held sway at court and prompted a harsh anti-Christian policy, which led to the execution of five Chinese Christian astronomers and the temporary closing of churches. But by the end of the decade the fury—and, with it, Yang's moment of prominence—was past.

The Jesuits remained in favor with the Manchu dynasty, most particularly with Emperor K'ang Hsi (1662–1722), through the late seventeenth century. So taken was this emperor with the faith of the Christians that he composed the following stanza in praise of Christ:

> With his task done on the cross,
> His blood forms itself into a streamlet.

> Grace flows from West Heaven in long patience:
>   Trials in four courts,
>   Long walks at midnight,
> Thrice denied by friend before the cock crew twice,
> Six-footer hanging at the same height as two thieves.
> It is a suffering that moves the whole world and all ranks.
> Hearing his seven words makes all souls cry.[23]

The second of the previously mentioned disruptions to the smooth flow of the mission was ultimately more serious than that caused by political upheaval in China; it resulted from the introduction of the Franciscans and Dominicans to China during the 1630s, which brought about the consequent intramissionary rivalry. The new arrivals had little of the Jesuits' regard for Chinese culture and even less of their tact. For them, the processes of Christianization and Europeanization were one and the same. Jesuit alarm that the newcomers would unsettle the Chinese with their crass attempts to disseminate the faith looked to the newcomers suspiciously like protective jealousy for their own order. Franciscan and Dominican protests at the Jesuits' alleged syncretism seemed like jealousy at what had already been achieved.

In favor of the newer missionaries it should be said that by mingling with the common people rather than hobnobbing with elite culture as the Jesuits did, the Franciscans and Dominicans came up against Chinese religious practices in their least sophisticated form. And in that context, ancestor ceremonies looked less like mere respect, or even "veneration," and more like "worship."

This phenomenon is a common one in religious matters. Sophisticated elucidations by Eastern Orthodox theologians of the significance of icons—veneration; worship, not of the icon, but of what it represents; the sanctifying effects of the incarnation upon the material world, thereby rendering religious art possible—and their dark insistence upon iconoclasm's implicit heretical dualism: all such arguments look less persuasive at street level, where actual practice manifests itself as what its Protestant detractors took it for all along: idolatrous worship. And so it was with the Chinese and their ancestor worship.

Ancestor veneration, though, was not the whole of it. Religion in many Chinese villages was essentially polytheistic. Divination was widespread. When working among the uneducated, one of the more entrenched practices the Franciscans and Dominicans came up against was that of feng shui. It was as well, perhaps, for the missionaries' peace of mind that they could not foresee the day when feeble-minded Europeans would think themselves sophisticated for allowing its considerations to dictate the specifics of their jacuzzis.

The dispute between the Catholic orders over the degree of permissible accommodation rumbled on. In 1693 the vicar apostolic of Fujian, Charles Maigrot, forbade accommodations with ancestor worship. The Jesuits made the tactical error of appealing over his head, not to the pope, but to the Chinese emperor, who naturally supported their own stance, thereby delivering the initiative to the Jesuits' enemies and to Eurocentric officials back in Rome.

Pope Clement XI outlawed the accommodations to native culture that the Jesuits had been making for a century and specifically ruled that the use of the term *T'ien* for God was not permissible on the grounds that its content was impersonal, in contrast to the personal (or three-personal) God of Christianity. This undercut Ricci's famous apologetic work as well as his attempt to shuffle the content of the term toward a closer approximation of the Christian idea. The so-called Rites Controversy (for the dispute centered upon the permissibility or otherwise of Chinese ancestor rites) was fought out with furious heat for several decades until, in 1742, Pope Benedict XIV found definitively against the Jesuits and accommodation.

By then, however, Emperor K'ang Hsi had reversed his earlier benign view of the Christians, correctly discerning their internal dissensions and the threat to Chinese values likely to be posed by European versions of orthodoxy. In 1721 he banned the religion he had done so much to promote over a long reign. The following year he died, and his successor began active persecution of Christians in 1723, a persecution that became more active from 1736, under Emperor Qianlong.

Unlike many persecutions, however, this one was more effective in the provinces than in the capital. The Beijing Jesuits were simply too useful to the emperors to be dispensed with. Their advice and technical expertise was still called for, and so the four churches in the city were allowed to function, even as those elsewhere were being closed down. By 1743 there were allegedly 40,000 Catholics in the city and a thousand baptisms annually—yet just four years later a significant number of Christians, including several foreign clergy, were executed in Fujian. Starting in 1760, the Dutch Jesuit Laimbeckhoven, bishop of Nanjing, spent over a quarter of a century in hiding, until his death in 1787.

By then the very order to which he belonged had been suppressed—not by the emperor in Beijing but by the pope in Rome. The cultural work in the capital continued under the auspices of the Lazarist Order. The church in remote Sechuan province, in the southwest, thrived during the late eighteenth century, increasing from 4,000 adherents in 1756 to 25,000 in 1792 and even operating a seminary, buried deep in the mountains, for fifty years until it was burned down.[24] But the wider project to Christianize China had stalled. It awaited further forward movement under the twin impact of the Protestant missionary movement and ever more aggressive European colonial powers during the nineteenth century.

The Philippines

None of the countries in Asia that we have considered so far made a generalized move toward Christianization, although progress in China during the late twentieth century has been such as to give rise to hopes that this may yet happen. But the Philippines witnessed early success. First contacted in 1521 as a result of Magellan's voyage, it was only in 1570 that King Philip II of Spain determined upon a vigorous forward policy of conquest and Christianization. Yet the mission proceeded smoothly enough that, in 1581, Domingo de Salazar was appointed the first bishop of Manila. Jesuits, Dominicans, Franciscans, and Augustinians—all became involved at an early stage.

The principal difference between circumstances in the Philippines and those elsewhere are to be sought, as so often, not so much among the missionaries (Spanish rather than Portuguese) as among the missioned. In Japan, India, and China the Christians found themselves face-to-face with venerable, long-established, and highly sophisticated cultures and the formidable religions that both shaped those cultures and by which they were enshrined. The Filipinos, by contrast, were mostly animists before the Europeans arrived. The major exception was on the southern island of Mindanao, which had already become partly Muslim. (As news reports remind us at regular intervals, it remains so.)

The great monotheisms, principally Christianity and Islam, have been able to make short work, in recent centuries, of animism. They have succeeded in converting its adherents and in transforming the cultures of the peoples who once adhered to it. But when they have encountered one another—or, for that matter, one of the other great religions with a long history of literacy, scholarship, high culture, philosophy, and sophisticated argumentation behind it—then the going has been tougher.

The Filipinos responded positively enough to Spanish attempts at Catholicization, though all of the usual hesitations—attachment to traditions, long-practiced ceremonies and festivals, or polygamy—needed to be overcome. As so often, the missionaries showed patience and flexibility.

The advice of Pope Gregory I, back in the late sixth century, concerning the conversion of the Anglo-Saxons continued to be remembered, as it had been throughout the Middle Ages:

> The temples of idols in that nation should not be destroyed, but . . . the idols themselves that are in them should be. Let . . . these same temples . . . be transferred from the worship of idols to the service of the true God; that, when the people themselves see that these temples are not destroyed, they may put away error from their heart, and, knowing and adoring the true God, may have recourse with the more familiarity to the places they have been accustomed to.[25]

Much of the liturgical calendar can be accounted for in this fashion. It was a policy calculated to minimize opposition where it existed and to keep things smooth where it did not.

The Philippines was a case in the latter category. In the Americas, the clergy and the monks had taken up the cause of the remaining, mistreated natives only once a vast amount of damage had been done and the hold of the Iberian conquerors upon the remnant was secure. In the Philippines, the process of evangelization encountered so little resistance that the missionaries felt sufficient self-assurance at a very early date to call for a stop to unwarranted political and military take-overs by their countrymen and coreligionists. One of de Salazar's first acts as bishop was to summon a synod of clergy, which opined that the Spanish king held no more than a "quasi-imperial authority" over the islands by virtue of having introduced the Christian mission in the first place. But "if the gospel were preached in places so well governed that there be no question of depriving the natives of their self-rule in order to establish the faith," if the populace broadly welcomed the process of Christianization and there was no hindrance placed in its path, "then they may not be deprived of their lands or of the right to rule themselves."[26] The strong implication was that in the Philippines those conditions might well be met, or nearly so, and that King Philip II should confine himself to protecting the mission with minimal force.

The Catholic Church continued to urge a softly, softly approach and to stress the rights of the native rulers. After Bishop Salazar's death in 1594, Philip was persuaded to return tribute money unjustly exacted from pagan chiefs by Spanish menaces and to deign to ask the conquered Filipinos whether they would voluntarily accept the king of Spain as their sovereign. It was not a technique that he had pioneered in the Netherlands. Perhaps if he had, much blood might have been spared—because it worked. (On the other hand, the fact that the

Philippine chieftains chose as they did may have spared them—and posterity—the grisly spectacle of what might have ensued in the event of a refusal.)

The Eastern Churches

In addition to the churches we have had cause to notice in this chapter thus far—and these have been European, or planted by Europeans— there were also a number of important non-European indigenous churches, to whose fortunes we must now turn. These were generally non-Chalcedonian; that is, they did not subscribe to the Christological definitions of the Council of Chalcedon in 451. In practice, however, such theological peculiarities counted for little—certainly by the sixteenth century. Instead, the distinctive natures of the various non-Chalcedonian churches enshrined important cultural and ethnic traditions.

Thomas Christians in India

The considerable overlap and interaction between the Thomas Christians in southern India and the Portuguese makes it appropriate that we should consider their case immediately after the other Jesuit missions and as a starting point for our overview of the other Eastern churches. We noted in chapter 1 that the encounter between European and Indian Christians, from the turn of the fifteenth and sixteenth centuries, had led to considerable and growing bewilderment on both sides. Initially at least, each needed the other. The indigenous Indian churches sought protection against their numerous enemies—protection that European weaponry was well able to provide. Conversely, the Portuguese needed a base of friendly natives in a complex, sophisticated society with which they wished to trade. But as the embrace between the two forms of Christianity deepened, it became clear that the Europeans would brook no divergence from their own, Western-Catholic norms.

The Indian Christians were required by their Portuguese masters to conform to Roman doctrines, particularly in respect to Christology and the veneration of Mary as "Mother of God" (rather than the Nestorians' preferred "mother of Christ"). The veneration of images was also an issue of contention, with the Catholics requiring it and the Nestorians suspecting it as smacking of Hindu idolatry. Francis Xavier's arrival in 1542, as the first of the Jesuit mission to India, served to strengthen the European side. The installations, depositions, and restorations of Indian metropolitans flowed thick and fast during the 1550s and 1560s, as one after another was displaced by the Portuguese and deported to Europe, there to be interrogated and "reeducated" into Western practices and ideas. Yet each time, the returning prelate would relapse as soon as he felt free to do so.

Finally, in 1575 the Portuguese determined that all future metropolitans would be appointed by the king of Portugal. The metropolitan, Mar Abraham, thereupon interceded directly with the pope in Rome. But for good measure, he sent warnings to the Chaldean catholicos in Syria that the Indian Christians were about to be lost to his patriarchate. In case this failed to move him, Abraham mentioned that this would, as a matter of course, entail the loss of their revenues. But even this consideration could not summon help where none was to be found, for the Syrian patriarch presided over a declining flock under Muslim control, while the Portuguese had both priests and soldiers on the ground.

When Mar Abraham refused to ordain students graduating from the Jesuits' seminary in Vaipikkottai in 1590 (a seminary founded three years previously), the bad relations moved rapidly toward terminal crisis. The native and Roman Catholic churches drifted toward schism. Pope Clement VIII in Rome issued orders to the Catholic archbishop of Goa, the principal base of the Portuguese, to arrest Mar Abraham. But the fear of popular fury served to keep the old man at liberty until his death from natural causes in 1597. Only then did Archbishop de Menezes seek to obey the Apostolic See (lack of such obedience being, of course, the primary charge against the Thomas Christians whom he was bullying). Menezes moved to frustrate the dying metropolitan's attempt to ensure a succession, by detaining any clergy who passed through Hormuz en route to India from western Asia. He then attempted to force Archdeacon George of the Cross, Mar Abraham's designated but as yet unconsecrated successor, to conform.

Despite native threats of violent reprisal, Nestorian libraries were destroyed in the Catholic campaign to expunge native heresy. The Synod of Diamper of 1599 completed and made official the work of European takeover. The local churches were to be reconstructed along Roman Catholic lines, the Nestorian patriarch of Babylon was anathematized, the legacy of the apostle Thomas was pronounced inferior to that of Peter, and the authority of the bishop of Rome was made binding.

But the Catholic victory was not quite complete. Over the next five and a half decades, George of the Cross and his successors maintained a shadow church, holding the real allegiance of the ordinary Christians who, unable to resist the Portuguese and their native supporters outwardly, nevertheless dissented inwardly from the foreign beliefs and customs being imposed upon them. Menezes had returned in triumph to Rome after Diamper, yet his Roman-appointed successors were unable to gain compliance from a population for whom, over generations, dissimulation, evasion, and subversion of stronger, alien rulers had become second nature.

Finally, in 1653 the Thomas Christians took courage and decided to consecrate their own patriarch, independent of both Babylon and Rome, thereby reconstituting their church. The move had such overwhelming support, and the failed attempt to impose an alien orthodoxy stood so discredited, that the Portuguese could do little but accept the fait accompli. Parambil Tumi was consecrated as Patriarch Mar Thoma I. His supporters insisted that only four hundred people remained loyal to his Catholic rival, Archbishop Garcia—a claim that would have served little purpose had it not been a reasonable approximation to the truth.

There remained for the Indian Christians the ticklish problem of Portuguese rule. But even this was dispensed with ten years later when, in 1663, the Dutch arrived and wrested control of Cochin and Malabar for themselves. Fearing the advent of Protestants more than that of Hindus or Nestorians, the Roman bishop swiftly consecrated an Indian successor (by delightful irony a cousin of Mar Thoma I) and left for home.

But the losses on the Indian side remained considerable. The unity of the local Christians, already under considerable strain from internal dissensions before the European meddling had even begun, was now fractured yet further. The link with Syria and Babylon had been broken. Perhaps worst of all, virtually all of the Thomas Christian literature and records had been systematically destroyed, both immediately before and in the aftermath of the Synod of Diamper. The Indian churches had been robbed of their history.[27]

Christians in the Ottoman Middle East

India apart, the Coptic, Syrian Orthodox, and Armenian Christians of the sixteenth and seventeenth centuries lived, for the most part, under Muslim rule—a circumstance that was seldom favorable to their prosperity and often capricious in its cruelty. The diplomatic leverage exerted by Christian powers could sometimes win concessions for Christians under Muslim rule, however. In 1597 French intervention with the Ottoman sultan persuaded him to revoke his own previous decisions to imprison monks in Palestine and to turn the Church of the Holy Sepulchre into a mosque.

The special relationship between the Most Christian Kings of France and the Muslim empire that threatened Christendom with obliteration was built upon the solid foundation of their shared enmity toward the Hapsburgs, both in Spain and in the Holy Roman Empire. Because of this, the French could take liberties with the Ottomans that other European powers would neither have dared nor attempted. Thus it was that in 1596 King Henri IV had obtained guarantees from the sultan protecting Western pilgrims to the Holy Land from mistreatment by Ottoman officials or from being subjected to forcible conversion to Islam.

The papacy was not above utilizing the same privileged relationship between Paris and Istanbul to forward its own purposes. French Jesuits, Capuchins, Carmelites, and Dominicans were all dispatched to the Ottoman lands during the 1620s and 1630s in order to persuade the sultan's Christian subjects to transfer their allegiances from their own churches to that of Rome—a move that could most swiftly be achieved by setting up Uniate churches that would bring about ecclesiastical loyalty while leaving cultural and, as far as possible, liturgical customs and sensitivities undisturbed.

But the Westerners were overreaching themselves. The Porte (the Ottoman government) allowed the missions to proceed, observed what was happening, and acted only when the missions appeared to have any prospect of success. For the sultan's Christian subjects to focus their religious identity in opposition to that of Rome suited him too well.

However, as the power of the Ottoman Empire began to wane, so too did its ability to resist the blandishments of the infidel powers. The Catholic missions enjoyed political protection and, for the Christian *reaya* (the "flock" of unbelieving subjects under the rule of the Muslim sultan), the kudos that naturally attended association with the Western powers. During the late seventeenth and the eighteenth centuries, Uniate churches—that is, bodies in union with Rome but continuing to practice their historic rites—proliferated until almost every one of the ancient churches of the East had suffered losses to Romanist schism. Their various patriarchs added to the clutter of rival pontiffs—Greek, Armenian, and Jacobite—in Syria and the Near East, with several in both Antioch and Jerusalem, each presiding over slowly diminishing flocks. A small Georgian Catholic Church came into existence during the same period as the other Uniate churches, reflecting the desire of some Georgians to keep channels open to the West.

Armenians in the Persian Empire

In 1604 war loomed between the Persians and the empire to their west—an event as ineluctable as the passing of the seasons, if just a little less regular and rather a lot more lethal. In the centuries before and after Christ it had been the pagan—and then later the Christian—Romans who were the Persians' enemy; during the Middle Ages it had been the Orthodox Byzantines; now it was the Muslim Ottoman Turks. But the contested ground remained the same as it always had been: a belt of territory running from the Caucasus Mountains southward, to the east of Anatolia, passing through Syria, and then petering out into the deserts east of the Jordan River. Being a contested borderland to which dissidents might flee and ethnic minorities find refuge—and where various groups had been left behind in the wake of advancing and retreating empires—had produced a rich diversity of languages, religions, and cultures, from the "anthropological zoo" of the Caucasian lands to the cultural melee of Lebanon, any and all of whom might suffer in the next bout of fighting or in the next maneuver for power by the great ones to the east and west.

In the fighting of 1604 it was the Armenians' turn to suffer—as it so frequently was. Christian Armenia had been devastated by wars between the two great Muslim powers since the beginning of the previous century, and it had been divided between them since 1555. But the part apportioned to the Persian Empire now found itself under attack from larger, superior Ottoman forces, who had been gradually overrunning Georgia and Azerbaijan since 1578. The Persian shah, Abbas I (1587–1629), determined upon a scorched earth policy that would leave the invading soldiers nothing to eat. The Christian Armenian populations of the city of Yerevan, of Mount Ararat (which overlooks it), of the trading city of Julfa (which had about 10,000 inhabitants), and of all the surrounding districts were cleared out by the Persian soldiers; all houses, crops, and food stores were burned.

The population of around 60,000 families was then shepherded toward the plain of Echmiadzin, the ancient religious center of the Armenian Church and whose name means "The Only-Begotten has descended"; it was the seat of the catholicos. From there, the terrified Christians were driven toward the Araxes River. The idea was to get them away from the advancing Ottomans, to whom they might prove as useful and profitable subjects as they hitherto had been to the shah. With too few boats available and the enemy arrival imminent, the panicking soldiers drove the Armenians into the river, heedless of their ability to swim. The result was a grisly massacre. Those who held back on the forced march or at the riverbank were beaten, mutilated, or killed. Two men, one of them the brother of Catholicos Arakel, were beheaded and their heads stuck on poles.[28]

Rapes and murders by the soldiers proliferated amid the terrified chaos. Those Armenians who succeeded in crossing the torrent found their forced marches continued on the far bank, until their Persian masters judged the pursuing Turks to be a safe distance behind. Other Persian military forces continued the deportation of Christians from the threatened regions for months afterward, killing thousands in the process.

But Armenian durability was legendary. The survivors who eventually reached the Persian capital of Isfahan were given land outside the city, and they established the town of New Julfa, complete with a cathedral and other churches decorated with frescoes depicting scenes of their Christian history and heritage. The late 1660s and the 1670s, under the reign of the debauched Shah Suleiman, were a troubled time when religious minorities of all kinds suffered from the whims of the monarch: thousands of Jews were killed while the Armenians were subject to crippling financial exactions. The unsettled conditions encouraged brigandage, which harmed trade by making travel unsafe.

Even as early as the mid-seventeenth century, however, the Julfa Armenians had established trade links in Vietnam, Java, and the Philippines. A few decades later, they were operating in Tibet, in time to greet the Catholic Capuchin missionaries who arrived there in 1707 and to act as interpreters for them. By the end of the seventeenth century, New Julfa was prospering and boasted a number of opulent mansions and wealthy traders. Even the more modest dwellings of the majority were distinguished by their order and cleanliness.

Tibet was not the only place where Catholic missionaries found Armenians waiting for them. They had been waiting for the Portuguese on the coasts of southern India two centuries before. When the Italian priest missionary Niccolo Lancilloto reached Cochin in 1548, he found an Armenian bishop who had been "teaching the principles of our faith to the Christians of St. Thomas" for forty years. Armenian Christian merchants had established themselves in the Moghul capital of Agra also. Though few in number, from the early seventeenth century they developed a talent for gaining the trust of the Muslim emperors. A number of Armenian women became royal wives or married powerful officials and influential European envoys in India. By 1666 Armenian Christians had settled in Madras also, but they did not succeed in establishing a church there until 1712. Sixty years later an Armenian press was set up in the city, publishing a book of moral theology the following year.

The intrepid Armenian Christians had penetrated Burma at about the same time they were getting settled in Agra. Their church in Syriam, near Rangoon, was attacked and burned down by raiders. But this did no more than dent the enormous commercial power they came to wield in that country and the consequent influence they had over the king.

The Armenians' abilities in trade and their consequent capacity for being transplanted from one place to another, renewing their corporate and religious life each time as if by miracle: these are qualities—and historical experiences—that closely parallel those of the Jews.

Last Remains in Sudan

The Sudanese Copts were less able to weather the terrible storms that came their direction. By the start of our period, they were already close to extinction under the weight of Muslim incursions.

Sudan had once been a flourishing Christian civilization, with several Christian kingdoms—most notably those of Nuba and Alwa—along the Upper Nile. A substantial argument can be made for the "Ethiopian eunuch," of Acts 8:26–39 being from this region, and it is certain that the bulk of the population was Christianized during the mid-sixth century. The Alwa kingdom collapsed to Muslim invaders in the late thirteenth century, and that of the Nuba suffered the same fate almost a hundred years later. But Christian influence persisted long afterward.

Indeed, it seems likely that Islam did not simply supplant Christianity but, rather, that Muslim incursions cut off the Nubian Christians from their traditional supply of foreign clergy and bishops and that this had the effect of strangling the churches. This is consistent with the report of Francisco Alvarez, a Portuguese who traveled in Ethiopia in the 1520s. He noted that during his time there a group of six Nubians had visited the Ethiopian king, requesting priests and monks to be sent back with them, since their supply of bishops from Constantinople had dried up long since and the Christianity of their people had lapsed. One of Alvarez's traveling companions, John the Syrian, found corroborating evidence of this state of affairs: 150 churches in Nuba, complete with crucifixes and mural paintings, though all were old and disused.

But no help came. Two hundred years later, in 1734, Ildefonso of Palermo, a member of the Franciscan mission to Upper Egypt, encountered reports of Christians in an outlying area whose religious observance was reduced to baptizing their children at an old church, using the ministrations of the last remaining priest. Eight years later, in 1742, other members of the same mission encountered more fragmentary evidence of vestigial Christianity in remote villages, including a monastery that was still used by the people although there were no monks and stories that had been handed down through generations of local Christians martyred at the hands of the Muslims. Even where all active Christian life had died out, folk customs continued to include the use of the sign of the cross to protect both grain stores and people, especially newborns. For most purposes, however, Sudanese Christianity was extinct, awaiting reintroduction by Western missionaries during the colonial age.[29]

4

THE CONFLICTS WITHIN CHURCHES

PROTESTANTS

▼

The fissures within Christendom were not only between churches but also within them. It had, of course, always been this way, but the struggles of the Reformation and Counter-Reformation had the effect of intensifying internal squabbles. This was because what was at stake was the definition of, for example, Lutheranism (or the Church of England or the Roman Catholic Church) and so also the definition of what was being contended for against the rival ecclesiastical bodies. To define the legacy of Luther in the way that Melanchthon wished to do was to lay down one set of markers vis-à-vis Catholicism and Calvinism; to define it in the way in which Melanchthon's enemy Matthias Flacius Illyricus (Matija Vlačić) wished was to fight those rivals on slightly different ground and with different levels of intensity.

The German Lutherans and the Formula of Concord

The opening of our period saw the Lutheran churches hopelessly divided along the lines we have just hypothesized. To be sure, Melanchthon himself had died in 1560, but his party, the Philippists, lived on. Broadly, this group stood for a flexible interpretation of Luther's theological legacy. Their opponents, the Gnesio-Lutherans (or Strict Lutherans) took the opposite stance.

The quarrel had its origins in 1547, when the armies of the Schmalkadic League, an alliance of Protestant German princes, had been routed by Holy Roman Emperor Charles V at the Battle of Mühlberg. For a few years it looked as though the Lutheran states might have to revert to Catholicism. Even Wittenberg itself had been captured by the victorious imperial forces. The religious settlement imposed upon the hitherto-Protestant states may have been called "the Interim" (implying a final arrangement at a later date), but it was harsh enough. The only Protestantism left to them was permission for clergy to marry and for the laity to receive communion wine as well as bread. (The Roman church, it will be remembered, was in the habit of compensating its own priests for their enforced celibacy by reserving the chalice only for them.)

At this, the nadir of Lutheran fortunes, Melanchthon had felt able to treat with the forces of Antichrist, conceding the return of a Latin liturgy, seven sacraments, and many other aspects of Catholic form and ritual. In this Melanchthon was probably accurately reflecting Luther in thinking many things *adiaphora* (indifferent or of secondary importance) if the gospel itself was left free. Even so, it is doubtful Luther would have approved the extent of the concessions. In any case, Melanchthon was repaid for his flexibility by a great loss of popularity among ordinary Lutherans and the emergence of an intransigent party under Matthias Flacius Illyricus, who left Wittenberg for Jena, which remained under Protestant control.

Flacius denounced all compromise and encouraged popular resistance to the Interim. He was rewarded when the political and military tide turned again in 1555, allowing the Protestant princes to extract a restoration of full-blown Lutheranism in those states that had held to it previously.

The Peace of Augsburg settled the religious conflict between Lutheranism and Catholicism within Germany for sixty-three years, but it did no such thing *within* Lutheranism. The question now was: what did full-blown Lutheranism mean? The Philippists had not merely been willing to deal with the Catholics on their right; they wished also to mend fences with the Calvinists on their left. This latter meant blurring the distinction between Luther's insistence that recipients of communion received the body of Christ "*in* the bread" and the Reformed, who shunned such physicality and taught that the body of Christ was received mysteriously *"with* the bread." The Gnesio-Lutherans, predictably, would brook no compromise on this either; for them, Luther's doctrine of communion was sacrosanct. Luther had famously retorted that, if he were ever forced to choose, he would rather "drink pure blood with the pope than pure wine with Zwingli";[1] Flacius continued to take the same stance, looking upon the Reformed as little better than heretics; the Philippists, he thought, were Crypto-Calvinists.

This last epithet bears more than a little irony. It refers, of course, to the willingness of Melanchthon's party to meet the Reformed halfway on the issue of sacramental theology. Yet, on doctrines of predestination and free will, it was the Gnesio-Lutherans and the Reformed who were at one (as Luther and Calvin had been); the Philippist party inclined to a belief in free will.

German Lutheranism continued to tear itself apart with these disputes for a generation. In 1577 an attempt was made to heal the breaches when Jakob Andreae (1528–1590), a theologian under the patronage of the Elector Augustus of Saxony, produced the Formula of Concord. This document's simple trick was to declare the match a draw by upholding one of the key Gnesio-Lutheran views (the doctrine of consubstantiation, the body of Christ being *in* the bread) and one of the key Philippist contentions (that people have free will). The first dispute, however, was universally perceived by Lutherans as more important than the latter, and so the formula was widely rejected by Philippists. The Danish king ostentatiously threw his copy into the fire.

Many Philippists were, in any case, slowly accepting the accusation that they were Crypto-Calvinists and drifting into the Reformed camp. This, of course, deprived them of any legal status under the terms of the Peace of Augsburg—but then Catholics, Lutherans, and Reformed alike were playing all kinds of dirty tricks with the stipulations of that treaty, and so Reformed influence in Germany was able to continue to grow during the later sixteenth century, its illegality notwithstanding. During the period from 1580 to 1605 the Palatinate, Bremen, Anhalt, and most of Hesse moved in this direction and subscribed to the Reformed Heidelberg Catechism of 1563.

If the Formula of Concord helped to bring at least some measure of greater unity to the Lutherans, its unbending stance on eucharistic doctrine helped to accentuate even further the differences with other Protestants. Lutheranism had become merely a conservative form of Protestantism, the religion of the Scandinavian kingdoms and the German principalities. Lutheranism was the only Protestant body to hold such "high" views of the Eucharist, and after 1577 it was the only Protestant

German Protestantism in 1618.

state church not to hold an unequivocally predestinarian stance. Thus by its distinctive quirkiness, Lutheranism made itself parochial. This was a tendency reinforced by the strong subjection of Lutheran churches to the secular governments that upheld them. In these respects, Lutheranism was coming to resemble Eastern Orthodoxy: content to cling to the popular, almost tribal, loyalty of certain populations and distant from the universalizing impulses present in Roman Catholicism, in Calvinism, and, later, in evangelicalism.

This is not to say, however, that Lutheranism failed to expand for a while. Prussia was consolidated, and several smaller states subscribed to the Formula of Concord during the last two decades of the century. Growth continued, however quietly and dangerously, in southern Germany and Austria until the beginning of the Thirty Years' War in 1618 utterly destroyed Protestantism there. But the original dynamism was gone.

The English Church (1570–1625)

The accession of Elizabeth to the English throne in 1558 had been both a great deliverance and a perplexing nuisance to those determined Protestants who wished for a clean break with England's religious past. It was a great deliverance because she replaced her deceased half-sister, Mary, who had spent her five-year reign in a determined, persecuting, but ultimately fruitless attempt to reunite the Church of England with Rome after its twenty-year separation. It was a perplexing nuisance because the newly re-separated Church of England that Elizabeth established seemed, in the eyes of many observers, to be barely Protestant at all. "We in England are so far off from having a church rightly reformed according to the prescript of God's word, that as yet we are not come to the outward face of the same"—so opined one Puritan tract of 1572, *The First Admonition to the Parliament*. According to its authors, Elizabeth's preferred liturgy, the form of church government, and the clerical garments that ministers were required to wear "are drawn out of the Pope's shop . . . antichristian and devilish."[2]

Whence this intemperate fury? It had been a decade in building but, even then, was shared only by a minority of radicals. The Act of Uniformity of 1559 had established a new Book of Common Prayer, modeled closely upon its predecessor of 1552 (which had been produced during the short reign of the boy king, Edward VI) but modified in a conservative direction. The language to be used at the celebration of communion was an exercise in studied ambiguity, allowing room for both "real presence" and memorial doctrines. Worst of all for consistent Protestants, ministers were required to wear surplice and clerical vestments, making it possible for traditionalists to appear as "priests" and for the communion service visually to resemble the Catholic Mass. Significantly, Elizabeth chose as her archbishop of Canterbury one of the few key Protestants who had not spent the previous reign in exile and so had not been exposed

Elizabeth I.
Illustration from The Royal Collection.

to the allure of the European Reformed hothouses of Geneva, Zurich, Frankfurt, Strasbourg, or Emden.

From a strictly pragmatic viewpoint, Elizabeth had, at the start of her reign, judged the situation correctly. Her subjects were tired of incessant religious change and would settle for a compromise between the old religion and the new. The vast majority of her subjects being peasants, like peasants everywhere, were attached to tradition for its own sake. So it was important that the strictly visual, experiential aspect of church services convey as much of a sense of continuity as was possible under the bewildering circumstances of the previous quarter-century, during which period ecclesiastical polity had been changed continuously at the drop of a royal hat. Whatever its theological demerits, the liturgy of 1559 achieved this. The Protestant intellectuals, however, were the only available source for Elizabeth's senior ecclesiastical officeholders, and these were weighed down with principles to a degree she could comprehend but not share. As an olive branch to these, therefore, the official theology of the Church of England was tilted, moderately but very definitely, in the direction of Reformed theology. In the serene assurance that, now as then, theology was an arcane art with which only the few would bother their heads, it was a concession Elizabeth could well afford.

That said, troublesome intellectuals can be . . . well, troublesome. And from the 1560s onward, many of them chose to be so. The Puritan movement sputtered into life over particular grievances, but its flames soon spread, and it became a consuming drive to *purify* (hence its name) the Church of England from "the rags of popery." The "rags" referred to the literal garments of priesthood; protests began over the use of surplices. When some ministers refused to wear them, they found themselves disciplined or even expelled from their livings by the bishops, some of whom went through agonies of embarrassment because they sympathized with those whom their office required them to rebuke.

Episcopal embarrassment, however, has seldom been a morally impressive sight, and by the early 1570s some of the more radical Puritans were switching the target of their attacks from individual bishops to the institution of church government itself. It began in 1570 when Thomas

Cartwright, Lady Margaret Professor of Divinity at Cambridge, gave a series of lectures on the book of Acts in which he pointed out that the early church had possessed a plurality of elders in each congregation and that the distinction between *presbuteros* and *episkopos* was a later development.[3]

Cartwright's reward for this contribution to knowledge was the loss of his job, but others followed in his wake. By 1572 the "presbyterians" were a well-organized force within the Church of England.[4] Two of the principal organizers were Thomas Wilcox and John Field, a twenty-seven-year-old clerical firebrand who, the previous year, had been debarred from preaching for eight years. It was this pair who orchestrated the petition to the members of Parliament known as The First Admonition to the Parliament.

As monarch, Elizabeth claimed the right to order church affairs herself. However, the combination of moderate price inflation and the tradition of needing parliamentary consent for most taxation gave the members of Parliament an increasing leverage over many aspects of royal policy—including religion. Back in the 1530s Henry VIII had required the cooperation of the political classes gathered in Parliament in order to make legal his royal divorce from his wife and England's concomitant ecclesiastical divorce from Rome. And Elizabeth's own 1559 Act of Uniformity had also entailed considerable participation by both the House of Lords and the House of Commons—including, of course, their final assent. So lobbying members of Parliament to bring about religious change did not seem a wholly unreasonable ploy to the presbyterians of 1572.

The result of the petition is more impressive if measured as a literary artifact than by its actual achievements—but the former is not to be despised. Rich in venom and ingenious in turn of phrase, the language of Shakespeare is clearly foreshadowed in its cadences and rhythms:

> This book [The Book of Common Prayer] is an unperfect book, culled and picked out of that popish dunghill the . . . mass book full of all abominations. . . . In all their order of service there is no edification, according to the rule of the Apostle, but confusion; they toss the Psalms in most places like tennis balls. . . . Such [unscriptural officials and unworthy clergy] seek not the Lord Jesus, but their own bellies; clouds they are without rain, trees without fruit, painted sepulchres full of dead bones.

The archbishop's court, which had been instrumental in disciplining so many Puritan agitators and expelling them from their livelihoods, was "the filthy quake-mire and poisoned plash of all the abominations that do infect the whole realm," while its junior counterpart, the commissaries' court, was "but a petty little stinking ditch that floweth out of that former great puddle."

What would have happened if the petitioners had stopped beating about the bush in this fashion and plainly spoken their minds, we may only conjecture. Even as it was, they were allowed to cool their heels in Her Majesty's custody for a year before returning to the fray.

The Puritan movement—including presbyterianism—was at its height during the 1570s and 1580s. It seemed to threaten drastic change to the forms of worship and government of the Elizabethan Church of England. Yet the storm was weathered, and the crisis, for the moment, passed.

Public opinion was indeed slowly moving in the Puritans' direction, but they were much too far in advance of it and represented too small a minority (however voluble and well organized) to bring about the decisive changes they wished.

They were also divided among themselves. The moderates among them wished for little more than abolition of surplices and amendments to those aspects of the ceremonial that they found most offensive. A sizeable portion, however, wanted the abolition of episcopacy and its replacement by a presbyterian system (that is, the supplanting of a hierarchy of clerical officeholders with a hierarchy of committees, beginning with the local parish presbytery or consistory made up of minister and lay elders, through a local governing body—the *classis*— up to regional and national synods). The most radical fringe wanted Independency—that is, the self-government of each parish within a loose, national framework.

Many—perhaps most—wanted what they called "discipline." According to the petitioners of 1572, this was one of the three "outward marks" of a true church. (The other two—"preaching of the word purely" and "ministering of the sacraments sincerely"—were uncontentious among Reformed Protestants of all kinds, but the third was more debatable.) *Discipline* would have empowered the clergy to act as religious policemen in their parishes, placing moral or spiritual offenders (the latter would have included those suspected of harboring Catholic sympathies) under excommunication, with strong pressure on them to conform and amend. It was emphatically *not* a call for a "believers' church" nor anything like it; the Puritans' Calvinism told them that they could not discern who was and who was not a "true believer" in any case. Instead, it was a demand for the outward conformity of the whole population to the moral and spiritual requirements of biblical precepts.

This was the Achilles' heel of Puritan popularity. Like most movements, whether political, social, or religious, its greatest appeal came from antithesis—that is, from its ability to sling mud at the shortcomings of the status quo. (As has often been remarked of Luther at the outset of the Reformation, he had found it easier to convince the Germans that the pope was Antichrist than to persuade them that the just shall live by faith.) The Puritans gained popular support as long as they were criticizing the very real lack of education of the older clergy who had served under previous dispensations (both Protestant and Catholic), as long as they were pointing out the evils of clerical nonresidence, as long as they targeted many aspects of the ceremonial as "popish," and as long as they were annoying bishops under almost any pretext. But when they sought to arrogate to themselves the right to order the lives of their neighbors, at that point their popularity failed them, and they became, in the popular imagination, what their detractors derided them for all along: self-righteous killjoys. The blustering defenders of the compromise that was the Elizabethan establishment, Crypto-Catholics, traditionalists, tavern blasphemers, and the religiously indifferent: all might combine at any moment to rain on the Puritans' righteous parade.

Nor was this all. The Puritans constantly foundered on the rock of implacable royal opposition to their aspirations. Elizabeth's church settlement may have been a quagmire of ambiguity and political pragmatism, but her personal Protestantism was quite principled in its own minimalism. She rejected popery, but she hankered after its trinkets, whether an ornamental cross in her private chapel or the maintenance of an unmarried clergy. (The legal status of clerical marriages remained in doubt during her lifetime, as Elizabeth was unwilling to give them unambiguous sanction.) Above all, she could see that Puritan preaching led to widespread involvement of ordinary people in public discussion, that presbyterian principles undermined hierarchy in the church, and that both were injurious to stable monarchy.

The Puritan high tide during the 1570s and 1580s, therefore, was tolerated by Queen Elizabeth for reasons that owed more to her political needs than to her real preferences. England was in a state of war (or quasi war) with Catholic Spain during this period, and the Puritans were her best nationalists and doughtiest antipapists. On the English side, much of that warfare was run on principles of private enterprise. Many of the famous attacks by English sea dogs on Spanish shipping, and especially upon the fleets bringing back bullion from the New World, were financed by Puritan merchant adventurer companies in London. Elizabeth could hardly press too hard upon a constituency whose support she so badly needed. So she humored them and merely contained their demands for religious change.

After 1588, however, the danger peaked out and Elizabeth had a freer hand. The failure of the Spanish Armada's attempted invasion of England in that year hardly dissipated the Spanish threat as a whole, but it did constitute the high-water mark. After that point, the military crisis gradually ebbed. And, with it, receded Elizabeth's need for Puritan support; she could thenceforward afford to be less placatory. Field died the same year, and so, shortly afterward, did several sympathizers on the Privy Council (effectively the government of the country) who had protected Puritans from over-rigorous prosecution.

The scurrilous anti-episcopal tracts published during 1588–1589 by one self-styled "Martin Marprelate" were a shot in the foot for the presbyterian cause because their language was perceived by many as beyond the bounds of legitimate public debate. The bishops were thus given the excuse they needed to crack down on Puritans generally.

Thirty years into Elizabeth's reign the monarch had succeeded in outliving her first appointments to the episcopal bench, and the new breed was more genuinely conservative, less mealymouthed and embarrassed in its attacks upon Puritans, and less inclined to view them as close brethren and fellow travelers. The vision of this second generation was summed up by Richard Hooker in his *Laws of Ecclesiastical Polity*, a work that eschewed narrow biblicism and viewed the English religious settlement as something positive—a blend of Scripture, reason, hierarchy, and tradition—rather than as a compromise fudge resulting from the politico-religious exigencies of 1559. The law of ex post facto rationalization (that faithful friend of all religious institutions) was coming into play. After a generation of relative stability—or at least of absolute existence and continuity—the Church of England had come of age.

A further positive vision of English Protestantism was fostered by a book destined to have a far greater impact than Hooker's. This was John Foxe's *Acts and Monuments of the Christian Church*, more popularly and excitingly known as the *Book of Martyrs*. Ostensibly covering all martyrdoms through Christian history, its principal subject matter was English martyrs in recent times, and especially those Protestants who had been interrogated and executed for their faith during the reign of the Catholic Queen Mary (1553–1558). In that respect, it conveyed English nationalism along with rabid anti-Catholicism.

Foxe himself was a moderate Puritan, and the second edition of his massive work, running to 2,312 pages, was published in 1570. Further, even more expanded editions appeared in 1576 and 1583. Any further expansions were prevented only by his death in 1587; clearly, these would have run the risk of collapsing under the weight of their own gravity, with

An illustration from
John Foxe's *Acts and
Monuments of the
Christian Church*,
1563, p. 1102.

The burning of Thomas Tomkins hand by Bifhop Boner, who not long after burnt alfo his body.

goodness-knows-what consequences for the creation of bibliographic black holes and the sucking in of the lexical heritage of the universe.

Even as it was, the legacy of Foxe's book is nearly as interesting, and just as apocalyptic. According to him, Queen Elizabeth was a new Deborah (the prophetess of the book of Judges), who was to lead the people of God (or England—it made little difference) on a crusade against the papal Antichrist. Elizabeth, of course, was far too realistic to do anything of the sort, but the idea was to have interesting consequences long after Foxe and his queen were both dead.[5]

Foxe's book was more widely read in England during most of the period covered by this present volume than any other work except the Bible itself. It was a principal agent of conveying virulent anti-Catholicism to the English mindset, teaching as it did that the Roman church was inextricably bound up with violent religious persecution, foreign influence, and tyrannical rule. As with Foxe's implicit apocalypticism, these ideas were to be full of consequences in the century that lay ahead.

By the time Queen Elizabeth I died in 1603, the Church of England was far from united, but it was more settled than it had been—or than it would be after the 1620s. The sheer length of her reign had made possible the progressive and solid Protestantization of the country. The Puritan movement continued to attract support but was mostly moderate and politically quiescent; it no longer presented an imminent threat to the hierarchy.

This reality was underlined at the accession of Elizabeth's successor, James VI of Scotland, who moved south from Edinburgh to take up residence in his new capital as King James I of England. Puritan organizers took the opportunity to acquaint their new prince with the "particular griefs" of "the ministers of the gospel in this land"—by which they meant, of course, of the Puritan fraternity. The Millenary Petition made requests ("demands" would be far too strong a term) so moderate in tone and expressed in language so expectant of denial that the astonishment inflicted by acceding to any of them would have been almost cruel. The Lambeth Conference, which James convened the following year to discuss the petition and to air his theological sophistication, rejected all the requests, though it did resolve to produce a new English translation of the Scriptures.

This Bible appeared in 1611 and is known as the King James (or Authorized) Version. Its paramount importance for English readers was only gradually achieved, having first to contend against the Bishops Bible (approved hitherto by the Elizabethan authorities) and the popular Geneva Bible (beloved of Puritans). The new edition, which gradually supplanted these, borrowed very heavily from Tyndale's translation of the 1530s. Its language and turns of phrase were to shape spoken English in countless ways during the following centuries and even today are buried deep in the speech patterns of the Jacobeans' secularized descendants. The reasons for that influence are to be found partly in the merits of the translation itself, and partly in the deep, Bible-centered religiosity of the seventeenth century. The congruence of the two phenomena made innumerable biblical or quasi-biblical turns of phrase the unreflective resort of godly and ungodly speakers alike, until the English Bible became an unwitting (but hardly unspoken) partner in every mundane conversation.

Though the reign of King James I was rich enough in political incident, it saw few other important religious developments, though it did see the first stirrings of a movement that would cause large amounts of trouble in the years after 1625. It should be noted that, hitherto, none of the Puritan concerns had touched upon matters of doctrine. Until the 1620s, Puritanism was concerned almost exclusively with ceremonies and church government. The reason for this circumstance is that the bishops and their Puritan critics had been in agreement on doctrinal issues; all had supported the Reformed theology of the Church of England's Articles. When Peter Baro, a foreigner teaching at Cambridge, had had the temerity in the 1590s to oppose Calvinistic doctrine, the Puritans immediately and successfully enlisted the support of the bishops to have him silenced. But this brief period of calm was about to change. In the process, the Puritans themselves were about to be transformed from critics of ceremonies and forms of church government into champions of Reformed orthodoxy.

It was the early seventeenth century that saw the first beginnings of a new form of High-Churchmanship that opposed Reformed doctrine and traditional Protestant practice. Its early adherents were few during the reign of James (though some were highly placed), and they wisely kept their heads down in order to stay out of trouble. Their most notable, learned, and saintly adherent was Lancelot Andrewes, bishop of Chichester. As we shall have cause to notice in the next chapter, the immediate future belonged to the High Church party; the only question was whether, given its extreme turbulence, that future was worth the having.[6]

The Dutch Reformed Church (to 1619)

About midday on 19 October 1609 a forty-nine-year-old professor of divinity at the University of Leiden died, succumbing to a fever that had plagued him for the best part (or rather, the worst part) of a year, had confined him to his house, and, for the last month, had deprived him of the sight of his left eye. Jakob Hermandszoon had been born at Oudewater, a small town in southern Holland, on 10 October 1560. His father, a cutler, had died a few years afterward. Later, while a student in Marburg, the teenage Jakob received the news that his mother, sister, and two brothers had been killed by Spanish troops destroying his hometown. Truly, he had little cause to sympathize with the Catholic faith or with its principal defender.

By the time of his death, Jakob Hermandszoon's name (Latinized as Arminius) was already synonymous with a theological party around which the infant Dutch Republic was exploding into theologically inspired political conflict. As has been seen in chapter 2, the Dutch Reformed were in the happy position of being seen as the champions of a "national" cause at a time when national consciousness was starting to mean something, at least in the more urbanized and economically developed parts of Europe, such as the Netherlands. The pressure of warfare against a larger and exceedingly threatening enemy in the form of Spain might have been expected to hold the Dutch Protestants together. Alas, it did no such thing. Although the name of Jacobus Arminius continues to be invoked as a description of all theologies espousing free will, just as that of Calvin is called upon to describe all kinds of predestinarianism, there is little justice in either usage.

Arminius.
Illustration from Jean-Jacques Boissard, *Bibliotheca Chalcographica*, Heidelberg, 1669.

The young Arminius had studied under Beza in Geneva, where he was thoroughly imbued with all of the usual Calvinist doctrines about sovereignty, predestination, and reprobation as well as with the further ramifications of these doctrines, upon which Calvin himself had not always insisted but his successors did. Indeed, the young Dutchman got into trouble as a student there for giving unofficial lectures on the ideas of Ramus (the herald of "Reformed scholasticism") in his room.

From Geneva, Arminius toured Italy for seven months before being recalled to Amsterdam in 1587 by the Merchant Guild. This body had recognized his outstanding abilities and had agreed to pay for his education. Now they understandably felt that he had had ample time in which to enjoy himself. The following year he was ordained as a minister of the Dutch Reformed Church.[7]

Arminius began his ministry by teaching on Malachi and Romans, but his new colleagues soon had a more pressing task for him. He was called upon to write a confutation of Dirck Coornhert, a layman (and, from 1572, Prince William of Orange's secretary to the Estates-General) who had written challenging the predestinarian orthodoxy of the Reformed church, had spoken out against the death penalty for heresy, and had declared, "I hold for brethren all those godly men who hold Christ for their cornerstone, whether they be priests, monks, [Ana]baptists, Reformed or Lutherans." Equally horrifying to the consciences of the Reformed, Coornhert also wanted changes in the Belgic Confession to moderate its Calvinism.

As a former student of Beza and a promising young scholar, Arminius was a natural choice to put the free-willer in his place. A distressingly high proportion of sixteenth-century publications, especially theological works, were written as a direct counterthrust to somebody else's book or tract—counterthrusts that then usually received a reply in their turn. These publications bear titles such as "An Answer to——," "A Reply to a Certain Calumniating Answer made by——," "A Further Confutation of the Dastardly Reply," "Calumnius Execrabilis." And so on, until even the writers got bored and the public literary exchange would peter out.

An unfortunate requirement of such exercises (though one from which some modern book reviewers have successfully liberated themselves) was, of course, that one read the works one was attacking. And during the course of this particular writing project, Arminius made the unnerving discovery that his designated enemy seemed to be in the right. It was a moment that was to shape the rest of his career, and from which ecclesiastical bodies around the globe have still not quite recovered. His opponent's arguments were strong—but then Coornhert had played this game before; in his dispute ten years previously with the Delft ministers Arnold Cornelisz and Reinier Donteclock, those gentlemen had, shortly after, renounced their belief in supralapsarianism.

This arid polysyllable, which was also at the heart of the debate with Arminius, is the notion that, not only has God individually preselected which individuals will be saved and which damned, but he has done this before the fall of mankind in the Garden of Eden (indeed, even before the act of creation)—and so he predetermined that the fall itself would happen. (Its alternative, infra- or sublapsarianism, allows for genuine human free will up to the third chapter of Genesis, with God's predestination and a deterministic universe then "kicking in" after that.) Free-willers of both right (Catholic) and left (Anabaptist and radical) had long claimed that denial of human free will was blasphemous because it made God the final author of sin, to which accusation the Calvinist rebuttals had been more rhetorical than substantive; supralapsarianism tended to make any rebuttal more difficult than ever.

Coornhert, busy fellow that he was, was also engaged in translating Erasmus's text of the New Testament into Dutch. It had been the persistence of the early sixteenth-century Erasmian mentality that had largely kept the Spanish from exploiting the religious disunity of the Dutch and creating the sharp polarization that had, for example, taken place in France. Dutch Catholicism retained this humane, Erasmian temperament even after the Council of Trent, but the same outlook guaranteed that the growth of Calvinism would also be slow and tempered by the demurs of the likes of Coornhert. Despite the official status of the Reformed Church, its flock accounted for barely one third of the population of the United Provinces, even by the early seventeenth century.

Arminius's defense of full-fledged Bezan theology never appeared, and he moved over, first to an infralapsarian view, and then, by 1590, to a rejection of individual predestination altogether. To have proclaimed such a conversion at once required more courage than Arminius was able to muster, but the change showed through his exposition of Romans, and the more theologically astute among his hearers began to suspect his orthodoxy. The following year he got himself into trouble with his exposition of the seventh chapter of that epistle by suggesting that Paul is there speaking in the (hypothetical or assumed) person of an unregenerate man struggling against sin. Arminius was obliged to defend himself before the ministers of the town, especially against Plancius, who countered Arminius's appeal to Erasmus and the church fathers with an appeal to the Belgic Confession and the Heidelberg Catechism. Plancius accused Arminius's teaching of affinities with Pelagianism (the idea that one can be saved by one's own efforts) and Socinianism (the minimizing or rejection of the deity of Christ). On the latter charge, Arminius did indeed refuse to use the term *autotheos* (God in and of himself) in respect of Jesus and tended toward subordinationism (the view that the Son is less than the Father).

Plancius's accusations were largely mere name-calling, but the row simmered on, and in early 1592 Arminius asked to have the matter sorted out in a meeting of the civic authorities with the presbytery. At that point Kuchlin, a minister and Arminius's uncle by marriage, replied that the civic authorities had no part to play in such ecclesiastical affairs. (The strict Reformed view was that magistrates' duty was to uphold the church and enforce adherence to it upon the populace, not to meddle in its workings.) The division on this point was indicative of things to come; Calvinists and Arminians were to characterize one another as theocrats (wanting a church-ruled state) and Erastians (wanting a state-ruled church).

Eventually, in May 1593, Arminius demanded that definite charges be brought against him. Plancius leveled various accusations, all of which, by judicious use of words, Arminius was able to answer sufficiently, even if not satisfactorily. To be fair, his opponents had real grounds for anger on this point; one of the things that most infuriated them was the deviousness of Arminius's approach. To search his writings for a clear, forthrightly argued statement of free will or for an unambiguous assault upon individual predestination is to search in vain. All is buried in obscure language, exhortations to moderation, attacks upon only the outer bulwarks of predestinarianism and seldom, except by implication, coming to the heart of the matter. His works seem almost designed to frustrate even those readers predisposed to agree with his central contentions, precisely because one has to wade through such a mass of verbiage to find them and cannot be entirely confident, even then, that one has really located them. In consequence, Arminius was accused of Jesuitical deception, of saying in private what he would not say in public, of expressing himself in forms of words that circumvented what everyone knew to be his real thoughts.

Similarly, Arminius's attack upon Calvinism was the sneak attack of "death by a thousand qualifications." His principal targets were two doctrines about which it remains a matter of (sometimes heated) debate as to whether Calvin himself ever even taught them. These are supra-lapsarianism and limited atonement.

The former we have described. The latter is the idea that, the New Testament notwithstanding, Christ did not die for the sins of the world but only for those of the predestined elect. The atonement is limited, therefore, to these in both its intentions and its effects (divine intention and effect being always identical in Calvinist theology, of course). The logic of this (and, if one accepts its shaky premise, it is perfectly logical) is that Christ cannot have died for the sins of those whom God had predetermined from before all worlds (or from Genesis chapter 3, according to the point of view) to damn because then, for them, Christ would have died in vain. The Calvinist universe, it must be remembered, is one in which the will of God is always done. Indeed, it is one in which there is only one real actor. Therefore, it is argued, if Christ died for a person, he or she must infallibly be saved. But since all are not, in fact, saved—it follows that Christ cannot have died intentionally for all, but only for those who are predestined.

Leaving aside the question of whether or not Calvin held to these positions—a question about which blood continues, occasionally, to be mingled along with the torrents of spilled ink—two things are quite evident.[8] First, his successors did so. Beza, in Geneva itself, and the large majority of Reformed and Puritan writers after Calvin's death taught these ideas. Second, they follow quite logically from the premises upon which they are based, namely a rarefied, philosophical view of God as prime cause of all phenomena and a tendency to read much of Scripture as anthropomorphisms. Clearly, for God to say, "Now take off your ornaments and I will decide what to do with you" (Exod. 33:5), or to speak of changing his mind (Exod. 32:14; Jonah 3:9–4:2) or to refer to his "patience"—and a lot else besides—cannot literally mean anything on a Calvinist reading, and so it must be a mere "accommodation" to human ways of talking.

By switching sides and turning against Reformed doctrines of predestination (in however cagey a fashion), Arminius set the Dutch Reformed Church in a turmoil, for he was hardly without supporters. When Trelcatius, one of the professors of divinity at the University of Leiden, died of the plague in 1602, the lay curators of the university and Arminius's friend Wtenbogaert secured an offer of the position for Arminius. He was at first unwilling to accept, but the High Calvinists kicked up such a fuss about the very possibility of Arminius as professor that he finally concluded that to decline would be tantamount to an admission of heterodoxy.

Immediately, Arminius found himself penned in with one of his bitterest opponents. Francis Gomarus was senior professor and had sought, unsuccessfully, to block his appointment. Friction developed rapidly, with Gomarus complaining if Arminius, in the course of lecturing on the Old Testament, made any references to the New—for that was Gomarus's province for teaching because of his seniority.

As students graduated from the university with the imprint of Arminius's ideas upon their minds, thence to impart these ideas to their flocks in the churches, so the concern of the Calvinist orthodox grew. Thus it was that in 1607 a meeting was called to prepare arrangements for a national synod. Many wanted an opportunity to discuss the precise theological status of the Belgic Confession and the Heidelberg Catechism and the relationship of both to Scripture. Gomarus claimed that they were a secondary rule, while Bogerman went one further and claimed that Scripture itself was to be interpreted according to them. As Arminius later wrote to Wtenbogaert, "How could one state more clearly that they were determined to canonise these two human writings?" If this line had been followed consistently, the Reformation itself would have been impossible. Arminius and his friends declared their readiness to accept the documents, not as a rule of faith, but as an agreed formula against which they would not teach.

By the following year, Arminius had become weary of the constant need to defend himself against new accusations. Articles had been circulated purporting to describe his teaching in terms that he considered slanderous, since he did not hold the views ascribed to him. In April, therefore, he and Wtenbogaert addressed a petition to the States of Holland, begging that the national synod might be held. The Great Council summoned Gomarus and Arminius to the Hague to settle their differences. True to form, Gomarus began by refusing to plead his case, denying the council's competence in such matters. The council took this tax upon their patience in their collective stride and responded very correctly by claiming merely a desire to know what the differences were, not the right to determine them.

Well might the magistrates remain in a state of confusion, despite the fact that heated debates had been raging for years. The Calvinists were quite right to claim that behind Arminius's constantly expressed desire for peace, circumspection, and orthodoxy, his ambiguous statements and varying pronouncements were being used to protect his irreconcilable differences with the locally prevailing orthodoxy. In July 1609, just three months before Arminius's death, he claimed, in terms that would have satisfied Beza himself, that "what man soever is called in time, was from all eternity predestinated to be called, and to be called in that state, time, place and mode, and with what efficacy, in and with which he was predestinated." Presumably he construed his own words in some sense that allowed for free will, for he added that he could not say in what manner the Holy Spirit effected conversion.

In the same year of Arminius's death, the translation of his and Gomarus's competing theses of 1604 on the subject of predestination began a long and bitter pamphlet war between the opposing sides. The United Provinces could afford, for the first time, the luxury of allowing this dispute to come fully into the public arena, for it was in this same year of 1609 that a twelve-year truce was concluded with the Spanish. The truce allowed political differences, buried in the wartime struggle for survival, to emerge into the light of day.

The major division was between Maurice of Nassau, the successful military leader of the last war years, and Oldenbarneveldt the Advocate, who had sought to bring about peace. The hard-line Calvinists, many of them originally south Netherlanders whose home territory in Antwerp and its environs remained unliberated and whose faith ill-disposed them to any letup against the Spanish epitome of Catholic tyranny, formed the backbone of the war party, while the Arminians drifted into natural alliance with Oldenbarneveldt, whose apparent lack—until the last stage of his life—of any strong theological convictions inclined him to the liberalizing tendencies of the Arminian party.

Wtenbogaert thought that if the coming of peace (however temporary) allowed for political differences to emerge at home, the new conditions allowed space for theological differences as well. In the summer of 1609, he argued that the teaching of Luther and Calvin on predestination had resulted only from their desire to remove the idea that people could be saved by works or attain divine grace by their own strength. Now that such notions had been dispelled there was room, he argued, for differences between Protestants on the subject of predestination that would not amount to schism or heresy.

Wtenbogaert privately called together a gathering of Arminian sympathizers at Gouda, with the purpose of drawing up a defense of their position to the Estates General. Their two protestations were, to say the least, somewhat in tension with one another: on the one hand they claimed that they desired no religious innovations and complained that the Gomarist form of Calvinism was innovatory; on the other hand they urged that the Estates General's order for the revision of the catechism and confession (that is, for changes) be carried out.

On 14 January 1610 forty-three preachers assembled, to be joined somewhat later by three others from Utrecht, and issued the famous Remonstrance, a summary of Arminian propositions in five points. These taught that election was "in Christ" (and so not necessarily individual); a universal atonement; mankind's lost state and need for regeneration; the need for both prevenient and cooperating grace; and the need for (but not the inevitability of) perseverance in a state of salvation.

On this last point, the Remonstrance was openly ambivalent, claiming that "this must be the subject of more exact inquiry in the Holy Scriptures, before we can teach it with a full confidence in our mind." The Arminian preachers in the churches, however, were less inhibited and openly taught the possibility of falling from grace.

The Remonstrance itself was unsigned, but is generally held to have been the work of Episcopius and Grotius. The former was the assumed name of Simon Bischop (1583–1643), one of Arminius's ablest students, who emerged as a leader of the party at this time. The latter was the name taken by Huig de Groot (1583–1645), the brilliant jurist who had been offered a doctorate at the age of fifteen. An even less acceptable leader in the eyes of their opponents was Konrad Vorstius (1569–1622), who was appointed as Arminius's successor at Leiden. His *Tractatus de Deo* of 1610 was widely attacked for its rationalism, and King James I of England ordered copies of the book to be burned, regretting only that its author could not share the flames.

The dispute widened during the years that followed to the area of natural theology. Much effort was expended on analyzing the passage in the first chapter of Romans in which Paul teaches that God may be perceived and revered through his creation. The Calvinists insisted that this referred to a mere mental deduction of God's existence from the existence of the natural world, the sole purpose of which deduction was to make each person inexcusable before God. Arminian theologians countered that such knowledge was itself a channel of grace whereby people might both attain to a more moral mode of life and apprehend their need of a Savior, thus preparing them for the preaching of Christ.

The Arminian party found its support among the higher political classes and prosperous burghers of the United Provinces. The more liberal theology held an appeal for them, as did the Erastian notion of secular political control over the church and a pacific policy toward Spain (good for trade). The Calvinists, despite the unattractive form in which their doctrines were often expressed, had more popular support. The continuing theological

The execution of Oldenbarneveldt. Illustration from Koninklijke Biblothek, Netherlands.

controversy became inextricably entangled in this political division. Oldenbarneveldt and his party were portrayed as unpatriotic. When the Synod of Dort was eventually convened in late 1618, the condemnation of the Arminian doctrines was already certain.

Holland and Utrecht, where Arminian sympathizers were strongest, had by now reversed themselves on the calling of a synod and, foreseeing its likely outcome, held out against it for as long as they could. Earlier in 1618 Oldenbarneveldt had foolishly attempted to take control of a local militia in Utrecht, but the attempt was nipped in the bud by Maurice of Nassau. It was this action, for which Oldenbarneveldt was executed the following year, that gave the synod an aspect of the deepest moment. The future of the state, national security, and the unity of the Dutch Reformed Church were all at stake.

Although the attendance of delegates from Switzerland, England, Scotland, Hesse, and the Palatinate guaranteed that the hardest line of Gomarist doctrine would not be taken by the synod, it also ensured that Arminianism would be rejected. This rejection was partly the result of a real insight into the Arminians' latent liberalism, and partly a result of their entanglement in the politics (on the losing side) of their day.

The Gomarists had responded to the Arminians, shortly after the publication of the Remonstrance, with a Contra-Remonstrance, which the Synod of Dort largely upheld. The five points of Arminianism were thus answered with the (rather more famous) five points of Calvinism, remembered in English by their acronym "TULIP." In brief, these are: Total depravity; Unconditional election; Limited atonement; Irresistible grace; Perseverance of the saints.

Any theology that denied that every aspect of human life and existence is tainted by sin would, presumably, be in serious danger of heresy. What Calvinists meant by *total depravity*, however, was altogether more depressing: each person is so depraved that he or she cannot, in their own nature, so much as wish for regeneration or choose to believe. If anyone actually believes, therefore, then that faith must itself be a gift of God to that individual.

Unconditional election is the idea that God chooses which individuals to save on the basis of no condition at all—not even faith. If a person has faith, then that is not the *cause* of his or her election but merely the *sign* of it. There is no condition at all to cause God to give it to this person rather than to that. As Calvin had once said, if God has chosen you, it was not because of your nice blue eyes. Very well, but if not for those, then for what? One might legitimately say that we cannot know why God chooses this person rather than that (i.e., it is a mystery), but that is not "no condition"—merely a condition that is unknown to us. To say, however, that there is literally no condition at all is almost meaningless. In effect, salvation is random and the personhood (let alone the three-personhood) of God is undermined.

Limited atonement was to have an interesting history. In Calvinist and Puritan thought, the person in the process of conversion needed to find assurance, not merely that Christ was a Savior who had died for sins, but that he or she was among those for whom Christ had died. Assurance of this latter stipulation was, obviously, rather harder to come by than the former. Some never came by it at all. Many died in despair, repentant of their sins and believing all of the essential doctrines of the gospel but convinced, nevertheless, that they personally were among those predestined to be damned. Calvinist pastors were to go through all manner of logical gymnastics to circumvent this, the inevitable outcome of their own doctrine, in their attempts to help parishioners somehow to find assurance. The despairing were the minority, however; human beings are, for the most part, incurably optimistic, and most managed, after some months or years, to persuade themselves that they were, after all, among the few for whom Christ had died. The experience made conversion in the Reformed tradition a somewhat long, drawn-out affair—with suspicion of "instant conversions" as being somehow necessarily spurious.

Irresistible grace was simply the corollary of the previous doctrines. If God purposes to save a person, then he or she cannot resist but is "savingly wrought upon."

The last of the five points, *perseverance of the saints* is the idea that a person who is once in a state of grace can never finally be lost. If God has predetermined to save certain individuals, they cannot become unsaved. What, then, of those persons who apparently fall away? Such cases simply demonstrate that we cannot trust the evidence of our own eyes and that they were never truly converted in the first place—which in turn demonstrates that no one can know of the saved-ness or otherwise of anyone but himself or herself. The number of true believers of whose identity a Christian can be sure is precisely one. Believers' churches are not possible, therefore, and the church is inevitably a mixture of the saved and unsaved. Churches cannot demand saved-ness as a condition of membership; they can only demand conformity and outward obedience.

In deference to this last principle, Episcopius, Vorstius, and the others were banished from the Netherlands. Grotius was imprisoned for life in 1618, though in 1621 he managed to escape to Paris. (The authorities in France, of course, were in the process of minimizing the toleration afforded their own Protestants, but they were prepared to stretch a point in the case of someone who had made himself so troublesome to the Dutch government and to Calvinism generally.)

In 1625, however, following the death of Maurice of Nassau, the Arminians were granted a degree of toleration in Holland and had built a church in Amsterdam by 1630 and a seminary four years later. As a denomination they never grew large. Episcopius led them gradually into an ever more rationalist direction, emphasizing Christ as an ethical example and the Trinity as symbolic—until they began to have affinities with the Socinians, thereby vindicating their adversaries' charges of a generation before.

Arminianism remains a synonym for the assertion of free will. It is interesting, therefore, that Arminius was very cautious about asserting anything at all. As we have seen, his version of free will stemmed from a liberalizing instinct and a wish to play down the strident pessimism of the strict Calvinists. In both flavor and effects, it had little in common with the evangelical free will of the Anabaptists nor with the semi-Pelagian free will of much Catholicism and Protestant High-Churchmanship (even though the last of these, in England at least, is usually designated "Arminianism"). In consequence Arminius, like Calvin and some other theologians, has this much in common with God: his name is taken in vain almost more often than it is invoked to serious purpose.

5

THE CONFLICTS
WITHIN CHURCHES

CATHOLICS AND ORTHODOX

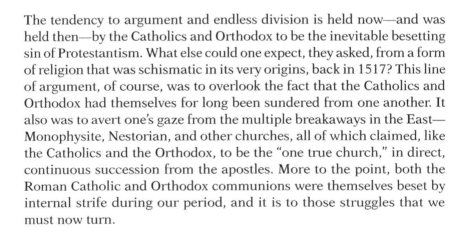

The tendency to argument and endless division is held now—and was held then—by the Catholics and Orthodox to be the inevitable besetting sin of Protestantism. What else could one expect, they asked, from a form of religion that was schismatic in its very origins, back in 1517? This line of argument, of course, was to overlook the fact that the Catholics and Orthodox had themselves for long been sundered from one another. It also was to avert one's gaze from the multiple breakaways in the East— Monophysite, Nestorian, and other churches, all of which claimed, like the Catholics and the Orthodox, to be the "one true church," in direct, continuous succession from the apostles. More to the point, both the Roman Catholic and Orthodox communions were themselves beset by internal strife during our period, and it is to those struggles that we must now turn.

The Roman Catholic Church

That the Reformation ushered in an unstoppable torrent of mutually anathematizing sects was the constant refrain of Catholic polemics, both in the sixteenth century and for most of the time since. On the other hand, differences of opinion or loyalty among Catholics, then as now, were enshrined institutionally in competing bodies within the Roman Catholic Church. Whether this finer instinct gives it a moral or spiritual advantage over Protestants may be debated. But it did not allow the Catholic Church to escape from acrimony during the later sixteenth and early seventeenth centuries.

On the positive side, the impetus of Counter-Reformation had spawned a whole raft of new orders, while the drive to renew the life of the church had encouraged a fresh upsurge of piety among many secular clergy, monastics, and laypeople alike. Capuchins, Jesuits, Theatines, Ursulines, the Oratory of Divine Love: all these engines of reform and renewal had been founded in the years immediately before the Council of Trent. The years following the council saw their increasing deployment.

Renewal Movements

In some cases, the new movements represented attempts either to escape or to renew older orders that had become lax or decayed. Such was the case with Teresa of Avila (1515–1582), a Carmelite nun who, from the mid-1550s, became a visionary and mystic. Acting upon her own remark, "No wonder the Church is as it is, when the religious live as they do," she founded in 1562 a new convent at Avila that observed the Carmelites' primitive rule. From the late 1560s, she was engaged in founding other houses for both nuns and friars. In a microcosm of the battle for renewal within the Catholic Church as a whole, her order, the Discalced (or "shoeless") Carmelites, came into considerable conflict with the unreformed, who preferred to keep their shoes on and their laxity intact. Professor Dickens has deliciously described these latter as "elegant hostels for gossiping women, with the occasional case of hysteria passing for sanctity."[1]

Teresa's principal assistant in the struggle, her fellow mystic, John of the Cross (1542–1591), was seized by his enemies in 1577 and imprisoned in the Castilian city of Toledo. After nine months of brutal mistreatment he escaped, and the formal separation of shod and unshod Carmelites followed in 1579–1580. John's troubles were not entirely over, however. In the last year of his life he incurred the wrath of the Vicar General of the order he himself had helped to found and was banished to Andalusia where, again instigated by rough treatment, he succumbed to illness.

Teresa's *Way of Perfection* and *The Interior Castle* have remained influential spiritual guides, as has John's *Spiritual Canticle*. His *Dark Night of
the Soul*, of course, casts echoes to the end of the universe.

If both Teresa and John left significant literary legacies, then the
Spanish Inquisition thought itself underemployed if it did not attempt
to poke them about a bit, together with their authors. Teresa herself had
an alarming brush of this sort in 1575 after her mentor, the Dominican
Domingo Báñez, thoughtfully passed her *Life*, an autobiography covering
the period to 1562, to the inquisitors. Thankfully, they left the author
unmolested, but they held the book itself back from publication until
four years after her death.

Fellow mystics Luis de Granada (1504–1588) and Luis de Leon (ca.
1528–1591), however, were given much harsher treatment. In mitigation,
it should be mentioned that the inquisitors' report recommended applying only "a moderate amount of agony" to the latter, who was in poor
health. Upon his release in 1576, after four years of such "moderation,"
Luis de Leon returned in triumph to the University of Salamanca, where
he had been a professor, and recommended his course of lectures with
words that have won him the grateful thanks of humanity ever since:
"As I was saying yesterday. . . ."[2]

The Inquisition

If Spain was the home of most late-sixteenth- and early-seventeenth-
century mysticism, it was also the home of the Inquisitors, and this body
perceived a fine line between ecstatic experience of God and heresy.
Its cautions applied particularly in respect to women, whose mystical
experiences were generally "an invention of the *alumbrados* [enlightened
ones] of this time, who thus detach daughters from service and obedience to their fathers, and wives from their husbands."[3] Certainly some
women mystics did gain unusual degrees of social influence through
the currency of their revelations. The nuns who lived within convents
could be contained to some degree by their own institutions, but the
beatas (women living separated, devout lives in their own homes) who
turned to ecstatic revelations threatened to overturn the social order.
One of the most alarming examples of this tendency for such women
to escape their proper sphere in life was that of Catalina de Jesus, who
preached, prophesied, and wrote in early seventeenth-century Seville.
She acquired a devoted following of about seven hundred people before
the Inquisition put a stop to her career in 1627. She was sentenced to
six years in a hospital.

The Inquisition, of course, was organized by the Dominicans—the chief and, before the advent of the Society of Jesus, the only exclusively academic teaching order of the Catholic Church. The inquisitors' working assumption—that talk of God was an intellectual parlor game and the Christian church a means of social control, with claims actually to have experienced God threatening to break the bounds of both—is one too frequently shared by modern historians. One of these has recently written suggesting that most such ecstatic experiences in this period were the result of sexual repression among nuns or attempts by nonconventual *beatas* to reject ecclesiastical patriarchy.[4] Why late-sixteenth- and early-seventeenth-century Spain would have hosted these feasts of sublimated sexuality and gender rebellion—when monasteries and convents had been celibate (at least in intention) for over a millennium and all the world patriarchal until about the 1970s—remains as mysterious after such explanations as before. We might suggest that the alternative possibility, that of divine encounter, should at least be seriously entertained.

Grace and Human Initiative

One of the more important quarrels to beset the Roman Catholic Church during the late sixteenth and early seventeenth centuries concerning the relationship between grace and human initiative mirrored that between Calvinists and Arminians in the Dutch Reformed Church. Within Catholicism, the chief protagonists were the Dominicans and the Jesuits. Both were primarily teaching orders, bidding for the allegiance of the intellectuals within the church. The Jesuits had dedicated themselves to teaching the faith: to the already faithful, in order to ensure their informed and continuing loyalty; to the inhabitants of the borderlands between Protestantism and Catholicism, so that a new generation would save themselves and their homelands from the alien herbs of heresy; and to the pagans beyond Christendom in Africa and Asia and in the newly conquered lands of the Americas. If the Jesuits saw their task as to propagate the faith, the Dominicans saw theirs as to define it. And inevitably, each trod upon the toes of the other. The Dominicans claimed seniority as the older of the two orders; the Society of Jesus, established only in 1540, was a mere newcomer.

The Dominicans' point of reference for dogma was, of course, Thomas Aquinas, whose status as *doctor communis* had been reaffirmed at the Council of Trent. By a sort of law of political gravity, therefore, it was necessary that the Jesuits define their distinctive doctrinal emphases at a distance from Thomism (though obviously within acceptable Catholic parameters).

It is a matter of some irony, then, that the book that ended two decades of subterranean rumblings of debate between the two orders by provoking open acrimony came from the pen of a Jesuit scholar who had spent his professional life teaching on the theology of Aquinas. Luis de Molina (1535–1600), a Spaniard, had studied—and then taught—at the universities of Coimbra and Evora, in Portugal. His *Liberi arbitrii cum gratiae donis, divina praescientia, providentia, praedestinatione et reprobatione concordia* (A Reconciliation of Free Choice with the Gifts of Grace, Divine Foreknowledge, Providence, Predestination and Reprobation), understandably known simply as the *Concordia*, was published in Lisbon in 1588, after the failure of attempts by his opponents to prevent its appearance.

The *Concordia*'s text was as cumbersome as its title. But in summary, Molina taught that our moment-by-moment sensation that our actions are freely chosen by ourselves is not, in fact, mistaken—though, of course, he had a more ponderous way of expressing the matter: "That agent is called free who, with all the prerequisites for acting having been posited, is able to act and able not to act, or is able to do one thing in such a way that he is also able to do some contrary thing."⁵ Quite. God foreknows all possibilities and our propensities, but he never actually determines what we will choose.

The Dominican champion, Domingo Báñez, countered that Molina's position was essentially Pelagian and flew in the face of the teachings of Aquinas. A trial run of this dispute had already taken place in the University of Louvain, where the Jesuit Leonard Lessius had been accused by the disciples of Michael Baius of diminishing the grace of God by his emphasis upon human free will. Baius himself had also clashed on the same subject with the great cardinal and Jesuit scholar Robert Bellarmine (1542–1621), who argued that freedom of the will could be squared with the teaching of Thomas Aquinas.

The Jesuits were not alone in treading on thin ice, however. Their opponents needed to be able to define their own position in such a way as not to give too much ground to the Lutherans and Calvinists. They needed to own Augustine of Hippo (354–430), the great theologizer of Christendom, without conceding an inch to the Protestant heretics who were reiterating and amplifying him. It was a delicate balancing act: Báñez averred that "the efficacy of divine aid, as it comes from the Holy Spirit, does not destroy liberty, but perfects it." The Jesuits, on the other hand, needed to demonstrate that they had not lapsed into Pelagianism;

their consolation was that they were able to claim the high ground of maximum distance from Wittenberg and Geneva and of greatest faithfulness to the intentions of the Tridentine decrees.

The dispute in Spain became irksome to King Philip II, and the pope was invoked to resolve it. Pope Clement VIII did what all leaders do when asked to adjudicate in a dispute in which they cannot afford to offend any of the chief protagonists: he began, in 1594, by asking both sides to desist from public debate and went on, in 1597, to establish a committee. The papal Commission on Grace met 132 times over the following decade (thereby achieving its first purpose, namely outliving its initiator). At the end of it all Clement's successor, Pope Paul V, decreed lamely that both sides might defend their opinions and requested merely that each refrain from denouncing the other as heretical. Things had indeed looked black for the Molinists for a while, but the intervention of Cardinals Robert Bellarmine and Jacques du Perron served to remind the pope of the Jesuits' enormous usefulness to the Holy See and to secure them from any danger of condemnation.

The dispute continued for much of the first half of the seventeenth century, and not just between Jesuits and Dominicans, until few leading Catholic figures could escape identification as partisans of one side or the other. Nowhere was this more true than in France, where Pierre de Bérulle and the Oratorians sided with the proponents of Augustine's doctrine of grace and their opponents included Francis de Sales and Cardinal Richelieu. De Sales (1576–1622), one of the greatest of Counter-Reformation saints and devotional writers, had undergone a terrifying six-week ordeal in which he was convinced that he was predestined to be damned. He had his revenge on such ideas by converting at least 8,000 Calvinist inhabitants of Chablais to Catholicism during the first decade of his ministry as a priest.

Jansenism

But the Dominicans and Oratorians were not the only Catholic champions of the primacy of grace over human initiative. The Flemish theologian and bishop of Ypres, Cornelius Jansen (1585–1638), protested against the Jesuits because of what he saw as their departure from historical orthodoxy. This orthodoxy he saw as best represented by the writings of Augustine. Jansen's most famous book, *Augustinus*, was not published until 1640, two years after his death, and in consequence much of the dispute surrounding his teachings was posthumous.

Cornelius Jansen.
Illustration from
Bibliothètheque de la Société de
Port-Royal.

Jansen emphasized the need for conversion along with the Augustinian doctrines of original sin, human depravity, and divine predestination. The Jansenists' opponents, quick to spot a chance of securing papal condemnation, called them Calvinists, though the new movement was loyal to the pope and loudly rejected Protestantism and its associated doctrine of justification by faith. It taught that Mass should be taken only infrequently and should be attended by the most scrupulous self-examination and confession.

The movement took particularly strong root in France. This was perhaps unfortunate, because Jansen had already made powerful enemies there in 1635 when his book, *Mars Gallicus*, had angered Cardinal Richelieu. That work had argued that Louis XIII, the Catholic king of France, had no business fighting on the Protestant side in the Thirty Years' War and that those soldiers who betrayed the faith in this fashion were imperiling their souls. It was a sensitive argument; back in 1610 a certain man named Ravaillac had made the identical point in respect of the previous monarch's intention to fight fellow Catholics by burying a sword into Henry IV.

Despite such embarrassments, Jansenism secured a strong base in the French convent of Port Royal, whose spiritual director was the abbot of Saint-Cyran, and whose abbess was Angélique Arnauld, a member of an influential family of lawyers. The convent also ran a number of schools. Their famous pupils included Jean Racine (1639–1699), who, though his future career as a playwright led him into liaisons with various actresses, later made a peace of sorts with the Jansenism of his youth.

A more faithful disciple, from 1646, was the mathematician Blaise Pascal (1623–1662). Pascal won several of his family to the movement, notably his sister Jaqueline, and later many of his friends. Pascal suffered throughout his short, brilliant life from ill health, and a time of recuperation from 1650 seems to have led to a period of diminished ardor in his piety. But a second conversion experience on the night of 23 November 1654 renewed him permanently. He had an overwhelming sense of the divine presence, which he recorded in scribbled, barely coherent notes as it happened: "From about half-past ten in the evening until about half past midnight. FIRE. The God of Abraham, the God of Isaac, the God of Jacob. Not of the philosophers and intellectuals. Certitude. Certitude. Feeling. Joy. Peace . . . Joy, joy, joy, tears of joy."[6] For the rest of his life Pascal kept a reminder of this experience in the lining of every coat he possessed. He also lived an ascetic existence, and wore a cincture of nails, which he would press into his flesh every time his conscience accused him of pride. Pascal planned a massive work of apologetics, but it was never completed; the preparatory fragments were sufficiently formidable and coherent as to be collected after his death at the age of thirty-nine and are now justly famous as the *Pensées*.

According to Pascal and the Jansenists, the Jesuits' utilitarianism, whereby they urged priests to be lenient in the practice of the confessional in order not to alienate those who might be useful to the church, was turning that sacrament into a mockery. It was also unduly optimistic about humanity's moral fiber and failed to confront the reality of human wickedness. The Jansenists, by contrast, stressed the pervasiveness of original sin and, like Pascal, adopted a moral rigorism to counter it.

Cardinal Richelieu was inclined to the lenient view on this point—not so much because it was lenient (we are, after all, dealing with the author of the immortal words, "Give me six lines written by the most honest man, and I will find something to hang him") but because it was more pragmatic. Any person might confess their sins and do penance from fear of God's punishment—and so that sufficed. Only a few experienced the real contrition that the Jansenists demanded and that flowed from a love for God rather than from a love of self-preservation. But this, for Saint-Cyran and the other Jansenists, was the entire point: only God could grant such a conversion, and he granted it only to a chosen few.

If Jansenists were so vociferous in their condemnations of Protestantism,

Blaise Pascal.

it was perhaps because they ran close to it themselves. And their opponents correctly perceived that focusing upon such direct contact between the believer and God in a matter that was essential to everyone (namely confession and pardon for sin) was to undermine the institutional power of the church. Similarly, a work by Antoine Arnauld, brother of Abbess Angélique, entitled *De la fréquente communion* (1643) tended to stress the importance of the disposition of the recipient of communion to the point of undermining the *ex opere operato* principle—and hence the intermediary role of priests. If the Jansenists could not perceive this, their opponents could, and Arnauld's book provoked a rare show of unanimity between Jesuits and Dominicans. Arnauld himself was deprived of his university degrees by the Sorbonne in 1656. In an unsuccessful attempt to prevent this deprivation, Pascal penned his witty and brilliant *Provincial Letters*, lambasting the Jesuits for their supposed laxity and badly damaging their public standing. Pascal's book, like Jansen's *Augustinus* before it, was placed upon the papal Index of Prohibited Books. Arnauld had to spend twelve years in hiding.

In 1653 Pope Innocent X had pronounced (definitively, as he thought) a condemnation of five key propositions of the *Augustinus*. However, the Jansenists evaded the judgment by agreeing that the condemned propositions were heretical while denying them to be a correct construal of their mentor's meaning—a morally casuistic argument that can only be described as Jesuitical. Thereafter, much of the debate centered upon whether or not the condemnations had correctly represented Jansen's teaching, though the Jansenist denial was itself condemned by Innocent X's successor, Alexander VII, in 1656.

But the wrangling outgrew Jansen's original theological concerns—or even his objections to the practices of the Jesuits—by some distance as it became embroiled in French politics and the complex relationship between the monarchy and the papacy. Jansenists tended to favor Gallicanism, the old idea that, in France, the king should have a prime say in the running of the church. The Jesuits, each of whom had, of course, taken a personal oath of obedience to the pope, were for ecclesiastical centralism. With differing theological positions, opposition over moral and pastoral matters (especially the frequency of taking communion), and conflicting political loyalties, the battle between Jansenists and Jesuits was irreconcilable.

If Jansen's principled stance over the little matter of the Thirty Years' War had been irritating to the mundane practitioners of Realpolitik, then later Jansenist support for Gallicanism should have endeared the movement to the French government, especially in its battles with the Jesuits.

In 1660, however, King Louis XIV chose to join forces with the pope and the Jesuits, and though the fury abated in 1668, the row erupted again with full force a generation later. Pasquier Quesnel published a French New Testament replete with Jansenist footnotes, which was condemned by Pope Clement XI. Papal bulls of 1705 and 1713 were directed against the Jansenists, and the aged Louis XIV closed the Jansenist nunnery of Port Royal. The Jansenists, however, survived all moves to suppress them, and in the Netherlands some of their adherents went so far as to renounce their obedience to Rome and set up a rival church, the Old Catholics, which persists to this day.

The Catholics of Protestant England

If intra-Catholic rivalries affected still solidly Romanist areas of Europe, this did not mean that minority Catholic communities, subject to persecution by their Protestant enemies, were therefore immune from them. English Catholics found that the pressures of minority status, the efforts of Rome to reclaim their kingdom for the old faith, and the peculiar politics that this experience imposed upon them led to serious internal tensions.

When Queen Elizabeth I ascended the throne in 1558, English Catholics found themselves somewhat bemused. Although the development was clearly ominous, the young queen, mindful of her extreme political vulnerability in the early stages of her rule, was politic in sowing confusion as to her intentions concerning future religious policy. In consequence, it remained possible to persuade oneself that she might be Catholic at heart. And even when the religious settlement emerged in the following year, conservatives of all kinds could take encouragement from its moderation, while committed papists continued to hope for a change, either in the regime's policies or else in the regime itself. After all, both had fluctuated wildly during the previous quarter century. And the latest young monarch remained unmarried, while her cousin and putative successor, Mary Queen of Scots, adhered to Rome. Even if Elizabeth proved implacably Protestant, the restoration of the one true church was no further away than a severe cold.

It was considerations such as these that inhibited any immediate upsurge of Roman Catholic resistance, still less of actual violence, during the opening years of the new reign. In any case, the mindset fostered by traditional, pre-Tridentine Catholicism left its adherents ill-equipped to respond to the new circumstances. Schism from Rome was unnatural, self-contradictory, and destined to perish of itself. The traditional order of the Catholic Church was part of the very order of the universe, since God had given it. Therefore, as a violation of this order, no schism could finally prosper; one needed only to bide one's time.

Many rural parish functionaries behaved in ways consistent with the belief that the new arrangements might be only temporary. Like the more daring of their Puritan counterparts, conservative-minded parish priests made tactical additions to and subtractions from the Elizabethan Prayer Book services—though in this case it was in order to adhere as closely as possible to the pattern of the Mass. Some retained images, holy water, and signs of the cross. Others provided the new, official services in public and the old in private. About 15 percent of all parishes were in trouble at some point during the 1560s for failing to remove images from their churches. Others were more seriously suspect as dens of secret papists when crucifixes and other Catholic paraphernalia were found hidden in barns or buried in shallow pits. The great minster church at Ripon suffered a spot of bother along these lines in 1567, when Catholic ornaments were found, preserved though dismantled, in nearby buildings. But such cases indicated a blurring of religious conservatism with mere financial prudence; the preceding thirty years had put parishes to no little expense in repeated jettisoning and replacing of church fixtures. Who could tell if the present order might not prove equally fleeting?

But a number of Catholics were moving beyond such irregularities and hesitancies during the 1560s and drifting into actual recusancy. Strictly speaking, this term referred to the absenting of oneself from one's parish church, an offense for which one could be fined. In practice, it was synonymous with principled Catholic objection to the Elizabethan Protestant church and a consequent determination not to participate in it.

In 1570 the bishop of Carlisle bewailed that "on all hands the people fall from religion, revolt to popery, refuse to come at Church; the wicked parish priests reconcile them to the Church of Rome and cause them to abjure this [Church of England]; and that openly and unchecked." The previous year's visitation report for the Chichester diocese noted, "When a preacher doth come and speak anything against the pope's doctrine, they will not abide, but get them out of the church."

Even if we make some allowance for the natural desire of the early Elizabethan bishops to harp on the terrors of a Catholic revival and to maintain maximum official backing and force for their work of Protestantization, yet the scale of localized resistance to religious changes still seems impressive. And if quantification is impossible, we may still note that conservative resistance was nowhere absent—the areas of

The Catholic Recovery ca. 1650.

strongest Catholic loyalty being in the north, the west Midlands, Wales, and Cornwall.

The Northern Rising, which began as the panic-stricken response to an embarrassing disclosure of plans to marry the Duke of Norfolk to Mary Queen of Scots, quickly took on the fully Catholic character that had always been implicit in the marriage machinations themselves. Some historians of Catholicism insist upon seeing it as merely a large and late example of decaying aristocratic feudalism, in which magnates had always made war upon their neighbors and upon central government. But that is a half-truth. Admittedly, the Northern Rising resulted in part from aristocratic faction-fighting and opposition to the upstart William Cecil (Elizabeth's chief minister and the son of a mere Northamptonshire squire) on the part of the Earls of Northumberland and Westmorland. At that level, religious traditionalism was a response to the (correct) perception that Protestantism was the religious arm of the expansion of central government. But the Rising had widespread support across the north and was by no means confined to the earls' retainers. Altars were reerected and Masses sung again in Durham Cathedral. The rebels proved no match, however, for the queen's ability to deploy military force, and the revolt was swiftly put down with hundreds of executions following.

From this point onward, survivalist Catholicism retreated into a sectarian movement, practiced with circumspection by country squires in out-of-the-way corners of England. It was a novel experience. Catholic gentry families needed to be persistently kind landlords to their tenants in order to gain their complicity or silence so they could survive with mere token gestures of conformity. A distinction was made between the bonds of loyalty in the family and locality, on the one hand, and the bonds that tied the heads of families to the queen.

Most Catholics, certainly after 1569 and many before, wished for nothing more than for the pope and the queen to make up—and at least to leave the Catholics of England free to reconcile their religious allegiance with their political loyalties as best they could. In this, neither pontiff nor monarch would oblige them. In April 1570 Pope Pius V declared Elizabeth excommunicate and absolved her subjects from their oaths of allegiance to her: "We charge and command" English Catholics "that they do not dare obey her orders, mandates and laws. Those who shall act to the contrary we include in the like sentence of excommunication."[7] On the other side, acts of Parliament of the following year made it high treason to call the queen a heretic or to bring papal bulls into England. A further act, passed a decade later, made it treason to reconcile anyone or to be reconciled to the Church of Rome. Recusancy fines were raised to levels designed to be ruinous for those subjected to them, though it should be mentioned that the fines were seldom fully enforced, especially in the north.

In this exceedingly difficult situation, what the Catholic gentry wanted was for government to refrain from interfering in a sphere—namely, religion—that did not, in the eyes of the successors to Thomas More, properly belong to it. "No prince [may] presume by any law to take upon him . . . a spiritual pre-eminence [which belongs] by the mouth of our Saviour himself . . . only to St. Peter and his successors."[8]

The Catholic gentry were becoming successors to More in another sense also; the notion of the godly and instructed household was perforce gaining ground. Priests were living secretly within the walls of the manor or else were employed outwardly as tutors or stewards. The priests' custodians, at the very moment of denying the validity of lay control of religion when exercised by central government, were achieving lay control within their own houses. Having a dependent, client priesthood released them from inappropriate sermons and ecclesiastical supervision alike. Lord Vaux, defending himself against recusancy charges in 1581, "did claim his house to be a parish by itself." The ability to sustain this kind of claim gave the gentry some protection and, curiously, brought them parallel with the same tendency among their Puritan equivalents to integrate religious instruction into the household. Indeed, when the appointment of George Blackwell as archpriest was made in 1598—an arrangement ominous with implications of institutional control and hard-line Jesuit influence—many Catholic laity and even secular priests appealed to Rome in protest.

But as early as the 1570s the quiet survivalism of would-be loyal subjects to Elizabeth was interrupted, even as it was coming into existence, by a new breed of more determined, Counter-Reformation harshness. This latter found its origins in the seminary priests who had been trained in the exilic English colleges at Douai, France (founded 1568), Rome (1575–1578), and Valladolid, Spain (1589). All these were founded by the expatriate William Allen (1532–1594), who was elevated to the cardinalate in 1587 and whose life task was the reconversion of his countrymen. It was under Allen's inspiration, also, that the Douai Bible was produced—the New Testament in 1582 and the Old Testament in 1609. Translated into English from the Latin Vulgate rather than from the original tongues, it was intended to act as a counterweight to Protestant translations.

Between 1574 and 1580 about one hundred seminary priests were secreted into England, though mostly without the benefit of much central coordination. Altogether, 438 were sent from Douai during the late sixteenth and early seventeenth centuries, of whom ninety-eight were executed. Better trained than the Marian priests who preceded them, they counseled stiffer resistance, principled nonattendance at parish church, and active attempts to reconvert neighbors to Rome.

Nicholas Sander (1530–1581), another expatriate who became professor of theology at Louvain, attained notoriety for writing a number of books in which he opined that the only hope for English Catholicism was a foreign invasion. In a convincing demonstration that loyalty to the One True, Universal Church is no sure rescue from myopic provincialism, he wrote to the Duke of Alva that "the state of Christendom depends upon the stout assailing of England."[9] By way of example of his conviction, however, he joined Catholic and Spanish forces in Ireland in 1579, determined to assist Irish rebels against Protestant English rule.

Sander was the mentor of a new, less complacent breed of English Catholic for whom the Anglican schism was less an unnatural anomaly than an intolerable affront to true faith. Neither was it destined to wither away by itself; it demanded to be destroyed by determined action.

As if all this were not unnerving enough, from 1580 onward the seminary priests were supplemented by the appearance of the Jesuit mission in England. Its leader, Robert Parsons (1546–1610), was definitely committed to the removal of the queen by any means available. Alerted to the Jesuits' presence, the authorities pulled out all the stops to apprehend them and, with the country too hot for him, Parsons returned across the English Channel the following year.

Parsons's assistant, Edmund Campion (1540–1581), was less fortunate. Campion is generally adjudged a better man than his leader (indeed, historians of all persuasions have lamented that Parsons was not the one who was caught and Campion who escaped), and it is certain that he was less obsessed with politics and more concerned with the spiritual welfare of the individuals he encountered. At Campion's trial, in which he stood accused along with other seminary priests and a layman, he protested that "if our religion do make us traitors, we are worthy to be condemned; but otherwise are, and have been, as good subjects as the Queen ever had." From this platform, Campion proceeded to demonstrate the eloquence and reasoning for which he (and his order) was so feared:

> In condemning us you condemn all your own ancestors—all the ancient priests, bishops and kings—all that was once the glory of England, the island of saints, and the most devoted child of the See of Peter. For what have we taught, however you may qualify it with the odious name of treason, that they did not uniformly teach? To be condemned with these lights—not of

England only, but of the world—by their degenerate descendants, is both
gladness and glory to us.[10]

Here, of course, is the strength of the conservative case at times of
cultural and ideological handover, when a society and its government
adopt and approve a new faith or ideology to replace the old. At that
point, the spokesmen for the old ideas can appeal with real force and
persuasive power to the sense of meaninglessness and of being cast adrift
with which such changes threaten the populace. Only once the new faith
has gained the dignity of age and can appear plausibly "natural" do the
backward-looking arguments begin to lose their force; and that point
had not been reached in 1581, when England's ties with Rome—and
even more the general catholicity of its religious past—were still well
within living memory.

Campion had been fearfully racked by his captors, who wanted information, not about his ideas and arguments, but about plots, assassina-
tions, and invasions. However, he was unforthcoming upon these subjects, concerning which he seems to have known nothing. In November
1581 he and his companions were condemned to be hanged, drawn,
and quartered—the punishment for treason. The two hundred or so
Roman Catholics, two-thirds of them priests, who were put to death
during Elizabeth's reign suffered, not as heretics (for Catholicism was
not officially considered to be heretical), but as traitors, for the government judged them to be giving allegiance to a foreign power that rejected
Queen Elizabeth's right to rule. In this way it was possible to argue
that Catholics were not persecuted for their religion but for treason. It
was a fine distinction that few found persuasive, even in the sixteenth
century.

The heroism of Campion and his ilk notwithstanding, the new breed of
seminarians made many English Catholics uneasy. A succession of plots,
either to cooperate with Spanish invasion or else to murder Elizabeth,
were unearthed by the government during the mid-1580s centering
around the figures of Francis Throckmorton (1583), Dr. Thomas Parry
(1585), and Anthony Babington (1586). The large majority of English
Catholic laypeople wanted nothing to do with any of them and were
suspicious of the new priests who seemed to be worryingly equivocal
on the point.

The Jesuits in particular found they had alienated most of the very
constituency they claimed to be helping. When Parsons published a
book in 1594 arguing that the strongest claim to the succession to the
English throne was that of the Spanish Infanta, English Catholics were

horrified and deeply embarrassed. The same year that Campion was executed saw Sir Thomas Tresham compose a declaration of loyalty to Queen Elizabeth and to her lawful successors (for the queen was already forty-eight and the succession issue was troubling Protestant minds) in the name of the Catholic laity. In 1588, the year of the Spanish Armada, leading recusants noisily and ostentatiously expressed their desire to fight the Spaniards. And the Puritans' Millenary Petition was not the only religious lobbying to pester James VI and I as he arrived in his new capital in 1604. The Petition Apologetical protested loyalty and promised that the Catholic gentry would exact an oath of allegiance from priests "before they shall be admitted to our houses, otherwise they shall not have relief of us."[11] It was an impressive claim; in laying to rest his own fears about a new priest (who might, after all, be of the Parsons type), the Catholic gentleman would furnish proof incontestable of his own loyalty to the Crown. Problem solved? It was a pity that the fiasco of the Gunpowder Plot (1605)—the failed conspiracy by Catholic zealots to detonate Parliament at a moment when the king was in attendance— lay just around the corner.

The Russian Orthodox Church

Not even the Russian Orthodox Church was spared the pain of inner conflict during the sixteenth and seventeenth centuries. In one case, that conflict remained "internal"—with the losing party being suppressed and maintaining a shadowy existence thereafter. In the other case, dispute led to secession—with violent consequences.

Possessors and Non-Possessors

The early sixteenth century saw the dispute between the Possessors and the Non-Possessors. The latter were the followers of St. Nil of Sorsk (1433–1508), who taught that monasteries should not possess serfs or large estates but that monastics should support themselves by their own labor. The former supported St. Joseph of Volotsk (1440–1515), who argued the opposite, on the grounds that this left the monks free to concentrate on prayer, care for the poor, and give spiritual direction. A lot was at stake, for the monasteries owned a quarter of all the culti-vated land in Muscovy.

Behind this simple debate, however, lay a far deeper division. The Non-Possessors held to a primitivist vision of Christian faith, which was ultimately focused on the individual's relationship with God, unentangled by possessions. The church should not be subject to the state, nor should secular force be used to punish heretics. Meditation, fasting, chastity, and prayer were more important than elaborate worship.

St. Joseph and the Possessors, however, thought that Christianity was about the whole society's relationship with God; the corporate life of the church was what mattered. According to them, every Christian home should be modeled on a monastery, with the father in absolute authority, leading daily worship at the icon corner of the house. The Old Testament was sufficient justification for the punishment by secular government of those who broke God's laws. Liturgical worship was of paramount importance—its correct performance brought ritual sanctification to the whole people.

No reader of this volume is likely to be so entirely free of cynicism as to be in any doubt about whose arguments were more likely to recommend themselves to the Muscovite princes. The occasion of the reckoning was a marital difficulty that bore remarkable similarities to that of Henry VIII of England and occurred at about the same time. In 1525 Basil (Vasily) III (reigned 1505–1533) wanted a divorce because he had no male heir by his wife. The Non-Possessors, true to their usual high-mindedness, took a strict New Testament line on this issue. But the Possessors supported Basil; considerations of national stability outweighed the rights of a childless wife. The Non-Possessors found themselves persecuted.

The offspring of Basil's second marriage was Ivan IV (reigned 1533–1584), who did well to survive his minority (at the age of three he lost his father and at age eight his mother, the latter probably to poison). He assumed personal control of government at the age of sixteen.[12] In 1551 Ivan IV convened a council of ecclesiastics to whom he presented the *Stoglav*, or Hundred Chapters, insisting upon reforms and tightening of the regulations concerning the behavior of monks and priests as well as halting any drift toward "the Latin heresy" in such weighty matters as beards and the correct manner of crossing oneself.

The Emergence of the Old Believers

The conflict between Possessors and Non-Possessors and the previously noted division in the Ukraine (see chapter 3) were not the only crises to afflict the Orthodox Church among the Eastern Slavs during the seventeenth century. The "Time of Troubles," a period of political upheavals in Muscovy during the years from 1584 (the death of Ivan the Terrible) to 1613 (the election of Mikhail Romanov as tsar), had greatly enhanced the power of the church, but the period from the 1630s onward saw a growing chorus of voices protesting about abuses within it. Furthermore, the Orthodox Church appeared to be threatened by the rising confidence of Counter-Reformation Catholicism, especially as reflected in the Polish state and its success in persuading so many of its Orthodox subjects to defect to Uniatism. The new Catholicism made Russian Orthodoxy appear rough, credulous, and unsophisticated.

The possible responses of reform movements in Muscovy were two-fold: one could make modernizing attempts to wrest the intellectual high ground from the Catholics, or one could press for moral improvements and the elimination of abuses. Unfortunately, reformist movements in Muscovy refused to see these as complementary positions: the modern-izers clung to their corruptions; the moral purists aimed at ceremonial retrenchment.

The latter movement, the Zealots of Piety (pompous names did not begin with the Soviets), consisted mainly of priests in the Volga region, though their influence spread soon enough. Archpriest Avvakum was one of their most fiery preachers. The prime target of their attack was the uncomfortable reality that Christianity was worn as a veneer over an underlying paganism and sub-Christian immorality, especially in the more far-flung rural areas of the vast country. But the Zealots also sharply criticized the often disgraceful behavior of clergy—including bishops and archbishops—in and around Moscow itself. They advocated a thorough-going, enforced religiosity on the population as a whole: frequent fasting, confession, and communion and the banning of alcohol sales on holy days. Perhaps their greatest weakness was their underlying anti-intellectualism; though they advocated improved education, especially for the clergy, they were extremely uncomfortable with the current, Renaissance-inspired forms of it, which were so alien to the traditional Russian mind-set and which Avvakum identified with Western *khitrost*, or "cunning."

The clash within the Orthodox Church began in earnest in the 1650s, when Patriarch Nikon (originally a Zealot, but whose elevation had pushed him decisively toward the modernizers) revised the ancient liturgy in line with classical Greek practice. He also insisted that the Russians abandon their old habit of crossing themselves using two fingers, and do so instead "with the three first fingers of the right hand. Any Orthodox Christian who does not make the sign of the cross according to this Eastern church tradition . . . is a heretic and imitator of the Armenians. He will be damned."

Whether the parents and ancestors of the existing generation of Russians had all been damned for this fatal ritualistic shortcoming he did

Patriarch Nikon of Moscow.

not explain. The peremptory changes were an unwise move in a country whose population had been taught to reverence the precise, and distinctively Russian, details of religious ritual and to believe that they were efficacious only because they were carried out in the correct manner. But Nikon was motivated somewhat by the Renaissance principle of *ad fontes* (the idea that one should go back to original sources and the earliest possible manuscripts) and even more by a desire to further his monarch's aspirations to the leadership of the Orthodox world, a goal that would require greater harmonization with Greek liturgical practices.

For extraneous reasons relating to his overweening power vis-à-vis the tsar, Patriarch Nikon fell from favor in the late 1650s and gave a dramatic public resignation in 1658. But Nikon's reforms were upheld by his successors and by Tsar Alexei himself.

Many ordinary people were horrified. For them, religion was not a matter of ideas but of forms, not of theology but of magic. They knew no preaching, and most priests were themselves illiterate. Everything depended upon maintaining faithfulness to the precise rituals of their ancestors. To abandon them was to come into league with Antichrist.

Archpriest Avvakum became an early leader among the Old Believers (or, more accurately, Old Ritualists—*Staroobriadtsy*). "If we are schismatics," they argued, using identical logic to that of Campion in England, "then the Holy fathers, Tsars and Patriarchs were also schismatics." The reforms were "introducing the alien Roman abomination." Avvakum was imprisoned in 1667, spent twelve of the next fifteen years in a pit, and was finally burned at the stake in 1682.

His xenophobic defense of his position bears sharp similarities to that of the Essenes, of the English Puritans, or of mid-twentieth-century

American fundamentalists: He repudiates as apostate the very country he claims to love. It and it alone has the possibility of purity and godliness, yet it is hopelessly contaminated unless and until it returns to a mythical past—an idealized past which, in reality, never was. In the meantime, the stance of righteous remnant is adopted; the group is self-defined by repudiation of the thing it loves and calls to repentance. For Avvakum, the Catholic Poles were "enemies of the Christians"; the Greek patriarchs must now "come to us to learn," rather than introducing an Orthodoxy that was "a varied mixture under the violence of the Turkish Muhammad." The Russian church had been "pure and spotless" before "the wolf Nikon along with the devil introduced the tradition that one had to cross oneself with three fingers."

One recent historian has argued that support for the Old Believers stemmed only in part from repudiation of Nikon's liturgical reforms and that concentration upon them was a later rationalization of eighteenth-century Old Believers, whose movement was originally motivated at least as much by a wide range of social grievances. Yet the later decades of the seventeenth century witnessed mass suicides, often by entire congregations setting their wooden churches ablaze—a likelier response to certain kinds of religious zeal than to more mundane disaffections.

The apostasy, as Old Believers saw it, of the Third (and final) Rome could only possibly portend the end of the world. (Moscow was widely believed, from the sixteenth century onward, to be the Third Rome; Rome, the first, had fallen politically to the barbarians and spiritually to apostasy in the early Middle Ages; Byzantium, the second, had fallen to the Turks in 1453; the task of being the center of the Christian world now devolved upon Muscovy and its rulers.) The end of the world was predicted for 1666, but its failure to materialize did not deter the movement. In 1684, after mutinous soldiers adopted the Old Belief as part of their own cause, the Empress Sophia introduced a comprehensive program of persecution. "Those who appear to be heretics or schismatics, . . . such persons are to be severely interrogated, under torture"; those who "remain obstinate and will not submit to the holy church" were to be burned to death. But the Old Believers were unmoved. Indeed, they were delighted: thousands rushed to embrace martyrdom at the stake. Others fled to areas beyond the reach of the persecutors, in the Arctic north or in Siberia.[13]

In the early eighteenth century, Peter the Great finally granted the Old Believers a limited toleration, replacing the death penalty with subjection to a double tax and other harassments. His pragmatic motives, however, smacked of the very secularism and rationalism that the Old Believers most detested. His moving of his capital from Moscow to St. Petersburg was blasphemy against "the Third Rome." The modernization of his court and his forcing of the boyars (Russian aristocrats) to abandon the wearing of beards were measures the Old Believers considered dubious, irreligious, un-Russian, and Western. Peter was well aware that the Old Believers were opposed to everything new, whether in religion or in politics, and as such would always seek to obstruct his project to modernize Russia.

Divided in Ukraine, suffering schism in Muscovy, fearful of Western encroachment, and eager for leadership of the Orthodox world, Russian Orthodoxy entered the modern era bruised and ill at ease with itself, yet certain of its messianic mission. The paradox was a metaphor for Russia itself.

6

MELTDOWN

THE CATACLYSM OF 1618–1648

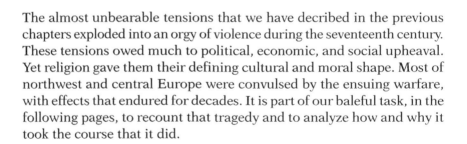

The almost unbearable tensions that we have decribed in the previous chapters exploded into an orgy of violence during the seventeenth century. These tensions owed much to political, economic, and social upheaval. Yet religion gave them their defining cultural and moral shape. Most of northwest and central Europe were convulsed by the ensuing warfare, with effects that endured for decades. It is part of our baleful task, in the following pages, to recount that tragedy and to analyze how and why it took the course that it did.

The Thirty Years' War

A "cold war" had been building in the Holy Roman Empire for several decades before 1618. The protagonists were two mutually antagonistic and suspicious confessional camps that, in 1608 and 1609 respectively, formalized alliances as the Protestant Union and the Catholic League. The former, however, suffered from the disadvantage that the chief Lutheran principality, Saxony, declined to join it.

152

The Empire itself consisted of a crazy patchwork quilt of small principalities, dukedoms, city-states, and ecclesiastical territories governed by prince-bishops, all holding general allegiance to an ever-less-powerful emperor in Vienna. So many of these small jurisdictions were embroiled in long-term strategies—or short-term opportunistic coups—aimed at territorial aggrandizement that political life was often interesting. The background of confessional rivalry and mutual terror at the prospect of ultimate triumph by the other, however, made interest obsessional. Travelers in Germany in the opening decades of the seventeenth century remarked on the arms buildup and the proliferation of castles.

As people in the second half of the twentieth century discovered, however, deterrence works best when each side faces the calming reassurance that it will be completely annihilated in the event of serious conflict. Central Europe in 1618 had no such confidence, and the arms buildup, therefore, led to its more usual outcome: war.

The trigger was Bohemia. Under circumstances going back to the days of the Hussites before the Reformation, the Catholic Church had no monopoly on the religious allegiance of Bohemia's two million inhabitants (indeed it was clearly in the minority), and Protestants were supposed to be tolerated under the terms of the Letter of Majesty, wrested from an unwilling Emperor Rudolf II in 1609. The theoretical toleration, however, constantly ran foul of actual practice.

The situation threatened to get worse when, in 1617, Archduke Ferdinand of Styria was named king-designate by Rudolf's successor as emperor, Matthias. Ferdinand was known to be both zealous and personally devout in his Catholicism. The Bohemian magnates correctly feared that his rule would bring a new round of centralizing measures, trammel their freedoms, and harass Protestantism yet further. For the moment, the Estates of Bohemia had little alternative but to accept Ferdinand tamely, in the absence of any alternative native leader or acceptable foreign candidate. Even more ominously, the new king of Bohemia was clearly the future emperor by virtue of precedent, of being the leading Hapsburg, and by being the only one of the Catholic majority of the imperial electors who was a layman.

In Styria Ferdinand had succeeded in suppressing Protestantism by giving the people a choice between conformity and exile, with the result that the Lutheran nobility were isolated in their recalcitrance and increasingly docile. This served to convince him that there was a link between ascendant Catholicism and monarchical power. A survey of the contemporary scene—Bohemia, Germany, France, the Spanish-Dutch conflict—would have served to confirm him in this view.

The outlook for Bohemian Protestantism being as ominous as it was, nobles from the committee of Protestant defenders convened on 21 May 1618, in violation of imperial wishes, to protest the flouting of the provisions of the Letter of Majesty. Two days later, several of these men decided to emulate their ancestors by carrying out a rerun of the famed "Defenestration of Prague." In the original event of 1418, Hussite leaders had propelled some unfortunate royal officials through a large window high up in the castle, sending them hurtling to their deaths on the flagstones below. The attempted reenactment of this quaint folk custom, by way of bicentennial celebration, led the Protestants to seize two leading Catholic nobles, plus a hapless secretary who found himself in the wrong office at the wrong moment. Everything worked perfectly until the moment that the three victims and several million shards of glass were in midair. At this, the crucial nanosecond of the entire exploit, it became apparent that the perpetrators had not done their homework. For in the intervening two hundred years there had grown up beneath the famous window a very large, brownish pile of waste matter. Into this the unfortunates—or perhaps fortunates—now descended, to emerge moments later with their clothes and dignity irreparably damaged, but otherwise unharmed. Marx's dictum—that history repeats itself, the first time as tragedy and the second time as farce—was never better illustrated.

It would have been good (though smelly) if the violence had remained at this level. Alas, the methane of the poisoned atmosphere was about to explode to far more lethal effect. The incident was the signal for rebellion. The Bohemian Estates elected a provisional government and raised a ramshackle army under Count Thurn. But raising 16,000 men is not the same thing as training, feeding, paying, and equipping them. Perceiving these shortcomings, the Duke of Savoy, a good enemy of the Hapsburgs, offered the Bohemians the services of a mercenary army under Count Ernst von Mansfeld. Mansfeld's troops, like his ducal paymaster, were Catholic, but one cannot be too fussy about religion if one wishes to fight for money, and they proceeded to capture the Catholic city of Pilsen for the Protestants in September. King Philip III of Spain, in a show of family solidarity, sent an army from Flanders to help his Hapsburg relative, Ferdinand. The following spring, the Protestant rebels were joined by troops from Silesia and Lusatia, Moravia, and both Upper and Lower Austria. (Ferdinand himself already held Inner Austria.)

At first the revolt went well. By June 1619 Thurn's army was camped outside Vienna, and the city was saved only by the arrival of a small cavalry force led by Ferdinand's brother, Leopold. However, the same month

Mansfeld's army was completely destroyed at Sablat, and the first force of the rebellion was spent. The Bohemian military position began to look vulnerable in the face of determined royalist and Catholic counterattack. That August, in desperation, the Estates declared Ferdinand deposed and, having given out broad hints in all directions concerning possible alternative appointees, ranging from the Catholic Duke of Savoy to the Protestant Bethlen Gabor of Transylvania, finally offered the Bohemian throne instead to the Elector Palatine, Frederick V. This was a piece of dangerous folly, matched only by Frederick's acceptance.

Frederick was no ordinary Protestant prince. For one thing, he was a Calvinist, not a Lutheran—and Calvinism had no legal recognition under the terms of the Peace of Augsburg of 1555. In the second place, he was the leader of the Protestant Union, the military alliance defending Protestantism inside the empire. In the third place, he was an elector, and accepting a royal title would have conferred upon him a second electorate. It was this factor that was the most crucial and far-reaching of all for, by accepting the proffered kingship, he was upsetting decisively the empire's entire, and somewhat intricate, religious balance.

There were seven electoral princes inside the Hapsburg realms. Their electoral status conferred upon them the right to choose the new emperor whenever the previous incumbent died or (as in the case of Charles V) retired. The fact that they always chose the next Hapsburg in line was neither here nor there; the principle was the thing. In any case, there could be situations when the succession was not entirely clear, and then the electors would arbitrate. Since the Reformation, the electoral college had consisted of three Protestant electors (those of Saxony, the Palatinate, and Brandenburg) and four Catholic electors (the archbishops of Trier, Köln, and Mainz, and the king of Bohemia).

No advanced training in mathematics is necessary, therefore, to envisage the potential results of Frederick's acceptance of a second electorate. For with it, the Protestants stood in possession of four votes, and thus of a majority. The religious future of the Empire seemed to be at stake. At one blow, the Catholics' world was swimming before their eyes. The fact that Ferdinand was successfully elected emperor just two days later (following the death of Matthias the previous March) was beside the point; the principle was the thing. The empire dissolved into war.

Frederick had a sincere concern for his Bohemian coreligionists. He had used his position as leader of the Protestant Union to try to obtain rather more military help for them than they eventually got (which was simply a decision to stop Spanish troops crossing Germany to fight for Ferdinand). But sensing that he was about to be sucked further into the unfolding morass, he felt himself out of his depth. "My God!" he exclaimed aloud to his adviser, Anhalt, "If they elect me, what should I do?" And to this, his Mephistophelean adviser could give no clear reply. Anhalt had machinated long and hard for just such an eventuality, but now that the moment had arrived, their forces were too weak to make acceptance practicable, their fellow Protestants too noncommittal, the Palatinate too vulnerable. When Frederick ignored practicality, accepted the offer, and entered Prague in triumph that November, friend and foe alike could foresee the sequel.

The first decade of the conflict is a catalog of Protestant defeats. Assailed by imperial forces, the Bohemian Protestants were unable to mount an effective resistance and were decisively defeated at the Battle of the White Mountain. Frederick was expelled from the country in early 1620, thus earning for himself the title of "the Winter King"—that being all the time he had managed to stay in place.

Ferdinand, determined to use the opportunity of his military advantage in Bohemia to maximum effect, did not wait for his victory there to be complete and the fighting to end but offered Frederick's original electorate to the Catholic Maximilian of Bavaria if he would help to invade the Palatinate. The offer was accepted. Even the Protestant John George of Saxony lent his assistance in this enterprise because, as a Lutheran, he was unhappy about the idea of a Calvinist prince in Bohemia.

But a Catholic emperor on the loose in Bohemia was proving hardly better. If John George was paying too scrupulous attention to Luther's famous preference for "drinking pure blood with the Pope" rather than "pure wine with the Reformed," then this was unfortunate, for blood was everywhere in evidence in Bohemia under the devastation wrought by the Catholic armies. The fighting was absolutely savage, a feature of the conflict that was to endure for most of its length. Fearful massacres were inflicted by the roving bands of soldiers on the civilian populations of the "wrong" confession. The *Hutterite Chronicle* records the appalling sufferings visited upon just one group, namely the communities of pacifist Anabaptists who were unfortunate enough to be overrun by the imperial forces. Boys and girls, as well as women, were subjected to brutal rape. Men of the settlements were burned with red-hot irons, their feet held in fires until the toes were burned off, gunpowder poured into wounds and ignited, eyes gouged out. As the chronicler comments, "Such things were openly practiced by the imperial soldiery who believed themselves to be the best of Christians."

Bohemia was forcibly re-Catholicized during the first half of the 1620s. More than 100,000 Protestants were expelled and the ancient

University of Prague was handed over to the Jesuits. Protestant states that might have helped failed, on the whole, to do so. The reasons for Saxon noninvolvement in the early stages of conflict have already been mentioned. The Netherlands declined to intervene because it had made a twelve-year truce, starting in 1609, in its endless war with Spain and was busily preparing to defend itself for the renewed onslaught—an event that happened on schedule.

Protestant England might have been expected to do something to assist. Since the later years of Elizabeth I's reign, it had been gently coasting toward the status of leading Protestant power (for none of the states that had embraced the Reformation was very big); furthermore, Frederick V's wife was an English princess, Elizabeth, daughter of James I. She (and because of his reputation, her husband) commanded a good deal of popularity among the English political classes, and James faced demands in Parliament that he come galloping to the rescue of his daughter and son-in-law—and of European Protestantism in its hour of greatest need. These were demands that were to pursue James's son, Charles I (Elizabeth's brother), in the years after he succeeded his father in 1625. None of this heartfelt compassion and Protestant solidarity, however, stretched so far as a willingness to vote for the kind of tax subsidy that would have been required to translate the fine sentiments into military effect.

Financial constraints were not the only reason that James and Charles declined the role of Protestant white knight that was being so urgently proffered to them by their Parliaments. James was furious at his reckless son-in-law for encouraging the Bohemian squabble to escalate into a European bloodbath. Besides, his own private fantasies included acting the part of arbiter and peacemaker of Christendom, designs that could hardly be furthered by becoming a party to the conflict. In any case, in the years around 1620 he was still attempting to marry off his son and heir to the Spanish Infanta—an aspiration that was scarcely consistent with taking the field against the Hapsburgs. Although this match never materialized, the son in question, Charles, was even less inclined than his father had been to get involved in the war, the whole mentality of Protestant internationalism and anti-Catholicism being generally repugnant to him.

The German Protestant princes, then, were left to struggle on alone. By 1623 Frederick had been expelled from his erstwhile electorate in the Palatinate. During the first half of the 1620s, Spanish and Hapsburg troops overran much of Protestant Germany, right up to the Baltic.

It was at this stage that the dissolute King Christian IV allowed his Protestant conscience to prick him into action. As ruler of Denmark, he had a marked preference for his southern borders to adjoin small, relatively weak German principalities rather than areas subject to strong, centralized control from Vienna. He had also been concerned for some time about Jesuit missionaries, who had been infiltrating his territory from the south. The likelihood of former church lands that he held in northern Germany being taken back into Catholic ecclesiastical ownership was hardly appealing to him either. In 1625 he entered the conflict and, until 1629, was the mainstay of the Protestant cause. It was not enough. Underfinanced and outgunned, he soon came unstuck, particularly when faced with the brilliant leadership of the imperial forces under Ferdinand's chosen general, Wallenstein. Wallenstein's army was partly financed by the Dutch Calvinist banker De Witt—but then, one cannot serve both God and mammon, and even bankers have to choose their priorities.

By 1629 Ferdinand was in a position to offer peace more or less on his own terms. The Edict of Restitution of that year restored all church lands that had been secularized since 1552, allowed Catholic rulers to expel any of their subjects who were Protestants, specifically excluded recognition of Calvinism anywhere throughout the empire, recovered five bishoprics, thirty cities, nearly a hundred convents, and countless individual parishes for the Roman Catholic Church, and appointed imperial commissioners who could enforce these rulings by calling in imperial troops to particular localities. It was the high point of the Counter-Reformation.

And it was too much. Even Catholic princes blanched at this vast extension of the powers of central government (that constant refrain of sixteenth- and seventeenth-century conflicts of every variety). To take the Palatinate away from its legitimate prince and offer it to another may have had a certain justice to it, under the circumstances, but it underlined the idea that princes held their positions courtesy of the emperor—and it set a dangerous precedent. A prince did not need to approve of Frederick's foolish actions, or even be a Protestant, to feel this.

Too many outside powers, also, had a vested interest in imperial weakness. The logic that had caused Francis I of France to resist moves a century earlier that might have ended the Protestant schism in Germany, thereby freeing the German emperor for more action abroad, continued to hold good. Other powers, Protestant and Catholic alike, were unnerved that the potential colossus that was the empire might finally be religiously and administratively united and thereby be in a position to overshadow its neighbors.

The Edict of Restitution was never universally enforced. In July 1630 Swedish forces landed at Peenemünde, in Pomerania, and the conflict

Gustavus Adolphus.
Illustration from German School.

entered a new phase. It was the beginning of Sweden's century of great-power status on the European stage. Faced with the prospect of an overly strong empire on the coasts facing him to the south, the Swedish king, Gustavus Adolphus, had decided to take up the challenge of containing imperial power. He was both a pious Lutheran and a brilliant military commander. Twisting the arms of the north German Protestant princes into a new alliance (this time with the Saxons included), he renewed the war.

The fighting had not become any less savage during more than a decade of conflict. Back in 1626, Wallenstein had asked the emperor "to be so good as to assure the city of Magdeburg that this is not a war of religion in any way; but that as a loyal and devoted city, their privileges of religious and secular peace will not be harmed in the slightest."[1] Five years later, however, the citizens' privileges were beyond further harm, for the majority of them were dead at the hands of the imperial troops. In May 1631 the imperial forces under Tilly captured and sacked Magdeburg, setting it ablaze from end to end.

The capture of Magdeburg was an atrocity that, though it pales into insignificance amid the total casualties of the war, was perhaps the worst single incident. Several hundred people inside the Protestant city were nevertheless on the side of the emperor. Thinking to rescue themselves from the general carnage that they were sure was about to ensue, they ran to greet the imperial forces as they broke in. But they merely became the first to be slaughtered. Citizens who fled into the churches were massacred inside them, including the church of St. John, which was locked and then burned, despite being crowded with women. The clergy were burned in their libraries, along with their books; their wives and daughters, singled out for special treatment, were dragged behind horses into the army camp before being raped and savagely treated. The Swedish report to the Riksråd (Swedish Parliament) noted that the Croat and Walloon troops spiked small children on their lances, waved them around, and threw them into the fire. In total, about two-thirds of the 30,000 citizenry perished.

The Protestants were not long in taking vengeance. Following Gustavus Adolphus's complete destruction of the main Catholic army at Breitenfeld four months later, his forces moved into the Rhineland and then Bavaria, where they devastated the countryside and slaughtered the peasantry. Von Grimmelshausen reported on the wanton destruction of peasant property by soldiers. In one settlement, a farmhand was thrown to the ground, a piece of wood was clamped into his mouth, and a milk churn full of dung water was emptied into him. Another was thrown alive into the baking oven. A third had a rope tied around his head and twisted so tightly that blood gushed from his mouth, nose, and ears.

The peasants, of course, were more or less helpless victims, but they took their revenge on stray soldiers as and when they could. The same writer noted being part of a troop that had scared off some semi-armed peasants before making a grisly discovery. A barrel had been poorly buried in the ground, containing a soldier, still alive. His nose and ears had been cut off. He and five of his fellows had been captured by a band of peasants. Forcing the six to stand closely in line, one shot was fired into them which, after piercing five bodies, failed to reach the sixth. The survivor was then mutilated, forced to lick the behinds of his dead comrades and buried alive.[2]

That such incidents have any place at all in a history of the Christian church is a condemnation, not merely of the participants, but of the entire phenomenon of a politicized Christendom whereby churches have, and claim, a legal monopoly on entire populations. The Thirty Years' War (like the Crusades or the Inquisition) is not an accidental product of this idea, nor an aberration, but its inevitable consequence.

In November 1632 the Swedes narrowly won the Battle of Lützen, though Gustavus Adolphus was killed. From then on, Swedish military strength started to wane.

During the 1630s the real nature of this war—as of all such wars and the parties that conduct them—began to show itself; that is, as a power conflict transposed into religious mode. But Protestantism had proved too weak to sustain the allegedly Protestant side of the conflict, and so alleged Catholics needed to come in to sustain it. We speak, of course, of France, which had in any case been giving heavy financial subsidies to the Swedish military effort every year since 1631. In 1635 France entered the conflict openly on the anti-Hapsburg side.

To confront this new (or rather, old) enemy with full force, Ferdinand instantly felt compelled to offer terms to the Protestants in the so-called

Peace of Prague. This move was at once condemned by Pope Urban VIII (1623–1644), whose military noninvolvement could afford the high ground of principle—the principle being, of course, that no compromise was to be made with heretics. His own compromises, however, stretched to having prompted Cardinal Richelieu and King Louis XIII to intervene in the first place. Lest this be thought strange, it should be remembered that the papacy, like everybody else, feared an overly strong emperor, who might put pressure on the papal states in Italy. Hence the papacy pursued a contradictory policy of seeking the destruction of the Protestants while nevertheless wishing to check the power of their principal destroyer, the emperor.

Given the papacy's double-dealing, it is perhaps understandable that Ferdinand did not allow his own Catholic zeal to extend quite so far as to put his realms at risk from French domination, and if averting that threat meant at least a temporary accommodation with the heretics, then it was a price he was willing to pay. The war continued, fitfully, for another thirteen years, though not for the reasons urged by papal pleading but because French intervention made peace impossible. Just as Protestant Denmark and Sweden had wanted—and continued to want—control of the Baltic coast (to the point of fighting one another from 1643), just as the papacy wanted the emperor weak in Italy, so the French wanted access into Germany and a weak, divided empire. The German princes, Protestant and Catholic alike, wanted autonomy from Vienna—though not at the price of foreign domination. The emperor wanted to salvage what he could from the ghastly mess.

The Peace of Westphalia and Its Consequences

The conclusion (perhaps *dénouement* is a better word) to the conflict was the agreements known collectively as the Peace of Westphalia of 1648. This confirmed that "the religious peace of 1555 . . . shall . . . be confirmed and observed fully and without infringement." So, on the matter originally contested for, an ocean of blood had been spilled to no good purpose.

But there were changes in practice. The treaty noted that, under the Peace of Augsburg, "the privilege of emigration was conceded to the subjects of such states if they dissented from the religion of their territorial lord"; this "privilege" would be taken advantage of—or enforced— often during the years ahead. It was decreed that "no one should seduce another's subjects to his religion";[3] the sharp practices of the prewar period were to cease. So too was evangelism, by either Catholics or Protestants. This stipulation marked the end of Protestant territorial expansion in Europe.

In fact, it marked its contraction. Bohemia and Hungary had been forcibly re-Catholicized. So too had large areas of Austria. Protestant advance in the upper Palatinate, Bavaria, and southern Germany had been stopped and reversed by force of arms. However, "those who are called reformed" were now subject to the same "rights and benefits" as the "Catholic and Augsburg faiths," though apart from these "none shall be received or tolerated in the Holy Empire."[4] The Palatinate was also restored to electoral status, but since the dukes of Bavaria had been rewarded early in the conflict with that dignity, which could not now easily be taken away, the number of electors was allowed to rise to eight.

The treaty was strong on state sovereignty, on territorial independence and integrity, and on noninterference in the affairs of neighboring states. Hobbes's *Leviathan* was coming into existence before the eyes of beholders. It is for this reason that the Peace of Westphalia is the starting point for students of modern international politics and the modern state.

From 1648 the emperor had almost no real power over the states of Germany; they were independent in all but name. Imperial energies were henceforward to be directed southward and eastward, expanding into the lands conquered from the slowly (later, rapidly) weakening Ottoman Empire or taken from Poland. The population of the old empire had, in any case, been devastated by the fighting. Germany suffered the loss of a greater proportion of its population than it was to lose during World War II. Overall losses may have been of the order of 30–35 percent, though some districts may have suffered double that. The population of Bohemia fell by about 50 percent during the conflict. These areas required the rest of the century, in some cases more, to recover from this demographic catastrophe. The religious geography of western and central Europe, in terms of its allegiance for or against the Reformation, had assumed something like its modern shape—until twentieth-century secularization and then immigration played new havoc with the previous longstanding loyalties.

The papacy might be thought, at first glance, to have gained by the war. The pope's flock now included large areas of central Europe that had previously been lost to the old faith, while the emperor's power in Germany was broken. Despite all logic, the contradictory policy had succeeded. Yet this would be a superficial reading. In reality, the papacy was the only political entity to lose even more from the conflict than had the emperor. The pope's political authority, even over Catholic monarchs, had been shown to be broken. The Peace of Westphalia, like that of Prague thirteen years earlier, had been made in the teeth of papal protests. Pope Innocent X's (1644–1655) *Zelo Domus Dei* had loudly decried the making of concessions to Protestants, but the Catholic monarchs of Europe had simply ignored it—and him. It had been a matter of some doubt whether "zeal for the house of the Lord" had been the papacy's only motivation in its own dealings since 1618; it had certainly ceased to motivate the kings and princes of Europe. *Raison d'état* was revealed as the sole determinant of decisions—but then, we have already mentioned that Westphalia was the beginning of the modern phase of international relations.

This was one of the signal effects of the Reformation, which the outcome of the last, and easily the bloodiest, of the wars of religion precipitated by it revealed: the throne was now mightier than the altar. Before Luther, the pope had owed no debt of gratitude to western European rulers for keeping their realms Catholic; any who failed to do so were positively inviting papally sanctioned rebellion by their vassals or displacement by other means. But once the Reformation had happened and been made to stick in significant areas of Western Christendom, the boot was on the other foot; the papacy was the debtor of any and every ruler who chose to uphold the Catholic faith and enforce it on his subjects. It was hard (nay, impossible), therefore, for the popes to dictate the precise terms under which it would be upheld. If the emperor, or the French or Spanish king, chose to make deals with heretics, or expel the Jesuits, or pursue a foreign policy of which the papacy disapproved, there was little that the Apostolic See could do about it.

The barbarity of the Thirty Years' War represents the logical conclusion of insisting that Christ's kingdom is indeed "of this world" (thereby rejecting a fundamental precept of Christ) and that Christianity was therefore a formula for ruling it. In consequence the churches, Protestant and Catholic alike, were dominated by politicians for ungodly, secular purposes. Rulers of principle, such as Ferdinand and Frederick, became, because of their very high-mindedness, the worst persecutors or most inclined to perpetrate religiously motivated acts of folly. Pragmatic politicians such as Christian IV and Richelieu were most inclined to abuse religious faith for cynical, power-seeking ends. And, as we have seen, the contradictory policies of the papacy left it guilty on both counts. Meanwhile, social and political struggles were transposed into a religious key to form rival powerblocks with rival cultures and rival military alliances. The resultant conflicts—and conflicts between rival cultures that threaten one another's existence are always savage—were then blessed as "wars for Christianity." Finally, when this led to military stalemate, the disguise was thrown aside, a secular international polity was ushered in, and Christianity stood discredited in the rising generation of thinkers in the ensuing Enlightenment.

The Coming of the English Civil Wars

Europe's offshore islands were also convulsed with their own violence during the later part of the Thirty Years' War—violence in which anxiety about the outcome of the wider, European conflagration played its part. England by the 1620s had a population rabidly and fearfully anti-Catholic, yet possessed of a church whose polity was somewhat ambiguous and was about to be nudged in a direction that many feared was an undoing of the Reformation itself.

In 1624 Richard Montagu, one of the small but growing party of English Arminians, succeeded in getting his highly controversial book, *A New Gagg for an Old Goose*, published. This followed the rules of all societies in which freedom of speech is restricted: writers praise what is supposed to be praised and vilify what is officially hated—but all readers know that the real message lies in the fine print, and the precise terms in which praise and vilification are stated. In form, at least, Montagu's book was a dutiful attack upon the Roman Catholic Church (the "Old Goose"), but its argument was so designed as to amount to a redefinition of the Church of England in terms that brought it much closer to Rome. Papists slandered the Church of England, argued the author, by their insistent pretence that it differed from Catholicism in countless ways. In point of fact, he insisted, there were only seven doctrines in contention between Canterbury and Rome. The papists lied when they claimed that the official theology of the English Church was necessarily Calvinistic.

The drift of this line of argument could hardly have been more clear, and Montagu was denounced by Members of Parliament. He defended himself the following year with a follow-up work, *Apello Caesarem*. The fact that he had succeeded in getting either publication through the censors was a clear enough indication, however, that he had already been doing quite a bit of appealing to Caesar—or, at any rate, to Caesar's closest henchmen—in private. In 1626 the new monarch, Charles I, appointed Montagu bishop of Chichester.

The accession of Charles in 1625 assured the ascendancy of the English Arminian faction in the Church of England. This group had little or nothing in common with the Dutch party that carried the banner of

Arminius after his death in 1609—nothing, that is, beyond a simple rejection of Calvinist views of predestination. For the original Arminians, the motivation had been, in a sense, Erasmian and liberal; in England, the enterprise was linked instead with a new High-Churchmanship. This entailed an increased emphasis upon the importance of sacraments as actually conveying the grace they signified and upon the priestly (that is, the intermediary) role of ministers.

Such ideas fitted well with Charles's all-consuming belief in the Divine Right of Kings. Briefly stated, this is the view that God has chosen that kings should rule and that they should rule absolutely. James I had also held to this doctrine, but he had not been so much of a fool as to take principle further than the traditional sympaties of his subjects and the opportunities presented by immediate circumstances would allow. His son, however, was only rarely even a good tactician, let alone a strategist, and his single-minded pursuit of the absolutist ideal was to lead himself, his throne, and his kingdoms into the abyss.

King Charles I's favored churchman was not Montagu so much as William Laud, an efficient, fussy little man, whose overriding concerns mirrored those of Charles himself: order, discipline, and decorum. The parallels with France's *eminence grise* (gray eminence), Cardinal Richelieu, are striking. The new king found himself, at his accession, encumbered with a Calvinistic, Puritan-sympathizing, but ineffectual archbishop in the form of George Abbot, but Laud was clearly the heir apparent to Canterbury from the moment the new reign started.

Charles appointed Laud to preach the sermon at the opening of the first Parliament on 6 February 1626. A wiser counsel might have led Laud to stick to the strictly platitudinous: the harmony of the commonwealth, the obedience of subjects, the love of a Christian king for his people, and the like. But he chose instead to harangue the assembled Members of Parliament, effectively accusing them of harboring presbyterians and even republicans in their midst. He knew, he said, that there were some who disliked the rule of each clergyman in his parish: "A parity they would have, no bishop, no governor, but a parochial [i.e. a parish] consistory, and that should be lay enough too." He went on, in belligerent tones, to insist that Christ himself had ordained the episcopal structure and that it had been universal in the church ever since.

This was a new note. The Elizabethan and Jacobean bishops had defended their office on much the same grounds that they had defended clerical vestments: the form of church government was *adiaphora*, a thing indifferent, about which the prince was to decide, and which the populace was then to obey for conscience' sake. The new English Arminianism, by contrast, rejected such pragmatic arguments and contended for epis-copacy *jure divino*, that is, by divine right. It was a doctrine that fit hand-in-glove with the Divine Right of Kings: both sought structure and hierarchy in an appeal to the timeless will of God.

But Laud was not finished. If a nonepiscopal system ever were in use "it might perhaps govern some petty city, but make it common once, and it can never keep unity in the Church of Christ." He moved swiftly on, but it was clear which "petty city" he had been taking a swipe at: it was Geneva, the city of Calvin and Beza. And his audience knew it. Finally, he concluded, "There is not a man that is for parity, all fellows in the Church, but he is not for monarchy in the State."

It was an astonishing speech. On one level, it used a standard ploy of theological and political debate throughout the ages: the "slippery slope" argument. To be a Calvinist, he implied, was to be a Puritan; to be a Puritan was tantamount to presbyterianism; and presbyterians were really antimonarchists. Every stage of the argument was palpably nonsense, but the regime's insistence that it was so became self-fulfilling during the next two decades.

Puritans may all have been Calvinists, but not all Calvinists were Puritans. The English Church itself, from 1559 onward, was moderately but firmly Reformed in theology; that was what the English Arminians wished to change. But to do so they needed, in order to excuse themselves from charges of innovation, to argue that the church had never, in fact, been really Reformed at all. Similarly, only the hard-core of the Puritan movement had ever espoused presbyterian sympathies—and they had been in eclipse since the Spanish Armada. Finally, the suggestion that there was any significant body of republican opinion—among presby-terians or anywhere else—in 1625 was completely preposterous. Even at the start of the Civil War itself, in 1642, virtually all parliamentarians wished, not to replace the king, but to force him to negotiate with his opponents; the parliamentarian armies went into battle crying, "For King and Parliament!"

Yet by seeking to overturn the Reformed nature of the Elizabethan and Jacobean church, Charles and the Arminian party terrified the moderate, overwhelming majority of English Protestant opinion during the 1630s and early 1640s into the arms of a revivified Puritan movement. Charles filled the episcopal bench with the tiny minority of English clergy who were Arminian in sympathy. (A joke of the 1630s ran, "What does the Arminian party hold?" The answer: "All the best bishoprics in England!") As a result, a strong body of opinion reemerged determined to remove, not simply *those* bishops, but *all* bishops.

When Charles lost the consequent war (1642–1646), he still refused to negotiate in good faith with his enemies, because his conscience told him never to surrender his Divine Right. Instead he succeeded in playing them off against one another and starting a brief second war in 1648. Consequently, a radical party determined that their own heads would never be safe on their shoulders until Charles (who had always been a short man in any case) underwent the removal of his own. In January 1649, the necessary surgery was arranged. For eleven years, England became a republic. The self-fulfilment of Laud's ridiculous speech was complete.

It need not have been so. Charles and the English Arminian party, however, chose to antagonize moderate and, by then, traditional Protestant opinion at every turn. During the 1630s, communion tables in parish churches were railed off from the congregation and, as before the Reformation, called "altars." The strong implication was that communion was a sacrifice, that only priests could come to the table, and that grace, encapsulated in bread, was to be doled out by them over the communion rails to those for whom they acted as intermediaries. Calvinistic doctrine and its ramifications were forbidden to be preached because of their contentiousness; in theory, the same restriction was placed upon Arminianism though, in practice, silence was applied only to the former. After Laud finally became archbishop of Canterbury in 1633, Puritans of all kinds found themselves disciplined, harassed, and prosecuted as never before. Some turned to Separatism; others turned to New England and emigration.

Charles's marriage to the French (and therefore Catholic) Princess Henrietta Maria had necessarily entailed the permission of a Catholic chapel at court, and therefore a tolerable exemption from the laws against popery. The chapel, however, was open to the public, and this fact, coupled with the rise of a fashionable Catholic proselytizing faction at court, caused widespread scandal. The laws against Catholicism fell into some disuse across the country, causing many to fear that Charles planned eventually to adhere to the Counter-Reformation. These fears can only have been heightened by the opening of diplomatic relations with the Vatican in 1636, the overtures made to the old enemy, Spain (and still, at least in the popular imagination, the most feared Catholic power), the continuing failure to participate in the Thirty Years' War—and so on.

The nightmare scenario that every Englishman and Englishwoman had come to fear from the pages of Foxe's *Book of Martyrs* appeared to be coming true before their eyes. What was Roman Catholicism all about if not tyrannical government, foreign influence, and religious persecution?

And what was Charles doing if not all three of these things? As for tyranny, he failed to call a single Parliament for the eleven years from 1629
to 1640 (a choice he had every right to make, but which was nevertheless
unprecedented), he attempted to raise money from his subjects by means
that were only dubiously legal, and he interfered with judges and courts
to enforce his will. As for foreign influence, Charles was more than usually devoted to his French, Catholic wife, who appeared to have a greater
say over policy than did the Privy Council, the normal government of the
land, which Charles chose to sideline. And as for religious persecution,
the imprisonment of Puritans and expulsion of clergy for doing no more
than preach traditional Protestant doctrine was every day in evidence. No
wonder that ordinary, moderate English gentlemen had the gut-wrenching
feeling that England as they knew it and liked it was about to be taken
away from them and replaced with a new, absolutist, popish model.

The ungluing was not long in coming. Charles attempted to impose
centralizing policies upon Scotland similar to those he was enacting in
England, and this included a push toward High-Churchmanship. His
father had known just how far to go too far with his unruly Scottish
subjects and had persuaded them to modify their preferred thorough-
going Presbyterianism to the point of accepting officials bearing the title
of bishops, though with very limited powers. Other changes were also
made, such as kneeling to receive communion and celebrating Christmas
and Easter, Ascension and Pentecost—but they were ill-enforced, and
James, a wise man, had chosen to leave many stones unturned. All of
these delicate operations had been managed by gently playing off the
Scottish nobles against the Presbyterian leaders. James's son, however,
was a man of principle and wished to go much further than his father
had done. Furthermore, he believed that he could do so by mere fiat;
after all, he was the king.

King he may have been, but he was a foreigner to most Scots. James
had chosen, after 1603, to rule Scotland from London (rather than
England from Edinburgh), but he could get away with this; he had more
than thirty years' accumulated understanding and good will from living
and ruling in Scotland to fall back upon. Charles had nothing but his
exalted views of kingship and a seat in distant London. Even his early
measures as king suggested a willingness to reclaim former church lands,
which had been alienated at the Reformation, from their new, secular
owners. If Charles had wished to unite the lords and the Presbyterian
leaders against himself, nothing could better have suited such a purpose.
He did not deign to travel north to be crowned king of Scotland until
1633, fully eight years after his accession. When he did so, he caused a

rumpus with his fussy, High Church coronation ceremony. His attempt in 1637 to impose an English-style prayer book on the Scottish church proved the last straw, provoking riots in Edinburgh. The Scottish nobles rose in revolt.

The rebels took the title of Covenant (a favorite term of Reformed theology and devotion) as a description of the oath they made, before God and with one another, to maintain Presbyterianism by force of arms. They easily trounced the feeble English army sent to oppose them.

If Charles wished to suppress the Covenanters, he would need a proper army, not the bands of county militia who could be made to serve only for a few days each year outside of their home shires. But proper armies are expensive things, and Charles had no means available to finance one—even by the strong-arm tactics he had used during the 1630s.

No means, that is, except one. Charles would have to call a Parliament. But, quite apart from his bad experience of these during the late 1620s, to request money from this body implied a parliamentary right of refusal, compromise, and horse-trading—all things which entailed an impediment of his Divine Right as monarch to rule unimpeded by mere subjects. To make matters worse, Charles had alienated the political classes by every means possible over more than a decade, and he knew it. To think that they would now come unquestioningly to his aid in imposing policies upon the Scots that had been—and still were—resented in England was, even for a person of Charles's high ideals, bordering on the unrealistic. Still, when the only course of action is an exceptionally difficult one, it nevertheless remains the only thing to be done.

To describe the Short Parliament of April-May 1640 as problem-free would, therefore, be stretching the facts. It was convened to raise taxes for a war nobody wanted in order to enforce policies that even the traditionally anti-Scots prejudices of the English were insufficient to incline their gentry and burghers to approve. Indeed, Charles had succeeded in achieving what no monarch had done before: uniting popular opinion north and south of the border. The demand for taxes was met with a long shopping list of grievances and requests from the assembled Members of Parliament. Charles demurred. It became apparent that no money would be voted unless the king would stoop to meet at least some of his subjects' requests. And then the Parliament was dismissed. The whole session had lasted a mere three weeks.

Heartened by this spectacle (for it is an ill wind that blows nobody any good), the Covenanters proceeded to march south into England during the summer and occupied Newcastle—that is to say, London's entire coal supply. The Scots then had the temerity to demand that the king pay £400 per day, not for his own, at that stage somewhat rarefied and hypothetical, army—but to defray the expenses of theirs.

Charles spent the summer confirming, by trying every other expedient with increasing desperation, that a parliament was indeed his only recourse. In the autumn he gave in and called another. And, this time, he knew that he would have to accede to at least some of its demands.

The convening of the Long Parliament (it was to meet, with intermissions and in various incarnations, for well over a decade) in November 1640 was the occasion for the suppressed fury of the political classes to be unleashed. Religious affairs were not their only target, but they epitomized the tensions that had built up during the course of the reign. The regime was so palpably in deep trouble that it immediately lost its ability, and sometimes the will, to enforce its rule. Puritan ministers celebrated communion in their parish churches any way they pleased, and they remained unmolested for it. Even various sectarians, such as Separatists and Baptists, emerged from their hitherto troglodyte existences and escaped, for the most part and unless local mobs chose to attack them, unscathed. The country had blundered into a de facto—though definitely not a de jure—toleration.

The Root and Branch Petition was drummed up by Puritan agitators, urging Members of Parliament to reform the Church of England along presbyterian lines, destroying episcopacy "root and branch." But the resultant debates in the House of Commons reached an impasse, for the members were more united in their opposition to the Laudian regime than about what should replace it. Already parliamentarians were beginning to divide between moderates and radicals. The former would later join the royalists in the Civil War, dreading anarchy and social revolution more than they feared what they fondly believed to be a chastened monarch.

Then, in the autumn of 1641, Ireland rose in revolt and the political crisis in England drifted ominously toward violence. English rule in Ireland already had a long record of brutality and tragedy to which the course of the Reformation had added to all parties an element of bitterness and desperation. Ireland was not a united society; it was divided into native clans, which the admixture of English and Scottish settlers over generations had further mutated into a kaleidoscope of potential loyalties and rivalries. The general pattern, however, entailed the dispossession of Catholic natives at the hands of Protestant settlers. The furious revolt of 1641 produced the worst massacre of civilians in the history of the British Isles. The figures have been much disputed but are now generally agreed to have been on the order of 7,000–8,000 settlers—men, women, and children. As traumatized survivors were washed up on the western shores of Wales and England, however, the terror their accounts unleashed spread across the country like an electric shock. The figure of 100,000 dead was widely believed, both at the time and for generations afterward—a figure that later demographic science has discredited.

If enough people believe a thing to be true, however, then for all practical political purposes, it is true. The papist Irish were coming across the water to massacre the English in their beds. Anti-Catholic hysteria, never far below the surface in seventeenth-century England, reached fever pitch.

Two points need to be made about this phenomenon, not so much in mitigation as in simple explanation. In the first place, the population distribution between the two largest of the British Isles was not nearly as uneven in the 1640s as it is today. Now, the populace of England, Scotland, and Wales is at least a dozen times that of Ireland. But in the seventeenth century the population was spread more evenly, so that the relevant ratio would have been perhaps just two or three to one. It did not seem so preposterous that an Irish rebellion might transform itself into an invasion of the larger island.

In the second place, one needs to remember the atrocious dynamic that had been set up in Anglo-Irish relations over the previous century. English attitudes toward the Irish whom they were colonizing can be likened to those of contemporary Israelis toward Palestinians, or of apartheid-era South African whites to blacks. In each case, the compound was of three elements: a real sense of cultural superiority and contempt for the hapless objects of rule; a suppressed sense of guilt (for the loud justifications of misrule were in precise proportion to the uneasy awareness that no one has any business to treat other human beings in such fashion); and the very real terror that one day, perhaps quite soon, the scales might be reversed and the despised party would wreak a fearful revenge. This particular combination of emotions is perhaps the most poisonous known to humanity, for the person who feels them will unhesitatingly treat the other party as subhuman gooks who can be wasted at will. This lethal cocktail was quite apart from the previously mentioned anti-Catholic hysteria of English society—except that it was not apart at all, for it was part and parcel of the same thing, each element intensifying the other. This needs to be borne in mind as a prime explanatory factor in some of the gruesome incidents that lay ahead.

The Irish rebellion raised a pressing, unavoidable, and agonizing question: Could the king be trusted with an army? If Puritan opinion was complacent about the need to pay for raising a military force against the Scots (who were, after all, pressing Charles to desist from enforcing High-Churchmanship on his subjects), no one could be in any doubt but that an army was needed—without a moment to lose—to suppress the scarcely human papist hordes in Ireland. But would the king, once in possession of the requisite force, not use them to suppress Scottish Covenanters and even (who could know?) overawe his English Parliament also? Might he not use armed force to gain what the constitution and the law of the land had denied him, namely an absolute rule? Certainly the experience of the 1630s did not dispose all parliamentarians to give their monarch the benefit of the doubt.

The most radical of the parliamentary leaders knew full well that their own lives were at stake in the answers to such questions, for the game had gone too far since the Long Parliament had convened, and the stakes were now too high to consider moving back from the brink. During the summer of 1642, England drifted toward civil war.

Fighting began in August. The first battles were small, scrappy affairs, as each side struggled to gain control of particular counties or of local arsenals. No pattern emerged until the end of the year and, as the fighting continued into the next, it became apparent that Parliament had control (give or take a few outposts of royal resistance) in the commercialized and Puritanized south and east of the country; the north and west, including Wales, formed a mirror-image of this scenario, with the royalists preponderant. The early military advantage lay with the king—an advantage augmented by the extreme unwillingness of the first parliamentarian generals (who were mostly peers of the realm) to accept the reality of what they were doing, namely fighting against their sovereign. Mostly they fought battles, not to win them, but to prevent the king from doing so. Clearly, this was an outlook that would have to change. The longer-term strategic and economic advantages, however, lay with Parliament.

To counteract the early inferiority in men and weapons, the parliamentarian leaders felt compelled to put out feelers to the Scots. The terms of the latter were to introduce strict, Scottish-style presbyterianism in England as the quid pro quo for help on the battlefield. And at this point the charming reticence of the English political leaders on the specifics of what kind of church they wanted (as opposed to the mere vilification of what they rejected) became a complete liability.

For much though religion was implicated in the Civil War, it had not begun over specifically religious causes. At its heart lay the resentment of the English gentry at the king's centralizing policies—and these had included the clericalism of the Laudian church (that is, the high place it gave to clergymen as intermediaries between God and the congregation) and especially to bishops, and the aggressive, centralizing way in which the changes had been pushed through, overruling the cozy, local influences that many gentry had long exercised over their parishes. In the dark years of the 1630s, presbyterianism had been a bride who had seemed beautiful from afar to the Protestant gentry; now that they found themselves being bundled up the aisle, however, she seemed, on closer inspection, to bear unnerving similarities to the dragon of English Arminianism. For Scottish-style presbyterianism would give every clergyman disciplinary powers over each member of his parish congregation—including the squire. And, astonishing though it may seem, the English gentry had no burning desire to be disciplined. Indeed, such an arrangement would amount to having "a pope in every parish," as one of them complained, struggling to import some hot-Prottery into his rationale for rejecting the ecclesiology of Geneva.

Parliament did what all political bodies do in such dilemmas: it hedged and played for time. During the summer of 1643 it was agreed with the Scots that the Church of England would be reformed to bring it into closer alignment with the Scottish form of Presbyterianism, "according to the Word of God." And who could disagree with that last phrase? And who could nail down what it might mean? Two exegetes, three opinions. So it had been for sixteen centuries since the resurrection. If the debates could be strung out a little longer, while the Scottish armies helped in the necessary business of prosecuting the war, consciences might be satisfied all round without the landholders of England losing one clerical master only to find another.

The Westminster Assembly was set up as a talking shop to spin out discussions while the new alliance had time to take military effect. The Westminster Confession of Faith, one of the main results of the assembly's deliberations, has remained a reference point for English-speaking Reformed Christians, and especially for Presbyterians, ever since. The assembly's ecclesiastical contribution, however, was less glorious, for it was effectively powerless, depending entirely upon the politicians for permission even to discuss anything. In August 1646 the Church of England was formally reorganized along the lines of a lame version of Presbyterianism (lame versions being the English speciality in religious matters), but it remained a dead letter in most areas and, in practice, each parish did that which was right in its own eyes.

During 1643 and 1644 the parliamentarians were discovering by experience (that is, by their mistakes) how to wage war successfully. By 1645 they had a national, standing army in place and a taxation system that went partway to financing it (that is, a lot further than the equivalent arrangements on the royalist side). The Battle of Marston Moor in the summer of 1644 inflicted serious damage on the king's forces and lost him control of most of the north. The Battle of Naseby the following year should have been the coup de grace, but the struggle continued hopelessly into 1646, when fighting petered out.

The king had lost. But who, exactly, had won? Parliament's army had become, by the end of the war, a political player in its own right—and it was a lot more radical than its theoretical masters in Westminster. A new party had emerged on the parliamentarian side, the Independents— a loose grouping whose ecclesiastical position was that each parish should be self-governing within a national framework. Some among them espoused a limited religious toleration for certain other kinds of Protestants.

Then there were the sectarians, who were particularly numerous in the army, in London, and among small traders. None of these was for letting the king return on anything but the harshest of terms, for if he had been disinclined during the 1630s to tolerate Puritans within the Church of England, then, if political arrangements depended in the least degree upon royal goodwill, the chances of his tolerating Separatists and Baptists outside of it were absolutely zero.

And what of the king himself? He was a prisoner, at first, of the Scots; but these, sensing a money-making opportunity, sold him (at a very fair price) to the parliamentarian politicians. This did not mean, however, that Charles had entirely run out of cards to play. His religious conscience told him that his captors, by virtue of being enemies of their sovereign, were therefore also God's enemies. Accordingly, it was no sin to deceive them or to negotiate in bad faith. He occupied his time in playing them off against each other in the hope of starting a new civil war that might return him to (absolute) power. In the spring of 1648 he succeeded: the Scots, satisfied that Presbyterianism in their country, at least, was now assured, found themselves more worried about the radicals in England than about any reversion to the 1630s, and they declared themselves for the king at the same moment as a new English royalist army was scraped together.

The Second Civil War was brutal and short. By October, it was all over. The radicals in Parliament and army judged that Charles was attempting to overturn the manifest providence of God expressed in the result of the First Civil War. (The thought that, using identical logic, the Laudian regime of the 1630s might have been providential and the parliamentarians therefore guilty of attempting to overturn *it*, seems to have occurred to none of them—for God was obviously a Calvinist and, indeed, a Puritan.) Charles was the "man of blood" spoken of in the Scriptures (2 Sam. 16:8), and it was therefore a religious duty to kill him.

In December the army purged Parliament of all but the most radical members ("the Rump," as one conservative sniffed—a name which has stuck ever since), and these agreed to summon a special court to try the king for treason. Various constitutional handstands and logical acrobatics had to be performed to make this process seem plausibly legitimate, and the vast majority of the populace at the time (and of historians since) have remained unimpressed by them. Nevertheless, they were duly executed, and in January 1649, so was Charles. He went to the block, maintaining to the end that he was "the martyr of"—not to—"the people." The British realms became a republic.

The English Republic 1649–1660

To describe the royal execution and the subsequent rule by the Rump Parliament as popular would be an exaggeration. Even the crowd who came to watch the royal abbreviation groaned as the blade fell. Domestic and foreign opinion alike received the news with unfeigned horror. As Third World states today continue to find, getting rid of the kings and empires is the easy part; finding alternative arrangements that all will accept as legitimate is well-nigh impossible. And, in the absence of a generally accepted legitimacy, the only instrument for fending off chaos is naked force.

Most dictators, however, find nakedness embarrassing and prefer to clothe their force in something or other, however skimpy and prone to fall to ribbons it may be. For the military men and parliamentary radicals that something was, until 1653, the Rump Parliament. From 1653 to 1658 it was the Protectorate, a novel and precarious arrangement in which Oliver Cromwell, as a leading republican and regicide, assumed monarchical powers in all but name. As both an erstwhile Member of Parliament and senior military leader, he alone could hold together the fragile forces wielding power.

Many of the members of the Rump Parliament were horrified at the sectarianism and de facto religious toleration that had grown up during the chaos of the war years, and they were determined to curb it. They knew that the great gentry of England, whom they still claimed to represent, were even more conservative in this regard. But the Rump Parliament's power was entirely beholden to an army that was more than sympathetic to sectarians of every kind, and in no small part composed of them. The army commanders, however, were unwilling to be seen to rule in their own name, for the cooperation of society's natural leaders, the gentry (and so of their mouthpiece, Parliament), was absolutely necessary unless each and every action of central government were to be exacted in every village by main force alone. The result was an irresoluble struggle between the conservative defenders of such shreds of legitimacy as had survived the regicide and the radical lovers of a freedom that could only be delivered at the barrel of a gun.

Like many a modern dictator (or, for that matter, the Anglo-American military protectorates of the early twenty-first century), Cromwell found himself hopelessly torn between a desire to grant religious freedom and the need to protect that liberty from the majority whose consciences it offended. In the name of freedom, therefore, he maintained a dictatorship. He called Parliaments but constantly felt the need to gerrymander them in order to exclude those who had fought for the king or were otherwise a threat to the Republic. Even then, the purged assemblies were too conservative for him, and they wished to bring back persecution in one form or another.

And what of the most religiously conservative (and therefore hungriest to persecute)—was he to tolerate those also? Officially, prayer-book episcopalianism of the prewar variety was banned, along with Catholicism. In practice, as long as one kept one's head down and out of major population centers, all manner of things was possible. The dilemma remains today: Should democracies tolerate communists and fascists (that is, those determined to destroy democracy)? Should the armed enforcers of "freedom" in the Western protectorates tolerate the mullahs who call daily for their blood? Such questions are delicate admixtures of principle and calculation, of common prudence and avoidance of provocation. All answers stand charged either with weakness or with oppression. And so also for Cromwell and his major-generals.

By the time of his death in September 1658, there had been four different constitutional arrangements, all of them fig leaves covering the reality of military dictatorship. The first of these, the Rump Parliament, had faced, among other emergencies, a renewed civil war in 1650–1651 when Charles II had returned from exile to claim his father's throne and found many Scots and some Englishmen ready to fight for him. The outcome was predictable, and its aftermath left an English army occupying Scotland.

There was also the unfinished business of Ireland to settle. Charles I had sought to recruit troops there in the 1640s, and such as had fallen into parliamentarian hands had been dealt with mercilessly. After the Battle of Naseby in 1645, the language of Welsh camp followers was mistaken for Irish by the pursuing parliamentarian soldiers (whose modern descendants are, after all, mostly unable to distinguish between French and Zulu), and they were butchered. Now that the fighting was over on the mainland, the Irish natives could be sure that the sectarian-backed Republic in London was unlikely to deal with Irish Catholic interests in anything other than the harshest manner.

And so it proved. Cromwell's massacres of prisoners and civilians at Drogheda and Wexford have passed, justly enough, into Irish folklore. He hoped, by a show of ruthlessness, to shorten the Irish rebellion. If anything, the tactic proved counterproductive and stiffened resistance. But the English New Model Army was by this stage the most formidable armed force in Europe, and the final military outcome was never seriously in doubt.

The London government spent much of the next decade sowing the seeds of the crises that have bedevilled Ireland ever since. Unable to pay the wages of the soldiery, the Rump Parliament and its successors rewarded them instead with land in Ireland, thereby planting new waves of Protestant English and Scottish settlers whose property consisted in confiscations from the native Catholics and whose prosperity, political privileges, and even survival depended upon the perpetuation of caste-like segregation. Truly, we have much to thank the English republicans for.

Back in England, the rising numbers of sectarians inadvertently fueled the forces of conservative reaction among the gentry. Cromwell was sometimes embarrassed by sectarian excesses (for example the extreme provocativeness of the Quakers), but he determined to protect them if he could. Indeed, the scope of toleration was widened in 1656 to include the Jews, who were formally readmitted to the country whence they had been expelled in 1290.

Cromwell's death in 1658, however, made the collapse of the ad-hocracy that was the English Republic simply a question of time. He had been the only person possessed of the charisma, personal connections, and respect to keep any kind of stability at all—and even he had more detractors than admirers, more enemies than friends. His son was briefly installed to replace him, but he spent 1659 proving what he already knew and everyone else suspected: that he was utterly unable to shuffle spoons as fast as his father. General Monck, commander of the English army in Scotland, moved south, entered the capital, and reinstated the

Rump Parliament, whose survivors were dragged out of retirement to do what the general had calculated that they would do all along: they recalled Charles II from exile upon his promises to respect "tender consciences" in matters of religion. In the spring of 1660 the king returned to general rejoicing, and the Republic was at an end. Legitimacy and episcopalianism were restored.

7

FRACTIONS OF FRACTIONS

THE PROGRESS OF SECTARIANISM

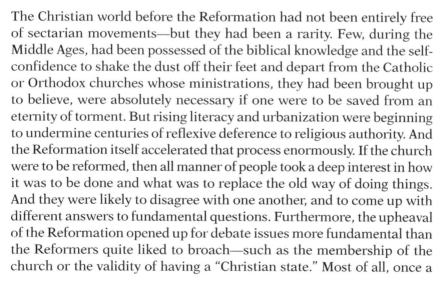

The Christian world before the Reformation had not been entirely free of sectarian movements—but they had been a rarity. Few, during the Middle Ages, had been possessed of the biblical knowledge and the self-confidence to shake the dust off their feet and depart from the Catholic or Orthodox churches whose ministrations, they had been brought up to believe, were absolutely necessary if one were to be saved from an eternity of torment. But rising literacy and urbanization were beginning to undermine centuries of reflexive deference to religious authority. And the Reformation itself accelerated that process enormously. If the church were to be reformed, then all manner of people took a deep interest in how it was to be done and what was to replace the old way of doing things. And they were likely to disagree with one another, and to come up with different answers to fundamental questions. Furthermore, the upheaval of the Reformation opened up for debate issues more fundamental than the Reformers quite liked to broach—such as the membership of the church or the validity of having a "Christian state." Most of all, once a plurality of churches had come about, the arguments against starting a new one seemed not merely less persuasive, but positively feeble. In consequence, our period saw an unprecedented constellation of new Christian sectarian movements, separating from the larger bodies and also from one another.

It is worth stressing that the terms *sect* and *sectarian* should not be construed in even the slightest pejorative sense; we use them here, not to denote any theological deviance (though, as we shall see presently, a minority of them certainly were heretical), but simply as a sociological description. The sectarians seldom sought, and never received, the support of the state. And this is no criticism at all, on either religious or secular grounds. Religiously, the early church was a sectarian movement in precisely this sense; and, from a secular point of view, sectarianism has been the making of the modern world.

Anabaptism in the Late Sixteenth and Seventeenth Centuries

Anabaptism, as we have already noticed, was of ill repute in late sixteenth- and seventeenth-century Europe. The stain of Münster clung to it, indeed, until well into the nineteenth century in Germany and elsewhere, seeming to bear out the accusation that religious radicalism of any kind would lead to anarchy, polygamy, communism, bloodbaths, and who knew what other horrors.

However, even as that appalling chapter had been playing itself out during the 1530s, cooler, wiser heads among the radicals themselves had been working feverishly to avert the catastrophe they so clearly foresaw and to establish a radical Anabaptist movement on a more solid, biblicist, and evangelical footing. Though they failed in their first endeavor, they succeeded in their second, painfully gathering up the fragments of shattered Anabaptism and constructing a new, more stable movement.

The reconstruction was a task made even less easy by the constant shadow of persecution. Even then a variety of factions, some crazed and others more mundanely heretical, continued to dog the progress of the biblicist groups. Evangelical leaders came and went during the late 1530s through to the 1560s, but the most successful of them all was Menno Simons. The conversion to Anabaptism of this Dutch priest from the village of Witmarsum had been as inauspiciously timed as it was possible to be, coming as it did while the Münster fiasco was unfolding little more than a hundred miles away, yet this former Catholic priest emerged as a devoted, clearheaded, unremittingly patient pastor and theologian. He spent a quarter century as a hunted fugitive, yet, by the time of his death in 1561, he was nevertheless the preeminent leader of a cohesive, firmly grounded Dutch and North German Anabaptist movement.

The achievement had come at a price. Disputes over both doctrine and practice, combined with the pressure of relentless persecution, had turned the Mennonites into a somewhat legalistic and inward-looking group. The early, eager evangelistic thrust had been dented, and it would continue to diminish during the years ahead as part of the price of rigid, stable group formation. There had been disputes during the 1550s over "the ban" (the process whereby erring members might be expelled from the community, and what measures should be taken against them). The resultant practice had led to the expulsion of some members for refusing to shun their own "banned" spouses. It also led to the elucidation of domestic arrangements that might be thought laughable, were they not so serious, and ungodly, were their protagonists not so certain of their godliness.

After the three synods of Strasbourg in the mid-1550s, the Dutch and North German Anabaptists separated from their less severe brethren from Switzerland and South Germany, among whom the humane councils of Pilgram Marpek (who had died the previous year) had prevailed. But the Anabaptists of the Middle Rhine could not stomach the North Germans' rigorism either. To compound the problem, a number of congregations in the Waterland district of Holland and West Frisia also adhered to a more moderate line on shunnings and exclusions, and they ended up breaking away from Menno Simons over the issue. Even the Flemish congregations declared themselves in sympathy with the broader view. A further round of splits over the same issue disfigured the late 1560s.

As if this were not enough, the Mennonites were saddled with Menno Simons's deviant Christology—a feature he had inherited from Melchior Hofmann, the founding father of all streams of Dutch Anabaptism, both evangelical and heterodox. This Melchiorite Christology was a species of Monophysitism (a term we include here merely to torment those who happen to be reading this aloud): This is the idea that Christ was possessed of only one (hence *mono*) nature (*phusis*), which was divine. He was, in fact, simply God in a human body. Few of the people and groups accused of teaching this have really done so; the concept is valuable mostly as an accusation to throw at teachings that do no more than incline in this general direction. And this was true of Melchiorite Christology also; what Menno and his circle had actually taught was that Christ had not taken his humanity from Mary but had brought it with him from heaven.

It was not very orthodox, of course, though the biblical arguments made in support of it were disconcertingly formidable. Menno had seen this "heavenly flesh" doctrine as the mandate for a spotless "bride of Christ" represented by the pure congregation of the faithful on earth—and therefore justifying his harsh views on employing the ban.

None of these considerations should be allowed to detract from the magnitude of Menno's achievement in reconstituting evangelical Anabaptism during the decades after Münster, in galvanizing the loyalty of doubting, confused, and frightened believers, in explicating a clear, biblical program and a credible theology. Above all, he was an extraordinary pastor and leader. In any case, there is strong evidence that he was badgered into his harsh stance on the ban by Leonard Bouwens, another leader. Certainly the resultant splits had distressed him greatly.

But during the decades after Menno's death, his followers succeeded in allowing the dubious theological heirloom represented by Hofmann's Christology to lapse and to be replaced by orthodoxy. The second of the Strasbourg synods had already prepared the ground for this shift by calling for all discussions of the incarnation to confine themselves to strictly biblical phraseology (for "heavenly flesh" teachings had little currency among Anabaptists from Switzerland and the south, where the name of Melchior Hofmann counted for little). The Waterlanders' Confession of Faith of 1577 also quietly dropped the doctrine of the heavenly flesh of Christ. One of their leaders, Hans de Ries, expressed the view the following year that Melchiorite Christology was a tolerable opinion—but he did not adhere to it himself. This became formal Waterlander policy in 1579.

Waterlander liberalism on the ban was extended further in 1581, when a synod affirmed that members might marry those who had never been part of the fellowship in the first place. They had for long recognized as Christians all who had experienced regeneration through faith in Christ—a recognition that earned them the dismissive judgment from Bouwens (who was an expert practitioner of judgmentalism) that they were a *drekwagen*, a "garbage wagon." Certainly the Waterlanders' broadminded approach counts as tantamount to frivolousness in the context of the mutual anathematizing and lack of any sense of proportion that so disfigured the age—and perhaps especially, alas, in its sectarian aspect.

Yet the Waterlanders were the key to the Anabaptist future. And their openhanded dealings were truer to the original Anabaptist insights than was the intransigence of Bouwens. The original insistence, it will be remembered, had not been that only Anabaptists were saved but the very different proposition that only the saved might become Anabaptists.

By the late 1570s their churches in the Netherlands, at least, could afford the luxury of a little openhandedness. In 1577 they were granted religious and civil liberty by William the Silent, who had become the effective leader of the Dutch revolt. But he did so in the teeth of Reformed opposition. And his newfound generosity of spirit was also a reversal of his own exhortations, back in 1566, to Margaret of Parma, the regent of Spanish King Philip II, to be particularly severe in repressing the Mennonites.

But that had been then. William had, in the interim, undergone several changes in his religious convictions—changes not unrelated to his political aspirations and the fast-shifting realities during the opening decade of the Dutch revolt. The new state that had emerged needed the loyalty of all manner of religious affiliates if it was to stave off defeat at the hands of the powerful Spanish army. And this dictum applied even to those who, like the pacifist Anabaptists, refused to lend a hand in the actual process of fighting. To generate wealth and to pay taxes was help enough.

The Anabaptists' troubles were not quite at an end, even in the Netherlands. Various zealous spirits in the Dutch Reformed Church continued to lobby for an end to toleration. Sometimes they were successful at the local level, as when Mennonite worship was prohibited in Frisia for a few years after 1596, when the local Calvinist clergy believed themselves to have worsted the Anabaptist leaders in debate at Leeuwarden.

Yet of all the radical writings, it was those of David Joris and, far more, of Sebastian Franck that continued to have the widest circulation in the Netherlands. Although these writings had the effect of dragging some biblicist Mennonites toward spiritualism, they had the same effect upon non-Anabaptists also, further inclining the already tolerant Dutch toward a softening of dogmatic boundaries and strengthening the hands of moderates in the Dutch Reformed Church who might favor religious toleration.

Those hands were already being strengthened, nearly two centuries before Adam Smith gave it a name, by the invisible hand of economic benefit. Religious toleration was simply too good for the Dutch economy, once its effects had become clear, to be dispensed with. When in 1601 the Calvinists Geldorp and Bogerman translated a work by Beza that urged the persecution of heretics, they were reduced to fending off the obvious objection by asking rhetorically, "Must Satan now, instead of God, promote our commerce?"

Some historians have argued, however, that in the long term at least, the Reformed faith was itself geared toward religious toleration. They have noted in particular that it was in lands where the Reformed church predominated (Switzerland and the Netherlands) that Anabaptist churches survived and were, eventually, tolerated. In Lutheran and Catholic states in Germany and Austria, by contrast, Anabaptism was eradicated. Other explanations of this phenomenon are possible than a supposed grudging, despite-it-all niceness of Calvinism. For the same strength of the mercantile interests that promoted Reformed expressions of Protestantism in the first place also, later on, promoted religious toleration.

But it is true that in central Europe Anabaptists continued to face persecution. One of the few exceptions, for a while and in limited areas, was the estates of some of the Moravian and Slovak lords who, for economic reasons, continued to harbor a variety of radicals, but most especially the communitarian Hutterites. This group had emerged, after much bickering and division, as a communitarian, biblicist evangelical movement. The first characteristic was, and has remained, the most eye-catching. The life of each community was centered upon a *Bruderhof*, where members lived and worked. This communal life was not always managed with easy amity and, partly for this reason and partly as a defense mechanism against the lures of rival radical groups, the Hutterites had become quite authoritarian in practice.

The Hutterites' principal bishop from 1565, Peter Walpot, was an able, intelligent, and dedicated leader. He had received the baton of leadership from a predecessor, Leonhard Lanzenstiel, who had led the movement into a period of stability and prosperity. Walpot was to take it further and, by the time of his death in 1578, there were perhaps 30,000 adult members in Moravia and Slovakia.

Every member and every child was taught to practice a trade. Literacy in the *Bruderhof* was virtually 100 percent as a result of the solid, basic schooling provided for all. It was an education that emphasized the fear of God, Bible reading, and personal hygiene. The communities were highly valued by the authorities for the extremely fine quality of their craftsmanship. It was a characteristic that brought them modest wealth—which in turn earned them the envy of their non-Anabaptist neighbors, and occasionally made them too tempting a target for expropriation taxes, theft, and communal violence. The *Hutterite Chronicle* lovingly and plaintively records the communities' story as a continual catalog of wrongs suffered at the hands of outsiders, many of whom persisted in believing the Hutterites to be wealthy, despite repeated denials. Prosperity, pacifism, and the social opprobrium toward them by outsiders also made this group of Anabaptists irresistible prey for plunder and attack during the early phases of the Thirty Years' War after 1618, a period during which grotesque and appalling suffering was inflicted upon many of the *Bruderhof* inhabitants of all ages and both sexes.

The *Hutterite Chronicle* itself was initiated at the behest of Peter Walpot, under whose encouragement an elder, Caspar Braitmichel, began the work by utilizing various Anabaptist documents available at Neumühl (Czech: Nové Mlýny) and Austerlitz (Slavkov) and following the story from the creation of the world, through a whistlestop tour of various righteous remnants discernible both in the Scriptures and during the ancient and medieval Christian eras, finally taking the story down to 1542. Braitmichel's ability to bring the work up to date was precluded by his death in 1573, but various successors continued the account down to 1665.

The *Hutterite Chronicle* was not the only major work of Anabaptist historiography from this period to set Anabaptist sufferings in a cosmic context. Thieleman J. van Braght's enormous *Martyrs Mirror* of 1659 rivals in scope and size the martyrology of John Foxe—only from an Anabaptist, rather than a state-church Protestant, point of view. Specifically, he focused upon the trials of Dutch radicals. In doing so, he drew upon court records, surviving correspondence, and earlier Anabaptist martyrologies.

According to van Braght, "The whole volume of Holy Scriptures seems to be nothing else than a book of martyrs." When one remembers Jesus's reference to the Old Testament history as running "from the blood of righteous Abel to the blood of Zechariah" (Matt. 23:35), it is clear that he had a point. But his central contention was that this biblical teleology was perpetuated through the history of the church, the lambs among wolves. "The bloody army of the spiritual champions, who fought unto blood and death for the Lord, commenced with the beginning of the world, as though God's saints were born to suffer and fight; and as though God had designed, that His church should be tried from the beginning and all through, even as gold in the furnace that her purity might become the more manifest."[1]

Van Braght was writing two generations after the end of persecution of Anabaptists in the Netherlands; he was passing on the memory and the martyr ethos to a generation that was beginning to lose it. Though their trials in central and eastern Europe were far from over, Anabaptists in the Netherlands could afford the luxury of feeling at least a little at home in the world.

For some sectarians, however, such at-homeness is perceived, not so much as blessing and respite, but as threat. Where this is the case, leaders prepared to re-create tension and distance are seldom lacking. In that rather perverse sense, Jakob Ammann was perhaps the man of the hour in Switzerland.

The Swiss Brethren had, during the later seventeenth century, reached a position of stability in some of the Swiss cantons and in Alsace and parts of southwestern Germany. Persecution remained a threat, but in practice and with the cooperation of sympathetic outsiders, the *Treuherzigen* or true-hearted, an agrarian life could be eked out in the mountainous fringes.

For Ammann (ca. 1644–1731), an elder in Erlenbach in the canton of Bern, this was all too easy. From 1693 he resurrected the old disputes about *Meidung* or shunning and the lengths to which this should be taken. He also went into battle against the growing opinion among his coreligionists that *Treuherzigen* might be saved. Alas, his protest was not founded upon some evangelical, faith-versus-works antithesis but upon the insistence that there was no salvation outside of the one true church—a contention that bore remarkable similarities to that of the See of Rome.

Ammann also insisted upon a footwashing ceremony as part-and-parcel of communion services and upon uniformity of dress among his followers, including the rejection of new fashions, to set up visible demarcation from "the world." Reist, Ammann's chief opponent, complained, "It is contrary to the Gospel to affix one's conscience to a pattern of the hats, clothes, stockings, shoes, or the hair of the head and to enforce such regulations with the ban." But by that stage Ammann was already pronouncing the ban against any and all Anabaptist leaders who would not follow his lead.

The disputes thereby engendered became both chronic and bitter during the course of the next four years, and they led to a complete separation between the Amish (as Ammann's followers came to be called) and the main body of the Swiss Brethren. Perhaps 40 percent of the movement went with the former, though they may have been a majority among the Alsace congregations.

The trivia that epitomized these distinctions is perhaps best illustrated by the names by which each party—at least in the Palatinate—came to be known. The Amish were the *Häftler* (hook-and-eyes people), while the Swiss Brethren-Mennonites were the *Knöpfler* (buttoners); the separation came down to the matter of how you did up your jacket.

From 1727 to 1780, the Bernese Amish began the process of immigration to Pennsylvania, where they have thrived ever since. Alsatian congregations followed to America during the early nineteenth century. Of those who remained in Europe, none maintained their rigid identity beyond the nineteenth century; most merged with ordinary Mennonite groups.

The Rise of English Sectarianism

English Puritanism was far from intrinsically sectarian. On the contrary, its central purpose was the purification of the national Church of England from the continuing elements of Roman Catholicism in its liturgy and government. The very idea of separation was anathema and smacked of Anabaptism.

Yet, the longer and more bitter the Puritans' hopeless conflict with the establishment became, the more likely it was that two developments would push at least some of their number along the path to separation. In the first place, heated rhetoric about the evils of the existing state of affairs in the English Church would translate itself, in the long run, into seeing that church, not so much as merely unsatisfactory, but as no true church at all. One cannot forever pillory one's spouse for his or her shortcomings without eventually running the danger of wishing for a divorce; the same applies to institutions. In the second place, the Puritans made no headway in seeing their demands met during Elizabeth's reign (or for long after); some began to lose patience. During the decades before the Civil War in England, many more began to despair that they would even be able to hang on to their consolation prize: the possibility of living a Puritan-style life within an imperfect church.

These considerations prompted at least a small minority of Puritans to separate. The memory of the Marian martyrs, especially as recorded by Foxe's *Acts and Monuments*, inadvertently provided an object lesson in how to conduct an illegal, properly Reformed church life while the establishment was apostate. As early as June 1567, ringleaders of a group meeting illegally at the Plumbers' Hall explained themselves to Edmund Grindal, bishop of London, by saying that "we remembered that there was a congregation of us in this city in Queen Mary's days."[2]

The following March an even larger group was discovered at a goldsmith's house in Westminster, including several renegade ministers from the Church of England. They appeared to have quite a sophisticated church organization. They were clearly Separatist, in the sense that they would not allow their members to attend the Church of England, since it was a false church.

It must be stressed (since distinctions that matter little in a postmodern, pluralist society were of extreme importance in this period) that the Separatists were not seeking to create a believers' church; neither did they think one possible. They would certainly have looked upon the idea of religious toleration with horror. They wished to separate from the ungodly, but they wanted the civil authorities to uphold their religion and suppress all others. Their final goal was the enforcement of the right religion—as conceived by themselves—rather than the current, wrong one. In that sense, of course, they were at one with the aims of the original Protestant Reformers.

This is made clear in the petition of an early Separatist group in 1571, which asks Elizabeth to "build and plant his holy signs and true marks" of the church, and to "utterly destroy . . . all monuments of idolatry"— meaning, of course, popery, which they took to include all vestiges of the old religion remaining in the Elizabethan church. Its authors took it as axiomatic that the Old Testament referred directly to England, to the point where they apparently found a reference to the British Isles in the prophets: "O England, if thou return, return unto me, saith the Lord, Jeremiah 4, verse 1." These Separatists desired "that the word of our God may be set to reign and have the highest place, to rule and reform all estates and degrees [of] men."[3] For them, as for the church they criticized, the rightness of the Constantinian alliance of church and state was so obvious as to be taken for granted. And it was all a million miles from Anabaptism and a believers' church.

Even the longest journey, however, starts with a small step. The Separatists themselves were to change—and their spin-offs were to change a lot more—until the end result was the very thing their founders had dreaded more than popery itself: a believers' church, practicing believers' baptism and espousing religious toleration. In the next few pages we shall navigate that long trek and explain something of its strange course.

Brownism

The most important—and by far the most radical—of the early Separatist leaders was Robert Browne (ca. 1550–1633), a Cambridge-educated Puritan who had embraced presbyterian ideals as a student and later went further, concluding that the ministry of those ordained by bishops—the whole English clergy—was therefore no true ministry at all. This, of course, led him out of Puritanism and into Separatism. In 1580 he and his co-worker, Robert Harrison, were arrested for organizing

Separatist assemblies in and around Norwich. Released the following year after the intervention of friends in high places, the two men led such of their followers as would come with them to the Netherlands.

In exile, the Separatist refugees fell out with one another. Browne's most famous tract, *A Treatise of Reformation without Tarrying for Any*, published the following year, was denounced by his friend Harrison as containing "manifold heresies." In this polemical masterpiece, Browne suggested that the godly neither could nor should delay until they had secured the backing of the secular authorities before reforming the church in line with Scripture, for this would be to hand a veto to those who may not be godly at all. In arguing this way, Browne was doing no more than articulating the rationale for what the Separatists had already done: they had created a church in line with their own beliefs, without official permission. Despite this rather obvious fact, most of his fellows were extremely uncomfortable with elevating it to the level of theory. The idea that the working assumption of reformers should be that the magistrates were not in a state of salvation smacked too much of Anabaptism. So too did his idea of religious voluntarism: "The Lord's people is of the willing sort. . . . For it is the conscience and not the power of man that will drive us to seek the Lord's kingdom." No later Separatist leader was to espouse such shocking principles again. Harrison, by contrast, held the more orthodox view that the magistrates had a duty "to strike with the sword everyone which, being of the church, shall openly transgress against the Lord's commandments."[4] Except for Browne, Separatists had no problem with the principle of religious persecution but only with the magisterial sword's current choice of themselves as suitable objects for being struck.

In point of fact, even Browne did not hold consistently to voluntarism, for he clearly believed that magistrates had a duty to uphold true religion and that the church should wield at least some secular power. He spoke of how the saints would "bind the Kings in chains, and the Nobles with Fetters of Iron."[5] Obviously, even Browne's eloquence was unlikely to have been equal to the task of squaring this with his voluntarism. Consistency was not his strong point; rather, it is the general direction and pattern that are significant—and later Separatism's overall orientation was to be emphatically more conservative than that of Browne.

In any case, Browne later defected from his Separatism. Having thoroughly fallen out with his congregation in the Netherlands, he went to Scotland and got himself imprisoned there, briefly, for attacking its Presbyterian Church. Returning from there to London, he recanted, made his peace with the Church of England, and became a schoolmaster at

St. Olave's School in Southwark (though he was suspected of continuing his Separatist activities in the capital), before moving on to become a rural parish minister. We last hear of him as an octogenarian, arrested again in the early 1630s for attacking a constable.

The name "Brownism" was gleefully hung around the neck of all later Separatists by outsiders, as a means of embarrassing them with the slur of both his one-time extremism and his later defection. But Browne's radicalism perpetuated itself in subtler ways through his ideas about church government, which continued to have their effect upon later Separatism and, through it, upon seventeenth-century Congregationalists and Baptists.

In the first place, Browne taught that a church covenant was necessary; members agreed together to "be church." This idea, so comforting and exciting to individuals who had undertaken great personal risks to follow their religious ideals, was subtly undermining of the "Christendom" ideal: easy to imagine on a sectarian basis, it becomes hard to visualize as part of compulsory parish life. The same could be said for his idea that all members shared responsibility for discerning the will of Christ, with the more gifted and mature members responsible for leading and teaching. It is doubtful whether a "Christian country" could be run on such a basis.

Finally, the congregation as a whole was to be responsible for accepting or rejecting those who applied for membership, for enacting the stages of discipline outlined in Matthew 18:15–18 (rebuke, condemnation, and exclusion), and for calling and appointing its own leaders. The ideals of congregational participation and autonomy, biblical as they are, were nevertheless hard to square with the ideals of a Christian country and a compulsory church in which the Separatists still claimed to believe.

True Confession

After Browne, the Separatist cause in England was led, first by Henry Barrow and John Greenwood and then, after their execution in 1593, by Francis Johnson. But the authorities were getting better and better at detecting them. Barrow and Greenwood spent the last three years of their lives in confinement, writing voluminously. As they passed the baton to Johnson, he found himself arrested almost immediately, along with many of his flock. The congregation removed itself, for the most part, to the Netherlands, where Johnson and the other leaders joined them upon release in 1597.

Barrow and Greenwood's outpouring of prison literature during 1590–1593 was partly for the benefit of such of their flocks as remained at large and partly for their own satisfaction, to unleash their vituperation upon the Puritan emissaries of the bishop of London, sent to visit them in their cells and convert them back to mere Puritanism. Increasingly, Separatism was defining itself in terms of a "not-ness"; they were the not-the-Church-of-England church. This is a trap into which small, pressurized minority confessions have continued to fall vis-à-vis whichever large, bullying confession they find themselves pitted. It is understandable, and makes the bullied feel much better. (After all, it is only a Nazarene carpenter and perhaps a few of his very closest followers who have entirely succeeded in keeping open hands when confronting their persecutors or quasi-persecutors.) But for a minority to define itself entirely by a negativity has the unfortunate effect of locking it into a social and intellectual ghetto.

The Separatists' *True Confession* of 1596 generally considered to be their definitive statement of faith, reflects this phenomenon precisely. Although it begins with a statement of Calvinist belief of a kind that every Puritan and most upholders of the hierarchy could accept, it is the following emphasis upon ecclesiology and exclusive true-ness and falseness that are more striking. A person's duty to leave the Church of England was, apparently, a matter of one's salvation: "By God's Commandment all that will be saved, must with speed come forth of this Antichristian estate, leaving the suppression of it unto the Magistrate to whom it belongeth." The unrealism of this aspiration, coming as it did at a time when the magistrates were busily suppressing its authors, is striking. Nevertheless, the *True Confession* insisted, Christ speaks to his church "by his own ministers and instruments only, and not by any false ministry at any time . . . by which Officers and laws he governeth his Church, and by none other."[6]

At least equally deserving of historians' attention, however, was an ecclesiological shift that was all the more significant for being almost certainly unconscious. The traditional Puritan demand had been for the disciplining and excommunication of open sinners from the parish churches, with a view to their correction. The more radical the Puritan, the greater the willingness to use such instruments, which they considered to be an essential mark of a true church. The Separatists, in theory, had always wanted the same thing; indeed, its absence from the Church of England as presently constituted was a major reason why they had chosen to separate from it. Yet their *True Confession* did not call for the exclusion of the unworthy minority from among the worthy majority; it called, rather, for the converse: "separating [Christians] from amongst unbelievers, from idolatry, false worship, superstition, vanity, dissolute life."[7] The godly were visualized as the minority, whose duty was to exclude themselves from the larger, corrupt mass. Tacitly, the Separatists had slid into an assumption of sectarianism.

This is what we mean when we say that doctrine follows life more frequently than life follows doctrine. It is a realization distressing to those whose career is built upon propounding abstractions, theological or otherwise. Neither is it without its dangers, for experience may lead us to justify anything. But the hypothesis that doctrine follows life (as a sort of ex post facto rationalization: "This is why we do this") is, in part, consonant with the behavior of the early church, whose exegesis of the Old Testament was driven by their experience of Jesus, and whose doctrines and creeds, including trinitarianism itself, were attempts to make sense of that experience of Jesus—and of the Holy Spirit—in alignment with the biblical data. For better or for worse, the Separatists' response to the same impulses caused their ecclesiology, with the passing of time, to reflect their daily lived experience as a de facto sect, and it caused their original rhetoric, about the kind of Christian state they wanted, to become more hypothetical and more incredible, even to themselves.

The Emergence of the General Baptists

In exile in the Netherlands, this process continued as the original group was joined by other Separatists who found the pressure in England too much to bear. Whereas in 1597 the number of English Separatists in Amsterdam had been not more than forty, by 1609 there were about three hundred. But in the fine tradition of Browne and Harrison, the exiled radicals fought like hens among themselves. An elder, Daniel Studley, stood accused of repeated immoralities. Francis Johnson and his brother quarreled, with the latter being excommunicated. When their father tried to mediate, he was cast out as well. There was a dispute with another Separatist pastor who came to Amsterdam from a church in the English West Country. A number of members left to join the city's new English Reformed Church, a congregation of English merchants, which was formally a part of the Dutch Reformed Church and so, theoretically, in communion with the Church of England. And in 1610, Henry Ainsworth, a respected leader, seceded with about thirty followers to form another new church.

But the most damaging argument was that with the group led by John Smyth. Smyth had come with a party of Separatists from the northeast Midlands. They were, on average, rather more bourgeois than Johnson's group and contained a high proportion of educated people and ejected former clergymen. Accordingly, they were less inclined to submit to Johnson's increasingly bossy ways, and it is possible that they never joined his congregation in the first place. Certainly their new Separatist church in Amsterdam took a more egalitarian line on many matters than did Johnson's.

But in late 1608, Smyth pushed what had always been a nagging question for the Separatists to an alarming conclusion. If the Church of England was no true church, then its ministry was no true ministry. By the same token, its sacraments were no true sacraments—and therefore its baptism was no true baptism. The implication of this impeccable logic was that the Separatists, who had all been christened as babies in their parish churches, had never been truly baptized and stood in need of being so now.

So which was it? Was the Church of England a true church? If so, then why not return to it? Or was it a false? In which case, its baptism was false also and the Separatists needed to rebaptize themselves.

The spectral presence of this difficulty had for long haunted their debates with Puritans, who had argued that the Brownists must either go forward to Anabaptism or return to the Church of England. For no one seemed in any doubt that Anabaptism was where the issue of rebaptism led. The hypothetical mediating position—that Separatists, being a true church, might practice a rebaptism solely to make good the defects of that administered by the Church of England, and then continue thereafter with infant baptism ministered by themselves—appears to have been overlooked by all. Instead, it was assumed on all hands that, if the principle of rebaptism was once allowed, it must inevitably lead to the abandonment of infant baptism altogether and to an adherence to believers' baptism—that is, to Anabaptism.

Baptism was merely the lightning conductor for a general tendency of all churches (and even factions within them) during the Reformation period. For all employed Aristotelian arguments to debunk churches that were more conservative than themselves and Platonic ones to fend off criticisms from radicals to their own left. Aristotelian arguments define things in terms of the sum total of their characteristics (or "accidents," to use the philosophical jargon). So if a church could be shown to have corruptions of various kinds (and critics were good at magnifying these), then it might be inferred that they were no true churches at all. This was the standard line of attack by Protestants against the Church of Rome, and it was used in turn by Separatists against the Church of England. Platonic arguments, by contrast, define things in terms of their supposed "essence," which is allegedly unaffected by mere empirical characteristics.

(Modern psychobabble plays the same game when it contends that the "real me" is somehow different from the person who has demonstrably just lied, cheated, or stolen.) So when the critics found the Aristotelian solvent applied against their own churches by those more radical than themselves, they reversed their previous arguments to show that unfortunate blemishes did not destroy the *essential* church-ness of their own favored institution.

The need to play this foolish game left many theologians, especially Protestant Reformers, engaged furiously in doublethink (or "balance," as their modern apologists like to call it). On the one hand, they expended unthinkable volumes of ink over mind-numbing deforestations of paper in tirades designed to demonstrate beyond contradiction that the pope was Antichrist. Then, a few pages later, they would reverse themselves to point out that the Church of Rome was, nevertheless, in some sense (they could not quite say how) a true church—at least insofar as the crucial matter of administering a valid baptism was concerned, though certainly no further.

The lightning conductor again. For, if the Aristotelianism were maintained to the last, then the christening that the entire population of newly Protestantized lands had received as infants under popery would be invalid. It would have to be performed afresh according to Lutheran or Reformed rites. This never happened; it would have been far too embarrassing—and that for two reasons. In the first place, the administrator of the new "true" baptism in a Protestant state church would, nine times out of ten, be the same person who had served as a Catholic priest at the original ceremony; the Protestant rhetoric about a clean break with the papist past would have a face-reddening brush with parish reality. Even more importantly, to perform rebaptism of any kind, with whatever claimed justification, considerably weakened one of the central arguments against Anabaptism. Better, then, to maintain that the Roman Catholic Church was simultaneously the whore of Babylon described in the book of Revelation *and* in some measure a true church—a body possessed by both Christ and Antichrist. It was all very Augustinian.

And it was a cleft stick of exactly this kind that confronted Francis Johnson, as the key leader of the Separatists, in fending off the arguments of Smyth, who was now contending for believers' baptism. In 1609 Smyth baptized himself (there being, in his estimation, no true church at whose hands he could be baptized) and then the others of his group, about forty in all, who consented to this radical step. The other, larger part of his congregation left him for the leadership of John Robinson. Francis Johnson, meanwhile, reversed his arguments of the past seventeen years to concede that the Church of England was, in fact, just sufficiently a true church to have administered a true baptism; the concession entailed that he had to say the same of the Roman Catholic Church—for the argument was all of a continuum.

Smyth soon discovered that this was not the only argument where one thing led inexorably to another: he moved a considerable distance during the following months toward many of the theological positions held by the Dutch Waterlander Mennonites, from one of whom he was renting premises in Amsterdam. The new English Baptists abandoned their Calvinism and embraced a belief in religious toleration. Smyth himself wished to go yet further in the direction of Mennonite theology, but in this he seems not to have had the full support of his congregation. Finally, he concluded that the baptism he had given himself had been a hasty mistake; he should have sought it at the hands of the Waterlanders who, he now realized, were indeed a true church. His quest for a third baptism was rejected, surprisingly, by only a minority of his followers. These insisted that they were already quite wet enough and that the quest for an apostolic succession of baptisms was pointless and likely to prove unfruitful.

This minority of about a dozen, led by Thomas Helwys, concluded that God was leading them back to England, there to face persecution. In 1612 they returned to their mother country and thereby became the first Baptist church on English soil. Their anticipation of sufferings proved correct; most of them were imprisoned. We possess a number of pleas for toleration, petitions to government, and doctrinal tracts, mostly written toward the end of that decade, and from all of them it is apparent that the Baptists had been dealt with harshly. Helwys himself died in 1616.

Our evidence of the life of these churches remains fragmentary, but it is clear that they succeeded in their mission, notwithstanding the heavy hand of persecution. By the late 1620s there were five General Baptist churches in England, though we know lamentably little about them, even concerning their size. To elude the attentions of authority is, for the most part, to do the same in respect of posterity, and the methods by which these churches were established is, sadly, unknown to us.

The Particular Baptists

The General Baptists did not, in any case, remain the sole representatives of Baptist opinion in England for much more than two decades. Sometime in the late 1630s (again, we cannot be much more precise) saw the birth of the Particular Baptists. If the Generals are named for their belief in a "general" atonement (i.e., Christ dying for the sins of the whole world, and so the salvability—but not necessarily the salvation—of all people), the Particulars are named for their adherence to a "particular" atonement (the Calvinist belief that Christ died only for the sins of the elect). The emergence of such a boiling-ice phenomenon as Calvinistic Baptists is so extraordinary as to demand our particular attention.

The story begins in 1616 with the Puritan agitator, Henry Jacob. On the spectrum of ecclesiological opinions, Jacob belongs in the slot labeled "Independent"—that is, he believed that each parish should govern its own affairs within a loose national framework. It was for this opinion that the existing national framework, whose leaders desired nothing of his looseness, had imprisoned him in the early 1600s. Upon his release, Jacob had made his way to the Netherlands where, although he met with the various brands of English Separatists who cluttered up the Dutch coastal ports, he never became one of them.

However, he did allow John Robinson, one of the more irenic Separatist pastors, to convert him to a belief that Christ was literally the immediate (i.e., unmediated) head of each congregation. This rather abstruse idea had the very practical effect of rendering national frameworks—whether loose or otherwise—more or less redundant. Direct congregational communication with Christ tended to dissolve the royal veto upon churches forming in the first place or upon their acting out the commands of Scripture as they understood it.

Thus emboldened, Jacob returned to London in 1616 and established a new, independent congregation, whose worship and discipline were organized along Puritan lines. By historians, this church is generally denominated "semi-Separatist" or "non-Separatist" because, although it made all of the usual and predictable criticisms of the Church of England, it consciously refrained from following through on them with the usual Separatist insistence that the national body was therefore no true church. Accordingly, Jacob's fellowship permitted its members to take communion in their parish churches on an occasional basis.

This unprecedented broad-mindedness had two immediate practical benefits. In the first place, it helped adherents (and the church as a whole) to avoid detection by the authorities. It also won Jacob's congregation the good opinion of Puritans who remained within the Church of England and who would have viewed principled Separatism as a cardinal sin.

The Jacob church (or rather, the one he founded, for he himself left for Virginia in 1622) was the big success story of the 1620s and 1630s. The trouble was that success brought official attention—and the attentions of the authorities were not tender. In 1632 the congregation was finally detected, and forty-six of its sixty members were imprisoned for eighteen months. Most left for America upon their release, but despite these losses and two secessions by strict Separatist breakaway groups during this period of turmoil, the church continued to grow fast.

The growth was largely courtesy of Archbishop Laud, whose policies were making life within the Church of England ever less tolerable for Puritans. The alternative to heading for New England was to join an illegal congregation such as that of the semi-Separatists and, during the 1630s, increasing numbers took this line of action.

But apart from the benefits of growth, the congregation founded by Henry Jacob was experiencing internal pressures. During the 1630s some members came to the conclusion that baptism was intended only for "professed believers." Under the pressure of a persecuted, sectarian existence, it had become tacitly accepted that one could tell, at least on a rough-and-ready basis, who the believers were—although the church's Calvinism continued to make this a matter of doubt, and so the adjective "professed" was usually added as a saving qualifier.

By 1638 John Spilsbury was leading a congregation of this sort, which had broken away from the mother church (pastored by this time by Henry Jessey) in terms so amicable that it hardly counts as a schism at all. Indeed, many of this new kind of Baptist viewed the issue of believers' baptism as a mere preference, a topic about which Christians might legitimately differ. Their brethren who believed in infant baptism evidently took the same view, for the most part, and there were to be several congregations during the 1640s–1660s that contained members of each persuasion.

In 1640 Richard Blunt led another Particular Baptist breakaway from the Jessey church, again under very friendly circumstances. Perhaps Blunt doubted whether Spilsbury was "doing it right." A Dutch-speaker himself, Blunt had visited the Netherlands shortly beforehand to witness how a congregation of Collegiant Rhynsburgers (an exotically named interconfessional group of Reformed, Arminians, and Mennonites) performed the ceremony.

Like the mother church from which they came, these Particular Baptists were Calvinistic in theology, Puritan in origin, congregational in church government, and non-Separatist in their refusal to deny church-hood to the Church of England. Although they practiced believers' baptism, they were astonishingly moderate in their espousal of it. For them, it was an issue in isolation rather than central for their ecclesiology—for the latter was rather vague:

Should there be a national church? No answer.

Was the Church of England a true church? Perhaps.

Should the church consist only of believers? Of "professed believers," yes; one couldn't really tell who true believers were.

Should there be a religious toleration? Well, within limits, perhaps—but not of all and sundry. Certainly Particular Baptists should be tolerated, but that was because of their orthodoxy, not because the state had no business to regulate religious belief.

If the questions seem to mock, that would be a shame. An overdose of principle was exactly what had held Separatists and the General Baptists back from making greater inroads than they had; pragmatism and theological confusion were exactly the medicine that English sectarianism needed.

So far were all these breakaways from depleting the numbers of the mother church pastored by Jessey that in May 1640, shortly before Blunt's secession, it had had to divide itself into two on strictly precautionary grounds; numbers were becoming too large for meetings to avoid detection. Although the East End of London congregation, led by the leather seller Praise-God Barebone (a man of evidently Puritan parentage), refused to countenance members who had suffered themselves to be baptized as believers, the West End of London congregation, which continued to be led by Jessey himself, absorbed head-moistened babies and soaking-wet believers alike.

The Consolidation of English Radicalism during the Civil War Period

Within six months of the precautionary split, most precautions were rendered redundant. The convening of the Long Parliament in November 1640 caused a breakdown in the ability—or of the will—of central government to enforce religious controls. Just as Puritan-minded parish ministers abandoned, either selectively or across the board, the wording of the Book of Common Prayer in celebrating communion, so sectarians also were able to emerge into the light of day. Still subject to the dangers of popular riot or of reactionary local magistrates, they could nevertheless operate far more freely and openly than before.

In this climate both General and Particular Baptists as well as Separatists began to proliferate, to the fury of the conservative majority. As king and Parliament drifted toward civil war during 1641 and the first half of the following year, so the various sectarians took courage from the prevailing conditions of political chaos to broadcast their message in print. When war itself began in the late summer of 1642, they almost inevitably found themselves on the parliamentarian side. It was not that the Members of Parliament were predisposed to grant them toleration (indeed, most looked upon them with horror) but rather the simple logic that any change could only be for the better. The sectarians knew for a fact that the king would persecute them; perhaps his enemies would be gentler.

The circumstance that English sectarianism was by now strung out along a continuous spectrum of opinion, the most conservative end of which blended with radical Puritanism inside the national church, gave some justification for this hope. Much though the Separatists and Baptists were excoriated by the Presbyterians, who dominated the parliamentarian cause during the first two years of the war, there were those in the Independent party who were prepared to countenance a limited toleration, and emergent leaders such as Oliver Cromwell, who were strongly in favor of it.

In the meantime the various radicals were protected, not so much by the force of law as by its weakness. Thomas Lambe, a soap boiler, had endured several imprisonments in the years immediately prior to the war for his activities as a General Baptist preacher. But by the mid-1640s he was presiding over a large, thriving, tumultuous congregation in the capital that exerted wide influence. In 1645 Parliament refused to prosecute Lambe for breaking its own ordinance against lay preaching, despite the exhortations of the Lord Mayor of London to do so.

The General Baptists may have had a high visibility presence in the capital, but they were unusual for being equally at home in the country. While their Particular Baptist cousins (or rivals) thrived, for the most part, in the same social milieu as the more radical end of the Puritan alliance did—that is, among traders and townspeople of the middling sort—the Generals picked up, in addition to some of these, many adherents who had never been Puritanized in the first place. The reason is theological: the rigorous Calvinism of the Puritan movement, a theology that the Particulars shared, had struck deeper roots in the towns and among the commercial classes than it had among the rural population. The Generals were able to capitalize upon this in the countryside.

The differences, however, should not be exaggerated. During the two decades of civil war and Republic, both species of Baptist developed successful trans-local organizations. The most striking General Baptist device was that of the "apostle" or "messenger," whose duty was to travel at the behest of his home congregation (for General Baptists were hyper-democratic and rigorously subjected shepherds to their flocks) in evange-lism and pastoral visits to far-flung converts. The Particular Baptists, by contrast, established a network of "associations," which tempered the Baptist emphasis upon congregational self-government with an admix-ture of quasi-Presbyterian collegiality: association meetings of pastors and elders from a region could not instruct their constituent churches what to do, but they might advise them.

By 1644 there were seven Particular Baptist congregations in the capital, and these combined to produce the *London Confession* of that year. It was an apologetic work, in both senses of the term. Its authors were anxious, not simply to explain the details of their doctrine (though the confession performed this function well enough), but to conciliate all those Puritans, Separatists, and others who might with any degree of likelihood at all be reconciled, be it to even the slightest degree, to the horrible spectre of "Anabaptism," which their public reputation held the Baptists to represent.

Indeed, the *London Confession* dedicated no small part of its efforts to distancing the Particulars from any imputation that they were aban-doning either Calvinism or a Christian magistracy. The explication of their ecclesiology was almost mouselike in its boldness. The usual sectarian (or, for that matter, state-church) insistence that theirs was the one and only way to organize a church, or was somehow possessed of exclusive purity, was entirely absent. Instead, the confession was a plea for respectability and for the forbearance of the wider Calvinist-Puritan fraternity, whose members so many Particular Baptists had once been, and whose approval they continued, albeit somewhat des-perately, to covet.

It is not a posture that one can easily imagine being adopted by their General Baptist counterparts. The General Baptists were indeed a vig-orous—sometimes even an ecstatic—movement, but they were already prone to the legalism that would prove an important part of their undo-ing. During the early 1640s they had fallen out among themselves briefly over the issue of whether baptism should be by affusion (the pouring of water over the head) or immersion, with the latter practice eventually prevailing. The following decade they fought again, more seriously, over the practice of laying on of hands for all newly baptized believers. But other ceremonies, such as footwashing and the holding of a precommu-nion meal, also occasioned bouts of ridiculous infighting—all stemming from the core idea that there was one and only one biblically acceptable model for doing everything.

The irritability resultant upon this central conviction helps to account for the fluidity of their membership during the Civil War period and the Republic. Their ideas were attractive and their organization dynamic. Nevertheless, these positive points were often negated by General Baptist congregational life, which could foster attitudes of rigidity that sometimes made it hard to hang on to new converts and, at its worst, could turn the movement into something of a revolving door: people were won over from the Church of England only to be lost to it again a year or two later. Leaders in Cambridgeshire in the early 1650s expended much of their pastoral energies in persuading individual converts to stay converted.

When they were not losing adherents back to the national church, however, the General Baptists sometimes lost them instead to yet more radical groups, most notably the Quakers. Contrary to popular belief nowadays, these latter were not "started" by George Fox; he was simply one among several leaders of advanced radicals (seekers and other kinds of independent, newly arisen congregations) in the late 1640s and early 1650s who began to cohere around a shared egalitarianism and a moderately spiritualizing exegesis of Scripture and rationalism to form the emerging Quaker movement.

The Quakers took General Baptist ideas on free will a stage further: not only were all people, potentially, able to be saved, but the divine light already lived in each person. People need to be "convinced" by "truth." Arguments about baptism were fruitless; what was needed was not an outward immersion in mere water but a baptism of the Holy Spirit. Church buildings were nothing but "steeplehouses." Christmas was a pagan festival. The days of the week were idolatrously named after Roman deities and should be referred to instead as "first day," "second day," and so on. Ministers of every kind interposed themselves between ordinary people and God; Quakers dismissed them all, contemptuously, as "priests." Removing one's hat in the presence of one's social superiors, or addressing them with "you"—rather than the more familiar "thou" and "thee" (as in French *tu*, German *du*, Welsh *ti*, etc.)—was to give honor to humans, rather than respecting the fundamental equality bestowed upon them by their Creator. Most of all, Quakers were confident, above all, that the debates about the meaning of Scripture could be resolved

George Fox.
From a painting by S. Chinon.

if people would only listen to the light within: what mattered about the redemption story was "the mystery, not the history." It was an appealing idea to thousands who had tired of the factiousness of religious life in mid-seventeenth-century England and of its propensity to contribute to the violent struggles of the 1640s and 1650s.

Most of all, the ideas struck a chord with those who had already imbibed and accepted the Baptist critique of the Church of England but who were becoming a little nervous about the legalism that such an acceptance appeared to entail. The breezy rationalism of the Quakers—replete with opportunities to thumb one's nose at authority and be righteous at the same time—appealed to many, though it often came at the price of fierce persecution.

Neither were the Quakers always pacifists; they became so only after the Restoration of the monarchy in 1660—and then as part of their assurance that they meant no one any harm and so should not be persecuted. Before that, however, they had been particularly numerous in the parliamentarian army.

That army had become a hotbed of sectaries from about 1644 onward. It had begun with the shocking disposition of Cromwell, at that time a rapidly ascending cavalry commander, to promote soldiers on actual merit rather than on social rank. Those he found most meritorious were the religious radicals—and if a man was godly, then Cromwell studiously refrained from enquiring too closely about the details of his theology. By the end of the war, many individual sectaries were not only immune from prosecution; they wielded real power in the localities where they were posted. It was a state of affairs that reduced the local gentry who had to deal with them to apoplexy. But it certainly wedded sectarians of all stripes to the most radical wing of the parliamentarian party; perhaps, after all, there would be a place for them in whatever new England lay on the far side of a postwar political settlement.

Many sectarians, especially those in the military, dallied with either or both of two political movements during the late 1640s and the 1650s. The first of these, the Levellers, were a secular political campaign to establish parliamentary sovereignty in theory (to augment the mere fact established on the battlefield), universal manhood suffrage (except for servants), equality before the law, the abolition of the death penalty for all offenses save murder and treason, and annual elections. Most importantly, they insisted upon religious toleration. Baptists, especially General Baptists, were among the Levellers' most ardent supporters. The movement emerged from the chaos of the mid-1640s and flourished briefly during 1648–1649, but it was scotched when army mutinies in its favor were crushed by Cromwell, with exemplary executions following, *pour encourager les autres*.

Shortly after this setback a new, explicitly religious political movement emerged: the Fifth Monarchy Men. Named for its interpretation of the five monarchies described by the Old Testament prophet Daniel, this was a radical, unstable form of postmillennialism.

Postmillennial doctrine was a novelty that had first emerged in the early part of the century through the writings of the English Puritan Thomas Brightman (1562–1607). Its distinctive feature is the insistence that Christ's second coming will be after (hence, *post*) the thousand-year (*millennial*) reign of the saints on the earth. The rather awkward and unavoidable conclusion from this premise is that the saints are thereby reduced to ushering in their own reign—rather than the neater, early church solution of a magnifical second coming of the Savior to tidy the earth up for them beforehand.

As it happens, postmillennialism was to have a rather respectable future in the eighteenth and early nineteenth centuries as the most frequent eschatology of evangelicals and their most convenient way of spiritualizing the humanist, Enlightenment myth of inevitable human progress: the earth would get better and better and more and more Christian under the tutelage of British imperialism and missionary movements. Such dignified optimism was not characteristic, however, of postmillennial teaching in its earliest decades. In particular, it did not characterize Fifth Monarchist postmillennialism in the England of the 1650s. The theologically Calvinist radicals—Independents, Separatists, and Particular Baptists—who were most prone to the movement's appeal tended to emphasize instead that government needed to be seized by "the saints" (by which they meant, of course, themselves) to establish a theocracy, with a view to mounting an international crusade against the forces of Antichrist (by which they meant, with an equal inevitability, the pope). As apocalypses go, this was not so much Eurocentric as downright parochial; but then, English sectarians were stronger on cosmology than on cosmopolitanism.

Despite the movement's strength among the soldiery, England was spared further army mutinies on account of the Fifth Monarchy Men. But a constitutional experiment in 1656, the so-called Barebones Parliament (scornfully named for the leather-seller-turned-preacher, who was held to typify its membership), appeared for a while to be about to usher in "government by the saints." Its failure and dissolution led many erstwhile Fifth Monarchists to abandon their millennial hopes and led others to transfer them to new schemes. But a tiny minority turned to violence.

Thomas Venner led a doomed, ridiculous uprising in 1657, with his few dozen followers running amok in the city of London waving swords. The clemency of the republican regime, and its unreasonable patience for godly eccentrics, saved Venner from the scaffold on that occasion. But there was no such mercy for him when he repeated the exploit in 1661, following the Restoration of the monarchy.

Sectarian strength in the army was sustained for the duration of the Republic (1649–1660). And it was during this period that the Separatists, Baptists, seekers, and others were augmented in the ranks by the new-fangled Quakers.

There are those historians (and they may be right) who think that it was fear of Quakerism that finally provoked the Restoration of 1660. From the point of view of conservative opinion, the Baptists were an intolerable affront to social religious solidarity—but they were relatively few and some of them, notably among the Particular Baptists, did at least aspire to respectability. The Leveller threat had been yet more ominous—but it had passed a decade before. The Fifth Monarchists were mad—but their appeal was limited, even among sectarians. The Quakers, however, were fearlessly provocative, openly dismissive of even outward deference to social superiors, and ferociously egalitarian. Worst of all, they were growing fast. By 1660 there were 60,000 of them, coming from nowhere to equal the combined strength of the two Baptist movements within a decade. They were present in every county of the land. Their willingness to "go naked for [i.e. as] a sign" (by which some of them became, in effect, pious, seventeenth-century-style streakers), James Naylor's blasphemous reenactment in Bristol of Christ's entry into Jerusalem, the interruption of parish church services by Quakers rebuking the minister: all of these stunts epitomized the image of madcap sectarianism and the threat it posed to established order, hierarchy, and property. Who knew how far they might go?

It was nervous cogitations of this kind that, from the death of Cromwell in 1658, propelled a critical mass of the gentry and senior army officers toward the conclusion that a restored monarchy would provide a better guarantee of law and order, of hierarchy, and of property than would the continuing sufferance of radical influence upon government. During late 1659 and early 1660, therefore, negotiations were entered into, with a view to safeguarding the political classes from any possibility of a future return to the politics of the 1630s or of a drift toward popery or continental-style absolutism. Once those essentials were assured, the big leap was taken: the son of the beheaded monarch was allowed to return from exile as King Charles II. The rejoicing that attended this event is usually described as "general," but it was not quite that; the sectarians, at least, had every cause to fear what would happen next.

The Further Fragmentation of Dissent from Russian Orthodoxy

The defection of the Old Believers—or *raskol'niki* (schismatics), as the authorities called them—from the official Russian Orthodox Church created at least the theoretical possibility of further splintering. As so often, it was the defectors who were themselves the subjects of such breakaways, known as *tolki* or *soglasiia*. Once one has already excommunicated the vast bulk of the population among whom one lives, then falling out with brethren who have done likewise becomes relatively easy.

The Dukhobors ("spirit wrestlers") originated in the Kharkov area of eastern Ukraine in the mid-eighteenth century. They were pacifist, believing in an "inner light" that was inherent, not just in people (in the fashion of Quaker belief), but in all living things. Such ideas went along naturally enough with other Quaker-type beliefs such as personal guidance from the Holy Spirit and the abandonment of all outward religious ceremonies.

The Molokans emerged in the same area and at the same time as the Dukhobors. Their name, "milk drinkers," arose from the fact that, unlike the Orthodox, they refused to abstain from all animal products—especially milk—during Lent. This apparently profound theological repudiation of trivial ceremonies was evidently not incompatible with their frequent observation of Old Testament dietary laws. Such legalism aside, they rejected all ritual as mere outward observances and were in some ways quite biblicist. They also accepted their nickname because, as they piously pointed out, they desired "the sincere milk of the Word"—an insistence that reflects their tendency toward biblicism. One faction of them was known to outsiders as Pryguny ("the Leapers") because of what they doubtless considered the revolutionary practice of jumping and dancing in their meetings. In matters of Christian worship, the historian is forced to conclude that the wheel is not merely forever coming full circle; it is constantly being reinvented.

Various factions among the Dukhobors and Molokans were to act, in due course, as the seedbed for the rise of native Russian and Ukrainian evangelicalism from the late 1860s onward. But that development, when it occurred, depended also upon interaction with other, foreign elements in Russian society, elements which, by the late eighteenth

century, were making the facade of monolithic Russian Orthodoxy
ever less credible.

In the first place, we should note the growing number of foreign merchants with more or less permanent bases inside the Russian Empire
from the eighteenth century onward. Mostly western Europeans, these
consisted religiously of Catholics, Lutherans, and Anglicans. Though few
of these were inclined to engage in proselytism, neither was it possible
entirely to insulate the native Russians from the religious influences
of the newcomers. St. Petersburg was a particular center of pluralism.
The capital was located close to the Baltic lands that had been recently
incorporated into the empire by the Treaty of Nystadt in 1721 and were
inhabited by Lutheran Estonians and Letts, as well as a German-speaking
aristocracy that had been greatly affected by Pietism. Peter the Great
granted complete freedom for Lutheranism in these lands as early as
1710. The Pietist German aristocrats had an important presence at court.
The estimate of some historians that, in the years before the Russian
Revolution, the population of the capital may have been as much as
10 percent Protestant is perhaps not as surprising as it might appear
at first sight.

But it was not just in the capital and the northeast of Russia that the
foreign Protestants made their appearance. German-speaking Lutherans
and Reformed were introduced into various parts of the empire as
merchants and traders but also as farmers in self-contained villages.
Many of these, like the Baltic-Germans, had been profoundly affected
by Pietism.

Finally, the Mennonites also immigrated to Russia. In 1780 significant numbers of them were invited to Russia by Catherine the Great
in order to settle the underpopulated steppes in Ukraine and along the
Volga. Later waves, however, moved into the Urals and Siberia. The
newcomers gained a respite from the persecution they had experienced
in the lands further west, especially in central Europe; they were also
given land and, in deference to their pacifism, immunity from military
service. The Russian state gained new settlers, excellent farmers and
craft-workers, and particularly profitable taxpayers. But the newcomers
were also required to keep their beliefs to themselves; proselytism among
the indigenous inhabitants was strictly forbidden. That the new settlers
kept their own language and lived in self-contained villages suited the
authorities very well. It was an agreement that did not start to break
down until late-nineteenth-century evangelical influences renewed the
Mennonites themselves and caused their witness to overleap the boundaries that had been laid down for them.

And what of the Old Believers themselves during these years? As we noticed in chapter 5, Peter the Great had suspended persecution on the pragmatic ground that many of the Old Believers, as so often with religious schismatics, were gifted businessmen whose taxable and economically beneficial activities he was loath to chase away. Among his successors, the Empresses Anna (1730–1740) and Elizabeth (1741–1762) were made of more principled stuff, but Peter III (1762–1763) and Catherine II (the Great, 1762–1796) allowed them to settle in border areas. Catherine's urban charter of 1785 even granted them some political rights, such as the ability to stand for election for municipal offices. The mercantile life of the city of Moscow was built upon these concessions, for Old Believer merchants moved to the city during Catherine's reign. As with the Jews, the ties of mutual trust and family bonds between them did much to make up for the absence of any proper legal framework for business in Russia—a shortcoming that hampered the growth of trade in the empire as a whole.

By the time Nicholas I (1825–1855) resumed persecution of the *raskol'niki*, the movement was too firmly entrenched to be susceptible to extermination—except, perhaps, in the longest of terms. Notwithstanding Nicholas's spiteful attempt to invalidate even the marriages of Old Believers, he might as well not have bothered, unless his real purpose was merely to inflict misery rather than to end the schism, because Old Believer numbers were almost certainly continuing to grow. From the beginning, back in the 1660s, the Orthodox hierarchy had justly feared that the numbers of ordinary people who sympathized with the Old Belief far outran those who actually joined it. Popular respect for the schismatics hampered the business of persecution at every turn and backfired in the form of diminishing respect for the official church. Nor does this dynamic appear to have changed over time. By the late nineteenth century there were an estimated ten million Old Believers. The list of draconian Russian policies which proved, in the end, to be self-defeating is long indeed.

Heresies

Heretic is a term that has been prone to overuse. Certainly early-modern Christians were not backward in applying it liberally to all whose opinions offended their own conceptions of orthodoxy. To Roman Catholics, of course, the term applied to all Protestants—simply by virtue of the fact that the latter had departed from the One True Church. In addition, most people considered radicals and Anabaptists to be heretics—though this was because they assumed them all to be potential Münsterites. The real "heresy" of most radicals, however, was social, not theological; they denied the legitimacy of the *corpus christianum*, or Christian state.

But beneath the fog of overuse, name-calling, and distortion, a number of heretical groups—defined strictly by departures from the historic orthodoxy of the early church as expressed in its creedal statements—were indeed at work in Europe during our period. Mostly, these represented one form or another of the ancient Arian heresy, which denied the deity of Christ and the doctrine of the Trinity. But other groups represented forms of mysticism so extreme that essential Christian doctrines were, in effect, denied. A few groups held to the messianic claims of their leaders—though most of these, like the leaders themselves, tended to be short-lived. The radical dualisms that had affected the early centuries and the High Middle Ages—Gnostics, Paulicians, Bogomils, and Cathars—were seldom present, biding their time until esoteric nineteenth-century cults and, in the late twentieth century, the New Age resurrected them.

The Family of Love

Partial exceptions to this last point, it could be argued, were the spin-off movements from the career of David Joris. A marginally orthodox Anabaptist in the 1530s and early 1540s, Joris had become ever more mystical and unorthodox in later years, hinting at his own messianic status, advocating dissimulation by his followers (i.e., conforming outwardly to the official church, on the basis that outward ceremonies were of no value and, therefore, didn't count) and perhaps (for they remain matters of dispute among historians) practicing immorality and countenancing polygamy.

With the exception of these last points, Hendrik Niclaes (1502–ca. 1580) picked up where his mentor left off. Though his group, the Family of Love, had a following in his native Low Countries, it flourished most profusely in Elizabethan England, where its adherents occasionally alarmed the episcopal authorities by their slipperiness in debate, by their unprincipled denials of their real beliefs, and by their *sotto voce* insistence that all things were to be renewed by "H. N."—initials that devotees insisted, when questioned by officials, stood for *homo novus* (new man); the fact that it was the acronym of their leader's name was purely coincidental.

The Familists' ideas were expressed in cloudy and elusive language, facilitating denials to the authorities or reinterpretation of their true meaning. Insofar as their spiritual verbiage was reducible to dogma at all, however, it amounted to an extreme form of spiritualism: the Bible was not to be understood literally (except where it suited their purposes); outward ceremonies and institutions were a matter of indifference (although the ceremonialist Catholic Church was to be preferred to less ceremonial, Protestant ones); the mutual anathemas of the Catholic and Protestant churches were uncharitable and led to confusion and strife (but the Familists' leader, a merchant of Delft, in the Netherlands, was the real messiah, and all who failed to recognize the fact and join his Family of Love were lost). Probing these paradoxes would be a pointless exercise; the movement was sustained by mystery, not by rationally explicable precept.

From the mid-1570s two Puritans, William Wilkinson and John Rogers, horrified by the rapidly proliferating works of Niclaes appearing in English translation, ventured into this jungle of spiritual jargon and went into print themselves in order to alert good Christians as to the devilish ideas being spread among them by the Familist heretics. Wilkinson's and Rogers's efforts, though workmanlike, were attempts to refute not so much the irrefutable as the indefinable. Both men had personal acquaintance with their heretical antagonists, though neither could bring himself so far as to assist the authorities in capturing them. However, several Familists were later arrested anyway, notably in the Isle of Ely, which, as Richard Cox, the bishop of Ely, was shocked to discover in 1579, was an area of particular Familist strength.

The good prelate need not have fretted. Examination of the artisans who formed the bulk of the Familists' membership proved that these sectarians, though devious, were entirely nonviolent and harmless. Their spiritualizing of doctrine was indeed heretical, being so extreme as to turn heaven, hell, and even their own apocalyptic rhetoric into descriptors of people's spiritual condition rather than nonsubjective realities. For this reason, and because of the esoteric nature of their beliefs, the extent of their appeal was always likely to remain as limited as they were socially innocuous.

Jesus excepted, movements that posit the messianic status of their leader cannot long survive that leader's demise. Though some historians estimate Hendrik Niclaes's death as having occurred in 1570, it is more generally accepted that he died in Cologne around 1580. The Familists continued to exist into the seventeenth century, but they entered upon a period of slow decline. By the midcentury, at the latest, they were on the verge of extinction.[8]

Unitarian Heresy

A far more important and enduring strain of heresy emerged with the uncle and nephew Laelio (1525–1562) and Fausto (1539–1604) Sozzini. Both were humanist scholars who had toyed with various shades of Reformed Protestantism and also with Anabaptism. But their final direction was that of Unitarian heresy, in a form named after them as Socinianism. In the year before his death, Laelio finally clarified what Calvin, Bullinger, and others had long suspected about him: he issued a radical exposition of the first chapter of John's Gospel in which he denied that Christ had existed before the creation of the world, that the *Logos* was identical with Christ himself, or that it was anything other than the message of God.

Fausto picked up where his uncle had left off. In his view, Christ was effectively adopted into the Godhead after the Ascension but was not God in and of himself. His crucifixion was not so much the work of salvation as his resurrection was a pledge of salvation to humanity. Sin did not require a penal satisfaction; instead, it was an offense or insult against God, which the Father, in consideration of the work of Christ, freely forgives or overlooks. So forgiveness is not an effect of the Passion that is in any sense transferable to others.

Socinianism spread widely during the late sixteenth and seventeenth centuries, but it prospered most in Poland and Transylvania. In both countries it tended to draw away supporters of the Reformed churches. In both countries weak governments afforded opportunities for independent-minded nobles to follow their own courses, religiously speaking, and so offered scope for heretical teachers to gain a local following that could be sustained. Jewish and Muslim objections to the allegedly compromised monotheism of orthodox Christian trinitarian beliefs were pertinent topics of debate; local Jewish strength and the proximity of Islam, in the form of the Ottomans, was also common to both areas.

In 1569 a Unitarian-Anabaptist community was established at Raków by Gregory Paul. Many of its adherents consisted of minor nobility. The colony propounded a variety of radical ideas,

FAVSTVS   SOCINVS .   Fausto Sozzini.

including community of goods, psychopannychism (the idea that the soul "sleeps" between the point of death and the resurrection to final judgment), and the imminent arrival of the kingdom of God. Fitful negotiations were entered into with the Moravian Hutterites during 1569–1571, but they broke down over social differences and over the nature of God. The Racovian emissaries complained that their hosts "passionately maintained a triune God," and held "obstinately to the common doctrine of the Trinity."[9]

The Transylvanian Unitarians, meanwhile, were mounting full-fledged assaults on the doctrine of the Trinity in print. Their chief spokesmen included Francis Dávid (ca. 1510–1579)—a one-time Lutheran, then a champion of the Reformed before becoming a protagonist for Unitarianism—and the Italian physician Giorgio Biandrata (ca. 1515–ca. 1585). Biandrata had given his medical services to royalty in both Poland and Transylvania before spending time in the Italian congregation at Geneva, where his persistent questioning of the doctrine of the Trinity had earned him Calvin's wrath, which made him feel it advisable to remove himself. But he went on to play a leading role in the schisms of the Reformed churches in both countries where he had formerly served as royal physician.

In Transylvania, the prince, John Sigismund, favored the heretics. In 1569 he presided over a conference of Reformed divines at Nagyvárad, which saw the decisive sundering of the Reformed church—the majority siding with the king and his principal theological spokesman, Francis Dávid. The new church was radically sacramentarian in its denials of the real presence in the eucharist and inclined to oppose infant baptism.

The new dispensation positively demanded an assertion of religious toleration if the country was to be saved from confessional conflict between Lutherans, Orthodox, Catholics, and the two varieties (trinitarian and unitarian) of Reformed. Accordingly, in 1571 John Sigismund decreed that "no one shall be harmed for any creed, neither preachers nor listeners; if, however, any minister would go to criminal extremes, the superintendent shall be permitted to judge and suspend him, after which he may be expelled from the country."[10] It was a remarkable circumstance in an age not always predisposed toward tolerance, and it reflected the curious limbo that the region, long on the frontier between the Catholic and Orthodox worlds, now found itself, sandwiched between the two multiethnic empires of the Hapsburgs and Ottomans, one avowedly Catholic and the other Muslim.

By the end of the 1570s Dávid was taking the Transylvanian Unitarians to new extremes. Jesus was not to be adored or invoked in prayer; he was

of the seed of Joseph; his teachings were important but less authoritative than those of Moses; Saturday was to be observed as a Sabbath.
Other "Judaizing" leaders were urging the observance of Old Testament
dietary laws.

Such innovations began to tax the patience of the prince, Stephen
Báthory, who had succeeded John Sigismund upon his death in 1572.
Báthory was a Catholic but, though he was realistic enough to pursue
a tolerant course in so religiously diverse a country as Transylvania,
the ever-spiraling derogations from orthodoxy by Dávid were testing
the limits of his policy. Biandrata, who remained court physician, took
alarm at the rashness of his coreligionists. Fearing that such excesses
would endanger the Unitarian project as a whole, he invited his fellow
Italian, Fausto Sozzini, from Poland to mediate and arbitrate between
the moderate Unitarians and the radicals.

It is dubious theological company indeed when an arch-heretic is
brought in as the voice of moderation, but the process went ahead.
Dávid declined to be overawed by his prominent antagonist. Remaining
unmoved, in the spring of 1579 he found himself arrested and brought
before the diet—not specifically for heresy (a borderline that had been
crossed long ago) but for innovation beyond what had been approved
by John Sigismund back in 1571. Astonishingly, the nobles at the diet
continued to back him, though the court Jesuits and the Calvinist clergy
were united in calling for his blood. So when Stephen Báthory merely
incarcerated Dávid in a castle, he was simply striking a prudent compromise. But it still resulted in the radical leader's death that November
from broken health—an outcome that cannot have been unwelcome to
the prince, to the Catholic and Calvinist clergy, or even to Biandrata.

The Transylvanian Unitarian Church was reorganized upon more
conservative lines, taking an adoptionist view of the deity of Christ (not
God in and of himself but adopted into the Godhead on account of his
life and deeds) and reaffirming infant baptism and the Lord's Supper.

Sozzini, meanwhile, continued his work in Cracow for Polish Unitarianism until his death in 1604. His theological writing formed the basis
for the Racovian Catechism of the following year, a document which
was to take a place as perhaps the most important Socinian statement
of faith.

Unitarianism, especially in its Socinian form, was to remain an important challenge to orthodox Christianity throughout the period covered
by this volume and beyond it. An English translation of the Racovian
Catechism was produced by John Biddle of Gloucestershire in 1652,
an exercise in free speech that transcended the limits of the relatively

tolerant English Republic; he spent the remaining ten years of his life in prison, the last of them under a restored monarchy even less inclined to put up with outright heresy.

Biddle, however, was not without at least a few followers. One, a wealthy merchant called Firmin, financed the publication of antitrinitarian writings from the late 1680s onward. The first of these, *A Brief History of the Unitarians, called also Socinians*, was actually written by a Hertfordshire rector—an indication that heterodoxy had made its home within the establishment. By century's end, Arians were cropping up among both Presbyterian and General Baptist clergy. Though both bodies sought to defend themselves from such encroachments, the efforts in each case were too feeble and too lacking in clear, coherent defense of orthodoxy; the progress of heresy continued unabated.

By 1710 the professor of mathematics at Cambridge, William Whiston, was expelled from his position for holding Arian opinions. Five years later, his colleague in theology, Richard Bentley, demonstrated that the so-called "Johannine comma," which had been believed to be the only part of the Scripture to refer, more or less explicitly, to the Trinity, was, in fact, a spurious interpolation by later writers—a conclusion with which scholars since have concurred.

This last revelation, coming as it did at a time when orthodoxy was coming under unprecedented pressure from rationalist critiques, only encouraged the advance of antitrinitarianism. Among the Presbyterians, the heresy took hold in the Exeter congregations during the late 1710s. The alarmed orthodox party in the city submitted their case to a committee of clergy from the main dissenting denominations meeting at Salters Hall in London in February 1719. But the divines voted, by a slim majority, that no human compositions or interpretations of the doctrine of the Trinity should be recommended as binding. It was a fateful move. The motives of the majority were biblicist: they claimed to uphold belief in the Trinity but would not enforce upon others doctrinal terminology that was not itself taken from Scripture. It was a fine argument, but one that gave de facto permission to heretics to continue in their persuasion of others. It was charity of a kind that wrought the utmost destruction upon those who proffered it.

By the late eighteenth century, the large majority of English Presbyterianism had become Unitarian. On the one hand, the longstanding Presbyterian stress upon the inscrutability of the elect made them undemanding in their scrutiny of those offering themselves for membership—and even for the ministry. On the other hand, their suspicion of antinomian brands of Calvinism, a mistrust dating from the civil war period, predisposed at least a minority of their clergy toward Arminianism of a rationalist type. This in its turn made for an easier transition to Arianism. Furthermore, the prosperous merchant congregations of many Presbyterian churches were among the classes most affected by the new intellectual fashions and most anxious to distance themselves from the slur of "enthusiasm," which attached to religious dissent of all kinds. Such affectations lent themselves easily enough to rationalist repudiations of trinitarianism.

Farther down the social spectrum, the General Baptists had a history of falling out with one another over footwashing and the laying on of hands—both disputes that reflect a fastidious attachment to biblical turns of phrase. But it also made them unwilling, when the doctrine of the Trinity and the persons of the Godhead became matters of frequent debate, to enforce anything but strictly scriptural language as tests of orthodoxy. Once again, the heretics in their midst were given tacit permission to proceed.

The dissenting academies continued—or rather, hastened—the process of theological erosion. Seen from a strictly academic point of view, these institutions were in some ways the glories of eighteenth-century English dissent. Established to provide a solid education for young men whose failure to be Anglicans barred them from access to Oxford and Cambridge, the dissenting academies succeeded admirably in their purpose. However many, perhaps most, of them came to be dominated by radical teachers whose Arian or Socinian opinions impressed themselves upon the developing minds of several generations of dissent's finest thinkers.

Of these, Joseph Priestley (1733–1804), who held a variety of pastorates and teaching positions, almost certainly counts as the most famous. A polymath, his interests took in history, electricity, philosophy, chemistry, and physiology—yet they all somehow folded back upon the concerns of theology. An advanced Socinian who considered mere Arianism to be as idolatrous as orthodoxy because it permitted the veneration of Christ as well as his preexistence, Priestley concluded from his scientific studies that all human thoughts are caused by physical sensations rather than free apprehensions of the real. Whether this insight invalidated itself (having been caused, say, by a surfeit of coffee at breakfast and of arrogance at lunch) he declined to elucidate. But he insisted, nevertheless, that this made humans purely material, rather than a compound of matter and spirit. It also made them subject to necessity, thereby guaranteeing God's control of the world and making God (as in certain varieties of predestinarianism) the final author of sin.

It was, perhaps, a perverse intellectual journey from the Calvinist Congregationalism of his boyhood. And Priestley was not the archetypical Unitarian. Nevertheless, his career illustrates the radical possibilities within Socinian thought. His sympathies for the French Revolution made him an object of popular loathing after 1789, and he found it advisable in 1794 to remove himself to the republican safety of the U.S.

If Unitarian heresy reflected the rationalist trends present in western Europe from the Renaissance onward, and particularly after the mid-seventeenth century, then it is perhaps unsurprising that the heresies peculiar to Russia should reflect the mysticism and irrationalism that were such a strong note in the wider popular culture of that vast country. Not all of the breakaways from Russian Orthodoxy were as moderate as the Old Believers, or even the Dukhobors and Molokans.

The Khlysty and Skoptsy

The Khlysty, or Khristovoverie, were an early breakaway from Russian Orthodoxy. The group originated in the late seventeenth century under the leadership of one Danila Filipov, an army deserter from the region of Kostroma who seems to have been a teacher among the "priestless" faction of the Old Believers before his career as sect-leader began. This movement emphasized the spirit within each believer, following leaders whom they called "Christs," in whom the fullness of God was believed to dwell. Filipov—who was, of course, one of the Christs—was said to be "godded." It was an expression that recalled a favorite phrase of Hendrik Niclaes, "godded with God." Doubtless the similarity was merely coincidental, yet many of the Khlysty ideas were similar to those of the Familists—and, indeed, to other Gnostic-type groups down through the ages.

In the first place, members were supposed to keep their adherence to the movement entirely secret, a ruse they were to maintain by remaining within the parish churches. In the second place, they looked upon outward ceremonies as being valueless. Like other Gnostic movements in history, the flesh was held to be evil in and of itself. They therefore refused to eat meat or even fish. They also approached the problem of the incarnation (enfleshment) of Jesus in ways similar to at least some of the heretics of the early centuries: the Christ Spirit fell upon Jesus at his baptism, signifying an adoptionist view of his deity. But the dualism also had implications for sexuality: marriages were repudiated by converts or else they were required to be celibate. Even more worryingly, neophytes entered "spiritual marriages" alongside and in addition to the actual marriages already contracted. Although these, likewise, were supposed to be celibate, the potential for temptation, self-delusion, and resultant bitterness and recrimination was obviously enormous.

The Khlysty used fasting followed by singing and dancing in order to reach a state of Spirit-filled (or, at any rate, spirit-filled) ecstasy. Many of their songs were composed in such a state of exaltation, and they were accorded scriptural status in their *Kniga Golubina*, or *Dove Book*.

The movement flourished early on in Kostroma, Vladimir, and Moscow, where in 1733 three hundred of the sectarians were discovered by the authorities. Of these, one woman was from the nobility and eighty were monks or nuns. Only a third were peasants. Just five were condemned to death; the rest were beaten with a whip or their tongues were cut out, followed by hard labor on the frontier with the Kazakhs or in Siberia. Undaunted, the sectarians continued their activities in the capital, though many others fled to different parts of the empire, spreading their heretical teachings as they went. A series of inquisitions in Moscow during 1745–1752 included liberal use of the rack and hot irons to extract confessions. Of the 450 victims who were punished, five were burned and another twenty-six variously executed. Most of the rest were exiled, several of them minus their noses. Two-thirds of the sufferers were peasants on this occasion—though that still represented a far smaller proportion of the sectarians than of the population as a whole, confirming that literate people and traders were particularly prone to involvement. Just 36 percent of those punished were Muscovites, the rest being from the upper Volga region. By 1900 the movement had well over 100,000 members and was particularly strong in the Baltic regions, where some Lutherans had defected to it, and in the Caucasus. Since the Khlysty were not supposed to have children once they had joined the sect, mere survival across the generations is impressive; growth, even more so.

However, the Khlysty were themselves prone to divisiveness, splitting several times during the course of the eighteenth and nineteenth centuries. The ominously named Skoptsy ("Castrators") were among these. They called their eponymous practice a "baptism of fire"—as doubtless it was. The purpose, of course, was to circumvent the need for battling against the desires of the flesh by a single action that would render any future battles redundant. Neither were the group's female adherents in any way denied the privilege of appalling self-mutilation; they cut off their breasts. Amazingly, the group survived into modern times.

The originator was one Andrei Ivanov, a peasant who also went by the name of Kondrati Selivanov. Around 1770 he emerged as the "Christ" of the Khlysty in Tula, where the movement was about a thousand strong. Considering the distinctiveness and legalisms of his brethren to be altogether too lax, he took the step of administering upon himself the operation casually referred to in Matthew 19:12, using a hot iron. This was sometime before 1772, since it was at that date that the authorities took note of his activities, for he had won over a number of followers, of whom thirteen peasants had embraced "the baptism."

Exiled to Siberia in 1775, Ivanov passed himself off as Peter III, the tsar who had been murdered (or rather, as he claimed, not really murdered) by his wife, Catherine the Great. He was far from being the only such impostor, and though few were taken in, he was shown mercy twenty years later and was allowed to live out his days in St. Petersburg. There, alas, Ivanov persuaded many—and not only the poor—to succumb to the peculiar temptations of his favored operation, and he is believed to have performed it personally upon as many as a hundred people. But there were many more who, though they chose to keep themselves intact, nevertheless revered him as a saint and a holy man.

The status accorded the memory of Filipov among the Khlysty was given to Ivanov among the Skoptsy. Whereas the myths about the former made strong parallels between his life and that of Christ, however, the parallels concerning Ivanov were all in the realm of eschatology; his followers expected him to come again. (It should be added that, in a feat of backward projection, they believed Christ had been emasculated, like a good Skopets.) The other beliefs and practices of the Skoptsy were in general one with those of the Khlysty. During the nineteenth century, they numbered in the tens of thousands.

8

THE RISE OF PIETISM

▼

When orthodox faith is under attack from rationalists, when the official churches are led by those more concerned with keeping order than with propagating belief, and when any religious activity outside of those churches is popularly identified with regicide or fanaticism—then the options facing true, devout believers are few indeed. Pietism was one response to this difficulty, yet it was far from unattractive and was to prove enduring in its influence.

What was it? Like *Puritanism*, the word *Pietism* has been credited for much and blamed for more over the years. Pietism stands at the fountainhead of modern evangelicalism—spawning Methodism and, through it, later revivalism and the Pentecostal and charismatic movements. Yet it has also been blamed for nineteenth-century liberal theology and for the passivity of German Christians in the 1930s and 1940s when faced with the Nazi regime. Today, "Pietism" is sometimes used as a put-down by professors in theological colleges, intending thereby to intimidate those students who place more stock in answered prayer than on the pop-philosophy passing itself off as doctrine touted by their instructors.

So what was Pietism originally? It was a form of Christian devotion emerging, for the most part, within the Protestant state churches of continental Europe and emphasizing personal renewal, growth in holiness of life, and actual religious experience of God. That such features should count in any way as distinctive tells us most of what we need to know about the sad state of church life in general. That being so, Pietism should count as a treasure to be cherished, not so much in memory as in emulation.

Arndt and Boehme

The period of the movement's first emergence and the identity of its first leaders are matters of dispute, mainly because there is no complete agreement as to what might count as Pietism. Some point to the devotional writer Johann Arndt (1555–1621) as a forerunner. Son of a pastor from Anhalt and a student at Helmstedt, Wittenberg, Strasbourg, and Basel, he studied under a variety of fiercely conflicting professors, from avid Gnesio-Lutherans to Crypto-Calvinists. As a pastor back in Anhalt, he came into conflict with the Reformed count, John George, in 1590 and was expelled for his failure to remove religious paintings from his church or to cease the traditional use of exorcism at infant baptisms. In his next pastorate at nearby Quedlinburg Arndt won the grudging respect of an ill-disposed population through his devoted faithfulness and pastoral care during attacks of the plague, notably that of 1598, which killed 2,000 of the town's inhabitants. The following year he moved to the St. Martin's church in Brunswick, where for a decade he again found himself caught in the furious crossfire of theologians. "I never thought," he confided in a letter to a friend in 1607, "to find such poisonous, evil people among theologians." That he could make such a remark at the mature age of fifty-two speaks volumes for his sanctity—or his naïveté. In 1611 Arndt was finally called to the position that gave him most satisfaction when the pious Duke Christian of Brunswick-Lüneburg appointed him general superintendent of the churches within his realms.

Arndt is best remembered for his writings, the most important of which was penned during the years of strife and venom in Brunswick and perhaps represents his reaction against it. The four-volume *Wahres Christentum* ("True Christianity") is mystical and devotional in nature, drawing upon the ideas of Bernard of Clairvaux, Johannes Tauler, and Thomas à Kempis. In it, Arndt stresses the importance of the mystical union between the believer and Christ, and he reduces the exaggerated emphasis that the Protestant Reformers had placed upon forensic justification. What is true of Arndt in microcosm—a retreat from confessionalist nastiness and bitter dispute into inwardness and deep relationship with Christ—is a bellwether for later Pietism.

If Arndt is a precursor of Pietism, others consider the mystic Jakob Boehme (1576–1624) to belong to the story also, though that is very contentious. Boehme taught a species of pantheism that postmodern adherents of the New Age have found highly congenial.

A Lutheran shoemaker from Lusatia, with only a basic education, he did not begin writing until 1612, when he was thirty-six years old. His early works caused a sensation, however, even though they were not immediately printed but were circulated in manuscript form. The reasons for the strong interest and for the failure to be printed were one and the same: Boehme's ideas were heretical. The senior pastor denounced him from the pulpit and the municipal council ordered him to desist from writing—an injunction which, until 1618 at least, he obeyed. He then took up his pen again, though his work remained unpublished until *Der Weg zu Christo* ("The Path to Christ") appeared at Görlitz on New Year's Day, 1624, ten months before his death from a short illness. Influenced by Paracelsus, his mysticism was of the kind that tends to spiritualize Christian verities such as heaven and hell: "I have said that Heaven is everywhere present . . . for God is in Heaven; and God is everywhere. I have said also, that Hell must be in like Manner everywhere . . . for the wicked One, who is the Devil, is in Hell; and the whole World, as the Apostle hath taught us, lieth in the wicked One."[1]

Slippery argumentation, this. It also rendered doctrine indistinct and so simultaneously reduced his own vulnerability to confutation and to conviction of heresy: "When the Ground of the Will yieldeth itself up to God, then it sinketh out of its own self, and out of and beyond all Ground and Place that is or can be imagined, into a certain unknown Deep."[2] So that makes everything clear. Suddenly, the mysteries of the Trinity and the incarnation look sharp and hard-edged by comparison.

His admirers were usually those from a higher social milieu than Boehme himself; mysticism has never been a religion of the people. Neither were the masses in early-seventeenth-century Lusatia eager to hear of the seven originating spirits or the three first principles of eternal nature. Boehme's following came from the same groups who had followed Gnosticism in the early centuries of the church, or who had looked to David Joris or the Family of Love in the Netherlands and England in the sixteenth century, or who look to the Moonies or to Scientology now: the spiritually bored among the middle classes. But that was enough to ensure that his writings were translated into Latin, Dutch, and French and, during the Cromwellian Republic, into English.

For understandable reasons, therefore, not all are happy to see Boehme typecast as a trailblazer for Pietism. Yet his rebellion against confessionalism and insistence that Christian faith should rest upon personal transformation and relationship with God, along with the fact that he was read and appreciated by some later Pietists, mean that he has earned at least an honorable mention in the Pietists' pedigree.

Spener and Francke

Less controversially, the laurel is usually handed to Philipp Jakob Spener (1635–1705), a Lutheran pastor in Frankfurt am Main, as pioneer of Pietism. His most famous book, *Pia Desideria* ("Pious Desires"), was published in 1675. In it he argued for Bible study by individuals, each of whom could expect to be illumined by the Holy Spirit; small group meetings to encourage personal spiritual growth; the participation in worship of all believers; and individual expression of actual practical piety.

Like most new movements (whether religious, political, or artistic) in most ages, this was partly a reaction against current trends and partly a reflection of them. On the one hand, it was a reaction against the heavy-handed confessionalism of the Reformation and Counter-Reformation periods and a call for a more practical, applied faith that entailed personal moral and spiritual transformation. To that extent, it was a repudiation of the recent past and much of the present. It was an attempt to escape the aridity to which confessional conflict had led and in which, as Johann Gottfried Herder (1744-1803) later remarked, "Every leaf of the tree of life was so dissected that the dryads wept for mercy." On the other hand, few programs could be calculated to undercut more comprehensively the power claims of institutional officeholders—and so it was a form of modernism.

Philipp Jakob Spener.
Illustration from Daniel Thülens.

On the one hand, Pietism was a reaction against the mere intellectualism of the looming Enlightenment and an appeal to the Holy Spirit and the naked authority of the text of the Word of God. Spener wrote in 1677 that Bible readers "should not let their reason be master." Yet on the other hand, he immediately went on to say that they "should give close attention to the words of the Holy Spirit, how they are framed, compare them with what precedes and follows, consider their meaning, believe that every word is recorded by the Holy Spirit designedly as it is, and also compare the portion read with other passages of Scripture."[3] In other words, they should take a modern, rationalist, contextual approach to the sacred text. Furthermore, by short-circuiting the philosophical arguments of the skeptics and deists, Pietism was, in some ways, capitulating to them and conceding that Christian faith may be rooted in realms impervious to reason.

On the one hand, Pietism avoided many of the doctrinal arguments that had set Christians (or alleged Christians) at one another's throats for over a century and took little notice of debates about the logicality or otherwise of the Trinity or of philosophical arguments about the very possibility of divine revelation or miracles. To that extent, it was anti-modern. On the other hand, it emphasized practicality and pragmatism (those most modern of virtues) in the religious life. Bible readers "should read all with application to themselves, how far it concerns them and may be serviceable for their edification." They should never read the Scriptures without "the purpose to admit a place in themselves for his [the Holy Spirit's] working and power."[4]

The counterweight to philosophically driven debunking of orthodox faith, then, was holy pragmatism: the Bible-centered life works! The pragmatic test had been the response of the Renaissance scholars to the arid, almost faithless scholasticism of the late Middle Ages. It is a quintessentially modernist approach. It represents practical knowledge gained—but only at the expense of putting ultimate epistemological questions on permanent "hold."

Pietism had a strongly egalitarian streak: "God has promised the Holy Spirit to all who call upon him in simplicity and, therefore, not only to the learned," so that they can "understand all in the Scriptures that they need for their salvation and growth in the inner man."[5] Such sentiments needed, in general, to be balanced by a strong ecclesiological and social conservatism if they were to escape imputations of the very "enthusiasm" and subversiveness that most contemporaries feared. Of course, they did not escape such imputations, but the political quietism of Spener and his successors mostly served to stifle them.

Neither did Spener's insistence that disputatiousness should be put to one side mean that doctrinal concerns were entirely eclipsed. Like many another good Protestant, he considered it axiomatic that the Church of Rome was the whore of Babylon spoken of in Revelation. The irenic spirit was, in seventeenth-century experience, not an absolute good, but very much a relative thing.

In the same way, Pietism's latent anti-intellectualism was balanced by a careful emphasis upon the academic life—as long as it was Bible-centered rather than revolving around speculative, philosophically driven theology. The University of Halle was founded in Germany in 1694 to reflect these concerns, and it rapidly became an influential center.

Spener had been appointed court chaplain to the elector of Saxony in 1686, but he soon found himself at the center of a whirlwind of accusations and conflicts between Lutheran factions, on the one hand, and those relating to the underlying tensions between Lutherans and Reformed, on the other. According to his opponents, Spener's call for active discipleship was a derogation from the Reformation doctrine of justification by faith. The latter was by this time being interpreted in a spare, cold sense, admirably conducive to the new role of the Protestant state churches as upholders of social order and respectability. In the process, they had become purveyors of what Dietrich Bonhoeffer, in the twentieth century, would later castigate as "cheap grace"—but which its advocates saw as a necessary fence against the perils of "enthusiasm." Since this last was the principal terror of the generations after 1648, Spener's emphases were perceived by many as far from innocent; they portended danger.

Within a few years Spener's position in the Saxon court had become untenable, and he removed to the rival court of electoral Brandenburg. Prince Frederick III adhered to the Reformed confession but was not ostentatiously pious. The implicit emphasis of Spener's teaching—that personal piety trumped ecclesial authority—suited him well, as did the fact that Spener had annoyed the Saxon authorities. During the early 1690s Spener was given a senior church position in Berlin, where his key students and disciples, most notably August Hermann Francke (1663–1727), were allowed to join him.

Francke became professor of oriental studies at the new University of Halle—an institution that was Brandenburg's erstwhile *Ritterakademie*, handed over to the Pietists by the elector and upgraded. Although it came under fire from the local clergy for being staffed by faculty who were both young and "enthusiasts," the university continued to enjoy princely protection and easily weathered the storm.

August Hermann Francke.
Illustration from Wolffgang, 1729.

Spener died in 1704 and Elector Frederick (who by that time was king of Prussia) a decade later. But their successors, Francke and the devout Frederick William I, cooperated even more closely.

For Francke, as for Spener, theology was of interest—and it *was* of interest—only insofar as it contributed to practical ends: a person in relationship with God, a transformed life, a renewed church, evangelization. The Lutheran Orthodox emphasis upon *reine Lehre*, or pure teaching, as an end in itself (or to confound non-Lutherans) was of no concern to the Pietist leaders, much though they were happy to remain within the fold of the church.

Francke had been converted, when already a young clergyman, through his own sermon preparation. His intention was to preach to his congregation at Lüneburg upon John 20:31, "These are written that you may believe that Jesus is the Christ, the Son of God, and that by believing you may have life in his name." He wanted to apply his text to the distinction between *fides*, a living faith, and mere *assensus*, or assent, to true theological propositions. This, of course, is the identical distinction between Menno Simons's doctrine of justification by faith and that which Simons accused the Protestant Reformers of teaching. But as Francke prepared, he came to the realization that he himself possessed only the latter, formal faith. In the wake of this discovery, he besought God for mercy, and he eventually found "assurance of the grace of God in Jesus Christ." "That, then," he later recollected, "is the time which I may really regard as my true conversion. . . . From that time on it was easy to deny ungodliness and worldly lusts, and to live righteously and joyfully in this world. . . . I now realised that faith as big as a mustard seed is worth more than a hundred bags of erudition."[6]

Unlike the Mennonites, however, Pietists did not conclude from their distinction between living faith and mere assent that the former was church-defining; instead of becoming Separatists, they practiced what has been called *ecclesiola in ecclesiae*, or church-within-the church. The Pietist assemblies and prayer circles met together within the structure of their parishes. Indeed, Francke discerned three levels of commitment: the small inner core; those who have made a start on the journey of faith but lack full commitment; and the outer circle who have no more than the form of godliness.

But it was no part of Pietist principles for the godly to cuddle their blessed experiences in a corner; they aimed to transform both church and world. Francke himself was an organizational genius. His *Grosser Aufsatz*, or "Great Project for a Universal Improvement in All Social Orders," envisaged a plan for rapid social advance driven by education that would prepare its beneficiaries for the bureaucracy and the army. In that sense, it epitomized the spirit of the Enlightenment. It also typified the state-fortifying pragmatism and inculcation of civic duty that would propel Prussia to great-power status during the course of the century; Pietist biblicism and Prussian militarism turn out to be entangled by common threads.

Francke was no mere empty dreamer, and he did far more than theorize:

His Orphan House became one of the wonders of the age, accommodating more than 3,000 people in a factorylike production line of care and instruction.

His dispensary became the first-ever producer of standardized medicines, and advertised itself and its wares across Europe in five languages.

His *Hallesche Zeitung* became the first Prussian newspaper, appearing three times a week.

The Halle printing presses provided Bibles and religious literature in German, Greek, and a variety of Slavic languages in both Roman and Cyrillic script, such that by 1800 one publishing house alone had distributed two and a half million inexpensive Bibles or portions of Scripture.

The University of Halle poured forth a thousand theology graduates annually, while its schools and teacher training institutes produced a myriad trainees at lower levels.

Everything about Halle, that pious reaction against faithless Enlightenment rationalism, spoke of rationalist calculation and pragmatism— and it did so on a scale and in a manner fully worthy of the dawning Industrial Age. The medicines and the publishing could be more or less self-supporting. The charitable appeals, which, together with engagement in all manner of trades and businesses, were necessary to provide the financial underpinning for all of the other enterprises, were as international in scope as the businesses themselves.

The Electorate of Hanover, whose prince was also King George II of Britain, had taken an anti-Pietist line. Even so, when George founded a new university in Göttingen, the minister of state in charge of organizing it, Baron von Münchhausen, was a Pietist sympathizer whose wife had been converted under Francke's influence; the university was given genuine intellectual freedom and exemption from the censorship laws and was soon emulating the Pietism of its rival institution at Halle. Within a few years, its converted students had founded, on the model of Halle, a school for the poor and an orphan house.

Swabia, in southwest Germany, became another center of Pietism during the first half of the eighteenth century—the University of Tübingen being a particular stronghold and training ground for generations of pastors. Johann Albrecht Bengel (1687–1752) was its greatest luminary.

Bengel's father, a Lutheran pastor, had died when the boy was just six and, the family home being destroyed shortly afterward by the tender mercies of Louis XIV's soldiery, he had been reared by a foster father. Devout from a very early age, Bengel had no dateable conversion experience and so, unlike the Halle notables, refrained from commenting or theologizing upon it or from insisting that the "new life" is encountered by any one particular method.

Bengel's overriding religious concern was the interpretation of Scripture. For him, this included first and foremost a reconciliation of the variant Greek texts of the New Testament; where these clashed, they seemed to threaten the integrity and authority of Scripture, the supreme reference point for the content of Christian faith. During a lifetime of teaching and study at Tübingen, Bengel's accumulated scholarship was massive. His primary intention was to reconstruct a New Testament text as close as possible to the original in order to give certainty to Christian pronouncements upon "what the Bible teaches." Bengel's magnum opus was the massive *Gnomon Novi Testamenti* of 1742, which gave variant readings and the critical commentary and techniques to discern between them.

In undertaking this work, Bengel was preparing the groundwork for the textual critics of the nineteenth century, so many of whom would undermine the authority of the very Scriptures he had sought to shore up. For the sometimes besieged German evangelicals of the late twentieth and early twenty-first centuries, he remains a hero who undertook critical, scientific study while yet coming to orthodox conclusions.

Orthodox, that is, except in one respect. Bengel's eschatological studies, undertaken entirely in a scholarly fashion and without the least influence from inspirationism or neo-Gnostic ideas, led him to the firm conclusion that the second coming was scheduled for 1836. Such was his authority in other areas that many believed him.

By the turn of the new century, however, Pietism had spread, with or without Bengel's aberrations and despite encountering resistance in most cases, throughout the Protestant state churches in Germany, Holland, Switzerland, and Scandinavia and also to the Germanic settlements in North America. The influence of Francke and the University of Halle continued to broaden through the launching of missions to South India, to the East Indies, and to the settlers in the New World.

Zinzendorf and Herrnhut

The eccentric nobleman Nikolaus Ludwig, Count von Zinzendorf (1700–1760), also played a major role in disseminating the Pietist movement, and especially in orientating it toward mission. His father died when Zinzendorf was a baby and, when his mother remarried, the young count was raised by a grandmother inclined to Pietism and Boehme's mysticism. While a student at Halle from 1710 to 1716, where he was taught by Francke, Zinzendorf was involved in a secret society, the Order of the Grain of Mustard Seed, whose aristocratic members pledged to use their positions in society to further the cause of the gospel. (When he resurrected the society years later, its members eventually came to include the archbishops of Paris and Canterbury and the king of Denmark.) During this period, Zinzendorf was torn between his desire to train for the ministry and the social expectations placed upon him by his hereditary role as a count.

After completing his studies, Zinzendorf went on the "Grand Tour" from 1719 to April 1720. This was a sort of early version of backpacking, but more civilized and restricted to aristocrats. Like its modern equivalent, it was designed as a diversion from the threat of useful work for those who could afford it; unlike the present, it was also intended to add a veneer of culture to those who undertook it. In Zinzendorf's case, it changed—or rather, focused—the direction of his life, for in Düsseldorf he saw Domenico Feti's painting of Christ crucified, *Ecce Homo*, bearing the legend, "This have I done for you—Now what will you do for me?" The young Zinzendorf was transfixed and, in a mystical experience, dedicated his life to serving the Savior.

Back home in 1722, Zinzendorf invited the persecuted Moravian Brethren (descendants, by way of several twists and turns, of Petr Chelčický's radical

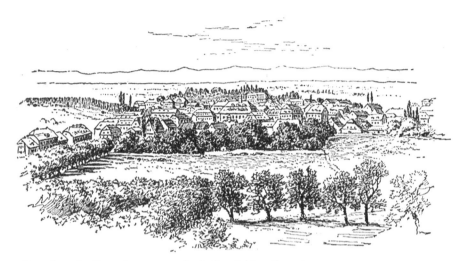

Herrnhut, the Moravian community, in the eighteenth century.
Illustration from *John Wesley the Methodist*, 1903.

branch of Hussitism from the fifteenth century) to cross the border and
take refuge on his estates in Saxony. Over the next few years the settlement, known as Herrnhut ("The Lord's Watch"), continued to receive a
bewildering variety of religious refugees from official persecution. Their
benefactor did not rest content with providing them shelter and then leaving them to shift for themselves; he took an active part in the religious
life and direction of the community, including the leadership of Bible
studies. The tensions created by the diversity of refugees, however, were
palpable. But in 1727, the entire community was shaken by a profound
spiritual awakening, triggered by guilt at their divisions, by their production of a document laying down basic Christian behavior to which all were
expected to conform, by the testimony of an adolescent girl, and, finally,
on 13 August, by a dramatic communion service in which there was an
overwhelming communal sense of the presence of God.

Four years later, following Zinzendorf's encounter with a West Indian
slave at the coronation of Christian VI of Denmark, the Herrnhuters
began their engagement with foreign missions. Beginning with work
in the West Indies, they later expanded to Africa, Greenland, and the
Americas. During the decades that followed, Herrnhut witnessed an
outpouring of missionaries preaching the necessity of new birth.

Zinzendorf traveled to several of these mission fields himself, seeking to evangelize the North American Indians, founding the town of
Bethlehem, Pennsylvania, and trying to persuade German Protestants in

North America to cooperate with one another. Despite his irenic inter-denominational position, some of his own measures were very contro-versial. As with the Wesleys in England (who had been converted under Moravian influence and who visited him at home in Herrnhut), under Zinzendorf's tutelage the Moravians permitted women to preach and to be ordained. This provoked sharp criticism from outside the community. But Zinzendorf's emphasis upon spiritual inspiration made this a logical step; if the Holy Spirit convicts, speaks to, and inspires all alike, then why may not women be involved in church leadership? It was a logic that Pentecostals were to follow in the twentieth century.

Pietism was, perhaps, one of the most important healthy signs for the future. In its insistence that prayer and mutual love should over-come theological wrangling, in its preference for religious experience and discipleship over doctrine, and in Spener's and Francke's emphasis upon the need for *Wiedergeburt*—being born again—Pietism is indeed "proto-evangelicalism."

The German Presence in Central and Eastern Europe

There is a certain game that would soon be over if played with an English-language map of Europe: How many towns and cities can we find whose name in English is written (rather than merely pronounced) differently from the official name in that country's language? A high proportion of capitals would count: the Hague (in the Netherlands), Brussels (Belgium), Copenhagen (Denmark), Rome (Italy), Prague (Czech Republic), Warsaw (Poland), Moscow (Russia), and many others. So too would a number of ancient Italian cities: Venice, Florence, Padua, Genoa, Naples, and a few more besides. There would be some German and Swiss cities: Cologne, Munich, and Nuremberg in Germany; Geneva and Berne in Switzerland, as well as several others. And then the game would be over.

To play the same game in German, however, would take several days. Countless cities, towns, and even villages across central and eastern Europe would bear different names in German than those of their Polish, Russian, Czech, Slovak, Hungarian, Romanian, Croatian, or Serbian equivalents—differences frequently much greater than those entailed in the English examples we have given.

The fact reflects one of the underlying social realities of Europe until modern times—a reality that, in the aftermath of World War II, has become nearly unsayable— namely, that many of the towns and, in the Russian Empire from the late eighteenth century onward, some of the

RUSSIA

● Novgorod

● Moscow

Volga

EDEN

C SEA

PRUSSIA

Don

● Warsaw

POLAND

HUNGARY

OTTOMAN EMPIRE

BLACK SEA

MONTENEGRO

Constantinople

The Church
in Europe
ca. 1700.

more prosperous villages were German-speaking islands in a Slavic (or Magyar or Romanian) sea. It was a situation that had come about since the central and late Middle Ages, backed by the political and military, but even more by the commercial, power of the Holy Roman Empire and its successor states. In much of central Europe, for example, this phenomenon is explained simply by the existence of the Hapsburg Empire, in which German was the most important language of the governing classes, and the movement within its frontiers of German-speakers was relatively unproblematic. But it was furthered also by the economic enterprise of the eastern European Jews, whose Yiddish language was a variant (sometimes a minimal one) of German.

The Reformation had caused the German diaspora to act as a conduit for the spread of Protestantism, for example in Bohemia and in the Hungarian lands. The advent of Pietism led to a repetition of the process. The awakening in the crossroads territory of Teschen, between Silesia and Moravia, for example, was furthered by Francke and his colleagues in Halle and touched first and foremost the German speakers of that territory and thousands of others who flocked to it for some relief from the official pressure of Catholicism. Yet it performed the same function for Czechs, Slovaks, and Poles, along with others, who came for the same reasons.

Pietism among the German-Baltic aristocracy would eventually bring biblicism to the Russian court; German settlers in the countryside would become, in the nineteenth century, the seedbed for Russian and Ukrainian evangelicalism. It was a process that would be repeated across central and eastern Europe.

One series of local evangelical awakenings in early-eighteenth-century Siberia had particularly remarkable beginnings: it took place among Swedish prisoners of war who had fought against Russia at the Battle of Pultava in 1709. About 20,000 soldiers and 10,000 civilian camp followers were among those captured and taken to Tobolsk, to the east of the Urals in Russian central Asia, passing by Moscow on the way. Although Swedish King Charles XII had fiercely resisted the encroachments of Pietist "enthusiasm" in his own country, he was powerless to prevent its spread among his soldiers held prisoner by the enemy. One of the most influential army chaplains, Curt Friedrich von Wreech, underwent a spiritual crisis that made him instrumental in leading a religious awakening among the prisoners. It happened shortly after he passed through Moscow, where he spent time with two pastors to the German community there, Thomas Roloff and Justus Samuel Scharschmid; both had good connections with Francke in Halle. Their ministrations to the Swedish prisoners passing through the city had already led to the conversion of a number of them. Von Wreech then subsequently experienced a similar crisis after being proffered books by Luther, Arndt, and Francke. In company with a German captain from the Swedish army, von Wreech's preaching caused many of the prisoners to be converted. Francke's machine kicked into action, sending religious literature and medicines to support the work, via the Germans in Moscow. Emissaries carried the work to other prison camps. Faithful to the Halle model, a school was begun in Tobolsk (for women and children were among the captive camp followers), which soon attracted children of the native Russian aristocrats.

The project was only temporary. In the early 1720s the prisoners went home and their institutions closed. But the influences lingered, and the reach of the German Pietist diaspora continued.

In the Baltic, the German aristocracy had made themselves unpopular with many of the natives. They had achieved this by reinforcing, with Russian help, the conditions of serfdom that the temporary Swedish hegemony in the area had been on the point of sweeping away. But even this was not sufficient to make the people of the Baltic regions entirely immune to the influences of German Pietists. The arrival in East Prussia and adjacent areas of Lithuania of many Protestant refugees from Salzburg in 1732 led a number of Lithuanians to convert. The arrival of Moravian refugees in Livonia (Latvia) and Estonia had similar effects, though the old paganism of those countries, the last in Europe to be Christianized, was in its lively death throes. Zinzendorf visited Livonia in 1736, establishing a seminary for Latvian teachers on the estate of Wolmarshof (*Valmiera* in Latvian), which belonged to a family friend.

By the following decade the majority of the clergy in the Baltic region were Pietists. Local revivals, such as that in Urbs, Estonia, in 1736, continued throughout the late 1730s and early 1740s among Letts and Estonians. By 1742, 14,000 of these, the majority Estonians, had joined themselves to the communion of the Moravian Brethren. In 1742 a revival among both Estonians and Germans in the village of Uppa bei Arensburg spread throughout the neighboring district and had such a powerful effect that the local court had no cases come before it for the entire period of 1740–1745.

In 1743, however, the Tsarina Elizabeth, intolerant of schismatics, forbade the Moravians to meet. Three of the local Pietist clergy were arrested, of whom one died in prison in 1750, another died in exile in Kazan in 1760, and the third was released two years later. Revivals broke out again, however, in the 1770s and 1780s. When Tsar Alexander I, a staunch friend of Pietism, legalized them again in 1817, 30,000 members in 144 congregations emerged at once from the murk of a subterranean existence.

9

THE CROSS, THE CRESCENT, AND THE STAR

CHRISTIANS AND JEWS
UNDER OTTOMAN RULE IN THE BALKANS

The extent to which the presence of Islam impinged upon Christians' consciousness of themselves and their place in the world has already been remarked upon. For some Christians, of course, Islam impinged upon their daily existence a good deal more forcefully than upon others. These were those who lived under Islamic rule in the Balkans and southeast Europe. We shall now have cause to notice them more closely.

The Turkish peoples came originally from central Asia—where many of them still live. From the ninth century onward, numbers of them had drifted westward, principally as warriors. From the Abbasid caliphs of Baghdad, under whom they took military service, they learned Islam. During the twelfth to fourteenth centuries, they moved into the rotting remains of the Byzantine Empire in Asia Minor—the area that would ultimately come to be named after them.

During the fourteenth and fifteenth centuries the Turks conquered the Byzantine territories in the Balkans, as well as the Bulgarian, Serbian, and Bosnian kingdoms and, in 1453, Byzantium itself. The 1520s brought into their possession most of Croatia, as well as Vojvodina, Transylvania, and the larger part of Hungary. Millions of European Christians, Orthodox and Catholic alike, thus found themselves under the rule of the infidel.

The blow, however, did not fall evenly upon the two confessions as a whole. The large majority of Balkan Christians adhered to Eastern Orthodoxy, not to Catholicism. Of Greek Christendom, only Russia and Ukraine remained beyond the Muslim yoke, and they had already endured pagan rule under the Mongols, a yoke which was only gradually supplanted by the rising power of Orthodox Muscovy. The fact that Turkish rule was to last so long in southeastern Europe (400 years in most areas, though as little as 175 in Pannonia and well over 500 in Macedonia) further deepened the gulf—already deep enough—between the experience and outlook of Eastern and Western churches. It continues to leave its mark even today.

Constantinople, it should be said, did not instantly—or even quickly—become a Turkish city. Even in the late nineteenth century, its population remained 50 percent Greek. De-Hellenization was achieved only much later by twentieth-century Greek and Turkish nationalism and the inability to live together that nationalism engendered. For Ottoman rule, though it could be extremely ruthless, had this much in its favor: it did provide a means of coexistence for a bewildering variety of races, religions, and tongues.

It was, of course, a coexistence on Muslim, Ottoman terms. All legal advantages were with those who adhered to Islam. Non-Muslims were expected to dress differently from Muslims and were forbidden to carry weapons. Muslims themselves were more likely to be burdened with military service, but they had legal advantages, and their testimony had greater value in court than did that of a nonbeliever. Non-Muslims suffered various indignities: they were required to dismount, if on horseback, when approaching a Muslim, and their churches had to be lower than any mosque in the same settlement.

Some churches were destroyed in the aftermath of conquest. Such was the fate of St. Naum, on the site of the monastery established by that saint in A.D. 900, south of Ohrid in Macedonia. But a new one was allowed to be constructed there in the sixteenth century. However, the cathedral church of St. Sophia, in Ohrid itself, was converted into a mosque, and its priceless frescoes and murals were whitewashed over; it was not to be reclaimed for the Christians until 1912. Hagia Sophia in Constantinople itself, a church that was one of the wonders of the world, suffered a similar fate and remains today firmly beyond the Christians' grasp. Because of that church's symbolic value for the overthrown Byzantines, it was confiscated immediately after the conquest in 1453, while the city's other churches (that is to say, those that had survived the violence of the siege and the ensuing carnage) were left unmolested for the time being. One by one, however, most churches were taken over and converted for Muslim worship or for secular uses, or else they were demolished and replaced by mosques. Mehmet II's respect for Hellenic culture and its faith was not inherited by his successors, for whom the Greeks represented just one more infidel subject people whee-dling for privileges on the basis of a historic prestige that seemed to count for little in the present. Although the capital boasted forty Greek churches in the eighteenth century, only three of them were continuing legacies of the Byzantine past; the rest were *Neubau* (newly built). Other major cities, such as Salonica and Athens, experienced the same tendencies, especially in respect of the centrally positioned, high-status places of worship; only in the Christian suburbs were churches left undisturbed.[1]

Above all, non-Muslims were subject to a poll tax. It was this that encouraged an incessant trickle effect of conversions to Islam during the centuries of Ottoman rule. Although Ottoman subjects could change their faith, apostasy from Islam was punishable by death. So conversion was effectively a one-way street.

The *devşirme* was one route of conversion to Islam. Christian popula-tions were subject to this cruel form of taxation, exacted during the early period of Ottoman rule, which was levied, not in money, but in human beings. Under the *devşirme*, young boys of about the age of fourteen were taken from their families, forcibly converted to Islam, and recruited into the janissaries, the sultan's crack troops. By the time the practice was discontinued in the early seventeenth century, perhaps 200,000 Bosnian boys had been taken in this way. There were also occasional—but rare and local—bouts of forced conversions. Mostly, however, Islamization was just the cumulative trickle effect of several centuries.

Conversion to Islam was particularly strong in areas where Catholicism and Orthodoxy had been in competition, such as in Bosnia and Albania. But it was also very marked in the Sandžak of Novi Pazar (that is, the area between Serbia and Montenegro), in Thrace (the area of Europe that today still remains a part of modern Turkey), and in Crete, which was not captured until the mid-seventeenth century but had been largely Islamized a hundred years later. Surveys of the Muslim population of Bosnia show it to have been around 45 percent during the 1520s and an actual majority by 1600.[2]

In most places, the rate of conversion was far less than this, but it existed everywhere. The names of Islamized Slavs, Greeks, and Romanians generally kept a non-Turkish form, so that records show Slavic Muslim sons of Christian fathers in one generation ("Hasan Mihailović") and then the perpetuation of the Slav patronymic form in the next generation ("Sulejman Hasanović").

Overall, it is the mutability of individuals' religious identities in this period that is most striking. Many Jews converted to Islam because their greater involvement in trade made the financial inducements more appealing. Nevertheless, one French traveler noted that "if a Jew desired to become a Muslim, he would not be accepted unless he previously had been baptized, that is, had become a Christian." In the second half of the seventeenth century, one group of Jews from Salonica and Bitola gave a splendid lesson in sincere pragmatism by turning to Islam and then later, after their relocation to Italy, either reverting to Judaism or converting to Christianity.

The various religious communities were largely self-governing (or at least, self-administering). The Ottomans governed their *reaya* (literally, flock) by dividing them along religious lines into *millets*. The Muslim *millet* included all Muslims, regardless of language. The Rum, or Orthodox *millet*, included administrative control over all Orthodox Christians as well as all Roman Catholics within the Ottoman realms. This control was exercised by the Greek patriarch in Constantinople since the Bulgarian patriarchate centered in Ohrid and the Serbian centered in Peć had been abolished by Mehmed II in the mid-fifteenth century—a point that was to store up resentments for the future. The Yahudi, or Jewish *millet* was administered by the chief rabbi (*Hakham Bashi*) in Constantinople. The Armenian *millet*, subject to the Gregorian (Armenian Orthodox) patriarch, included everybody else: Armenians, gypsies and (mostly further east) Assyrians, Monophysites and Copts, Maronites of Lebanon, Uniate Armenians of Cilicia and Palestine.

Jews in the Ottoman Empire

The empire had a large, thriving Jewish population. The original Romaniot Jews had mostly welcomed the Turks as liberators from the anti-Semitism of the Byzantines. The Ottomans were quick to spot the commercial advantages of giving the Jews freedom to operate; the *millet* system gave the latter a sense of self-government while yet remaining under the canopy of final Ottoman control.

The fact that Jewish emigrants from Christendom flocked to the Ottoman realms tells its own story. They were not subject to bouts of persecution as they were in Christendom, and as a result many fled to Constantinople and the Balkans, especially after the expulsion of the Jews (300,000 of them) from Spain in 1492. Jews from Sicily and southern Italy, Portugal, and Provence were also driven out during the same decade, and many of these also made their way east. Most of the newcomers were Sephardic Jews (i.e., Iberian in culture and speaking Ladino); almost all were urban. Salonica, in particular, became a largely Jewish city, its Sephardic inhabitants outnumbering the Christians by three to one by the early eighteenth century.[3] This city, the "mother of Israel," kept its huge Jewish population until the catastrophe of the Nazi Holocaust of the 1940s. There were also large Sephardic Jewish communities in Bitola and Skopje. Together with the Armenians, Jews often dominated trade in the Ottoman Empire, but they also brought with them many kinds of technical knowledge: medicine, crafts, manufacturing, financial expertise, linguistic skills. The combination of (mostly) decent treatment at the hands of the Turks along with a strong awareness by the Jews themselves of the alternative from which they had escaped meant that the sultan could be very sure of their loyalty.

The Jewish population was supplemented, from time to time, by influxes of Askenazim (i.e., Jews of German culture and speaking Yiddish). This trend was particularly marked during the sixteenth century and later, in the years leading up to and during the Thirty Years' War (1618–1648).

None of this is to deny the frictions and mistreatment that could occur. Jewish industriousness did indeed bring benefits to the Ottoman economy, but sultans, like other premodern rulers, were only dimly aware of such abstractions; they were much more impressed by the benefits that Jewish commercial enterprise brought to the Porte (the government of the Ottomon Empire) in the form of tax revenues. This was another constant of premodern societies; merchants were more vulnerable to the fiscal depredations of government than were peasants, simply because so much of their wealth was in the form of cash. (The massive commercialization of Western societies since the Industrial Revolution has been, for precisely this reason, a godsend to the taxman.) The only restraint upon government rapaciousness, then as now, was the danger of killing the goose that lays the golden egg. The list of taxes exacted from Jewish traders was very long, and it sometimes led to protests and, even more often, to attempts at evasion. Evasion, if detected, was simply asking for trouble, but even protests could be dangerous. When Rabbi Judah

Kovo was sent by his community to Constantinople in 1637 to protest against the level of taxation on broadcloth in Salonica, his petition was refused by the sultan, who, to save the expense of the rabbi's return journey, had him hanged.

Nor was this all. Unruly janissaries often mistreated Jews. Bandits also made them a particular target, making the transport of goods a risky business and sometimes paralyzing commercial activities. Jewish women, who had a reputation among both Turkish rulers and in Macedonian folk-songs as being famously beautiful, were particular targets for abduction by Muslims.[4] Jews were required to live in their own quarters and were forbidden to inhabit anywhere close to a Muslim religious school (*medresa*), dervish lodge (*tekke*), or bath (*hamam*). A host of regulations prohibited Jews from flaunting their wealth by wearing fine clothes or jewelery and thereby offending the sensibilities of their less enterprising Muslim rulers.

Ecclesiastical Corruption and Islamization

Each *millet* had its own legal system and courts, which governed all cases involving two parties from the same *millet*. (If the parties came from different *millets*, then Muslim law predominated.) Ecclesiastical courts had full legal powers in matters of marriage, divorce, and inheritance. The Ottomans also imposed corporate responsibility on *millets*, towns, and trade organizations, so that it would be in the self-interest of the building-blocks of society to stifle dissent and resistance at the root. In this way, local, traditional institutions were co-opted into instruments of rule. This had the further effect, hardly unintentional, of corrupting the churches as they were used, for example, in the collection—and even assessment—of taxes. Yet the clergy themselves were given an exemption from the *kharadj*, the poll tax levied upon non-Christians. It was a surefire way of binding the clergy to the sultan while simultaneously robbing them of any possible moral high ground vis-à-vis their own flocks.

If the sultans had been unaware before the conquest of the benefits of ecclesiastical financial corruption, then it was a lesson they learned early, for within a few decades of the capture of Constantinople, the Greek patriarchate became the subject of chronic, competitive simony. The sultan received the bribes; the obvious source of recouping them was from the lower rungs of the ecclesiastical ladder, from bishops and other office holders who recouped their own payments in the same way—and ultimately from ordinary Christians—until the whole edifice was corrupt. When sultans came to demand an annual payment from the patriarch, in addition to that given upon taking up office, the downward path accelerated. The average tenure of a patriarch during the seventeenth century was just twenty months (though many served for multiple reigns). Since the average sum paid to the sultan upon election was 20,000 piastres, this amounted to a revenue from the Phanar (the seat of the Greek patriarch in Constantinople) of 1,000 piastres a month.[5] By 1672 Sir Paul Ricaut noted that the patriarchal office owed more to the Porte than it could easily meet the interest payments for.

In addition to financial corruption, clergy at all levels were weighed down (or perhaps privileged, according to point of view) with all manner of administrative authority over their flocks. The lives of ordinary Christians depended upon their priests, and differences between them tended to be fought out within the realm of the church. At the highest level, this process tended to dovetail with the aforementioned simony, as Wallachian princes, the monks of Mount Athos, the kings of Georgia, and the wealthy Greek merchants of Constantinople all vied for influence over appointments to the patriarchate.

The secular governors and administrators in the empire were, of course, generally Muslims—either individuals who were imported into an area or else recruited from among those who had converted from the local population. In consequence, the towns of the Balkans were much more strongly Muslim than the countryside.

The tendency for towns to adapt more quickly to major cultural and political changes, however, is a universal trend. When the original apostles, recorded in the book of Acts, carried out their missions, they headed for the population centers, made converts, and then moved on, allowing the new churches to evangelize their own rural backyards. The pattern continued during the next three centuries so that when the late Roman Empire ceased persecuting the church and adopted Christianity as its official religion, it was the country people who were the last to conform to the new faith. The Roman word for "rural," *paganus* or "pagan" (cf. French *pays*, English *peasant*) remains as a linguistic fossil of that process. When the Arabs invaded North Africa in the seventh century, it was the towns that first abandoned Christianity and succumbed to Islam. When the Soviet Bolsheviks tried to wipe out all religion during the twentieth century, it was the *babushkas* in the countryside who clung to the ancestral faith; similarly, when Communism itself collapsed, it was the aspiring middle classes in the big cities who embraced capitalism with most fervor, while the countryside often remained the electoral stronghold of *stari kommunisti* and assorted postcommunist strongmen.

Always, the urban centers embraced innovation early on; the countryside lagged behind for as long as possible.

So it is no surprise that it was the towns of the Ottoman Balkans that were Islamized first. One long-term consequence is that, even today, Bosnian Muslims are strongly concentrated in cities like Sarajevo, whereas the Bosnian Serbs (i.e., Orthodox) tend to be most numerous among peasants in the villages.

Syncretism

One favored line of Muslim proselytizing was to stress the similarity of Christianity and Islam. A seventeenth-century Franciscan in Kosovo reported in scandalized tones:

> Those impious people also said that the difference between them and the Christians was small; "After all," they said, "we all have only one God, we venerate your Christ as a prophet and holy man, we celebrate many of the festivals of your saints with you, and you celebrate Friday, our festive day; Mohammed and Christ are brothers. . . ." And this error was so widespread, that in the same family one person would be Catholic, one Muslim and one Orthodox.[6]

Many Catholics did indeed celebrate Friday. They did this in order not to grate with the Muslims and promoted the cult of *Sancta Veneranda* (or, more plainly, Saint Friday) to justify it. Trimming on this scale clearly took the utter ignorance of ordinary believers for granted.

One might think that Muslim arguments of the kind cited by the Franciscan would make people more unlikely to change their religion. (After all, if all religions are really the same, why bother to change?) But in fact the long-term effect was the opposite: once a person had accepted that Muslims, too, could be saved, the reasons for hanging onto Christianity, when the *practical* advantages (in terms of tax, legal benefits, etc.) all pointed the other way, seemed weaker. The closing of some monasteries and churches and their conversion into mosques shortly after the invasion left some people isolated from any nearby church.

In general, Orthodoxy among the masses was often reduced to "folk religion" even more than was the case in rural Catholic areas of Europe. This owed something to the lack of theological education of so many of the clergy, since the university in Constantinople and many of the provincial academies had collapsed at, or shortly after, the conquest. All that remained was the Patriarchal Academy, attached to the Phanar, and a body of expatriate scholars in the Greek diaspora—most notably in Venice, where an academy was attached to the Greek church.[7] Indeed, it was this last point—the tendency of many Greek scholars and would-be scholars to base their activities in Italy and the West, which did something to temper the anti-Western bent of senior Orthodox clerics and to mitigate the isolation of the Greek church from developments in the Catholic (and, later, also the Protestant) world. Under the influence of men who had studied in Padua and Rome, the Patriarchal Academy began to upgrade its own curriculum from the late sixteenth century onward.

Even so, scholars became the exception rather than the rule; the standards of the academy were not replicated elsewhere until an Athenian academy was established toward the end of the sixteenth century. A number of schools, offering a more basic education, were founded in the Balkans during the seventeenth century, but permission for their existence depended, not upon imperial policy, but upon the wishes of local governors, who were often unenthusiastic about promoting the education of subject infidels. In Asia Minor and the eastern provinces, such schools were even fewer and further between. The best Greek education in the eighteenth centuries was provided by those situated within Hellenic cultural space but outside—technically or actually—Ottoman political control. This left the semiautonomous Danubian provinces of Moldavia and Wallachia, where academies flourished in Iaşi and Bucharest respectively, and the Venetian-controlled Ionian islands.[8] Certainly the ignorance of most ordinary clergy struck visitors from western Europe forcibly. The longstanding truism about "the learned East and the barbarian West"—a perception that preceded the rise of Christianity itself and a contrast that had been at its most stark during the Middle Ages—became a thing of the past.

The "Christianity" of many ordinary folk was in any case simply folk Christianity, and so not too different from folk Islam. Holiness, blessings, and curses were associated with various places, holy men, dates, celebrations, and rituals; the theological content put upon any or all of these was a secondary consideration—and sometimes not even that.

The Turks on the island of Lemnos, for example, turned out dutifully to observe the Christians making cakes of earth on the Feast of the Transfiguration and using them as a cure for dysentery and snakebites or as a balm for wounds. Ogier Ghiselin de Busbecq, a traveler around the year 1555, noted this and recorded the Turks' approval: "The ancients, they say, knew and could see more than they can, and customs which they approved ought not to be wantonly disturbed." Many Muslims in

Kosovo sought Christian baptism because they believed it would help them to live longer, protect them from mental illness and from being eaten by wolves, and save them from smelling like dogs.[9] (Whether this last belief in salvation from body odor is an indication that full immersion—with soap—was practiced may be doubted.)

Syncretism of this kind was common, especially because Constantinople often exiled its mystics, such as the Sufis and dervishes, to the Balkans—and the Islamic mystics tended to be the most syncretistic of Muslims. One group who took this process furthest of all was the Bektashi, a movement that was particularly popular among the janissaries, many of whom had, of course, been brought up as Christians and then forcibly converted as adolescents. Ostensibly Muslim, the Bektashi allowed the drinking of wine, ignored the fast of Ramadan, and had a quasi-trinitarian theology. At a more moderate level, however, many ordinary Bosnian Muslims drank *raki* (a Turkish liquor), and their women often did not wear the veil.

Catholics in Kosovo lent holy oil to their Muslim neighbors because of the belief among the latter that it protected children from eye infections. When Pjetër Bogdani, a Catholic envoy, visited Prizren in 1681, he preached at a mountaintop celebration observed (with slightly differing rationales, to be sure) by Muslims, Catholics, and Orthodox alike, and afterward he was wined and dined by the local Orthodox bishop. Good relations between Catholics and Muslims at the local level extended to the habit of the former appointing some of the latter as godfathers to their children.

Perhaps there is more to this striking instance of intercommunal intimacy than meets the eye, for many men in Kosovo, northern Albania, and Constantinople itself turned Muslim for official purposes (i.e., to avoid the poll tax) while their wives remained Christians. When priests were invited to the house, ostensibly to minister to the wives, the husbands also partook of the ministrations, including sacraments. One priest in Kosovo in 1651 recorded with disapproval, "Some of the men (and there are very many of these) say: 'We are Christians in our hearts, we have only changed our religious affiliation to get out of paying the taxes which the Muslims imposed on us,' and for this reason they say . . . 'dear Reverend, come and give us confession and Holy Communion secretly.'"[10]

Both Orthodox Church authorities and Catholic popes strongly disapproved of practices of this sort and tried to forbid priests and junior bishops from giving the sacraments under these circumstances—but their protests were in vain. Such pretences (known technically as "Crypto-Christianity") were sometimes kept up in families for generations, with their descendants emerging as open Christians in the nineteenth century.

Not All Christians Are Equal

The Ottomans favored the Orthodox Church over the Catholic for a variety of reasons, some of which were identical for the same preference shown by Communist regimes during the twentieth century. In the first place, Eastern Orthodoxy had no ties of obedience and loyalty to anyone outside Ottoman territory. The believers looked to the Greek patriarch in Constantinople, who could not help but be a compliant tool of state. In the second place, Orthodoxy in its own nature had always emphasized loyalty to secular government in much more unconditional terms than had the Roman Church. (Indeed, the second reason is hardly unconnected to the first; Orthodoxy had no independent power-base from which to exert political—or even moral—leverage upon government.)

The other reason for this preference for Eastern Orthodoxy over Catholicism was more peculiar to the Ottoman situation—though one can discern yet further parallels with the twentieth-century Cold War. The long-term antipathy between Greeks and Romans made the Orthodox loyal subjects of the sultan in most conflicts with the European powers. (In the same way, the resources of Orthodox resentment toward the Catholic West would later provide a fund upon which the Communist Soviet, Romanian, and Bulgarian regimes were able to draw in ruling their culturally Orthodox populations.) Anti-Westernism was an important requirement for any serious candidate for the patriarchal throne.

The Christians who occupied perhaps the most prominent place in the Ottoman Balkans were those who were Greek-speaking. They, along with the Albanians, dominated maritime trade and the fleet (for the Ottomans were soldiers, not sailors). All the coasts of the Aegean Sea and its countless islands were populated principally by Greek-speakers—a situation that did not change significantly until the massive bloodletting of 1922–1923. The relatively high numbers of educated people in the Byzantine realms meant that Greeks continued to be influential in administration, and very many official interpreters (dragoman) were Greeks. From the early eighteenth century the tributary principalities of Wallachia and Moldavia (in modern Romania) were, for example, governed by Ottoman-placed Greek hospodars (governors). Above all,

Greeks dominated senior church positions, even in Slav- and Romanian-speaking areas. The prominent—especially ecclesiastical—Greeks were referred to as Phanariots, after the Phanar district of Constantinople from which so many had originally come, and where the patriarch was—and is—based.

All of this gave influential Greek-speakers a great stake in the Ottoman Empire. It became possible to think of it as a continuation of the Byzantine Christian realm it had supplanted—or at least as a protector of Greek and Orthodox cultural space against the encroachments of the Catholic West. Despite this Greek domination and the previously mentioned corruption, the church identified with local populations throughout the Balkans and, in the long run, became a seedbed for the eventual mutation of religious identity into national identity in modern times.

One exception to the pattern of Greek domination is the case of the Serbian church. Mehmed Sokolović (Mehmet Sokollı in Turkish) was a Bosnian who had been drafted in the *devşirme* as a boy and rose to become grand vizier (1565–1579) under Suleiman the Magnificent. While still only a senior vizier in 1557, he managed to have the patri-archate at Peć reinstated, with his brother Makarije as patriarch. Yet the later, eighteenth-century alliance of Porte and Phanar eventually proved too strong: the patriarchate of Peć was suppressed again in 1766 (though it had been in the hands of Greeks for a generation in any case); that of Ohrid followed shortly afterward. All church schools gave instruction in Greek; Slavic and Romanian pupils who attended them frequently came to see themselves as Greeks and their mother tongue as a mere uncouth dialect for the peasantry from which they had escaped.[11]

The Hellenization process was helped in Moldavia and Wallachia (the Romanian-speaking provinces) by their political situation. As quasi-autonomous principalities, they provided a potential haven for Phanariot wealth; property held there would be safe from the ever-present danger of peremptory confiscation by the sultan. Wealthy Greeks from Constantinople had the same insight, and during the sixteenth and seventeenth centuries, many of them married into the Moldavian and Wallachian nobility and invested in land. The establishment of Greek academies in major cities we have already noticed. And the local princes took pride in being the last remnant of the Byzantine world with any independence from the Turks; it suited them to have so much attention from the Phanar and from wealthy Greeks, as a confirmation of their fantasies—that they represented a continuation of the Eastern Roman Empire.[12]

The Beginnings of Muslim Retreat

The beginnings of the reversal of the Muslim tide are clearly discernible from the late seventeenth century. Though many of the territorial gains of the Christian powers, principally Austria, were short-lived, there could be no doubt after the campaigns of 1689–1690 that Ottoman power was on the wane.

In 1689 the Austrian armies broke through the Turkish defenses and swept the enemy back hundreds of miles south of the Danube. The victorious Christians briefly found themselves chasing the Turks into Kosovo and Macedonia. In Kosovo some Serbs, including Patriarch Arsenije III, rose in support of the Christian invaders, in a rare instance of ignoring Orthodox-Catholic distinctions. Many more, though, viewed the Catholic invaders with suspicion. Those who chose to revolt, however, soon came to feel that they should have kept their prejudices intact; to their dismay, the Austrians' military gains were reversed as swiftly as they had been made. The Kosovo Serbs who had rebelled, justly fearing Ottoman reprisals, joined the retreating Hapsburg armies heading north.

Thus began the Orthodox admixture to the population of Vojvodina, a large, fertile, flat land immediately to the north of the Danube that remained, until 1919, a part of southern Hungary. This episode, the so-called *Velika Seoba* (Great Exodus), has passed into Serbian folklore as a key stage in the history of the martyred nation. The events of 1689 are perhaps more important today than they were at the time: various late-nineteenth- and early-twentieth-century nationalist depictions of the *seoba* are ubiquitous in Serbian homes, public buildings, calendars, and publications, with Patriarch Arsenije III leading his flock wearisomely and sadly into exile from Kosovo, "the heart of the Serbian lands."

The numbers involved in this migration have often been exaggerated, and they may not have far exceeded 50,000 or so. It is quite possible, however, that it was from this time that Albanian speakers began to outnumber Slav speakers in Kosovo; certainly, modern Serb nationalists emphasize that when the Serbs left, they were replaced by the Albanians. These tended to be loyal subjects of the Muslim Turks and more prone to conversion to Islam—although before this Albanian speakers had been mostly Catholic in the north (Ghegs, Kosovars) and Orthodox in the south (Tosks).

From the 1680s and 1690s, however, all of the lands north of the Danube and Sava rivers were reincorporated within Christendom. Hungary, Croatia, Slavonia, Vojvodina, and Transylvania all now fell into the Hapsburg—and so Catholic—realms. In many places, few records survive from the period of Turkish occupation. Osijek, in eastern Slavonia, is a case in point; its documentary history is fragmentary before the last three hundred years.

One consequence of these Turkish defeats, and the subsequent re-Christianization of vast tracts of territory, was the rapid removal of the Islamic populations of these lands. The Muslims now retreated south in order to remain within the *dar al Islam* (realm of Islam), to escape Christian retribution, and to maintain their somewhat privileged status. Such migrations of people, of course, had the effect of intensifying the concentration of Muslims in those parts of southeastern Europe that remained in Ottoman hands—a process that was to become more marked as the territorial contraction proceeded apace during the nineteenth century.

10

MISRULING ONE ANOTHER

The period between the mid-seventeenth century and the late eighteenth—that is to say, the age generally termed the *ancien régime*—saw an end, more or less, to religious warfare. But it did not witness the universal triumph of the Sermon on the Mount. For one thing, the odd brutal skirmish recurred intermittently, by way of reminder of the divisions that remained from the Thirty Years' War and from the civil conflicts within the British Isles. More importantly, Protestants continued to suffer under Catholic rule and Catholics, especially in Ireland, did likewise under Protestant governments. In England, Wales, and Scotland, Protestants managed to inflict grief upon one another.

Dissent in Restoration England

The Restoration is notorious for the vicious vindictiveness of the jubilant royalists. The bodies of Cromwell, his son-in-law Ireton, Bradshaw, and Pride were dug up and their corpses decapitated, quartered, and publicly displayed. Several of the surviving regicides, who had not had the good fortune to be buried first, found themselves facing similar treatment. But if the new king was able to stem the flow of official vengeance to just a few prominent victims, he could do little to stop outbursts of popular anger in the localities. Baptist and Quaker meetings were broken up by royalist mobs throughout the country, their members arrested, and their goods seized. George Fox, the prominent Quaker, was imprisoned in Lancaster.

The Restoration Parliaments are a story of initial moderation turning swiftly to hard-line royalism by 1661. The first, the Convention Parliament of 1660, contained a large minority who continued to favor presbyterianism, but these failed to secure the transfer of the "liberty for tender consciences" promised to them by Charles II at Breda into actual practice. Episcopalianism was obviously about to be restored now that the monarchy had been, so the Presbyterian strategy was to seek comprehension somehow within the national system, perhaps by securing a limited form of episcopacy. Charles seemed ready to listen to them, appointing some of them as his chaplains and offering bishoprics to others, such as Richard Baxter, who declined.

But the Parliament contained also a small number of Independents, who calculated that if the Presbyterians were included inside the national church, then the numbers outside (which would obviously include themselves) would be too small to have any significant chance of toleration. So, in a reversal of Lyndon Johnson's famous political dictum, beefing up the sheer numbers of those who would eventually be excluded from the national church was a way of securing legality for all of them. Paradoxically, therefore, the Independents joined the Episcopalians in opposing the comprehension of Presbyterians within the Church of England. By opposing the bill for making the King's Declaration Touching Ecclesiastical Affairs effective (to be fair, the king's own ministers opposed it too), it was lost by 183 votes to 157. The Presbyterians joined the Independents out in the cold.

The comprehension question having been decided, that of toleration remained. But the Cavalier Parliament of March 1661 returned a large Royalist-Episcopalian majority, with the Presbyterians reduced to about sixty. It became clear that the Independents' Machiavellian calculations were of no avail, and that there was no chance of toleration for any of them.

The Royalist majority were fortified in their determination to be nasty by a Fifth Monarchist uprising the previous January. All religious radicals, the conservatives sniffed, were of one piece: better to suppress them all. On that logic, though, they should probably all have been tolerated. The state had not even wobbled as Thomas Venner's Fifth Monarchy Men ran through the streets waving swords and shouting "For King Jesus!"; there had been just thirty of them.

The Corporation Act of that year obliged all officeholders to take oaths of allegiance and supremacy, abjuring the Solemn League and Covenant (the oath most of them had made in the 1640s, swearing to uphold Presbyterianism), and to pledge nonresistance: "It is not lawful upon any pretence whatsoever to take arms against the king." It was the anthem of the new age.

At the Restoration, the English gentry finally achieved what they had been struggling for through all the vicissitudes of the previous three decades: a tame church, controlled at national level by Parliament and at local level by a strong partnership between squire and parson—with the former in charge. The gentry were determined to have a settlement of religion (which remained, after all, the primary means of social control) that was under their jurisdiction; for the same reason, all forms of "enthusiasm" were to be suppressed. The Act of Uniformity and the Book of Common Prayer of 1662 brought back the outer trappings of Laudian episcopalianism, though shorn of its political powers over the gentry.

The Great Ejection of 1662, whereby Presbyterians and Independents lost their livings in the Church of England, is famous as a landmark in dissenting history. In one sense, it is justly so, for it marks the painful point at which Puritan-minded ministers of all stripes had to decide what they would do now that they could no longer keep trying to reform the unreformable and had to find something more constructive to do with their lives. In another sense, however, the Great Ejection is impressive, not for how many ministers were expelled from their parishes, but for how few. About 2,000 (out of a total of 9,000) lost their positions during 1660–1662 and were replaced mainly with men nominated by lay patrons (i.e., by local gentry). Of those ejected, the vast majority were Presbyterians and about 200 were Independents.

This left 7,000 men (or almost 78 percent) in their original posts, who, after serving the various Puritan regimes of the preceding twenty years, were now prepared to see out their days dangling the baubles of Antichrist. The expression "Vicar of Bray," used to describe an unprincipled timeserver who will loudly justify each new dispensation (and then equally loudly denounce it after every change at the top), was not coined in the 1660s, but perhaps it should have been. Apart from giving us an insight into the parish clergy at the time of the Restoration, this statistic also, by reflection, should make us less impressed with the depth of radicalism that had been on such noisy display during the period of the Republic.

The Puritans' hope of reforming the Church of England from within was now definitively dead. Their moment had come and gone. And it was very obviously never coming back. This left the difficult question of what Presbyterianism and Independency now meant. Each was designed to be a national church—but the national church had just expelled every last spokesman for them. Neither movement could ever be a believers' church, for they espoused infant baptism and a theology that assured them that you could never know who was a believer in the first place. So what were Presbyterianism and Independency after 1662? All that could be said of them was that each embraced the adherents of a particular set of religious principles. Each was a "denomination," and 1662 is the first occasion when we have justifiable cause to use that collective noun in its modern sense.

The Separatist dream of combining a gathered church with a national church framework (always a half-baked idea!) was dashed, and so nothing now divided the Separatists from the Independents (or Congregationalists). The uniting of the Separatist and Congregationalist churches in Yarmouth in 1660 is symbolic of the fact that both sides of that particular, very slight difference of opinion recognized the new realities. The aspiring state churches of the Presbyterians and Independents had ceased to aspire; they had become no longer nonconformists to the Prayer Book but part of "dissent." This left them in outer darkness with the Baptists (both Particular and General) and the Quakers—the other sectarians from the Civil War period having been too ephemeral and disorganized to survive a change in the weather, let alone a change in the state. Even so, it was company the ejected Puritans did not much fancy.

Dissenters were persecuted with varying degrees of viciousness, depending on the local officials. A primary motivation was sheer malevolent vengefulness by gentry who had suffered for their royalism in the years before 1660 and by many who had not, but had nevertheless endured the radicalism of the Republic in impotent fury. The circumstances of the Restoration allowed them to wreak their revenge, while persuading themselves that they were preventing the disasters of the 1640s and 1650s from ever happening again. The Conventicle Acts of 1664 and 1670 subjected all attenders at illegal religious meetings ("conventicles") to stiff penalties. Dissenters were not subject to execution, but they could be imprisoned for long terms in conditions that were often tantamount to a death sentence and even more frequently to broken health. Fines were often intended to be ruinous of whole families, and beatings by soldiers and others coming to arrest dissenters (of which a number died) were hardly unknown. They were harassed at every turn by authorities who were convinced that every religious dissident was a would-be regicide, and they were attacked by mobs with the connivance or encouragement of local clergy, justices, and gentry. It was not a circumstance conducive to calm, theological reflection or development.

The most famous victim of all this fury was, of course, John Bunyan, a tinker and preacher from Bedford who spent the years 1660–1672 in prison. Baptists and Congregationalists continue to claim the great author of *Pilgrim's Progress* and *Grace Abounding* (along with many other works) as their own; both are right. The Bedford Meeting is now the only church remaining that continues to be simultaneously Baptist and Congregationalist. The bizarre circumstances of the emergence of the Particular Baptists were such (see chapter 7) that many saw themselves as Congregationalists who chose to baptize adult professing believers, rather than as believers' churches in any strict sense. That being so, both forms of baptism continued to exist within the same congregation, members exercising a touching forbearance of one another on the matter, which neither they nor any others exhibited elsewhere on any other point of theological difference. Certainly no forbearance was shown by the magistrates toward Bunyan, who used his enforced leisure to produce some of the greatest and most enduring works in the language—though with a didacticism which has recently become less acceptable to a generation that will tolerate anything except being instructed.

If Parliament and the gentry were intent upon persecution, the king himself was inclined to toleration. This was, in part, because he secretly favored Catholicism and knew that he stood no chance of imposing it on a still hysterically antipapist country; the best hope for gaining at least a permission of his favored faith in England was to establish the principle of latitude, by giving toleration to the Protestant dissenters first. Accordingly, in 1672 Charles II issued a Declaration of Indulgence, which allowed dissenters to meet so long as they got licences for their meeting houses and which simultaneously permitted Catholics to celebrate Mass in private houses. Most dissenters accepted the royal favor with mixed feelings, uneasy about benefiting from a toleration that was to be extended also to Catholics.

The following year, Parliament saved their consciences by forcing the king to withdraw the indulgence, and persecution of all and sundry recommenced. The newly built chapels were confiscated or destroyed, and ministers were arrested.

Charles died in 1685, declaring on his deathbed his allegiance to the Roman Church. He had children enough, but none of them legitimate, so the throne passed to his brother James, who had declared himself a

Catholic long before prompted by mortality to do so. It was a moment to hold your breath. Politicians had been queasily aware for some time that their next monarch was likely to be a papist, but they now found themselves boxed in by their own exaggerated emphasis upon constitutional and royal legitimacy and by their own doctrine of nonresistance. In any case, many were confident they had the measure of their man and that he would not attempt anything rash. They would hardly have been human, however, had they refrained from watching like a hawk for any moves toward a Catholicization policy, and James would hardly have been a Stuart had he refrained from the folly of making such moves anyway. The result was not altogether a surprise.

Though James II survived with some ease two rebellions by panicky Protestants, his machinations finally got him into more serious trouble. He tried to appoint his coreligionists to military and official positions, notwithstanding the Test Act, which had been designed specifically to exclude them. Finally, in 1688 he attempted to repeat his brother's Declaration of Indulgence of 1672, granting a toleration to dissenters that was really aimed at Catholics.

The dissenters' Protestantism, which caused them to seek a toleration for themselves only upon terms that would exclude Catholics from the same benefits, finally won their political rewards in the next reign, as James II was forcibly replaced by his daughter and Dutch son-in-law, Mary and William of Orange, in the Glorious Revolution of 1688–1689. William succeeded in having the Toleration Act of 1689 passed by Parliament. This, it averred, granted "some ease to scrupulous consciences in the exercise of religion," provided that oaths of obedience were taken on appropriate occasions, that no meetings be held behind locked doors (to assuage the continuing paranoia about political subversion), that meeting houses be registered with the local bishop (so: no chance of dealing with well-disposed officials), and that tithes and parish rates be paid as if the dissenters were parish churchgoers.

At least it was a start. Furthermore, the crisis of the Glorious Revolution had caused the emerging Whig party to drift into alliance with those to whom Protestantism and the will of Parliament counted for more than strict royalism and any-price legitimacy of succession. The dissenters thereby found themselves embraced (more or less) by one of the leading forces in the new political landscape. It was an alliance that was to endure for two centuries. Their rivals, the Tory party, consisted of the staunch supporters of the established church and those whose loyalty to the new monarchs still left them room for pangs of conscience about the legitimacy of the Glorious Revolution that had installed them.

It might have been expected that the Toleration Act of 1689 would see the beginnings of a new and glorious chapter in the life of English dissent. In point of fact, it ushered in a century of decline. Of the five denominations, only the Congregationalists weathered the eighteenth century with their orthodoxy untrammeled and their numerical strength unharmed. For that which persecution had failed to achieve, for the most part, was accomplished by the new conditions of relative ease.

The Presbyterians accounted for slightly more than half of all dissent in the late seventeenth century. They were, after all, simply erstwhile mainstream Puritans from the Church of England who had now been ejected—and there had been a lot of them. Like their Puritan antecedents, they were strong in the towns and among the trading and mercantile classes. Their areas of greatest strength were in those regions where Protestantism had had to struggle, during the sixteenth century, to overcome Catholicism or traditionalism. With no further hope of forming the national church, however, they tended to become inward-looking and to focus mostly on matters internal to their own affairs. And that, obviously, was not good for numbers in the longer term.

In any case, the internal affairs of the Presbyterians soon began to look less than pretty, for by the end of the century they came to embrace a wide range of opinions and asked only for a degree of religious knowledge rather than any evidence of actual conversion. (Presbyterians, after all, believed one couldn't tell who was saved or lost.) As a result, they soon included liberal free-willers and, later, Socinians. This last inclusion was disastrous and, during the course of the eighteenth century, English Presbyterianism largely collapsed into Unitarianism.

The Independents, or Congregationalists, constituted about 18 percent of all dissent by the early eighteenth century. They had no theological differences with Presbyterians (prior to the deterioration of the latter into Socinianism) and sometimes cooperated with them. Like them, Congregationalists were mostly urban, but they were strongest in the old Puritan heartlands of East Anglia and Northamptonshire and also in areas of South Wales, such as Carmarthenshire, where Presbyterianism was weak. Indeed, the patterns of distribution between the two denominations bear an inverse relationship to one another, leading to the suspicion, in view of their similarities, that they functioned as effective alternatives to one another. However, the Congregationalists did not, on the whole, decline from their evangelical Calvinism either in the late seventeenth century or during the eighteenth—a feat they achieved by excommunicating heretics in their ranks.

One of the most illustrious names in the Congregationalist pantheon is that of Isaac Watts (1674–1748), who published his *Hymns and Spiritual Songs* in 1707. His most famous composition is perhaps "When I Survey the Wondrous Cross," but this was far from being the only song adopted by a wide range of churches, including, in the end, the Church of England. In his own day, though, congregational singing was opposed by some of his brethren as an innovation involving both regenerate and unregenerate people singing together words that are appropriate only to the former. (The criticism shows how far the original Calvinism had slipped, over the years of a de facto sectarian existence, into the assumption that members in good standing were among the elect.) Furthermore, it was complained by Watts's detractors that hymns involve women singing rather than keeping silent in church—a prospect even more frightful to the Almighty than that of the unregenerate piping up.

The long-run success of churches is perhaps best gauged, however, by how well they refuse to take seriously their own internally-generated nonsense. On this scale, the Congregationalists passed well enough.

But a very different fate awaited the Particular Baptists. They had been strong in Bedfordshire, Hertfordshire, Radnor, and Gwent, reasonably strong in the south and southwest, and very weak in the north. In 1660 there had been 30,000 Particular Baptists, and they continued to grow during the period of persecution until 1689. Thereafter, their growth trailed off, and the eighteenth century saw them enter upon a phase of at first gradual and then very rapid decline. The cause of the decrease was simple: it was their growing tendency to adopt hyper-Calvinism.

It will have escaped the notice of few readers that one of the greatest providences of God in the ordering of the universe is the way in which he appears to deliver almost all ideologues, Christian and non-Christian alike, from following through on the logic of their own ostensible ideas. That is to say, most of us are better than our principles. It is all the more shocking, therefore, when we encounter those relatively infrequent incidences where, instead of this, God has evidently stayed his hand and exposed an idea's badness by the simple expedient of allowing its full consequences to be played out in actual practice. (As has often been observed, the *reductio ad absurdum* is God's favorite argument.) Such was the appalling fate marked out for John Gill (1696–1771), the Particular Baptists' most influential theologian, read overwhelmingly by ministers of his own denomination and of others besides, and evidently a man whom God wished to harden.

Following in the doomed footsteps of some seventeenth-century Church of England writers such as Tobias Crisp (1600–1642) and the

Presbyterian Joseph Hussey (1659–1726), Gill concluded from his belief in predestination that since it had been decreed from all eternity which individuals would be saved, and since Christ had died for those and for those alone, it would therefore be an insult to the providence of God and a farce on the human level to waste time evangelizing people who, by reason of being reprobates, were utterly unable to repent and believe. Gill's fellow Particular Baptist, John Skepp (1670–1721), took the same dismal view: evangelistic preaching was "of little use to such a dead or disabled soul," while invitations to turn to Christ "amount to no more than a dead and helpless exhortation."[1]

Indeed. Whereas in 1715 the Particular Baptists had still been possessed of 220 churches, thirty-five years later this number had fallen to 146. Gill and Skepp must have taken a modest pride in such a success. And, if they did not, they had the consolation of knowing that the collapse had been decreed from before the foundations of the earth.

Perhaps even they were not, after all, quite consistent enough. For, using the identical logic, it could be demonstrated that their writings and sermons to Christians about the truth of hyper-Calvinism were as pointless as evangelistic preaching; those who were predestined to take such ideas seriously would do so regardless, while those who would not, would not. Truly consistent fatalists, like rigorously consistent existentialists (who cannot, after all, be quite sure that the rest of us actually exist to digest their opinions), would simply keep silent—a consequence as devoutly to be desired as it is unlikely to be met with.

In the latter half of the eighteenth century, Andrew Fuller (1754–1815) and others started to restore some sanity, under the influence of Methodism and the Great Awakening, and to lead the Particular Baptists back toward a more evangelical form of Calvinism.

If the Particular Baptists' self-inflicted fate looks harsh, that facing the General Baptists was worse yet. They had started at the time of the Restoration with the same numerical strength as the Particulars and were numerous in Lincolnshire, Cambridgeshire, Buckinghamshire, Kent, and Sussex. While they had a significant presence in five other counties besides, elsewhere they were quite weak. They were not a force to be reckoned with on a national scale. Although they had proved better able than the Calvinistic groups to penetrate the countryside as well as the towns, this may have acted as a liability for them in the longer term because their congregations became isolated backwaters that were less able to stand up against pressure from landlords during the persecution and in less contact with their brethren during times of peace. They were also more prone than other dissenters to lose members to Quakerism, with whom they shared some similarities. By 1715 they had already been reduced to 146 churches—and that was just the beginning of the downward path.

In the 1680s Matthew Caffyn, the pastor of the General Baptist congregation in Horsham, Sussex, turned to Arian heresy, and attempts to discipline him failed. It was the beginning of serious doctrinal difficulties, as a significant faction became established sharing these views. In 1697 the orthodox organized themselves to form the General Association, which broke away from the General Assembly (that is, from those who had become nontrinitarian or else were prepared to compromise with false teaching). Although the two groups reunited in 1731 on the basis of the six principles of Hebrews 6:1–2, the use of such a formula, bearing as it did little relationship to the substantive differences at issue, was really a compromise in which the Arians and Socinians won out.

By 1750 the General Baptists were reduced, under the debilitating effects of rationalism and heresy, to just sixty-five churches. The end seemed near. However, their original principles were rescued—and not a moment too soon—by Dan Taylor (1738–1816) who, in 1770, led a new secession on the same issue. Taylor had been greatly influenced by the Methodist movement and its strident evangelicalism. He observed that the General Baptists' predecessors in the seventeenth century had "maintained that the Death of Christ for the sins of men was the only foundation of the sinner's hope," and that the preaching of this gospel had brought numerical growth. When heresy had started to take root, he pointed out, some had "sounded the alarm, but they were calumniated as defective in charity. Many yielded so far as to trim and to temporise, and treat the fundamental doctrines of the gospel as matters of indifference. . . ." In consequence, "they degraded Jesus Christ, and He degraded them."[2]

No longer. Taylor's group, the New Connection of General Baptists, laid aside such misplaced "charity" and opted decisively for orthodoxy. They grew rapidly by aggressive evangelism from just seven congregations with a thousand members between them at the time of founding to thirty-one churches with 2,367 members in 1786—and onward and upward from there.

It was not quite enough. The Particulars had emerged from their own problems in slightly better shape than the Generals (who had, in truth, survived by the merest hairsbreadth). As a result, when the Baptists entered into the (for them) more glorious nineteenth century, it was the Calvinists who were to be the dominant strain.

The Old Connection of General Baptists, meanwhile, simply disappeared to death or Unitarianism, thereby joining the former Presbyterians. It was an ironic outcome for both groups, considering the vast gulf that had separated them in 1660.

The Quakers underwent the classic transformation from vibrant new movement to established and somewhat stagnant religious community during the century after the Restoration. They had begun in a position that was simultaneously strong in terms of numbers and extremely vulnerable politically. With 60,000 adherents in 1660, they had a presence in every county. While, like the General Baptists, they were strong in the countryside, they also accounted for more than 6 percent of the population of Bristol. None of this, however, prevented their decline over the next century. As provocative after the Restoration as before it, the Quakers often took the full force of the persecution of dissenters during the years before 1689, refusing to compromise on their various eccentricities and often scorning even to meet in secret.

But much of what had started as enthusiasm descended into mere legalism during the later seventeenth century. The emphasis upon group norms such as plain speech and plain dress began to seem tiresome after the first flush of rebelliousness was past. George Fox's wife, Margaret Fell, complained in her later years of the "silly, poor gospel" that "we must be all in one dress and one colour."[3] In the eighteenth century, Quakers continued to wear aspects of seventeenth-century dress (e.g., wide-brimmed hats for men) that made them look merely quaint and old-fashioned. Thus the Quakers demonstrated that they were not immune to the incorrigible human instinct for attempting to catch and bottle the Holy Spirit.

At the same time—and also following the classic trajectory of new religious movements—the early prophetic and enthusiastic elements in early Quakerism were downplayed. Revelation was routinized and rendered less exciting. When John Hall predicted an earthquake in 1693, he found himself reproved by Bristol Quakers. George Fox's *Book of Miracles* was never published, and his claims to have healed people were considered an embarrassment by the end of the century.

In every decade from the 1670s to the 1790s, the number of Quaker deaths exceeded the number of Quaker births. This would have been less important if the early missionary spirit had prevailed, bringing in new members by conviction rather than by procreation. But in fact the early proselytism declined and, by the mid-eighteenth century, probably 80 to 90 percent of Quakers were children of the previous generation of Quakers rather than converts.

In summary, by the time of the Great Awakening, Old Dissent in England was spiritually very lethargic. It required the birth and growth of Methodism to provoke it, at first to jealousy, and then to emulation. Only then did it revive.

Protestants in Catholic Europe

It should not be imagined that European governments were above mistreating their subjects for confessional causes simply because the Thirty Years' War was over and a period of generalized reaction against religiously dominated foreign policies and religious warfare had set in. Far from it. *Raison d'état*—or simple political pragmatism—may have been triumphant in interstate relations, but religion was still overwhelmingly the most useful and credible tool of social control at home.

People who were adherents of a confessional minority in states where the ruler adhered to the local majority could, therefore, find themselves subject to serious pressures. Nowhere was this more true than in the Catholic-ruled principalities of Germany.

Germany and the Hapsburg Lands

The danger for Protestants was that more and more of these states might acquire Catholic rulers as princes whose families had for generations adhered to the Reformation began, one by one, to turn their backs upon it. Such was the case of Augustus the Strong of Saxony in 1697. Back in the sixteenth century, the advantage for rulers had seemed to lie in embracing Protestantism, with all of its concomitant gains in the form of a church ruled within each state's political frontiers, the financial rewards of confiscating monastic lands, and so on. But now that the Reformation had happened, the pope's power was humbled, and the medieval balance of power between church and state had been resolved decisively in favor of the latter, the reasons for rejecting the Church of Rome seemed less persuasive. Indeed, the hierarchical nature of Catholicism, implying as it did a similar hierarchy in secular society, held a great attraction to royalty. So too did its emphasis upon works rather than faith and upon pomp and ceremony rather than austere sermons—as a way of keeping their subjects obedient and in awe. Princes might have other, more individual reasons for conversions to the Roman faith: Elector Augustus II of Saxony made just such a switch in 1697 in order to obtain election to the Crown of Poland.

The new princely conversions to Rome, however, were seldom a real threat to the Protestantism of their subjects in those places, such as Saxony, where the Reformation had become firmly and uniformly entrenched—though in states where the situation was less clear-cut it might have ominous implications. The extinction of the Reformed branch of the ruling house of the Palatinate and its replacement by a Catholic branch of the family led to all kinds of unseemly squabbles over jurisdictions and rights to particular churches during the eighteenth century, but it did not alter the religious orientation of the bulk of the populace.

The worst burden was borne by those Protestants who lived in areas where the majority of the population was Catholic or where the results of the Reformation had been largely undone by the Thirty Years' War. In the mid-1680s some thousand or so Protestants of Defereggental, in Austria, were expelled from their homes and had their property and children confiscated from them. The same fate befell some sixty Protestant miners from nearby Berchtesgaden during the later part of the decade. One of these, Josef Schaitberger (1658–1733), whose wife died shortly afterward from grief at the loss of their two daughters, turned to evangelism and the writing of tracts to encourage the remaining Protestants of Inner Austria in their faith. Over forty years later, in the winter of

Protestants expelled from Salzburg in 1731.
Engraving by David Böecklin, from *Die Freundliche Bewillkommen*, Leipzig, 1732.

1731–1732, as many as 30,000 Protestants were expelled from Salzburg; all were familiar with and had been nurtured by Schaitberger's literary outpourings. A number of Protestants from Carinthia and Styria who were unwilling to apostatize also made good their escape during these years into friendlier territories. By the late 1730s the only Protestant churches functioning openly in the Hapsburg lands outside of Hungary and the small territory of Teschen in the east were those attached to foreign embassies in Vienna. Other Protestants survived without the benefit of a functioning, institutional church to sustain their faith. The invasion of confessionally divided Silesia by Frederick the Great of Prussia in 1740 did at least release the Protestant half of the population there from the need to scurry to the border simply in order to go to church.

Two-thirds of the fleeing Salzburgers had in any case gone to Prussia, where they were resettled, especially in its eastern territories that had just been depopulated by plague. Prussian agents met them in Swabia and marched them in columns to their new homes, paying them a daily subsistence en route and providing them with plots of land or positions in service at the end of their journey. The entire operation cost the Prussian government half a million thalers—about twenty-five thalers per immigrant, and cheap at the price.

The Prussian kingdom had already benefited from the persecuting misdemeanors of its rivals. From the mid-seventeenth century through to the mid-eighteenth, the Prussian lands welcomed an influx of persecuted souls: Waldensians, Mennonites, Scottish Presbyterians, Jews, and even some Catholics fleeing the more rigorously Protestant regimes. Prussia, like America after the Revolution, valued loyalty to the state-as-abstraction over mere confessional conformity; in that respect, it was the very model of pragmatic, Enlightenment polity. And like the United States at a later date, by welcoming the outcasts, it could be assured of their gratitude and loyalty. The only compulsory religion of Prussia was the secular one of civic duty.

Not all of the Hapsburgs' Protestant subjects chose Prussian exile, however. The earthly salvation of those who survived the sundry mistreatments of the century and a third following the Peace of Westphalia lay in the fact that such depopulation could not long be afforded. Emperor Charles VI (reigned 1711–1740) and his successor, Empress Maria Theresa (1740–1780), sought to extend their empire to the south and east, thereby absorbing new subjects while nevertheless keeping—nay, making—those subjects entirely Catholic. Such a contradictory policy could not endure. For the emperor stood sorely in need of the loyalty of people—the inhabitants of the border realms of Hungary—whom his religious rigorism threatened to oppress.

In this situation, something had to give, for the emperor was periodically reduced to rebuking the rulers of neighboring Saxony for their presumptuousness in accepting the steady stream of Moravian refugees from his realms. In 1781 the attempt to enforce Catholic conformity was abandoned and the Patent of Toleration finally lifted the burden of persecution (though not always of devious and petty administrative and social discrimination) from the Protestants' shoulders. The churches that thereafter emerged into the light of day included a thousand pastorless Reformed churches in Hungary as well as congregations in Austria, Moravia, and elsewhere.

Poland

In Poland the situation of Protestants, which had looked so hopeful in the late sixteenth century, slid remorselessly backward from the late seventeenth century onward. The Reformed church, which had seemed so appealing to elements among the *szlachta*, or nobility, as a means of keeping the Crown weak, began to seem less appealing as priorities switched to keeping the kingdom intact against its foreign enemies. Furthermore, the succession of wars and invasions to which Poland was subjected from the mid-seventeenth century onward caused the loss of precisely those territories where the minorities were strongest. Even more ominously for Protestants, the fighting led to a rising Polish national consciousness of a kind that tended to identify itself in religious, Catholic terms, thereby branding non-Catholics as at least potentially disloyal.

This last tendency was increased by two factors. In the first place, the various invaders—Lutheran Swedes, Orthodox Russians, Lutheran-Pietist Prussians and Saxons—ruthlessly appealed to adherents of their own confessions among the Polish population. The invasion by King Charles XII of Sweden in the first decade of the eighteenth century saw an improved standing of Protestants and a spate of Lutheran church building. In the second place, the Marian cult picked up a full head of steam in Poland from 1655 onward when the icon of the Black Madonna of Czestochowa was believed to have helped the monastery there to withstand a lengthy siege by the Swedish army. The important Polish role, under the leadership of Jan Sobieski, in saving Vienna from the Turks in 1683, intensified the religiously Catholic self-image. But this drift toward an entrenched Catholic consciousness was confirmed by the experience of the Great Northern War of

1700–1721, when Poland was overrun by Swedes and Russians and left in a condition of vulnerability that would see the state disappear altogether before the end of the century. In 1717 at Czestochowa the Virgin, already Queen of Heaven, was ceremonially crowned queen of Poland also: a national totem was thereby set up which Protestants and Jews could not share.

The aftermath of the war saw the new Protestant churches in Poland torn down again as well as the loss of some of the old churches. The mostly Protestant town of Thorn was stripped of its Lutheran place of worship and forcibly re-Catholicized in 1724 after provocative actions on both sides. The Protestants were increasingly seen as a fifth column for German and Swedish influence.

The degree of mistreatment should not be overstated. A huge Uniate population continued in the south and east of the kingdom—though they, of course, owned allegiance to the pope. The Jewish population remained large, though they were required to keep to their own villages in the countryside and to their own ghettoes in the towns. There were even a hundred or so mosques, which met the needs of the Crimean Tartars whom the government hired as mercenaries for its army. But the strength of the Protestants continued to wane.

The Revocation of the Edict of Nantes and Its Aftermath

The Edict of Nantes of 1598 had left the Huguenots (or, more formally, the *Églises Réformées de France*) in a vulnerable position yet simultaneously a privileged state-within-a-state. Such a circumstance gave the Catholic forces of French central government both incentive and opportunity to encroach upon the edict's provisions.

During the reign of Henry IV, however, many Huguenots continued to hold positions of responsibility and influence. Protestant architects were employed in the beautification of Paris, and one of them, Salomon de Brosse, was even chosen by the canons of Orléans to rebuild the cathedral, which had been seriously damaged during the Wars of Religion. There were other high-profile instances of such heartwarming cooperation, but these did not reflect the general temper of the country and were more pronounced in Paris than in the provinces, where the two religious communities lived largely segregated lives.

Hundreds of churches, of course, had been devastated by the fighting; the inevitable reconstruction caused both friction and recriminations. The new, or renewed, buildings acted as bridgeheads for the reintroduction of

Catholicism in areas that had been largely Protestantized—an opportunity that the Catholics were not slow to utilize.

The Huguenot revolt from 1621 to 1628 was the occasion of a fresh round of conversions to Catholicism by the Protestant nobility, many of whom simply refused to take up arms against the king and chose apostasy as the simplest way out. The Peace of Alès of 1629, which ended the conflict, signaled the beginnings of a narrower interpretation of the edict by the Crown.

With the loss of support among the upper echelons of society, the Huguenot churches began to lose their impetus. Traditionally, they had been organized on the presbyterian system, with a hierarchy of committees ascending from parish consistory upward through layers of synods and culminating in the spiritual stratosphere of a national synod. However, though this last institution met every three years up until 1626, its sacred deliberations became ever rarer thereafter, and only four meetings (1631, 1637, 1645, and 1659) were held after the Peace of Alès.

By the time of the last meeting, the writing was already on the wall for French Protestantism. National synods required special royal permission to occur at all by this time, and Louis XIV's chief minister, Cardinal Mazarin, made it plain that the 1659 synod was to be the last. Royal contributions to ministerial salaries and ecclesiastical expenses (which were supposed to be one of the benefits under the terms of the edict to compensate for the Huguenots' enforced payment of tithes to the Catholic Church) had also long since become a merely occasional benefit, most likely to be forthcoming when foreign war loomed, as a way of securing Protestant loyalty. Churches were thrown back onto their own financial resources—and these, too, were becoming ever more slender. The conversions to Catholicism of local noblemen often deprived rural churches of their largest financial contributors and made them unviable or could at least set hungry ministers at odds with their financially overstretched congregations.

Even as the king issued a special declaration of 1662, promising to uphold the Edict of Nantes in recognition of Huguenot loyalty during the Fronde uprising, he was privately preparing for ever narrower definition of its terms; eventual revocation was already a virtual certainty. Louis XIV's Declaration of Forty Articles in 1669 was tantamount to such an action, authorizing the destruction of Protestant temples and a whole raft of administrative harassments and restrictions. Most feared of all by ordinary Protestants was that they would be subjected to that greatest of calamities that could befall an early-modern household, the billeting of troops. The issuing of the Revocation of the Edict of Nantes in 1685,

Revocation of the
Edict of Nantes.
Illustration from
Jan Luiken.

which demanded
that all remaining
Protestants abjure
their faith forthwith
and adhere to the
Catholic Church,
simply formalized a
state of affairs that
had for long been
impending.

The alternatives
facing the remaining Huguenots in 1685 were broadly the same as
were faced by other religious minorities confronted with the prospect
of persecution. Apostasy, exile, equivocation (or "Nicodemism"—that is,
continuing secret adherence to the proscribed faith), or resistance. Many
saved their property and lives, though at no little expense to their souls,
by seizing upon the first of these. Many thousands more, especially those
possessed of crafts and professional skills, fled abroad—some at once,
more during the succeeding decades. Emigration, however, was illegal,
and so it was undertaken at the risk of being sent to the galleys—a fate
that befell many.

King Louis XIV had no wish to be deprived of so many productive
subjects, and he offered no escape from his demand for obedience. But
this did not prevent the exodus. Estimates of the numbers who escaped
varied widely at the time, and have continued to do so since, but the
figure of 200,000 would be a not unreasonable estimate. Those who left
were disproportionately young, single men. Favorite refuges included
Switzerland, Brandenburg, the Netherlands, and England—all of which
countries reaped substantial economic benefit from their enemy's self-
inflicted wound. In Brandenburg and England the refugees' arrival
had political effects also. In the Edict of Potsdam, Elector Friedrich
Wilhelm of Brandenburg positively urged the refugees to come to his
territory. He was a Calvinist prince over a Lutheran population, and
the arrival of his coreligionists strengthened his hand. He set them up
with accommodation and start-up loans. By 1700 one inhabitant of
Berlin in three was French; they had their own churches and a grammar school. England was on the brink of the Glorious Revolution, and

the influx of refugees from Catholic tyranny provided an object lesson
for those who were already fearful of what a continuance of James II's
rule might bring.

Back in France, the Nicodemists and equivocators among the
Huguenots faced risks of their own. Those who abjured formally but
were later found guilty of being relapsed heretics faced being sent to
the galleys, having their property confiscated, and of their heirs being
dispossessed.

Boldest of all were those who chose to continue to practice their faith.
(Clearly, the line between this last group and the previous category could
often become blurred.) Many of these included the peasants of the Midi,
who were in any case seldom in a position to uproot themselves and
offer skills to commerce in other countries. The French Reformed had
for long lived a sectarian existence, but they were otherwise unencum-
bered by the pacifist squeamishness that would have restrained, say,
Anabaptists in the same plight. The Protestant recalcitrants attended
their secret meetings armed; if royal troops discovered them, then the
religious service became a scene of battle.

Violent resistance of the Protestant *maquis,* or militias, quickly became
a frequent feature of the aftermath of the Revocation of the Edict of
Nantes. Neither did it die away swiftly, but it continued sporadically
for decades after 1685, especially in the woods and mountains of the
Cévennes and the plains of lower Languedoc. Just when the revolt seemed
to have died down, it flared up again from 1702 to 1704 in the revolt of
the Camisards, which was quelled only with difficulty by 20,000 French
troops.

The suffering and extreme tension in which so many of the resisters
lived for years produced spiritual renewal, sometimes in surprising new
forms, among those who clung on. This was ironic, for it is generally
agreed that the French Reformed church had become characterized by
dry orthodoxy during much of the seventeenth century. The calamities
that had engulfed the community since 1685, however, caused many to
indulge in apocalyptic speculations and to understand their sufferings
in eschatological terms as a sign of the imminent return of Christ. The
fugitives included a woman preacher in Périgord and a fifteen-year-old,
illiterate shepherdess, Isabeau Vincent, who both preached in her sleep
and prophesied deliverance for the people of God. From 1688 the prophetic aspect of the movement became more pronounced over a wide
area, as a number of lay preachers took to prophesying. Many attenders
at clandestine meetings exhibited shakings, falling over, and weeping. The
soldiers discovered one of these assemblies and massacred the attenders,

but they did not stop the movement's progress into the 1690s. In 1701 there was a fresh upsurge of prophecy, including hundreds of children who, of course, would all have been born since 1685 and had no experience of normal conditions. Attached to the guerrilla units in the Camisard rebellion, these prophets were sometimes active participants in violence and were even consulted about whether God willed prisoners to be killed or allowed to live. The "French prophets" outlived the rebellions and even affected the early Wesleyan movement in the 1730s.

The Protestant militias and Camisards were sustained (as so many guerrilla movements are) by a sympathetic populace, consisting largely of people who had abjured their Protestant faith unwillingly and were trying to live lives of minimal conformity to the Catholic Church. There is evidence that children of abjurers were brought up to despise the official church—or else made that judgment for themselves as young adults. Despite all the force Louis XIV could bring against them, the Huguenots did not go away.

Persecution dragged on through the eighteenth century, with the Huguenots given no formal recognition until 1802, more than a decade after the French Revolution. But local will to exact the letter of the law had been lacking long before. Pastors risked the gallows for their activities: Jaques Roger in 1745 and François Rochette in 1762 were among the more prominent casualties. But neighbors and local officials often connived at what they knew to be happening; indeed, without such connivance survival of the movement on any scale would have been impossible. Yet survive it did. And in that survival, the limitations to the power of the modern state in general, and of the absolutist model in particular, are clearly visible.

The Tribulations of Scotland, 1660–1745

Scotland was unique in the sixteenth century in being an economically underdeveloped society that became predominantly Protestant. That exceptionalism was underlined by the immoderate version of Protestantism that prevailed there; where Catholic resistance was fiercest, hard-line Calvinism was the Reformation's most valiant recourse. And everything about Scottish political life was fierce, elemental, and violent. Even Calvin's measured and qualified respect for legitimate rulers had to be modified or reversed by his advocates on the ground; Luther's exaggerated respect for lawful princes would never have served as a sufficient instrument for reforming Scottish religion.

Presbyterianism had struggled to maintain itself in Scotland, ever since its stormy inception in the 1560s and 1570s. After John Knox died in 1572, his position as flag-bearer of Presbyterian truculence was taken up by Andrew Melville. He faced a country in which factions fought for custodianship of the boy-king, James VI, where churchmen were regularly murdered, and where England and France constantly intervened both diplomatically and militarily, the former to secure its northern frontier, the latter to destabilize it.

Amid the chaos of Scottish politics, Melville succeeded in persuading the General Assembly of the Kirk to accept the rigorous *Second Book of Discipline* in 1581. This asserted the independence of the church from state control. It was a position easy enough to maintain while even the state was beyond state control. But by the time James VI had disentangled himself from his latest group of kidnappers (the Ruthven Raiders) in 1583, he was close to attaining his majority. The Parliament of the following year obediently insisted that the king was the head of the Kirk, with the sole right to call an assembly and appoint bishops. The right of clergy to freedom of speech in their pulpits was denied if they touched upon political matters.

These acts of Parliament, the "Black Acts," proved mere statements of royal intent for over a decade, but in 1596–1597 a series of ecclesiastical disturbances played into James's hands, and by smart political footwork he was able to translate the aspirations into reality. The bishops, though, had more symbolic than real authority over what remained, in many respects, a presbyterian system of church government. James's episcopacy emerged by gradations, via positions as representatives of the Kirk in Parliament and permanent moderators at synods; only from 1606 were the prelates unambiguously "bishops."

The drift toward episcopalianism was brought to a shuddering halt when Charles I attempted, in 1637, to impose High-Churchmanship. Lairds and commoners rose in revolt in the Covenanter rebellion to restore full-blown Presbyterianism. Accordingly Scots fought, for the most part, on the parliamentarian side in the First Civil War of 1642–1646. Then, when confronted by an English Parliament that seemed to be in the hands of radicals and sectaries, they changed sides and fought for the king in the brief Second Civil War of April–October 1648, on the basis of his vaguely worded and scarcely-to-be-believed "Engagement" to permit Presbyterianism.

Apart from ushering in defeat, the war of 1648 also divided the Scottish Presbyterians between "Engagers," who had found radicalism and social upheaval more alarming than an untrustworthy king, and the more hard-line "Resolutioners," who had opposed the switching of sides. Although the war ended soon enough and the king himself was executed the following January, the difference between Engagers and Resolutioners refused to remain academic, for the dead king's son, Charles II, landed in Scotland in June 1650, and the decision about what to do with him returned to haunt both groups. This time both decided, rather unwisely, to give providence another nudge. The resultant Third Civil War of 1650–1651 returned the same military verdict as its predecessors, however, and from 1651 Scotland found itself treated as a conquered country, occupied by an English republican army. The affair split the Resolutioners into moderate and hard-line factions, with the former allying themselves with the Engagers in their resentment at republicanism and military rule, while the latter (the Remonstrants or Protesters) were prepared to cooperate, however grudgingly, with their new masters. Samuel Rutherford (ca. 1600–1661), the famous theologian and professor of divinity at St. Andrew's, supported the latter, though he had written fiercely against religious toleration in his 1649 work, *A Free Disputation Against Pretended Liberty of Conscience*.

The paradox of the 1650s and 1660s, therefore, was stark. The former decade gave Scots the unmolested Presbyterianism they wished for, under the auspices of a regime they despised. Yet though the Restoration of the monarchy in 1660 was ushered in as rapturously in Edinburgh as in London, it left the Kirk at the mercies of a monarch whose promise "to protect and preserve the Church of Scotland, as it is settled by law, without violation" was scarcely credible.

Indeed, as with the witches' promise to Macbeth, which the audience knows will prove false somehow (the only suspense being the difficulty of guessing how), the Presbyterian settlement of Scotland was undone by the simple expedient of declaring all laws passed since 1633 invalid. By the Act Rescissory of March 1661, the present arrangements turned out not to be those "settled by law" after all. Charles now promised "to maintain the true reformed protestant religion in its purity of doctrine and worship as it was established within this kingdom during the reigns of his royal father and grandfather of blessed memory."[4] So it was to be episcopalianism. By dying the same month as the passing of the act, Rutherford skillfully evaded both an impending treason charge and being forced to witness the undoing of all that he had worked for.

The Presbyterian defense collapsed swiftly. The Resolutioner James Sharp proved less resolute in the cause than had been expected. Sent to London to negotiate with the episcopalian enemy, he found himself swiftly persuaded of the value of hierarchy to the extent of accepting office as primate and archbishop of St. Andrew's. All but three of the new episcopal bench were, like Sharp, instant converts to the cause they had thitherto spent their careers combating. It was not an impressive sight.

Even under the new arrangements, however, presbyteries continued to exist—but with no laymen and little power. They were overseen by moderators—but these were chosen by the bishop. Ministers were exhorted to gain the help of prominent laymen "to oversee the manners of the people"—but they were no longer referred to as "elders." As for national synods, they were to include bishops and archbishops but in other respects they were to meet as before, the king having sole right to summon them—though, in point of fact, he never did summon one at all. Those Presbyterians of all shades and factions who took it upon themselves, during the course of the next three decades, to resist these arrangements are frequently referred to as "Covenanters" (i.e., by the same name as their pre–civil war counterparts).

The existing clergy who had been appointed during the period of Presbyterian ascendancy were not required to undergo reordination under episcopal auspices (for it was part of the strength of the self-confident Restoration regime to know just how far to push its luck), but they were required to attend their new bishop for collation. The sole condition for this confirmation in office *was* the willingness to apply for it; the purpose of the exercise was to persuade the parish clergy, with genial threat of sudden unemployment, to recognize the new episcopal authority. The deadline for submission was 20 September 1662.

Broadly speaking, the north and east of Scotland assented with few demurs. The south and west were far more problematic. Even after extensions and amnesties, 270 ministers were ejected and their places taken by more compliant men. These latter were scorned as "curates" by many of their parishioners, who continued to attend upon their former ministers.

The government had anticipated just such an eventuality. Meetings outside of parish churches were declared to be illegal conventicles; former ministers were required to remove themselves by at least twenty miles from their previous parishes; anyone failing to attend the official services for three consecutive Sundays was prosecuted as a recusant; troops were brought in to exact the ruinous fines that resulted from this legislation. The autumn of 1666 saw a revolt in the southwest of Scotland, but its participants never included more than 3,000 people of fairly humble circumstance, and it was squashed with ease.

Nevertheless, the period from 1669 to 1674 saw a succession of attempts by the Crown to accommodate all but the irreconcilables.

Ejected ministers were allowed to return or to be appointed to new parishes elsewhere without being required to give a full submission to the bishops. Only a minority availed themselves of such opportunities, preferring an untrammeled but illegal Presbyterianism to an indulged comprehension at the hands of the prelates.

Where carrots were insufficient, however, central government had a ready fund of sticks. Field preaching became subject to the death penalty in 1674. Lairds were made liable for the conventicling misdeeds of their tenants, and when, in 1678, the landowners of the southwest protested their inability to police their people in such fashion, 6,000 Highland troops were billeted upon them to assist.

It was the spark for new insurrection. In May 1679 archbishop Sharp made the mistake of venturing beyond St. Andrew's, and he was cut down on Magus Moor. And when a troop of cavalry made the mistake of attacking a conventicle at Drumclog, they discovered that the Presbyterians harbored more than psalmbooks under their cloaks; it was the soldiers who were routed.

However heroic, and however gratifyingly dizzying the success of destroying the local instruments of repression, such provincial uprisings could never succeed against the resources that central government could eventually bring to bear. With weary inevitability, therefore, the rebels were crushed by the army of the Duke of Monmouth. The reprisals were savage.

They were not savage enough, however, to dissuade one Richard Cameron, a young field preacher and the emergent leader of the Covenanters, from riding into the small market town of Sanquhar, Dumfriesshire, in the summer of 1680 and reading a paper from the market cross. This declaration professed to

> disown Charles Stuart, that has been reigning, or rather tyrannising, as we may say, on the throne of Britain these years bygone, as having any right, title to, or interest in, the said Crown of Scotland for government, as forfeited, several years since, by his perjury and breach of covenant both to God and His Kirk.

The authors also declared

> war with such a tyrant and usurper, and all the men of his practices, as enemies to our Lord Jesus Christ, and His cause and covenants; and against all such as have strengthened him, sided with, or anywise acknowledged him in his tyranny, civil or ecclesiastic.

It was immediately apparent that the Cameronians had been goaded into this startling call to arms by years of repression: "we hope, . . . none will blame us for, or offend at, our rewarding those that are against us as they have done to us, as the Lord gives opportunity."

"As the Lord gives opportunity": the very language of the authors of the Sanquhar Declaration betrays the fact that they knew full well that their "war" could never be more, for the foreseeable future at least, than a guerrilla campaign. The government responded, however, with full force. Cameron did not survive the year; his successor as leader failed to survive the next. James Renwick, their successor in turn, managed to elude capture for longer, but he was finally caught and executed in 1688. The years between have become known as "the Killing Time," after the ferocity and mercilessness with which government troops persecuted and summarily dispatched hundreds suspected of sympathizing with the Cameronians.

Yet deliverance was not far away. The death of Charles II in 1685 passed the crown to his Catholic brother, James VII (James II in England). And curiously, the outcome of the new king's meddling in the institutions of public life in Scotland was exactly what the Sanquhar Declaration aspired to, for James was forced to flee the country in 1688 and was replaced by his Protestant daughter and son-in-law, Mary and William. When James's supporters in Scotland tried to reverse this tide of events, several military engagements ensued, during which the Cameronians, as stalwart champions of the new regime of William and Mary, proved their mettle and found an opportunity to gain a measure of revenge on their tormentors.

The new monarchs summoned a Convention of Estates in Edinburgh in March 1689. Since the Scottish bishops had failed to follow the example of their English brethren in lending support to the change of regime, the new joint monarchs were spared overmuch anxiety on account of them. Therefore the following July, barely a month after the redesignation of the Convention of Estates as a Parliament, this body knew itself to be on safe ground in repealing the legislation enshrining episcopacy. The next year, it proceeded to scrap the royal supremacy over the Kirk. Presbyterianism was reestablished, the Westminster Confession reinstated, and those "curates" of the southwest who had not already been routed from their parishes by mobs in late 1688 now tasted the experience of ejection firsthand. The wheel had come full circle.

Just as the Restoration Parliaments and senior officials had been more inclined to persecute and harass their Puritan, Presbyterian, or dissenting enemies than had been Charles himself, so the Privy Council and the General Assembly were now minded to harsher measures against the episcopalians and their sympathizers in the universities than was William. The monarch saw that bare obedience sufficed and that to exact more risked provoking conscience-driven revolts. Senior officeholders, however, could see only that their opponents questioned the legitimacy of the change in regime and that such mental reservations augured ill for future security; the more dubious the state of legitimacy, the greater the imperative that all be seen to have participated in it, by way of making a reversal to the *status quo ante* more difficult. But as with the previous change in 1662, the Crown ensured that many ministers, on this occasion mostly in the north, who were willing to continue to serve, did not need to register an explicit approval of the new form of church government in order to remain in office. Nevertheless, a number of principled episco-palians eventually left the establishment and became, in effect, the very thing they most despised: a dissenting denomination. More ominously for the future, they were overwhelmingly Jacobite in sympathy; that is, they rejected the legitimacy of the Glorious Revolution of 1688–1689 and continued to view James VII and his heirs as the rightful claimants to the throne.

On the left of the spectrum, only the most intractable of the Cameronians remained outside of the new arrangements. These judged the Kirk to be Erastian still and noted that the new monarchs had not "taken the Covenant" themselves but merely assented to the reinstatement of Presbyterianism. Fortunately, it was not necessary to attempt to satisfy those who, like enough, could never be satisfied.

There were to be two serious episcopalian and Catholic challenges to the new religious and political establishment in the years ahead. The year 1715 saw a poorly managed Jacobite uprising in favor of the "Old Pretender," James Edward Stuart, son of James VII. But the 5,000 clansmen who rose for James were matched by those who refused. The final, insubstantial coalition consisted of 5,000 Scots, some Lancashire Catholics, and a promise of help from Ireland, which did not materialize until far too late. The rebellion was suppressed with ease. In 1745 the unequal contest was rerun—with a similar, if bloodier result—when the same constituency rose for Bonnie Prince Charlie, James VII's grand-son, Charles Edward Stuart. This time, thanks to bungling by central government, the rebels advanced as far as Derby. But then the clansmen began feeling homesick (their concerns were, after all, mostly local or extended, at best, only to Scotland), and the Young Pretender's army began melting away around him. No amount of boldness made a rapid march on London appear feasible; the Jacobites retreated again into

Scotland but were caught at Culloden, where they were crushed by the Duke of Cumberland's redcoats.

These interludes apart, the first half of the eighteenth century saw Presbyterian church order and discipline govern every aspect of the lives of most Scots. It was strict and unrelenting. Cursing, swearing, drunkenness, sexual sins, and Sabbath-breaking all bore penalties: excommunication, penance at the pillory, and, worst of all, subjection to the endless admonitions of the clergy. The Sabbath was observed with the kind of strictness more usually associated with orthodox Judaism; religious activities and observances were the only "work" permitted—though elders allowed themselves the additional task of patrolling the parishes to make sure that others were not absconding from church. Church services were lengthy, consisting of little by way of liturgy, and mostly of extemporaneous prayers, the singing of metrical psalms (hymns and the instruments that generally accompanied them being alike disapproved of), and long sermons, prepared in advance but delivered as though they had not been—that is, the preacher spoke without the benefit of a manuscript—and in which hell was a favorite theme.

At best, such an atmosphere evoked a piety of unusual sternness. More often it led to a dark, gloomy legalism. Yet participation was, in many areas, wholehearted. Communion was celebrated rarely, and with great earnestness and solemnity. The "communion season" commenced weeks beforehand, when ministers and elders would visit their parishioners, admonishing them to repent of particular sins, to be reconciled to neighbors with whom they had quarreled, and generally to put their spiritual houses in order. No offense was too small, no rumor too flimsy to be ignored. Toward the latter end of the week before communion itself, preaching services were held, often in the open air to accommodate the numbers, where all were exhorted to repentance and warned of the judgment that would befall those who participated in the bread and the cup unworthily. The designated Sunday was one long string of communion celebrations, followed the day after by a service of thanksgiving.

The need for open air meetings highlighted a problem of the church in Scotland: church buildings were often small and falling into neglect. The country itself was so poor that maintaining churches—or paying ministers a reasonable salary—was beyond the ability of many parishes, some of which struggled even to afford communion wine. The fervor amid the poverty, of course, was all the more touching and poignant.

Seriousness on this scale, however, provoked reaction and repudiation. The scornful portrayal of its brooding Calvinism by the poet Robert Burns (1759–1796) was understandable, though cruel:

O Thou, who in the heavens does dwell,
Who, as it pleases best Thysel,'
Sends ane to heaven an' ten to hell,
A' for Thy glory,
And no for ony gude or ill
They've done afore Thee!

Scottish Calvinism was an abettor in its own downfall. By emphasizing the otherness and inscrutability of God, it made him more distant from ordinary people—who were thereby made more amenable to the claims of the deists and rationalists of the rising Scottish Enlightenment. These turned divine inscrutability to their advantage by downplaying revelation and emphasizing God's role as distant originator. In the same way, the Calvinists' "providence" was increasingly stressed as being exemplified in and mediated by the laws of nature, until any sense of divine immediacy was lost.

The early eighteenth century saw the rise of a new breed of ministers within the church whose faith was tinctured by modern, rationalist considerations of this kind. These, the so-called Moderates, found an ally in the century's most unpopular religious institution: patronage. The Union of the Scottish and English Parliaments occurred in 1707, and five years later the new, combined institution undertook a measure that its purely Scottish predecessor, so much more closely answerable to Scottish political pressures, would never have dared: it reinstated the system of patronage, whereby gentry or other local worthies, rather than the elders and the congregation, could nominate a minister to a benefice. This allowed ministers with unpopular, rationalist opinions to be inserted over the protests of parishioners. Their progress was marked by a series of secessions. By midcentury, however, the national church was dominated by the supporters of the spirit of the Enlightenment.

British Rule in Ireland

We have noticed aspects of English rule in Ireland in earlier chapters. After the union of the Crowns of England and Scotland in 1603, the de facto situation became that of British rule, even if monarchs in London liked to speak of their three kingdoms, including Ireland, as if they were all somehow on a par. Religion remained—and remains—as part cause and part effect of the conflict engendered by the original conquest of Ireland by the Anglo-Norman kings and the subsequent attempts, down through the centuries, to maintain that rule.

The strength of Catholicism in Ireland was not unconnected with that country's economic and social backwardness, as measured against the relatively advanced state of much of England. The social and economic factors that contributed to Protestantism in England, the Netherlands, and the trading cities of Germany and Switzerland simply did not exist in Ireland, which had few towns of any size and none of native origin and was also characterized by low literacy and a mercantile class of minimal size. But Catholic allegiance did not merely reflect material conditions; it was also an instrument, after the Reformation, of resistance to alien rule. Of course, as the religious conflict deepened across Europe in the wake of the Reformation and Counter-Reformation, the mistreatment of the Irish Catholics by successive London governments and the resistance of the Irish to Protestantization (that is, to the religious policy of London) intensified one another, until each side scared the other witless.

It was not as simple as that, of course—except for the resultant witlessness. The established church in Ireland—established, that is, by the Irish Parliament of 1560—was a Protestant echo of its counterpart and model in Canterbury. It was augmented in 1592 by the founding of Trinity College, Dublin, for the provision of Protestant education. But the church held the allegiance only of the settlers and the Anglicized. The vast majority of the populace remained Catholic in both sympathy and practice—for the authorities could hardly stamp out Catholicism when it was in a position of such strength. The rebellions of the last quarter century of Elizabeth's reign had succeeded in embroiling England's nemesis, Spain, on the side of the Irish Catholics. But they had failed to overthrow Protestant rule. Defeats of the rebels had been followed, as surely as night follows day, with further expropriations of Irish land. If the native Irish refused Protestantization, their land would be given to Protestants from outside, who would be politically loyal to the monarch in London and form the basis for a new, Protestant element in the population.

This was made easier for the government in London by the flight of the Catholic earls from Ulster (the province that had formed the backbone of the rebellion in the 1590s) into exile on the Continent in 1607. A systematic "plantation" was begun, with Protestant settlers brought from England and, even more often, from the Scottish lowlands. Forests were cleared and Irish pastoralism replaced by arable farming. New towns and a commercial economy in Ulster began to replace the primitive subsistence economy of the native Catholics. It all had to be defended against the likelihood of revenge from the indigenous population, who were reduced to the status of laborers and servants—and sometimes tenants, though increasingly confined to the least profitable land.

The situation of apartheid made the native Irish all the more receptive to the outpouring of attention and fraternal help from Rome when it came. The Counter-Reformation was enthusing Catholics everywhere for mission, for education, and for heightened religious commitment. There could be no one better to make the objects of this newfound energy and beneficence than the Irish Catholics, under pressure as they were from infidel rulers.

The Protestants' most illustrious churchman during these years was James Ussher (1581–1656), archbishop of Armagh from 1625. Born in Dublin and a committed Calvinist, he steered a course of moderate Protestantism in an age when that was becoming difficult. A brilliant scholar, he was the first to provide the evidence necessary to distinguish the seven genuine epistles of Ignatius of Antioch (the late-first-century and early-second-century bishop) from the spurious ones. Ussher also produced a scheme of biblical chronology, according to which the creation of the world was calculated to have occurred in 4004 B.C.

A third of the land in Ireland was held by the so-called Old English aristocracy, descendants of Norman and subsequent newcomers. These had been indigenized but still thought themselves a cut above the "true" natives, though they remained, like their tenants with whom their lives were bound up, recalcitrant in their Catholicism. For this, they had just cause to fear that the monarchs in London did not trust their loyalty.

It was into this rather delicate situation that the somewhat less-than-delicate person of Sir Thomas Wentworth (later Earl of Strafford) was dropped, as the king's new Lord Deputy of Ireland, in 1633. In December 1634 he leaned hard on the Convocation of the Irish Church, persuading it to adopt canons approximating to the Church of England's Thirty-Nine Articles, thereby replacing the Calvinist articles that Ussher had introduced in 1615. The following year, he clashed with Ussher again, persuading the convocation to set up a Court of High Commission, also on the English model. By the end of the decade, every bishop in Ireland was an Englishman; the episcopacy had no native roots and no reserves of influence upon which to draw.

Protestants in Ireland knew themselves to be adrift in a Catholic ocean. Moderate charting of a course close to that of the opposing side is not a natural response in such circumstances; antithesis is. By background (Scottish Presbyterianism and English Puritanism) and by circumstance, therefore, Irish Protestants would be little inclined to Charles's High-Churchmanship. Neither was there anything to be gained by it tactically for, to committed Catholics, all varieties of Protestant heresy were alike; quasi-papist, High Church Arminianism stood no chance of winning them over merely because Calvinists disliked it. Charles's policies of enforcing Laudian reforms on the Church of Ireland thus alienated natural allies among the Protestants without winning many new friends. Strafford's highly effective policy of recovering alienated lands for the church from their "new English" landowners compounded the problem.

But if, in Catholic eyes, all forms of Protestantism were alike in dragging their disciples down to damnation, they were certainly not equal in their political consequences. From that point of view, Charles's policies were less harsh than was the likely program of his Puritan opponents. The rebellion of 1641 arose in part from Irish Catholics taking fright at developments in England and Scotland. In Scotland the Presbyterians had risen in revolt against Charles's church policies. The English Parliament also seemed set to impose more hard-line Protestant policies upon the king. Neither augured well for the future direction of English rule in Ireland or for the toleration of Catholicism there. But the king's difficulties and the divisions opening up on the mainland of Great Britain also presented opportunities. The leaders of the rebellion decided that the Irish rebels would deny that they were rebels at all, that they would take an oath of loyalty to the king and claim to be protecting him from his mutinous subjects in England and Scotland.

Alas, one of those who knew about the uprising planned for 23 October 1641 had a wee dram too many the night before, as a result of which word leaked out, many of the ringleaders were apprehended, and the intended attack on Dublin Castle never took place.[5] But the uprising elsewhere went ahead anyway. The decade-long revolt commenced with a massacre of English and Protestant settlers numbering in the thousands; it was only brought to an end eight years later, after the counter-massacres inflicted at Drogheda and Wexford by Cromwell's forces in 1649.

The stakes could not have been higher. Ominously for the rebels, the English Parliament borrowed, as early as 1642, large sums on the security of Irish lands it expected to confiscate, thereby confirming Catholic fears. The

Protestant depiction of Irish rebels massacring Protestants in 1641.
Illustration from Matthew Taylor, England's Bloody Tribunal, 1772.

Catholic rebels in turn confirmed the fears of the Protestants (apart, that is, from massacring the Ulster planters) by welcoming the papal nuncio, Archbishop Rinuccini, and the leadership of returning exiles.

Following the suppression of the rebels by Cromwell's forces in 1649, his soldiers were paid in kind—that is, in expropriated Irish land. Only a minority stayed to farm it for themselves. The majority sold out and returned to England. But the native Catholics were seldom in a position to repurchase their own property; the Cromwellian expropriations created new classes of Protestant landlords and Catholic landless across the length and breadth of Ireland. In 1641 Catholics had continued to hold 59 percent of the real estate in Ireland; only in Ulster and its adjacent counties, Wicklow and Kilkenny, had the majority been in Protestant ownership. By 1688, however, Catholics retained only 22 percent of the land, holding a majority only in Galway. By 1703 the proportion had fallen to 14 percent, and in 1778 to 5 percent—this despite the fact that Catholics continued to constitute three-quarters of the population. This was not construed as injustice in quite the sense insisted upon by today's protagonists of identity politics—for those who had always been mere tenants cared little about who their landlord was; nor the longtime landless, about the religion of the landowners. But it did create a new class of malcontents, who knew that their own poverty was recent and directly related to the elevation of the current landholders (or of their recent ancestors). It also created a cultural chasm between property owners and the propertyless, analogous to that in Russia, and so to an absence of the usual paternalism or of any sense of community interest—things that did so much in most of Europe to mitigate the inevitable social, economic, and legal distinctions between rich and poor.

The Restoration of the monarchy in 1660 led to a partial return of the confiscated lands—enough to make Protestants feel insecure in their tenure but not nearly enough to satisfy more than a small number of the most fortunate Catholics. The question of formal toleration for Catholicism in Ireland continued to press upon both sides.

In practice, each side made concessions to the other. In particular, the secretly Catholic-favoring (indeed, probably already secretly Catholic) Charles II did what he could to shield papists from the full wrath of Protestant intolerance. In return, the Catholics sought to ingratiate and facilitate where they could. When a new Catholic archbishop of Dublin was appointed in 1669, the man chosen was Peter Talbot (1620–1689), a member of a family that had long been in the royal favor. Knowing that his status as a Jesuit could only fuel the flames of Protestant hostility, the general of the order gave him special permission to renounce his membership in the Society of Jesus before taking on his new office. And although his consecration as archbishop reflected the church's illegality by taking place in the safety of Antwerp, his ministry was exercised openly in Ireland.

Talbot was able to hold his first diocesan synod in Dublin the following year, when the Franciscan Peter Walsh presented a proposed Declaration of Allegiance, demanded by the Duke of Ormond, Lord Lieutenant of Ireland, as a condition for granting formal toleration to Catholics. But the declaration explicitly denied the pope's right to depose a king and was considered too categorical for acceptance by the assembled bishops; so the matter went into abeyance.

The synod also debated the vexed question of primatial authority in Ireland. Did it inhere in the archbishop of Dublin, as claimed by Talbot (who just happened to hold the office in question), or in the archiepiscopacy of Armagh, as argued by Oliver Plunkett (who, entirely coincidentally, was the incumbent of that archbishopric)?

Meanwhile, the Catholics' enemies desired that neither archbishop be able to function at all. When the Irish Catholic gentry sent a representative to the court in London to petition for the redress of grievances, Parliament responded by petitioning the monarch to banish Talbot from the kingdom and "that all convents, seminaries, and popish public schools be suppressed; that no Irish papist be admitted to inhabit in any corporation of that kingdom; that all the Irish Papists might be disarmed, and no Papist be either continued or admitted to be a commander or soldier in that Kingdom."[6]

In 1673 the Members of Parliament got their wish and Talbot was exiled, though he was allowed to return shortly after. In 1678, however, he was implicated in misdeeds through the hysteria aroused in London by Titus Oates about a "Popish plot." Already a sick man, Talbot was arrested, and he died in prison in 1680. His antagonist, the archbishop of Armagh, reconciled to Talbot in prison, was hanged, drawn, and quartered for treason at Tyburn the following year.

Catholic hopes in Ireland rose when Charles's successor, his brother, James II, came to the throne in 1685. James was openly Catholic and consequently had understandable difficulty in persuading his Protestant subjects, in both Britain and Ireland, that he was not inimical to their interests. Their confidence was hardly increased when Talbot's brother, Richard, a longtime friend and confidant of James, was put in charge of the army in Ireland and made Earl of Tyrconnell. Shortly afterward he became the first Catholic viceroy for over a century. Tyrconnell then used his appointive power to promote Catholics to public positions in the government and judiciary of Ireland and to promote Catholic interests (and disadvantage Protestants) through the mechanisms of administration, touching church finance and town charters.

But what Catholic erstwhile landowners wanted above all was the return of their property. Tyrconnell's regime presented an opportunity to reverse the land settlement. The situation for bringing this about had never been so propitious; it was now or never. Tyrconnell utilized again the gerrymandering that had previously been used to produce an exclusively Protestant Parliament in Dublin, this time with the intention of creating an overwhelmingly Catholic one which, in the anticipation of royal assent, would draft the legal changes necessary to restore Catholic land.

The window of propitiousness, however, was smaller than Irish Catholics had realized. Significant sections of the political classes in England lost their nerve completely and in 1688 invited the redoubtably Protestant William of Orange to accept the throne in place of his papist father-in-law.

This was a catastrophe for Irish Catholic hopes. Tyrconnell held on, in anticipation of military help. James fled to France, but in March 1689 he was coaxed to land at Kinsale, bringing French money and weapons. War followed, though the Catholics were hampered by the unwillingness of their English leaders to do anything that would undermine English rule in Ireland in the long term. In the short term, however, there was a significant redistribution of property and a declaration of religious toleration. But Catholic Europe was itself divided; the peace settlements of 1648 had ended the system of confessional power blocs, and a good enemy of Louis XIV's France, such as Protestant Britain, could only be seen as a friend by Catholic Austria and Spain. The crisis straddled the reigns of two popes, Innocent XI and Alexander VIII, and even they took a dim view of James, simply because his chief patron, Louis XIV, was in conflict with the Holy See.

The armies fighting in Ireland were quite international in composition. James's troops were mostly French and Irish, though the former returned home in late 1690 after William's army of British, Dutch, Germans, French (Huguenots), and Danes had relieved the siege of Derry (Londonderry) and then defeated the Catholic army at the Battle of the Boyne in July. The back of Irish resistance was broken during 1691, and peace was made that October in return for the promise "that the Irish in Ireland should, in their lives, liberties and property be equally protected" and should have "the free and unfettered exercise of their religion." The promise was scarcely believable, but the overwhelming force of British arms made it necessary that the vanquished act on the premise that it was. About 14,000 Catholic Irish troops went into exile at the end of the war, emulating the 30,000 who had left after Cromwell's victories a generation earlier. This from a population of some two million was no insignificant loss of able-bodied men.

The supposed toleration soon proved itself an illusion. In 1694 the Act for the Better Securing of the Government against Papists decreed that no Catholic might bear arms. Three years later, the Banishment Act expelled all Catholic clergy under pain of transportation (if they refused) or of being hanged, drawn, and quartered (if they dared to return). Further legislation excluded Catholics from public office and from all civic and commercial life.

The eighteenth century was dominated by these notorious penal laws against Catholics. However, the legislation against their public worship fell into disuse from the second decade of the new century, and the church was enabled to organize itself properly, with the erection of chapels (the term *church* being reserved for the Protestant establishment) across the country and a full complement of bishops and hierarchy in place by the midcentury. Yet, as in England, papists and Protestant dissenters alike remained liable for payment of tithes to the established state church. For most poor people, it was this last measure that was resented above all the rest.

Other aspects also remained grim. In an effort to keep the subject population ignorant and powerless, Catholic education was strictly forbidden. A variety of "hedge schools" (that is, establishments operating out of doors) sprang up to circumvent this prohibition but, dependent as they were on the occasional clemency of the Emerald Isle's climate, the schooling they delivered was patchy. And damp.

The irony of the social apartheid was that it boxed in the Protestants also, to the extent that for the most part they did not even desire the conversion of their Catholic neighbors to Protestantism. The reason was simple: if too many abandoned what had become a subjugated caste, then the privileges of the existing Protestants would be eroded.

As the century progressed, Catholics found their own ways to enter public life. The Catholic Committee was set up in the late 1750s and reorganized by Charles O'Conor and John Curry in 1760. Pressure began in the direction of emancipation, which led to a series of Catholic Relief Acts from 1778 onward, culminating in the emancipation of 1829, which gave Catholics the vote on the same terms (ownership of property) as that of Protestants. But Ireland, as is well known, is a country with a problem for every solution. And the snag with the emancipation of 1829, as the legislators well knew, was that property was the central commodity that had been taken from Catholics long before, leaving few of them eligible to benefit from the supposed grand egalitarianism of the act's provisions. Ireland's problems were destined to grumble on. And whether we shall be entirely free of them this side the *parousia* is a theological question which, mercifully, we cannot pursue here.

11

LATIN AMERICA

▼

The Spanish and Portuguese Empires in the New World had been established, almost by definition, when those powers were vigorous engines
of intellectual energy, military strength, and spiritual creativity. But by
at least the middle of the seventeenth century they had ceased to be so.
Portugal had been absorbed into the Spanish kingdom and then, in 1640,
unabsorbed again. But in both countries, and especially in Spain, the
fire had gone out. Such military and political advantage as there was
to be gleaned from shipping all of that precious metal back to Europe
had been gleaned, spent, and, for the most part, wasted. Certainly Spain
noticed no economic advantages. It had entered upon its long, slow
decline in relative power, economy, and population that would not be
reversed until the death of Generalissimo Franco.

The definitive Counter-Reformation power in the late sixteenth century, it was in no small part the effects of its religion that had had such
deleterious effects upon Spain. An excessive fearfulness of religious
deviation and an exaggerated emphasis upon honor are not simply characteristic of poor societies; they are a recipe for creating them. Spain's
intellectual life had become closed-off and inward-looking even as its
monarchs had run out of resources to prosecute several wars at once—or

even one at a time. Hyper-Catholic crusading may be all very well while there are new worlds to conquer and treasure and slaves to be plundered, but when one's new rivals depend instead upon the despised, constructive activities—such as trade and manufactures, science and technology—then one must adapt or decline. One must choose the world either of Amsterdam and London or of *Don Quixote*. And Spain had opted for the world of *Don Quixote*. This was a shame, because even Cervantes had summoned it into existence only in order to ridicule it.

For Latin America, all of this meant an increased reliance upon its own resources. Having inherited the Iberians' religion and language through conquest, forced enculturation, and something approaching genocide, the resultant population, which was itself the product of widespread ethnic mixing, began to develop the distinctive religious and cultural resources available to it in new directions.

Inevitably, the debt to Spain remained large. Most bishops were still Spanish. The leading positions among the monastic orders continued, for the most part and to the chagrin of Creole monks, to rest in the hands of *peninsulares* (recent arrivals from Spain). Political control likewise remained in viceroys sent from Madrid. The splendid baroque architecture of the churches was imported—even if the Latin Americans developed upon it and embellished it.

Latin American society was unavoidably a mixture of the survivors from among the Indians, of the Iberians who had invaded them (both *peninsulares* and Creoles), of the black slaves (whom the invaders had imported from Africa), of the *mestizos* (people of mixed white-Indian ancestry), and of the mulattos (people of mixed white-black parentage, who were generally distinguished into subcategories according to what proportion of white or black they were). By the mid-seventeenth century, people of mixed race were the largest population group in cities and mines.[1]

The religious differences among the ethnic groups were considerable. The Iberians, of course, were Catholics. So too, at least ostensibly, were the Indians, many of whom, as we noticed in chapter 3, were governed by Jesuits in those places where mission villages had been created. Apart from these special situations, however, the Indians often received little pastoral attention, and for many of them in remote areas, their Catholicism was a veneer overlaid upon more traditional beliefs. The black slaves were the least evangelized of all. Their numbers were greatest, obviously, in those areas where plantations were easiest to establish: Cuba, Hispaniola, Venezuela, and parts of Brazil. The monastic orders had been most solicitous for the welfare of the Indians; the sentiment was expressed more weakly—and later—in respect of the Africans. And in any case, the Jesuit tactic of protecting Indians from European culture by physically separating them from it where possible could hardly be repeated in respect of slaves whose whole existence was fated to be subject to Europeans. In consequence, many slaves were not Christianized at all or else generated heavily syncretistic forms of Catholicism. Hence the strong persistence today of voodoo in Haiti, for example, and of Afro-Brazilian cults.

Christianizing the Indians

Latin America's Indians were often particularly good at feigning obedience and deference to their conquerors while practicing their traditional religion away from the latter's surveillance. And who could blame them? The Spanish invasions had devastated their societies, reducing indigenous populations to a mere remnant of what they had been. Open defiance did occur, but in most cases it was worse than risky; it was suicidal. And so Gonzalo de Balsalobre, the priest of a village near Oaxaca, Mexico, was shocked to find that for a century and a quarter the natives who formed the bulk of his parish, and who appeared outwardly good (or at least compliant) Catholics, were in fact worshipers of thirteen traditional deities. He had been priest of the parish for twenty-two years: "desiring with tireless care by all roads to set them upon that of the State of Blessedness, I have always found them inwardly very far removed from it, although outwardly they show the contrary." But in 1653 he discovered that all along they were quietly observing their own calendar, resorting to their own pagan priest (a man with the obediently Hispanic name of Diego Luis), using traditional charms to get good hunting or recovery from illness, making auguries, sacrificing dogs and chickens, and visiting the old pagan shrines. The pagan priest delivered his verdict about which would be good or bad days to give alms in the parish church. If the augurs were good, then candles were lit at the altar of the Virgin—though the goddess being worshiped was, in fact, Nohuichana.[2] Clearly, Father Gonzalo and his predecessors had not been paying attention! Even his account of what his charges had really been up to was obtained only by instilling his informant with the "fear of punishment."

The Jesuit Antonio Ruiz de Montoya had a lesser but not entirely dissimilar experience. In 1639 he published an account of the successes of his order in central South America, in which he related also an instance of serious backsliding from the faith by Guaraní Indians. Montoya and his fellows had trouble one Sunday morning in getting the Indians to answer the bells that summoned them to Mass. "Then, in great secrecy, a young man revealed to one of the Fathers that there were three dead bodies, on three hills, that talked; they were warning the Indians against listening to the Fathers' preaching." Further inquiries unearthed a pagan temple, complete with priests who consulted with a skeleton, suspended in netting from the ceiling, along with offerings of crops. The dead oracles were believed able to confer health and fertility upon people and crops.[3]

Father Balsalobre in Mexico and Father Montoya among the Guaraní were not alone. By about 1610 the Catholic authorities in the archdiocese of Lima had come to the conclusion that a population they thought to have evangelized successfully was not really evangelized at all. The Indians had been practicing idolatry in secret all along. The Catholic Church girded itself for a new campaign of eradication, complete with *visitadores de idolatría*, directed against the Andean Indians. It would blend instruction of the misguided, investigation of the erring, and punishment of the obstinate. Its activities lasted throughout the century, spilling over a little into the next.[4]

One striking success story of Christianization of Latin American Indians itself betrays something of the ambiguity of the process. Our Lady of Guadalupe has become an integral part of Mexican national consciousness and the most famous Marian shrine in the New World. According to the received story, the Madonna appeared to a Christianized Indian boy named Juan Diego in 1531, just a decade after the capture of Tenochtitlán by the Spanish. She appeared, not as a white European, but as a dark Indian. She instructed him to have a temple built for her "on this spot"; he was to go to see the bishop of Mexico City to arrange the matter. The bishop in question was Juan de Zumárraga, who treated the boy kindly but did not at once accept the reality of his revelations. Eventually, however, Bishop Zumárraga was persuaded when the boy brought him the sign of flowers that had bloomed out of season and which, when he dropped them on the floor, left an image of the Virgin on the boy's cloak, in which they had been carried.[5]

The story is charming, of course. But it is first recorded 118 years after the events it purports to describe. And it is set down by a priest, Luis Lasso de la Vega, who had charge of the Shrine of Our Lady of Guadalupe. The identical problem that confronts most medieval miracle stories and miraculous accounts of saints' lives immediately present themselves: the earliest written records of such stories date from many generations after the events they purport to describe, and the chronicler

is an interested party in magnifying the importance of the spiritual institution (abbey, cathedral, minster, or shrine) which he or she happens
to serve. (This is not a problem, be it noted, that besets either the New
Testament accounts or the recorded miracles from the early centuries
of the church.) Furthermore, Tepeyacac, the site of the shrine, had been
the site of a pagan temple of Tonantzin, "Mother of the Gods." Had this
mother of the Indian deities mutated into an Indian apparition of the
Mother of God? Should we perhaps understand the development of the
cult of Our Lady of Guadalupe as one more instance of the phenomenon
that attended Christianization elsewhere, including Europe in the early
Middle Ages, where ancient gods were newly baptized as Christian saints
and ancient temples rededicated as churches with local significance?
It accorded with the early-seventh-century advice of Pope Gregory the
Great—advice we had cause to notice in chapter 3 of this book.

Certainly the continuity between preconquest paganism and colonial-
era Catholicism was considerable. In the mid-eighteenth century Joseph
Och, a German Jesuit, recorded the persistent difficulties of persuading
the Indians of northwestern Mexico to give up their traditions.

> In their customs the Indians are secretive towards the missionaries. Even
> among those who otherwise are good Christians there always clings some-
> thing of the former odour of impiety. . . . At the tender age of six to twelve
> months [the] children must endure a cruel torture. All the hair is pulled
> from the child's eyebrows and the little holes or pores are enlarged with
> a thorn.

He described how the child's lips were reshaped even more cruelly, then
added that

> Women far advanced in pregnancy are driven from the house and absolutely
> forbidden to give birth within it, for such women are looked upon as being
> poisoned. The Indians believe that a birth deprives arrows of their power
> so that they will never be able to hit a mark.[6]

Houses in which a person had died were burned down "because the dead
one had returned to it" as a ghost.[7] But by giving Christian instruction
to these Indians—instruction that included the use of whiplashes—Och
was able to persuade them to desist from these practices. Or possibly
secretiveness reasserted itself, so that he just thought they had.

Indians in Latin America were seldom trusted with the responsibilities of leadership in any case. The priests remained Spanish, with few
exceptions, until well into the eighteenth century. *Mestizos* were also

excluded for the most part—not on overtly racial grounds, but because the vast majority of them were illegitimate, the offspring of casual dalliances by Iberian men, and so they were excluded from eligibility for the priesthood. Though Pope Gregory XIV, anxious for the Catholic Church to be rooted firmly in American soil, waived the traditional rule and gave express permission for such ordinations in 1576, facts on the ground went essentially unaltered by his concession to broadmindedness. During the first generation after the conquest of Mexico, Bishop Zumárraga established a college at Tlatelolco to train Indians for the clergy, but though the college continued, none of its graduates was ordained, celibacy proving a yet more insurmountable obstacle in Indian culture than it had in Europe. Instead, its graduates became clerical assistants of various kinds, especially in enabling a Spanish-speaking clergy to communicate with Indian parishioners.

So the gloomy dance continued through the sixteenth and seventeenth centuries and on into the eighteenth. Of the four conflicting elements in the political mixture of Latin America, three were espousing self-contradictory positions. The Catholic missionaries, often enough, cared passionately about both the spiritual and material welfare of the Indians—though not all monks and clergy were so high-minded. The most principled among them wished to protect the natives from the brutalities of the missionaries' fellow Europeans as well as from the brutalizing effects of contact with them. The most radical among the missionaries, such as Bartolomé de las Casas, deplored the Spanish invasions in their entirety; many others were at least ambivalent about them.[8] Yet their only hope of mitigating the appalling effects of enslavement and mistreatment was to strengthen the power of the Spanish Crown over the cruel underlings who were carrying out misdeeds in the name of Spain. The Crown, the second part of the mix, much though it lent a sympathetic ear to the pleas of the friars and the Jesuits, and much though it wanted its own authority enhanced in the New World, was far distant from the field of action and with highly uncertain control even over its own agents. Moreover, it relied for such power as Spain had in its colonies upon the exertions of the conquistadors and their successors, the *encomenderos* (soldier-landowners)—men whom it could seldom afford to antagonize. The royal writ did not always run reliably in European provinces; to expect its commands to be met with instant and uniform obedience half a world away was unrealistic. The Indians, the third element in the mix, were often ambivalent or worse about the new faith that was being so urgently proffered to them. Yet the Christian missionaries offered them the only protection they were likely to get from the depredations of the dreaded Christians. Outward compliance was generally necessary to ensure at least this much respite.

All told, it was a pretty pickle. The only group relatively unhampered by such inner conflicts was the colonizers and *encomenderos* themselves. They had residual respect for the religion whose spread had, to some degree, justified their conquests in the first place, and they knew that if the Indians accepted this religion it could only serve to make them more docile for the future. But the *peninsulares* and Creoles knew what they wanted: land, slaves, silver, and sugar. And they were the ones with power on the ground. Everything conduced to ensure that, struggles along the way notwithstanding, it was their objectives that were most likely to be realized. It should be little cause for astonishment, therefore, that the net result was a continent whose religious observances were rather superficial, served by a missionary clergy desperate to convert nominalism into real devotion, and torn between anger at mistreatment of the Indians and a desire to explain Iberian rule as, nevertheless, a harsh instrument under God to bring the natives to the One True Faith.

Slavery

The one major interest group excluded from these calculations was that of the African slaves. These were all but powerless and so, deplorably, can hardly enter into the kinds of considerations we have been describing. Although it was cheaper to enslave a local Indian, rather than bring an African across the Atlantic, it was not the Crown's ineffectual attempts to outlaw the enslavement of Indians that caused that practice to decline. Rather, it was because Iberians preferred Africans as laborers, considering the natives too weak to withstand the burdens their European masters wished to lay upon them. There was an ever-spiraling demand for sugar in Europe, which in turn stimulated demand for slaves in Brazil and elsewhere.

Indeed, many enslaved Indians died in the earliest years of the sugar plantations. The enraged Jesuit priest José de Anchieta (1554–1594) exclaimed:

The number of Indians that have been destroyed in this captaincy of Baía in the past twenty years passes belief; who would think that so many could be destroyed in so short a time? In the fourteen churches maintained by the Fathers they had brought together 40,000 souls, by count, and even more, counting those who came after—yet today it is doubtful whether the three churches that remain have 3,500 souls together. . . . Now look at the sugar-mills and plantations of Baía, and you will find them full of Guinean Negroes but very few natives; if you ask what happened to all those people, they will tell you that they died.[9]

Anchieta went on to complain that thousands of Indians had been tricked out of the forests, up to 300 miles inland in the interior, with promises of settlements on the coast, by Portuguese slavers who said that they would escort them to the Jesuit churches, "for it is common knowledge in the backlands that only the Indians in the churches where the fathers reside enjoy liberty and all the rest are captives."[10]

About a million black slaves were imported into Spanish America during the three centuries to 1820.[11] And about 600,000 more were imported to Brazil during the seventeenth century; by 1800 their descendants (and, of course, Africans imported later) constituted a third of the population. During the mid-seventeenth century two heroic Jesuits, Alonso de Sandoval and Pedro Claver, and their African translators were almost alone in ministering to the spiritual and material needs of the half-dead, disoriented slaves being disembarked from the floating hellholes of the slave ships at Cartagena. Sandoval went into print in 1627 to denounce the appalling treatment of the captives, but his efforts were in vain.

Though emancipation of slaves was more frequent in Latin America than in North America, eventually producing a significant number of free blacks, the phenomenon remained the exception rather than the rule. Each plantation had its own church where the priest, generally a secular cleric (i.e., not belonging to an order), was under the domination of the plantation owner, ensuring that the kind of Catholicism imbibed by the workers would reinforce, rather than undermine, their subjection. Indeed, the Jesuits themselves—so commendable in many aspects of Latin American life—were not above being slaveowners themselves. Jesuit estates near Quito, the capital of modern Ecuador, were worked by slaves in the 1620s.[12] By the time of the Jesuits' expulsion from Brazil in 1759, it was the colony's largest institutional slaveowner.[13]

African slaves had appeared in South America very early during the conquests. In the initial period they were accorded a social status intermediate between that of Europeans and Indians. But the growing slave trade during subsequent years meant that black people in the Americas could no longer be viewed by any of the parties as part-and-parcel of the European colonizing population. As the enslaved Indians died out, so the arriving blacks inherited the bottom positions in Latin American society. Amedée François Frezier, a French military engineer who spent the period 1712–1714 in Brazil, reported his surmise that blacks outnumbered whites in Baía by twenty to one. He expressed his astonishment at the way the former were treated, even though "when they have been baptised," they supposedly had "the dignity of sons of God." This comported ill, he maintained, with the "great outward show of religion" among the Portuguese in Brazil.[14]

Christianization of Africans generally followed enslavement, but since they were excluded from the priesthood, they formed *cofradías*. These were lay brotherhoods similar to those that had prospered in Renaissance Italy, promoting spiritual life, organizing participation in religious festivals, and providing rudimentary social security in matters ranging from sickness to burials.

One of very few black Christians to come to prominence during this period was Martin de Porres (1579–1639)—and he was a mulatto. Since the Dominicans of Peru were forbidden to accept blacks or mulattos as lay brothers, let alone to train them for the priesthood, he persuaded them to accept him as a voluntary servant at the order's infirmary. Legends grew about his sanctity even during his lifetime. The monks came to seek his spiritual counsel. "His boundless charity brought crowds of Indians and blacks to seek help. He spent his nights in prayer and penance. Even animals did as he told them." And it was apparently his humility, rather than any biting sense of ironic humor, that led him to refer to himself as a "mulatto dog."[15] In the ordinary run of such extraordinary things, Porres would have been an early candidate for sainthood. But again his color got in the way; though he was eventually canonized, it was not until 1962.

The Old Church in the New World

Organization and structure, of course, were the Church of Rome's strong suit. With the passing of time and the dedication of exceptional individuals, a pattern of organization emerged comparable to that in Europe. One of the early heroic churchmen was Archbishop Toribio de Mogrovejo of Lima, appointed by the Spanish king, Philip II, in 1580. Mogrovejo reorganized the Catholic Church in Peru and gave it a sense of cohesion and corporate identity by summoning, during the twenty-six years of his archiepiscopate, three provincial councils and ten diocesan synods.

One of Mogrovejo's top priorities, as befitted a former official of the Inquisition, was the eradication of idolatry. The provincial council of 1581 pronounced that all Indians living in the Americas before the arrival of the Spanish were in a state of eternal damnation. This verdict was arrived at under the guidance of José de Acosta, the provincial superior of the Jesuits in Peru and the man whom Mogrovejo had appointed as the council's chief theologian. (This appointment had been somewhat surprising in view of the bitter rivalry between Jesuits and Dominicans for the intellectual driving seat of the Catholic Church.)

In the Americas it was the Dominicans who, their responsibility for operating the Inquisition notwithstanding, often took the more liberal and accommodating line theologically. Bartolomé de las Casas had been of this school, and his fellow Dominican, Francisco de la Cruz, had followed in this tradition. But Acosta succeeded in having him condemned.

Yet it was doctrinal rigidity of this kind that produced the greatest operational and cultural flexibility. Mogrovejo's catechism, when it was published three years later, appeared in Spanish, Quechua, and Aymara. Acosta's dismal diagnosis of the Indians' spiritual state was certainly not based upon ignorance; he was massively well-informed about the Americas, as he demonstrated in his *Historia Natural y Moral de las Indias* (Natural and Moral History of the Indians) of 1590. According to him, the Spanish conquest had no moral status at all; it was a political fact like any other. Its importance lay in the providential use to which God was putting it, in bringing the Indians within the fold of the Catholic Church. Precisely because the Jesuits espoused such pessimism about the state of the Indians outside of the church, they were willing to make all kinds of cultural adaptations to further their salvation and to act as vocal advocates for their welfare. Acosta himself was just such an advocate. He urged missionaries to learn local languages, customs, and beliefs, and where these "do not conflict with the Faith or Justice, I do not believe that it is reasonable to change them."[16]

Doctrinal hardheadedness, then, was by no means incompatible with enlightenment; as our own age is proving, it is a condition for it. The phenomena of theological rigidity, on the one hand, and cultural flexibility and political solicitousness, on the other, are not incompatible; on the contrary, they are complementary, as evangelical missionaries have demonstrated again in our own day. But it was not—is not—a position that was altogether stable. Indeed, in Asia, as we have seen in chapter 3, Jesuits came to espouse positions equivalent to those held by the Dominicans in Latin America. Where culture leaves off and doctrine picks up can be a moot point. Or, to put the matter in McLuhan-esque terms, distinguishing between the medium and the message can be problematic.

Though the Indians of South and Central America continued to be excluded from the clergy during the seventeenth century, in practice, boundary lines could become blurred. The incompetence or corruption of Europeans opened the window. Thus it was that Felipe Huamán Poma de Ayala (1532–1615), an Indian Christian descended from an Inca chief, wrote in the last years of his life to the Spanish king, Philip III, a massive letter in which he noted that gifted Indians found employment in the church as singers and clerks.

> Because of the incompetence or absence of the priests they soon find themselves burying the dead with all the proper prayers and responses. They take vespers and look after the music and singing, as well as intoning the prayers. On Sundays and holy days they conduct the ceremonies as well as any Spaniard. In default of a priest they baptise the babies with holy water. . . . On Wednesdays and Fridays Indians conduct the early morning service. . . . However, they get nothing but interference from the priests themselves.[17]

Poma de Ayala was careful to commend a minority of the clergy, especially the Jesuits and Franciscans, but he found the other orders and the majority of the secular clergy to be corrupt, failing to live by the rule of celibacy, carrying weapons, indulging in trade alongside church work, and mistreating Indians. His long work of 1,190 pages gave a history of Peru interwoven with biblical history. According to him, preconquest Indians were Christians notwithstanding such technicalities as never having heard of Christ or the gospel, since they "observed God's commandments and the good works of compassion."[18] This goes beyond even the position of the Dominicans and comes closer to the twentieth-century thinking of Karl Rahner (a Jesuit!), whose concept of "anonymous Christians" is perhaps less innovatory—though no less contentious—than has been supposed.

Not only did Poma de Ayala's appeals never appear in print, but they had no effect upon Spanish colonial or ecclesiastical policy, and the document itself disappeared into utter obscurity, turning up by chance in the royal library in Copenhagen almost three centuries later, in 1895. But his work does illustrate the thoughts and attitudes of one particularly thoughtful Indian, whose reinterpretations and appropriations of the Christian faith, along with his protests at continuing, all-but-universal mistreatment of his people, were in all likelihood shared by the vast majority whose detailed reflections have gone unrecorded and must be reconstructed speculatively from the scattered details that are known of their actions.

The fact that printed books published in Spanish America were over-whelmingly religious in nature tells us more about the distribution of literacy (probably about 10 percent) than it does about the devoutness of the population—for the clergy made up a disproportionately large section of readers. Indeed, of the 26,500 population of Lima in 1611, exactly 10 percent were clergy or in religious orders—though it would be very unwise to extrapolate a similar proportion for the population as a whole since Lima was, after all, the administrative center of Peru. In fairness, the fact that most published books were of religious material reflects the strong drive to evangelize the population with the assistance of literature, which, if its intended audience could not read it, could at least be read aloud. But progress was slow. Only eighteen cities in Spanish America had printing presses during the eighteenth century; Brazil had none at all—a circumstance decreed by law—until 1808.

Unsurprisingly, then, the church was poorer and weaker in Brazil than elsewhere in Latin America. The country had only three bishoprics as late as 1700 and continued to be without a university during the eighteenth century. Its clergy were completely subject to the landowners, while, of the regular orders, only the Jesuits had an independent economic base. The actions of the Portuguese Crown during the course of the century weakened the church yet further.

Brazil was also more vulnerable than many of the other colonies; its population was small (perhaps a million in 1700, two million by 1800) and concentrated in coastal towns and the plantations a little inland. The colonizers had found no instant wealth to plunder, as in Mexico and Peru, nor any advanced Indian cultures like those of the Aztecs and Incas. In the mid-seventeenth century, Brazil's vulnerability was exposed when the expansionist Dutch East India Company successfully seized Pernambuco in 1630 and held it until 1654. Their territories included Recife, in north-eastern Brazil. The new, Protestant settlers were soon augmented by Calvinist pastors, who began work among the Indians. Worse yet from a Catholic point of view, a significant number of so-called New Christians inhabited the areas conquered by the Dutch. These were Iberian Jews who had been forcibly converted after the defeat of the Moors in the Iberian Peninsula during the fifteenth century. Their conversions remained a matter of legitimate doubt—partly because the inquisitors needed some-body to persecute and so suspected their orthodoxy, their sincerity, or both, and partly because, in this respect, the Jews felt an obligation to oblige them. With the restraining hand of the Catholic authorities gone, a number of the New Christians in Pernambuco came clean and declared themselves Jewish—a circumstance that hardly troubled the Dutch, who already had thousands of Iberian Jews back home in Amsterdam whom religious liberty and free enterprise had turned into honest men.

Unfortunately for both Jews and Protestants, the Catholic inhabitants of the Dutch-held territories united against the new rulers from 1645 onward, and in 1654 the Dutch gave the settlements up as a bad job, leaving the Jews in a woefully exposed position. Many of them were now forced to leave, though some later returned. In the early eighteenth century, for example, a curate of Baía who was a New Christian escaped and made his way to Holland, where he declared himself Jewish.

Catholic cultural identity for Central and South America was never seriously challenged. And inevitably its art, like its faith, was largely imported from Europe. Many of the baroque churches of Spanish America in the seventeenth century, for example, were as magnificent as those in the Old World. But sculpture enjoyed a more prominent place in decorating them than it did in Europe, where painting was more important. But often the different media were used in close combination and proximity. Much of the art was necessarily close to, or identical with, the mannerism and other styles of Catholic Europe, especially Italy and Spain. But Indians, though they learned the skills and techniques of their colonial masters, introduced elements of their own. It may have been simple enculturation or it may have indicated an element of protest that, in sculpture, "the Indians' favourite figures were lacerated, bloodstained figures of Christ, to whom the sculptor often gave Indian features."[19] Poma de Ayala, whose chronicles were mentioned earlier, commented that "Indians are skilful at the decorative arts such as painting, engraving, carving, gilding."[20] He hardly needed to mention himself as an example, for his work was illustrated with almost five hundred of his own drawings, which have "become the most popular focus of study in recent scholarship on cultural hybridity in Peru."[21] During the eighteenth century, the old Incan capital of Cuzco became the center of a school of religious art that combined Christian art with traditional and native motifs.

The seventeenth and eighteenth centuries were characterized by the advance of the parish system beyond the Iberian-dominated towns and into the wider dioceses. Nonurban areas had, in the early days, mostly been divided into *doctrinas*, that is, large districts under the ecclesiastical supervision—and frequently the secular jurisdiction—of a mission or other body of men in orders, especially the Jesuits. The extension of the parish system entailed conflict between these and the new, mostly Creole priests who were replacing them. But it also entailed yet further erosion of the Indians' culture and land. The missions had almost always operated in Quechua, Aymara, or such other languages as were spoken in the areas where they operated, but the new Creole priests were mostly unconcerned with such niceties and were generally uninterested in learning the tongues of a culture they considered destined and fit for destruction.

The Jesuit Missions

The Jesuit work fell back upon the most remote forest and jungle areas, which were those that in any case most interested them. Here the pure gospel could be preached without corrupting European influences. It was a vision that the other orders were unwilling, or unable, to share to the same degree of thoroughness, entangled as they were with the mundane politics of colonial urban life. The Jesuits, meanwhile, enjoyed a uniquely centralized structure of authority that was answerable only to the pope and agricultural wealth in Latin America that made them less susceptible to pressure from bishops and secular governors.

Such lofty principles—and such independence—won the Jesuits powerful enemies. The eighteenth century witnessed a crisis of vituperation against the Jesuits almost everywhere in Europe and its colonies, a crisis that would culminate in the suppression of the order itself in 1773. In Latin America, their determination to protect Indians from slave traders and from the colonial administrators who were often de facto in league with them enraged the colonial authorities. The fact that the Jesuits had independent sources of finance and wealth as well as a more direct line of authority to the Vatican enabled them to speak with an air of moral and spiritual authority that could leave secular governors exasperated.

Jesuit missions deep into the interior had begun in the early seventeenth century. From 1691 onward, ten missions were established in Bolivia, bringing Indians into settlements (*reducciones*) gathered around mission churches where they practiced agriculture and were educated by the Jesuits. One writer enthused in 1648 that they were "*nueva planta de la primitiva Yglesia*" (new growth of the primitive church).[22] And indeed the *reducciones* in Paraguay were a cause for particular wonder among contemporaries, with their enormous, highly distinctive churches, including countless altarpieces decorated with gilt and painted statues crafted by the Guaraní Indians. The Jesuits worked hard, not only to ensure that all was done through Indian languages, but to encourage related ethnic and linguistic groups to unify, where possible, in order to create more resilient, Christianized cultures.

But the colonists wanted Indian cultures that were less resilient—not more. And unfortunately for the Jesuits in Latin America, events in Europe were playing into the hands of their enemies. Portugal was increasingly dependent upon revenue from its huge colony across the Atlantic, and the Crown's able and energetic chief minister had a scheme to exploit the potential of the interior. Seen in this light, Jesuit opposition to the new policy was perhaps a mistake. Government fury may have been authentic, but it might as well have been manufactured, for the consequences of expelling the order from Portugal and its empire in 1759 included the opportunity for the Crown to seize Jesuit property in Brazil, which was vast and included estates, ranches, sugar plantations, colleges, and other urban property and investment holdings. And, as we have noted, the Society of Jesus held large numbers of slaves. Churches were handed over to secular clergy, as were the missions. Colleges were closed down and often converted into military uses.

The Jesuits continued their operations in Spanish-held territory, most notably their *reducciones* in Paraguay. Indeed, a new mission was started at Belén by Fathers José Sánchez Labrador and José Martín Mantilla in 1760. The Indians who had requested the establishment of the mission were the Mbayás, who had a long history of conflict with the settlers and for whom Christianization at the hands of the Jesuits now represented the best hope of protection from the other colonists. But even the commander of the priests' military escort viewed the enterprise less than favorably and looked upon his priestly charges with some irritation. Belén was a success, but in 1767 the settlers got their way when the Society of Jesus was expelled from Spanish territory also. The mission continued, but its prosperity declined. The secular clergy called in to replace the Jesuits were less well acquainted with Indian culture; some were actually fearful for their lives.[23]

It should be added that, however enlightened their tutelage in other respects, the Jesuits' failure to recruit Indians to the order itself made their missions perpetually dependent upon the cultural outsiders who had begun them. In this circumstance, the Indians were kept in the permanent status of "children."

12

NORTH AMERICA

TOLERATION AND NONTOLERATION

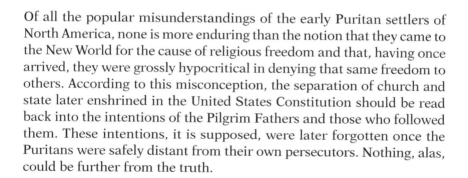

Of all the popular misunderstandings of the early Puritan settlers of North America, none is more enduring than the notion that they came to the New World for the cause of religious freedom and that, having once arrived, they were grossly hypocritical in denying that same freedom to others. According to this misconception, the separation of church and state later enshrined in the United States Constitution should be read back into the intentions of the Pilgrim Fathers and those who followed them. These intentions, it is supposed, were later forgotten once the Puritans were safely distant from their own persecutors. Nothing, alas, could be further from the truth.

The Christendom Model in America

The Separatists who sailed on the Mayflower in 1620 sought refuge from persecution, of course. But their settlement of Plymouth enshrined the notion, not that human communities should embrace a variety of religious beliefs, but that their own holy experiment might be played out in this remote corner of the earth, not only unmolested by episcopal authorities, but untainted by heretics or the ungodly. They came to establish a "city on a hill," not a Babel of competing religions such as the one that some of them had witnessed in Amsterdam. "All Familists, Antinomians, Anabaptists and other Enthusiasts," declared Nathaniel Ward in 1647, "shall have free liberty to keep away from us, and such as will come to be gone as fast as they can, the sooner the better."[1] As we have seen in chapter 6, the Separatists no more countenanced religious toleration than did their official persecutors in England; the former differed from the latter only on the question of which church was to be enforced and which persecuted. These were convictions that crossed the Atlantic with them.

The non-Separatist, Independent Puritans who, during the 1630s, followed the Pilgrim Fathers to New England had essentially the same vision of what a truly godly polity should look like; the only substantive distinction between them—Separatism and non-Separatism from the Church of England—tended to become somewhat hypothetical once both groups had, in practice, separated themselves by three thousand miles of cold salt water from the dubious ecclesiastical body that held sway in their native land. So it was only a matter of time before the Separatists merged with the far more numerous Puritan arrivals during the 1630s to form New England Congregationalism, which constituted the official church of Massachusetts and its neighboring colonies.

The Puritan emigrés and their descendants continued to do their utmost to ensure that the North American colonies—or those, at least, in which they themselves had the preponderance—really would be the "city on a hill" that they had come so far in order to establish. It was not until the end of the seventeenth century, and arguably not until the Great Awakening, that that dream began to subside once and for all. When it did so, it was as the result of undergoing a number of storms, five of which we shall now discuss in turn: (1) the furor around Anne Hutchinson's preaching and biblical expositions; (2) the question of how the Puritans would pass on their religious heritage to future generations; (3) the need to fend off attempts by the government in London to increase control over its colonies; (4) the Salem witch trials; and (5) the rise of religious sectarianism and religious pluralism.

The Massachusetts colonists of the first generation had granted political rights only to church members. The churches, in turn, had given membership only to those who could satisfy the clergy and elders with a credible evidence of having been converted. Truly, it was intended to be a reign of the saints.

The tangled connections between convertedness, church participation, and civic order had frequently been bothersome ever since Luther's disturbing announcement, over a century previously, that a person could know himself or herself to be in a state of salvation—a salvation that was not on the basis of good behavior but of faith in Christ. The portents of social anarchy that this analysis implied had then been addressed—and very quickly—in order to keep the Reformation in existence. The instability could be fended off one way by saying that only God could know which individuals he had chosen to have this saving faith—and so all could continue, *mutatis mutandis*, as before: everyone was required to submit to and participate in an official church, for the exact eternal destiny of one's neighbor was, thankfully, unknowable. The alternative resolution, that of the Anabaptists, had been to accept that true Christianity did not underwrite social stability. They denied that the identity of the regenerate was unknowable (along with the predestinarianism upon which such nescience rested), and they sought to restrict the church to those who knew themselves to be saved—with the consequence that not everyone could, or would, belong. This in turn demanded a breakage of the link between church and state. No rulers were prepared to take this second resolution in the early-modern period, with the result that predestinarian theology of one sort or another, moderate or virulent, was the sine qua non of state-church Protestantism.

Yet enthusiastic Protestants kept returning to tinker with the problem, dissatisfied that the Reformation had not, after all, produced a church of people decisively godlier than its Catholic rival. English Puritans, in particular, had scratched around for ways of restricting communion to those they approved of and at least of disciplining parishioners who lived scandalous lives. The breakaway groups of Separatists and semi-Separatists in the late sixteenth and early seventeenth centuries had spoken of "visible saints"—people who were "not ignorant in religion, nor scandalous in life"—as the only proper material for church membership. This way of talking blended easily enough, with the passing of time, into the assumption that one could, after all, make a rough-and-ready guess as to who might be saved. Finally, as we noticed in chapter 6, some of them had talked themselves through from this point to believer's baptism, thereby bringing into existence Calvinistic Baptists.

In America, the Separatists who had come over with the Mayflower, and the non-separating, Independent Puritans who had followed them a decade later, had not moved so far. Yet they also came in practice to the view that, their own Calvinism and the secret election of God notwithstanding, one could demand that church membership should be restricted to those who could give a credible account of conversion. By 1636 the Congregationalist clergy actually demanded such a test. The more strictly and traditionally Reformed aspect of their theology, on the other hand, continued to convince them of both the possibility and the desirability of a Christian state. Hence the connection between church membership and political rights. Hence also the affirmation of the Cambridge Platform, a synod of Congregationalist divines in Massachusetts in 1648, that the state should punish heresy in the interests of maintaining civil unity.

The Anne Hutchinson Affair

It was not an arrangement, then, given to religious toleration. Even dissenters from within could be subject to harsh treatment, as Anne Hutchinson (1591–1643) found when she started expatiating upon her pastor's sermons to other parishioners of Boston. The furor around her preaching and biblical expositions constituted the first of the major storms to break over the great Puritan experiment in the New World. The pastor in question was John Cotton (1584–1652); both he and the Hutchinsons had come to New England in 1633 from their native Boston, in Lincolnshire, England. (Countless settlements in the Americas were immediately named for the place of origin of their new, European inhabitants.)

Cotton's preaching hinted at Calvinism's antinomian potential: that, if God's grace did all and if faith was the sole requisite in human beings, then works of the law were redundant. It was a potential that Hutchinson did not hesitate to embrace and upon which she began to elaborate to the women who crowded her home for midweek meetings, which were intended to discuss Cotton's deliberations of the preceding Sunday. Sanctification, it seemed, was no evidence of justification. That conclusion was step one. The second step was the insistence that the Holy Ghost dwells in each justified person—an idea entirely unremarkable among Christians today yet feared by seventeenth-century Puritans, who saw it as but a step away from claims to personal illumination. And, indeed, just such a claim was Hutchinson's step number three: each justified person could tell who were the other justified souls, by a revelation of the Spirit, helping him or her to discern between those who were "under a covenant of grace"—and so saved—or "under a covenant of works"—and so lost. This, along with the unflattering implication that people who disagreed with Hutchinson were in the latter camp, threatened to undo the entire Puritan enterprise in North America.

It bears repeating that Reformed theology gained its strength by keeping the exact identity of the elect a closely guarded secret, known only to God in his inscrutable providence; only so could evangelical soteriology subsist with a state church that maintained social order and exacted outward moral obedience from every person. Hutchinson's ideas threatened to undo that linkage, fracturing the church by divisions between those who were sure, not only of their own salvation, but of that of other people, and those who were less sure. It also jeopardized moral order by undermining the importance of the moral law to salvation.

John Winthrop (1588–1649), the founder of the Massachusetts Bay Colony, began to have serious qualms about Hutchinson's meetings as early as 1636. Nor was he much reassured when, in January 1637, her brother-in-law John Wheelwright intemperately stood up at the close of a sermon to declaim against supposed legalists who thought sanctification to be evidence of justification: "We must kill them with the word of the Lord." Metaphorical language or not, the very stability of the colony appeared to be at stake.

Worse still, the young governor of the colony, Henry Vane (1615–1660), son of the English Secretary of State, sided with Anne Hutchinson. He had been elected to his position at the tender age of twenty, but despite his undoubted talents, his support of the troublesome faction now inclined the majority of electors to repent that they had chosen him. In 1637 Winthrop successfully stood against him for governor, determined upon the restoration of order.

Finally, that November the nettle was grasped. Anne Hutchinson was called to account in a lengthy judicial proceeding that lasted into 1638. Embarrassingly, she acquitted herself admirably, showing a knowledge of the Scriptures and an ability in interpreting them every bit as good as those of her official opponents. But her success in debate merely served to confirm the fears of her antagonists. For it was not only her ideas but, as the minister Hugh Peter declared at her trial, she in her own person who constituted a threat to social order: "You have stepped out of your place, you have acted rather like a husband than a wife and a preacher than a hearer; and a magistrate than a subject."[2]

It was Hutchinson's claim to divine inspiration that proved her final undoing. When confronted on the thorny issue of how she could be so sure that it was the Holy Ghost who was speaking to her, she unhesitatingly responded, Jesus-like, with a question of her own:

Hutchinson: How did Abraham know that it was God that bid him offer his son, being a breach of the sixth commandment?

Officer: By an immediate voice.

Hutchinson: So to me by an immediate revelation.

Officer: How! an immediate revelation.

Hutchinson: By the voice of his own spirit to my soul.[3]

However appealing, it was a fatal mistake. If the state churches of all hues, Catholic and Protestant alike, were agreed upon anything, it was that God cooperated with official religious leaders by revealing his will exclusively through them. Augustine, back in the early fifth century, had helped to theologize Christendom by declaring that the charismata were a thing of the past: the whole point of official religion was that it left the Holy Spirit redundant for all but rhetorical purposes and theological disquisitions. Hutchinson was now threatening, like the Anabaptists and enthusiasts, to take the genie back out of the bottle and to return to the pre-Constantinian situation. And the infection was spreading: already the young Henry Vane was reportedly going so far "as to maintain a personal union with the Holy Ghost."[4] It could not be allowed. The court pronounced: "You are banished from our jurisdiction as being a woman not fit for our society, and are to be imprisoned till the court shall send you away." When she enquired, "Wherefore I am banished," she was commanded by a stern-faced Winthrop, "Say no more. The court knows wherefore and is satisfied."[5]

If the cause of unfitness was left vague, then the same could not be said for the verdict. Hutchinson and her followers made their way to Rhode Island, where another group that had recently drifted away from the Puritan "city on a hill" and shuffled off into outer darkness was establishing a new colony.

The Half-Way Covenant

The second serious challenge to the New England Way was the vexed question of how the Puritans were to pass on the baton from one generation to the next—and then to the next. What should be done with those children of church members who, once grown up, remained unable or unwilling to give accounts of their own conversions? Such a failure to testify to conversion would have political effects, for the numbers of voters and people eligible for office would start to diminish—certainly proportionate to the population, and perhaps even absolutely. And what of the next generation? If the babies born in the 1650s and 1660s went unbaptized, they might lose all connection with the church. The "city on a hill" would fall into decay and ruin.

The current generation of unconverted adults, offspring of the first settlers, had received infant baptism on the basis of their parents' faith. Might they qualify for church membership? The answer, it seemed, was "no." Might they receive communion? Again, no. Might their children be baptized? Apparently, the answer to this was "yes, if the parents would subscribe to the faith and discipline of the church." Such was the decision of Congregationalist ministers meeting in synod in 1662. Their compromise solution, known to posterity as the "Half-Way Covenant" was aimed at balancing the idealism of a church of saints with participation of as wide a proportion of the populace as was practicable. It sought to keep society religious, even as society itself was becoming a little less so. And it sought to square the demands of godliness with the requirements of political stability. But it administered a severe jolt to the confidence of early Puritan New England.

Inevitably, the decision caused controversy. Some congregations denounced it as a slide away from primitivist rigor and into formalism. Others worried that, on the contrary, it did not go far enough, and they reasoned that the sacraments themselves were "converting ordinances." Notwithstanding its implicitly "catholic" ecclesiology, Solomon Stoddard, Jonathan Edwards's grandfather and minister of Northampton, Massachusetts, took this latter view. Increase Mather (1639–1723), son-in-law of John Cotton and one of the most influential Massachusetts clergy in his own right, was at first inclined against the innovation. But later he changed his mind and wrote a book in 1675, *First Principles of New England*, proving that the founders would have supported it and had shown more latitude on the question of who may be baptized than he and his contemporaries had suspected.

Political and Military Stresses

Though the colonies endured frightful losses to Indian wars in the mid-1670s, in which several thousand settlers died and half of the New England towns were destroyed or damaged, the fighting, once contained, did not threaten to overturn the essential basis of the Puritan dominance in New England. Instead, the third challenge came, not from the understandable fury of the natives, but from the relationship between the colonies and the mother country. In the early part of the century, when English power had been weak, the reach of royal government barely extended across the Atlantic. That, indeed, was precisely why the religious dissidents had gone there. In consequence, the regime in London was obliged to indulge political arrangements among their wayward subjects, be they ever so few and feeble, of which it can hardly have approved and which, under Charles I, with his attempted absolutist rule and Laudian church regime, it would have viewed with detestation. But, though English monarchs, civil wars, and republics came and went, by later in the century London's reach had lengthened. During the 1680s London made attempts to introduce episcopacy to its truculent subjects in the New World. In 1684 the charter of Massachusetts was revoked, and the following year the new Catholic monarch, James II (1685–1688), replaced all of the colonial assemblies of New England, along with those of New York and New Jersey, by an administrative Dominion authority. His purpose was to curb the autonomy of his distant, but fervently Protestant, subjects.

The Dominion did not last any longer than the monarch who introduced it. But the new charter of 1691, granted under the Protestant monarchs William III and Mary II, gave the vote upon the same basis as that prevailing in England: property. Not God, but mammon—at least to the extent of a freehold (outright ownership of land) worth £2 per annum—would henceforth determine who did, and who did not, possess the vote. The quasi theocracy of Puritan New England seemed to be at an end.

As if to vindicate these fears, some of the New England clergy toyed with episcopalianism or with "high" views of the sacraments. In response, their alarmed brethren reestablished local associations of clergy (they dare not be called presbyteries, for the Congregationalists had no truck with Presbyterianism), which had existed in an earlier generation but had been allowed to lapse.

Lapse, indeed, was what many of the New England firebrands believed had happened to far too many features of their forefathers' religion. Zeal had abated; this was why mammon had made so many inroads among them.

Worse was to follow. In 1698 the minister Thomas Brattle introduced a new clergyman to his Boston church whose sole title to clerical status was the fact that he had been ordained in England. Ordained in England! So the man had bowed the knee to a bishop. The only acceptable route to a pastorate among Congregationalists was by election of church members and with the approval of fellow ministers. An incandescent Increase Mather fretted:

If we espouse such principles as these, namely that churches are not to inquire into the regeneration of those whom they admit into their communion; . . . that the essence of a minister's call is not in the election of the people, but in the ceremony of imposing hands; that persons may be established in the pastoral office without the approbation of neighbouring churches or elders, we then give away the whole Congregational cause at once.[6]

The Salem Witch Trials

In point of fact, Congregationalism was already in the process of giving itself away or at least of undermining its own credibility. More than three centuries after the Salem witch trials of 1692 (the fourth of our tropical storms to beset the "city on a hill"), those proceedings remain a byword for Puritan obtuseness, cruelty, and bigotry. Indeed, in an aggressively secular age, they have become a stick with which to beat religion of all kinds out of the public square—or even, as the playwright Arthur Miller found, to attack the holding of any public beliefs at all.

Yet witchcraft remained a punishable offense in Europe, where executions were still not infrequent. The twenty deaths at Salem, Massachusetts, in the summer of 1692 were a heavy blow but not a catastrophe by the standards of, say, Germany. Yet the comparison would be a contrived one, for the New Englanders were not, for the most part, transplanted Germans but transplanted English people. And by 1692, the deaths of so many people as the result of witch trials counted as a catastrophe. No one had been burned, at least, for that offense in England for more than eighty years. The encroaching rationalism of the Enlightenment—influences from which the New World was by no means immune—were beginning to treat the very categories of witch investigations with some skepticism.

A court in Quaker-dominated Pennsylvania nine years previously had been faced with an accusation of witchcraft against a Margaret Mattson and Yeshro Hendrickson. The court investigated the matter thoroughly and, somewhat wearily, found Mattson guilty of "having common fame of a witch." Both were released.

In Salem, however, a range of factors came together to produce an altogether more violent outcome. One recent historian lists them as:

political strife between Salem Village and the larger town of Salem, voodoo practices associated with a West Indian slave, the recent republication of an ancient book presenting ways to combat witchcraft, recent tension with marauding native Americans and their French allies, judges and

ministers nervous about the colony's spiritual decline and eager to find
ways of checking it, simmering community hostility against a few lonely
old women and a few new families, a wide range of occult practices, and
adolescent hysteria in a few teenage girls along with judicial hysteria in
a few old men.[7]

Not much room for accidents there, then. Any combination of two
or three of these circumstances might have been enough to prompt
fears about witches during the early-modern period. Almost always such
excitements prospered in ethnically and linguistically marginal areas,
particularly where towns were skirted by large areas of uncultivated
forest or mountain. Economic and political instability was strongly
correlated with propensities to seek explanations for hardship in the
activities of people in league with the devil. And almost always such
agents of darkness were social outsiders of one kind or another. It has
become a commonplace for feminists to point out that the accused were
mostly women. But everyone who has ever heard a fairy story knows
more about witches than this: they lived in the forest (either literally
or metaphorically) and they lived alone (and again, the quality may be
literal or merely metaphorical).

The pressure upon the accused at Salem was such that they tended
to identify others as suspects, either to relieve the pressure upon themselves, to pay out grudges, or because the power of suggestion was so
powerful. Belief in witches was self-reinforcing. And in any case agents
of the devil, like Communists in McCarthy's America, were unlikely to
have acted alone.

More than a hundred people were accused of witchcraft during 1692,
of whom twenty-seven were tried, nineteen hanged (thirteen women
and six men) and one, Giles Corey, an octogenarian, was pressed to
death for refusing to testify. In addition, at least four people, but perhaps as many as seventeen, died while in prison. By the end of it all,
serious doubts had taken hold among the accusers and prosecutors
themselves. If the devil had been active—as clearly he had—it may
have been in an ironic sense rather than in the mode they had fancied.
It was a shattering thought. Increase Mather had turned against the
trials when accusations began to be leveled at upstanding citizens and
notable saints. Social insiders could not be witches—especially if they
were pillars of the church.

Five years after the frenzy had died down, one of the judges, Samuel
Sewall, read out a personal confession in church, repenting of his part
in the appalling business. As a result of the devil's work, rationalism had
taken another step forward in Puritan New England.

Unstoppable Pluralism, Inevitable Toleration

Yet it was the fifth and, of those that we shall be considering here, the last of the tempests to strike the Puritan vision of a "city on a hill" that was to prove its final undoing: the rise of religious sectarianism and the unstoppable force of religious pluralism. The most important early actor in that aspect of our drama was Roger Williams (ca. 1603–1683), a minister who had fled Massachusetts in January 1636, almost two years before the expulsion of Anne Hutchinson, in order to elude arrest and deportation back to England. (Strangely enough, Winthrop had tipped him off before the court officials arrived.) Williams's offense had been to argue that secular government had no business enforcing religion upon the population but only in upholding moral order. According to Williams, analogies between Old Testament Israel and the population of any given modern polity were false and biblically indefensible. As he later wrote, "The state of the land of Israel (the kings and people thereof, in peace and war) is . . . figurative and ceremonial, and no pattern nor precedent for any kingdom or civil state in the world to follow."[8]

As if this were not bad enough of him, Williams had also pointed out that moral order was hardly compatible with the settlers' expropriation of the Indians' land and property. Christian profession, he argued, should confer no special civil privileges, nor its absence among the natives justify Europeans in mistreating them: "We have not our land by patent from the King, but . . . the natives are the true owners of it, and . . . we ought to repent of receiving it by patent."[9] If the whites wanted land, they should purchase it from those who truly owned it.

After his midwinter escape from Boston, Williams would have perished had he not been taken in by the Indians, for whom the experience of a plain-dealing white person was—and would mostly remain—novel. The winter over, Williams, along with several families from Salem whom he had, while still at liberty, persuaded to his opinions, went on to establish Providence Plantation. The new settlement lay just outside the jurisdiction of the Massachusetts authorities. In due course, it developed into the colony of Rhode Island.

Williams's religious principles implied religious toleration and a believers' church, so it can have come as little surprise to Winthrop back in Boston (though he recorded the report to his diary in scandalized tones) that his departed antagonist had subsequently turned to "Anabaptistry"— under the influence, it turned out, of one of Anne Hutchinson's sisters. The date was March 1639.

This conversion to believer's baptism, fleeting though it was (for he had changed his opinion again by the end of that summer), places Williams at the fountainhead of the American Baptist tradition, which has since proved so vastly influential. This fact alone makes the event significant. But Williams himself came to think that his believer's baptism had been a hasty mistake. If the sacraments of the early church had become corrupted by the rise of priestcraft and popery then, although the corruptions might and should be rejected, it did not lie in the power of the godly in the present age to reinstitute the true ceremonies; this was the prerogative of the Holy Ghost.

Williams's concern for religious toleration, however, never wavered. He can only have been strengthened in this conviction by hearing of the final consequences of Boston's expulsion of Anne Hutchinson. In July 1643 she, her children, and her servants were scalped by Siwanoy Indians, who were taking revenge upon whites for a massacre of eighty Siwanoy men, women, and children by Dutch soldiers a few months earlier.

The following year, Roger Williams published in London his most famous book, *The Bloudy Tenent of Persecution for Cause of Conscience*. In it, he urged that "a permission of the most paganish, Jewish, Turkish, or Antichristian consciences and worships be granted to all men in all nations and countries. . . . Enforced uniformity, sooner or later, is the greatest occasion of civil war, ravishing of conscience, persecution of Christ Jesus in his servants, and of the hypocrisy and destruction of millions of souls."[10]

This tract, a devastating attack upon official intolerance, provoked a torrent of printed confutations—more than a hundred—during the rest of the decade from the outraged supporters of official religion, most notably that from John Cotton, who had been one of the principal targets of the original work. Cotton's own book was given the prim title, *The Bloudy Tenent Washed and Made White in the Bloud of the Lamb*:

> It is a carnal and worldly, and indeed an ungodly imagination, to confine the Magistrates' charge to the bodies and goods of the Subject, and to exclude them from the care of their souls. . . . Hath God committed to Parents the charge of their children's bodies, and not the care of their Souls? To Masters the charge of their servants' bodies, and not of their souls? . . . Shall the Captains suffer false worship, yea idolatry, publicly professed and practised in the camp, and yet look to prosper in the Battle?[11]

Cotton clearly thought these questions rhetorical; they answered themselves. Few today would share his confidence—even, in many cases, in respect to parents and children. His last remark puts one immediately in mind of the fourth-century Roman Emperor Constantine, who believed that the Christian God was the deity who won his battles for him—a conviction that was passed down through the centuries, as if via genetic inheritance, by all spokesmen for state-sponsored Christianity.

Neither did Cotton think Williams's argument to be truly a plea for conscience. For conscience was only itself when it was in accordance with the truth. Erroneous conscience was no conscience at all.

> In Fundamental and principal Points of Doctrine and worship, the Word of God in such things is so clear, that he cannot but be convinced in conscience of the dangerous Error of his way, after once or twice Admonition, wisely and faithfully dispensed. . . . So that if such a man after such Admonition, shall still persist in the Error of his way, and be therefore punished, He is not persecuted for cause of Conscience, but for sinning against his Conscience.[12]

This was becoming a less and less convincing argument, even in the seventeenth century. Those churches that would continue to persecute, for more than another century, tended to steer such discussions away from the dangerous ground of personal conscience and back onto safe rhetoric about defending the glory and honor of God or else about the necessary order to be maintained in a Christian commonwealth. By entering too closely into considerations of individual conscience, the New England Puritans had all but sold the pass.

Williams's counterreply was groaningly entitled *The Bloudy Tenent yet More Bloudy*. It was all standard form for the period, but the issues at stake were crucial—both in themselves and for the future of America. Yet it was not at all clear, at first, that that future lay with the cause of religious toleration. But the sectarians and dissidents would eventually overwhelm, by their sheer numbers, the adherents of the Congregationalist establishment, making a mockery of Cotton's rhetorical questions and rendering impossible his strictures about the secular punishment of heretics.

The Agents of Religious Toleration

It was the Baptists and the Quakers who first, after the Hutchinson and Williams episodes, presented serious principled problems for the New England authorities. John Clarke (1609–1676) of Suffolk had had his weapons confiscated by the Boston authorities shortly after his arrival in the New World in 1637 because he had even then been suspected of being "tinged with anabaptism." Such prognostications later proved all too correct: fourteen years afterward, in 1651, Clarke was again arrested in Massachusetts, by which time he was Baptist pastor of Newport, Rhode Island. Obadiah Holmes, one of Clarke's two companions on this occasion, was brutally flogged on the orders of the magistrates, leaving him unable to walk for weeks and his back a mass of scars for the rest of his life. But worse was to come. The advent of the Quakers in New England from 1656 onward led to several actual executions, along with more numerous mutilations, imprisonments, and banishments before the attempt to impose orthodoxy in such fashion was tacitly abandoned.

The Quakers

One of the most troublesome of the early Quakers was Mary Dyer (1611–1660). She had been a friend and accomplice of Anne Hutchinson. Back in 1637, Mary had given birth to a stillborn and grotesquely deformed baby, a tragedy that also befell her friend and mentor two and a half years later. The stern Calvinism of the Bostonian divines had seized with triumph upon both stillbirths as evidence of God's judgment, while others went so far as to hint that such portents indicated the women were tainted by immorality and witchcraft.

But it does not seem to have been any anger at Calvinist providentialism over such distasteful and heartless moralizing that drove Mary Dyer to embrace the nascent Quaker movement. Rather, she seems to have been driven by the more general logic of religious individualism, spiritual illumination, and social radicalism. Although Anne Hutchinson herself did not live long enough to see the rise of the Quaker movement, there is every reason to think that she would have become a participant. The faction of the Newport church to which she had adhered, which emphasized the inner light, and which in 1641 had broken away from Clarke's Baptist faction, later became Quaker.

Mary Dyer's conversion to Quakerism, however, did not occur in Newport but back in England. Residents of Rhode Island after the expulsion of the Hutchinsonian faction from Boston in 1639, the Dyer family returned to England in 1650, where they embraced the Quaker movement. The year 1656, however, saw them back in Rhode Island, determined to propagate their new faith. Roger Williams looked with ill favor upon the new movement, but his own principles prevented him from taking action against them on that account.

Not so in New England. By openly defying the Massachusetts authorities, who had decreed that Quaker missionaries who returned after two banishments should be executed, she submitted to the various indignities inflicted upon her early visits and continued to return to preach her faith. Faced with the choice between the public opprobrium that would attend them if they hanged a peaceable (though, in truth, extremely trouble-some) woman and the disrepute that their authority would come into if they failed to exact the prescribed penalty after repeated offenses, the Boston magistrates chose the former course. In June 1660 Mary Dyer attained her martyr's crown.

Two Quaker men had been hanged the previous year for the same cause. A third man suffered the same punishment in March 1661. By then, however, the throne in London was reoccupied, following the implosion of the English Republic, by a man whose hostility to Puritan theocracy was fueled by something far deadlier than his father's high-minded High-Churchmanship. King Charles II was a careless worldling and bon vivant to whom the Boston magistrates were not so much insufferable as irrational. At home in England, he had promised his subjects an "indulgence of tender consciences," and he half meant it. Untroubled by an overactive conscience himself, he could see the need for a religious establishment that would play its accustomed role of keeping social order, yet he wished to make that function as painless as possible, lest it lead to conflict—concerning which his life experience hitherto had given him every justification for being cautious—or to harmless people being hurt. And, in his judgment, the Quakers were harmless. Having met George Fox, one of the Quakers' leaders, in person, the king took the view that the fellow was more amusing than dangerous—an assessment that would have devastated the utterly humorless Fox, as it was perhaps intended to do.

Charles's reign in England was marked by fitful attempts to mitigate the persecuting zeal of his own Royalist supporters. And in 1661 he chose to alleviate the plight of the New England Quakers, at least to the extent of keeping them alive.

It was not quite the end of the contest. Quakers and Baptists continued to be on the sharp end of persecution in New England, even if it was no longer lethal. But gradually the conflict dissipated, as the sectarians made converts in the remoter settlements, from thence to renew their assaults upon Puritan Boston at a later time. Indeed, there was a Baptist congregation functioning in the city from 1665, which was possessed of its own building by 1679—though official harassment continued, and members often arrived to find the door nailed shut. Many other sectarians chose to avoid such ongoing unpleasantness by settling in Rhode Island or further south in the newly opened lands of Pennsylvania—colonies that enshrined religious toleration.

This was the strength of the state-church principle in the New World: in theory, no mechanisms needed to exist for accommodating or tolerating dissenters, for they could be chased away and made to start a new colony elsewhere in the vast, underpopulated landscape. But it was also its weakness; by the time this process had played itself out very far, a good number of colonies would exist, several of them advocating religious toleration and competing favorably for new settlers who could not—or would not—fit into the compulsory arrangements elsewhere. Furthermore, even within those colonies possessed of compulsory churches, the will to persecute settlers who dissented gradually ebbed away—not on grounds of enlightened principle but because of simple pragmatism. If religious dissidents removed themselves to new homesteads twenty or thirty miles into the wilderness, what satisfaction was to be gained by sending the constables all the way out to round them up and bring them back to the local jail? And would that satisfaction match the cost of doing so?

Slowly, geography reduced one local official after another, de facto, to the principles of Anabaptistry or of Brownism: it would have to be "the conscience and not the power of man" that would "drive [people] to seek the Lord's kingdom"[13]—for the power of man tended, in the long term, to peter out amid the trackless wastes of the New World. The Anglicans, Presbyterians, Lutherans, and Reformed—the Protestant state churches of the Old World, each designedly monopolistic within its own territory—needed to do far more than merely come to terms with the sectarians among them. The very fact that each of these churches found itself confronted by the others meant that, even without a Baptist or a Quaker in sight, America would inevitably have to function upon the sectarians' own terms.

It was Pennsylvania that, more than any other North American colony, became synonymous with religious pluralism. The son of an admiral, William Penn (1644–1718) turned to Quakerism during the mid-1660s and was imprisoned in 1668 for writing a tract. From his cell in 1669 he wrote his most famous work, *No Cross, No Crown*, on the subject of suffering for Christ. In it he exudes a warm, discerning, and confident piety for a twenty-five-year-old:

> But deliberating is ever worst; for the soul loses in parley: the manifestation brings power with it. Never did God convince people, but, upon submission, He empowered them. . . . Heaven is the throne, and the earth but the footstool of that man that hath self under foot. And those that know that station will not easily be moved; such learn to number their days, that they may not be surprised with their dissolution; and to redeem their time,

because their days are evil (Eph. 5:16); remembering they are stewards, and must deliver up their accounts to an impartial judge.[14]

Out of prison again, Penn resumed his Quaker activities. Fortunately for the Quaker movement, land was about to become available in which the Quakers, rather than establishing any "city upon a hill" (for they did not believe in such visions), could at least find a refuge in the wilderness. In 1673 John Fenwick and Edward Byllinge, two Quakers who had served as soldiers in Cromwell's army, paid £1000 for West Jersey, in the Delaware Valley. The vendor was Lord Berkeley, who had been given it by James, Duke of York (and the future King James II), who had received it from his brother, King Charles II—whose soldiers had conquered it, along with New York, in 1664 from the Dutch.

Though it was not the stated purpose of Fenwick and Byllinge to provide refuge for their persecuted coreligionists, it can hardly have been far from their minds. George Fox had just returned from one of his missionary journeys to America and had as early as 1659 enquired about the possibility of Quaker settlements there. The two new proprietors soon quarreled, and the young William Penn was brought in to manage the colony's affairs. Fortunately, the impecunious Charles II chose to settle a royal debt of £16,000 owed to Penn's deceased father by giving away lands to the south and west of New Jersey that were not (at any rate, in Roger Williams's understanding of such matters) quite his to confer upon anyone. Thus it was, in 1681, that the vast area of land that would become known as Pennsylvania—Penn's woods—in the New World came into the possession of Penn and, thereby, to the use of those committed to religious toleration.

As with Quakers and Baptists generally, Penn's opposition to persecution did not stem from the accidental fact that he was among the persecuted. Even where Quakers were in the political driving seat, they would offer toleration to others. Penn thought little of Protestants who opined otherwise. He taunted those dissenters who pleaded the badge of honor for their own sufferings but, because they wished merely to displace the established Church of England with their own preferred model, took Cotton's side of the question rather than that of Williams:

> You, who refuse conformity to others, and that have been writing these eight years for liberty of conscience, . . .

William Penn.
Illustration from (After) Benjamin West.

what pregnant testimonies do you give of your unwillingness to grant that
to others you so earnestly beg for yourselves? Doth it not discover your
injustice, and plainly express that only want of power hinders you to act?
But of all Protestants in general I demand, do you believe that persecution to be Christian in yourselves that you condemned for antichristian in
the Papists? You judged it a weakness in their religion, and is it a cogent
argument in yours?[15]

The restrictions placed upon Penn by the charter granted him were,
from the standpoint of his purposes, trifling. There was an express provision that episcopal worship was to be tolerated; the colony was also to
appoint an agent to represent itself to the government in London. Both of
these provisions reflect royal resentment at the failure of Massachusetts
to do either of these things. The first stipulation was no burden at all to
Penn, for he was determined to tolerate all comers in his "holy experiment." And the second was reasonable enough, too, for he intended no
disloyalty or incipient republicanism.

The following year, 1682, Penn sailed for America, leaving his wife
and children in England for the time being. Most of the ship's hundred
passengers were Quaker, and some thirty died of smallpox during the two
months at sea. Work was begun on establishing a new city of Philadelphia;
by the end of 1683 the rush of new settlers—Swedes, English, Germans,
and Welsh—had completed 357 dwellings, laid out in a checkerboard
fashion that was to characterize the city. That same year, Germantown
was founded by German Mennonites and Dutch Quakers, whom Penn
had invited there for the purpose. His colony offered respite to all of
the numerous minorities and sectarians who so sorely needed it, both
those in Britain and those in continental Europe, and whose stories we
have reviewed in chapters 6 and 10. Pennsylvania imposed the death
penalty for just two offenses—murder and high treason—compared to
Massachusetts's fifteen, which included witchcraft (as we have seen),
idolatry, blasphemy, adultery, the bearing of false witness, and cursing
or smiting parents.

The willingness to tolerate all comers who subscribed to monotheism
produced two consequences—and both led to the eventual erosion of the
Quakers' control over their own colony. In the first place, religious toleration led to an influx of the godly of all persuasions. In the last two decades
of the seventeenth century, a bewildering variety of German sectarians
made their way to the refuge in the wilderness, until much of it was a
wilderness no more. Mennonites, Dunkers, Schwenkfelders, and a host
of now-forgotten groups settled Lancaster County and further afield. In
the early decades of the eighteenth century, they were supplemented by

German Lutherans and Reformed, as Queen Anne's government sought to bolster the British colonies with reliable opponents of Catholic France and Spain. As with the Netherlands from the late sixteenth century and with England later, this development created the perfect conditions for rapid economic growth—a circumstance that tended, with the passing of time, to make Pennsylvania less austere and narrowly spiritual than its founders had intended.

In the second place, the Quakers soon found themselves at first merely outnumbered and then progressively reduced to a less and less influential minority in their own colony. The Anglicans who settled in Philadelphia—a small but very vocal and influential minority who, after Penn's death in 1718, included his sons—took an assertively anti-Quaker line on almost all political and administrative questions. Even during the 1680s and 1690s the governor (often a non-Quaker) clashed with the Quaker-dominated assembly, especially over such issues as defense and the need for a militia. The outlook of the latter was greeted with incredulity by Anglicans, some of whom petitioned the Lord Commissioners for Trade and Plantations in 1697 that "the principles they maintain do militate against the very end and essentials of government. . . . No bill can pass for the forming of militia . . . by which means the country lies naked and defenseless and exposed to be ruined and made a prey of by any enemy that shall first invade it." This last concern was hardly hypothetical, and the issue reached crisis point when the coming of the French and Indian War (1756–1763) provoked the colonial administration to a definitive abandonment of Quaker pacifism.

Back in England, the early Quakers' spirit inspiration and principled informality had, by the end of the seventeenth century, evolved its own rigidities and legalisms as well as its own mixture of affected behavior that passed for "being spiritual" within the Quaker subculture. But it was no surprise that the same developments occurred in America also. So when Peter Kalm, a Swede, visited a Quaker meeting in Philadelphia in 1749, he recorded his experiences with some bemusement:

> We sat and waited very quietly from ten o'clock to a quarter after eleven. . . . Finally, one of the two . . . old men in the front pew rose . . . and began to speak, but so softly that even in the middle of the church, which was not large, it was impossible to hear anything except the confused murmur of words. Later he began to talk a little louder, but so slowly that four or five minutes elapsed between the sentences; finally the words came both louder and faster. In their preaching the Quakers have a peculiar mode of expression, which is half singing, with a strange cadence and accent, and ending each cadence as it were, with a half or . . . a full sob. Each cadence

consists of two, three, or four syllables, but sometimes more, according to
the demand of the words and means; e.g. my friends / put in your mind / we
/ do nothing / good of ourselves / without God's / help and assistance. . . .
At the end, just as he was speaking at his best, he stopped abruptly, sat
down and put on his hat.[16]

Other Quaker idiosyncrasies were altogether more constructive.
During the eighteenth century, Friends were to become known for their
principled stand against slavery. It was a stance in which they were to
be joined, after the Revolution at least, by most of the Methodists. And
though it was the latter movement that was rewarded by picking up
significant black support (and many of the separately constituted "black
churches" that were beginning to come into existence by century's end
were one variety or another of Methodist), the Quakers nevertheless
deserve honorable mention for the persistence and consistency of their
position on the subject of slavery and for trying to bring about an end to
the practice. Even so, it was the following, nineteenth century that would
witness both burgeoning numbers of slaves in America and burgeoning
Christian polarization over the slavery issue. It was also the nineteenth
century that would experience the bloody cataclysm that resolved it.

The Baptists

If the Quakers left an indelible print upon early American life, it was
the Baptists who shaped the future. Their earliest decades were fairly
unimpressive, and by 1700 there were only some two dozen Baptist congregations in America, for the most part unconnected with one another
and with a combined membership well below a thousand. They were
also dogged by controversies of various kinds—though these were not
always signs of spiritual vigor. The long-term impact of the Baptists
upon America, however, has been so great—and even by the end of the
eighteenth century they had grown to become the largest denomination
in the young republic—that their early tiresomeness simply must be
borne with. Indeed, it must be understood in order to comprehend the
significance of the later rapid growth, and the reasons for it.

The church led in the 1640s by John Clarke, whom we had cause
to notice earlier, seems to have been, after Williams's congregation in
Providence, the earliest Baptist church in America. It was not peaceable.
The brethren were divided between Particulars (Calvinists) and Generals
(free-willers). Division eventually resulted. In 1671 the movement split
again over the Sabbath; Stephen Mumford taught that Saturday, not

Sunday, should be observed, and he made a point of plowing on Sunday just to make his point.

A Baptist church had been founded at Swansea, Massachusetts (located at a prudently close proximity to the border with Rhode Island), in 1663 by refugees from Ilston, near Swansea, Wales. They correctly anticipated that Charles II's "indulgence of tender consciences" was unlikely to span the chasm separating rhetoric from practice and so had crossed the Atlantic to escape the consequences. Their pastor was one John Miles who, back in Wales, had performed the unlikely feat of serving as parish clergyman in the Cromwellian establishment while simultaneously organizing a Particular Baptist church.

In the New World, however, Miles exhibited a different kind of theological eclecticism, and his church embraced both Particulars and Generals. This arrangement did not endure beyond 1680, when the congregation split over the issue.

Two years later, a Baptist church was established in Maine, but it faced persecution. So in 1696 the congregation emigrated en masse to Charleston, South Carolina, which, although it was ostensibly Anglican, permitted religious freedom in practice; indeed, there had been Baptists in Charleston from the 1680s.[17] The arrivals from Maine were all Particulars, but they blended well enough with the existing Baptists, many of whom were Generals.

Churches were established in the middle colonies during the same decade: at Cold Spring, near Philadelphia, in 1684 and at Pennepek, in the same region, four years later. The latter of these was founded by Elias Keach, who had the disconcerting distinction of being converted under his own preaching. Son of the famous London Baptist pastor, Benjamin Keach, he had arrived in America in 1687 in an unregenerate state and took it into his head to preach at a Baptist gathering, on the strength of his father's reputation, by way of a jest. But his own words got the better of him, and he broke off partway through his sermon to confess to his hearers the sin that he was at that moment committing. Despite their consternation, his listeners were inclined, once the shock had worn off and the new conversion definitely established, to take a phlegmatic view of his little joke. Keach went on to have a highly successful ministry, avoiding the controversies that dogged Baptist life and establishing several new churches.

It was the separatism of the Baptists and their oddness that seems to have held them back from rapid growth, at least until the Great Awakening channeled their energies into constructive directions from the 1740s onward. The earliest American settlers seem, as often as not, to have felt that their transatlantic migration (or that of their immediate ancestors) had already made them quite separate enough; emphasis in the early colonies was upon order and the maintenance of social cohesion—qualities that the elementary facts of a sparse population in an immense wilderness made even harder to come by than was usual in the premodern world. If the difficulties of law enforcement in North American conditions made it almost impossible to prevent Baptists and Quakers from existing, then the same facts also made the social deviance of sectarianism even less admired than it was back in England. By the 1740s, however, this picture was starting to change. On the one hand, the Baptists themselves had mellowed and were a little less obsessed with their own peculiarities and distinctives. On the other hand, the population of North America had grown more numerous; social conformity was at less of a premium than it had been in the early days.

13

NORTH AMERICA

COMING TO TERMS WITH PLURALISM

▼

Religious pluralism was a fact of American life, whether the Puritans—or any other actual Americans—wanted it or not. With religious tolerance, as in so much of Christian history, precept followed, rather than preceded, practice.

Catholics, Anglicans, and Presbyterians in a Sectarian Continent

Clearly, the practice in question came harder to traditionally magisterial churches than to their sectarian counterparts. However, as we shall see, most of the former had successfully negotiated the leap before the American Constitution set such principles in granite.

Roman Catholics

If South and Central America belonged to Catholicism, then North America was the Protestants' continent. The early Spanish settlements in Florida and the southwest apart, the Catholics of North America were necessarily guests in territory occupied primarily by heretics whom their spiritual head in Rome had pledged himself to eradicate.

But Catholic minorities in the Protestant states of Europe had achieved a way of living with their minority status, even if that involved secrecy. In America the hostility toward them was more muted, yet Catholicism entailed significant disadvantages for those who adhered to it. Popery everywhere incurred the same suspicions as in England. Most Protestants took it for granted that Catholicism was a persecuting creed allied to a preference for absolutist monarchy—and so a serious threat to those very freedoms (either principled, as with the Baptists and Quakers, or merely for themselves, as with the Puritans) they had come to America to enjoy. Anti-Catholic sentiment in such an environment was unsurprising.

By the 1780s there were probably no more than 25,000 Catholics out of the four million inhabitants in the territories that were becoming the United States. Of these, the large majority lived in Maryland, with some thousands more in and about the city of Philadelphia.[1] The colony in Maryland had been founded in the seventeenth century by George Calvert and his son Cecilius, the first and second Lords Baltimore, with at least half an eye on its becoming a refuge for English Catholics. Settlers only arrived in 1634, two years after the death of George Calvert. There were a little over two hundred of them, mostly Catholics, and including two Jesuit priests. A number of Protestants followed them in 1638, but within the year most of them had converted to Catholicism under the influence of one of the Jesuits, Andrew White (1579–1656). White went on to reduce the language of the Piscataway Indians to writing, the better to produce a catechism for them.

But the second Lord Baltimore faced multiple embarrassments. Catholic success in proselytizing—whether of Protestant settlers or of Indians—drew attention to the Catholic nature of the enterprise and risked hostility. In any case, settlers in significant numbers were needed if the enterprise was to be a success—and it was inevitable that most of these would be Protestants. Furthermore, the Jesuits had a habit of becoming so well embedded that they threatened his seigneurial authority. For a raft of reasons, all of them at least analogous to the considerations that brought Catholic gentry into conflict with overly zealous Jesuits and other missionaries back in England, Baltimore decided to rein in the Catholicization of Maryland. With the agreement of the Vatican, he secured the withdrawal of the Jesuits (whose very name was enough to make a Protestant Englishman's blood run cold) and their replacement by Franciscans and secular priests. And he made it plain that Maryland would be a colony committed to religious toleration; its Toleration Act of 1649 made it clear that religious considerations were emphatically secondary to the overriding concern that settlers "be not unfaithful to the Lord Proprietary [i.e., to Baltimore], or molest or conspire against the civil Government established or to be in this Province under him or his heirs." Within those political constraints, all those "professing to believe in Jesus Christ" were deemed acceptable.[2]

The act, of course, was passed just at the moment when England was at the point of becoming a republic. The Cromwellian regimes of the 1650s were disposed to religious toleration—but certainly not of Catholics. Protestants took control of Maryland during the 1650s, repealed the act, and began oppressing the colony's papist inhabitants. The Restoration monarchy took a more amiable view of Catholicism but nevertheless made the Church of England the established religion in Maryland. Notwithstanding this official position, the dynamics of American life that we have already observed ensured Catholics a continuing place, albeit attended by prejudice from outsiders and a need for the constant exercise of tact by Catholics themselves. In the long run, this was to breed a very different kind of Catholicism from that to be found in the Old World or in Latin America: more liberal and genuinely tolerant, and more attuned to the needs of living in a modern, industrializing society. Though Catholic numbers remained low before the Revolution, they mushroomed to 160,000 by 1820, making them the third largest denomination in the United States.

In the meantime, a larger number of Catholics, some 60,000, lived in the province of Quebec, which was ceded by France to Britain in 1763 after its principal city had been captured by General Wolfe. Ironically, the British authorities—so heavy-handed in their treatment of the colonies further south—swiftly succeeded in befriending their new subjects: the Quebec Act of 1774 was controversial with Protestants for the privileges it bestowed upon the Catholic Church within the territory, giving it the right to levy a tithe upon its adherents and even granting Catholics full civil and political rights—which was more than their coreligionists had in Britain itself. It was a generosity that was amply repaid a few years later when the Catholic bishop of Quebec proved a firm supporter of the British during the Revolutionary War, pointing to "the remarkable goodness and gentleness with which we have been governed by his very gracious Majesty, King George the Third . . . in restoring to us the use of our laws and the free exercise of our religion." Though most Québecois remained neutral during that conflict, Bishop Briand went further and urged his flock that "your oaths, your religion, lay upon you the unavoidable duty of defending your country and your King with all the strength you possess."[3] Politics in the New World has never ceased to make remarkable bedfellows.

The Church of England

The Anglican presence in the New World was far more considerable than that of Catholicism—at least during our period. The Church of England was the established church in Virginia, the Carolinas, Georgia, and after 1691, as we have seen, also in Maryland. Its authority even extended to parts of New York.

Yet the problems facing the Church of England were vast. Space was one. Most parishes were hundreds of square miles in extent. The very different nature of American society—especially in the southern plantations—was another. The willingness of King Charles II to grant lands to supporters or (as with Pennsylvania) to creditors gave the proprietors a nearly exclusive authority in key matters of governance in the middle and southern colonies. And those proprietors were generally anxious to take settlers where they could get them—which generally meant among the disaffected in England, who were frequently dissenters, or else from other countries whose inhabitants, whatever else they might be, were unlikely to be Anglicans. In Georgia, founded in 1732, and the Carolinas, flanked as they were to the south by the hostile Spanish in Florida, this was a matter of real urgency. So, except for the Catholics in the south, the predominantly Anglican colonies were not disposed to be too fussy about who might settle.

The absence of a bishop made almost everything problematic. A bishop, in episcopalian systems, is necessary to ordain a new minister and even to perform confirmations. Because of the latter, the real status of Anglican laity was necessarily ambiguous. Provincial governors were given power to appoint and induct ministers. The situation also led to ongoing conflict between Anglican clergy and laity. The planter aristocracies came to dominate the parish vestries, which, with the bishop 3,000 miles away and clergy in short supply, soon came to have strong control over parishes. Yet in spite of these problems, the church was not geared toward organizational adjustment or the creation of new dioceses.

This last failing can be exaggerated, however. Dr. Thomas Bray (1656–1730) spent just four years in the New World, from 1696 to 1700, when he served as the bishop of London's commissary in Maryland. As a result of his stay, he established two agencies that were to have ongoing importance. In 1698 the Society for Promoting Christian Knowledge (SPCK) was founded to educate the children of the poor and to provide literature that would support the church's work. Its first publication, six hundred copies of Bray's own book, *Discourse Concerning Baptismal and Spiritual Regeneration*, appeared in 1699. Described by the Catholic Encyclopedia as "the greatest and most important society within the Church of England," its early luminaries included Bishop Gilbert Burnet of Salisbury, John Strype, the antiquary and historian, and John Evelyn, the diarist, horticulturist, and political writer. Another was Rev. Samuel Wesley, whose sons John and Charles spent a brief, unsuccessful, and deeply unhappy period as missionaries to Georgia in the 1730s. Bray's other foundation was of the quaintly named Society for the Propagation of the Gospel in Foreign Parts (SPG). This was set up in 1701, the year after his return to England, to promote missions to the Indians as well as work among the settlers and slaves in North America and the Caribbean. Its first ministers and schoolteachers arrived the following year, and by the time of the Revolution, some three hundred missionaries had been sent.

During the Great Awakening of the late 1730s and early 1740s, a number of dissatisfied New England Congregationalists turned to the Anglicans as a refuge from the turbulence and emotionalism of the evangelicals, thereby doubtless vindicating the sentiments of the latter that the Church of England was a home for the spiritually tepid. Pointing in the same direction, perhaps, is the fact that four of the first five United States presidents were Virginians who adhered to the Anglican Church—and inclined strongly toward deism.[4] Anglicanism remained strong among the landowners and planters of the southern colonies, in societies that continued to be based more upon agriculture and land than upon trade in manufactures and services.

Yet it was the ongoing absence of a bishop that caused the greatest practical difficulties for Anglicans in the New World, and it was the fear that one might be appointed that, in the decades before the Revolution, caused the greatest friction between Anglicans and non-Anglicans. In 1767 Rev. Dr. Thomas Bradbury Chandler wrote an *Appeal to the Public in Behalf of the Church of England in America* with the intent of allaying non-Anglican suspicions about the consequences of appointing a bishop for the colonies. But many of his arguments had the opposite effect of what he intended, and he convinced many who were hostile to the church that the coming of a bishop would strengthen royal authority, impose costs that would then be defrayed by the imposition of taxes upon non-Anglicans, and mark a step down the slippery slope to forced religious conformity. Non-Anglicans did not necessarily approve of the fact that Anglican churches across the entire continent fell under the ecclesiastical jurisdiction of the bishop of London; they approved instead of the weakness this fact imposed upon the Church of England in America. Meanwhile, back in London itself, John Ewer, bishop of Llandaff, preached the annual sermon to the SPG in which he excoriated the colonists and their religion: the Puritan founders had moved to the New World "without remembrance or knowledge of God" while, for their present-day descendants, religion was "but an impediment in the way of avarice." Little could be further removed from the truth or more likely to provoke outrage on the other side of the Atlantic. Upon hearing of it, American clergy of various stripes shot off bitter rejoinders.[5]

The Presbyterians and Reformed

Presbyterians and Reformed churches are virtual equivalents. Since the Dutch dominated New York (New Netherland) until 1664, it is unsurprising that their brand of Reformed churches were strong in that area. Their first minister had arrived in 1628, but the Dutch colony suffered economic, social, and military setbacks during the following decades and can hardly be described as having been a godly province. Peter Stuyvesant, a Reformed elder and son of a pastor, took over as director general for the Dutch West India Company in 1647 and proceeded to crack down on the previous practice of tolerating religious dissenters. Even the highly respectable Lutherans found themselves fined and imprisoned for organizing services and were refused permission to build a church.

It was the arrival of twenty-three Jews from Brazil in 1654 that brought matters to a head in New Netherland. The Jews were fleeing the wrath of the Catholic authorities and the Portuguese, following the collapse of the Dutch colony in Pernambuco.[6] Both the Reformed clergy and the director general urged their respective masters, the Amsterdam Classis and the Dutch West India Company, to be spared such infidel incursions. But it was the company that had the final say, and the same commercial considerations that had brought about pluralism and toleration in the Netherlands conduced in the same direction in the Dutch colony. Jews were key shareholders, and their coreligionists could not lightly be mistreated with impunity.

Though the Dutch Reformed were "presbyterian" in polity, they had no need to go by that name, since they had had no Reformed rivals from

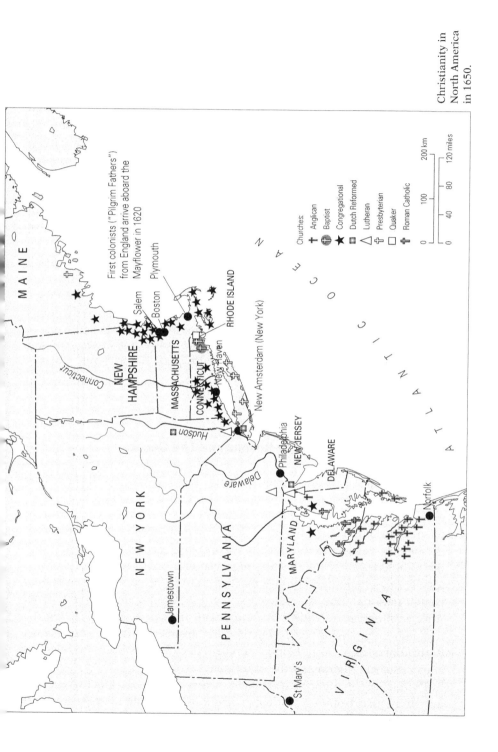

Christianity in
North America
in 1650.

First colonists ("Pilgrim Fathers")
from England arrive aboard the
Mayflower in 1620

MAINE

NEW
HAMPSHIRE

MASSACHUSETTS

Salem
Boston
Plymouth

CONNECTICUT

New Haven

RHODE ISLAND

New Amsterdam (New York)

NEW YORK

Hudson

Jamestown

PENNSYLVANIA

Delaware

Philadelphia
NEW JERSEY

DELAWARE

MARYLAND

Norfolk

St Mary's

VIRGINIA

ATLANTIC OCEAN

Churches:
+ Anglican
⊕ Baptist
★ Congregational
■ Dutch Reformed
△ Lutheran
⊕ Presbyterian
□ Quaker
✚ Roman Catholic

0   100   200 km
0   40   80   120 miles

whom to distinguish themselves in the mother country. But immigrants from Scotland and Ireland did, and so are known by the name of their form of church government rather than by that of their theology. The first Presbyterian congregation in America was established at Snow Hill, Maryland, in 1684. Its founder was an Irishman, Francis Makemie (1658–1708). Over the following two decades, he worked toward cooperation with later Presbyterian arrivals, and in 1706 he helped form the Presbytery of Philadelphia. (We note that in the process he was setting up home in the Catholic heartland and his presbytery in a city founded by Quakers. Pluralism was an inescapable fact of American life.) Many of the early Presbyterians were Scotch-Irish (or Ulster Protestants) like Makemie himself. The Scottish and Irish Presbyterian custom of holding "communion seasons" (which we noticed in chapter 10) was also introduced in the middle colonies.

Scottish and Irish Presbyterians became one of the most important elements in the population of Pennsylvania during the eighteenth century. Along with the Anglicans there, they chafed under the dominance of Quakers in the legislature and eventually succeeded in overthrowing it. With the passing of time, Presbyterians and Reformed became one of the most influential sections of opinion throughout the middle colonies, and it is certainly possible to view their influence as crucial in supporting the Revolution when it came. The British occasionally referred to the Revolutionary army as "Presbyterian."[7]

Religion and the American Revolution: The Debate

All around the world, the most absurd and partisan claims are made about the past. The reason is that any discussion of history is unavoidably, by an extension so minute as hardly to constitute an extension at all, about the present. Historical debate is a chronological extension of the field of battle about today's news, in which facts are mere scaffolding to hold together the real arena: interpretation. In few aspects of history is this phenomenon more marked than in respect of "the national past"—national, that is, relative to wherever one happens to be talking. American neoconservatism and American liberal secularism being the mutually antagonistic beasts that they are, this means that one of the most hotly contested areas of history in recent decades has been the relationship between religion and the American Revolution.

Predictably enough, both neoconservative and secular-liberal readings are often distortions—or, rather, projections back onto the past of values actually held by present protagonists. Some right-wing evangelicals have lately been conducting a veritable harrowing of hell in their efforts to reach into the grave and convert the dead; the assortment of eighteenth-century deists who formed the bulk of the revolutionary leadership are being recast as orthodox Christians (preferably evangelicals) who favored a "Christian America." On the other side, the evangelicals' secularist opponents are endeavoring to turn the separation of church and state, which the founding fathers intended as a freedom *for* religion, into a freedom *from* religion, whereby no sacred symbol or theological (or even traditionally moral) opinion may have any place in the public square. As with so many such stand-offs, each side justifies its own absurdities by pointing insistently at the absurdities of the other.

How far are the American Revolution and patterns of American religiosity connected? The Great Awakening of the late 1730s and 1740s had certainly energized many of the denominations in the North American colonies and set into motion a vigorous evangelicalism, which remains a crucial element in American life today. But can it be argued that this development helped form the impetus for rebellion against Britain—or for democracy, or a republic?

There is nothing, of course, in the doctrine of justification by faith that positively demands any particular political arrangements in the state. Yet the personalized nature of evangelical faith, which encouraged each believer to understand that he or she was dealing with, and being dealt with by, God directly, tended toward the voluntarist principle. And though Reformed theology and the Puritan tradition had worked for long to keep that voluntarism at bay, yet American conditions, as we saw earlier in this chapter, finally overcame them, even within the Presbyterian and Congregational churches. (The eighteenth-century American revision of the Westminster Confession deletes those clauses of the 1648 English original that had stipulated and provided "that all blasphemies and heresies be suppressed" by "the power of the Civil Magistrate.") The Great Awakening, then, heightened—or elevated to the level of principle—the unavoidable fact of religious pluralism in America and thereby laid stress upon personal autonomy. And personal autonomy in religious affairs prepares the ground for claims to personal autonomy in the lesser aspects of life. By this circuitous means it may be argued that the rise of evangelicalism helped prepare minds for republican and democratic ideals. Why it failed to do so, by and large, in Britain is not explained. It is safest to conclude, therefore, that if widespread evangelicalism might plausibly be claimed as a facilitating cause of the American Revolution, it was by no means a sufficient or principal cause.

In any case, the prominence of evangelical churches in American life during the run-up to the Revolution should not be exaggerated. Historians debate whether the numbers of evangelical churches fell between the 1750s and 1770s or merely reached a plateau, to start rising again during the 1790s. No one claims, however, that the movement continued to grow, proportionate to the population, during the generation before the Revolution. And this fact suggests that the relationship between evangelical faith and the American Revolution is both indirect and partial: a strong and direct connection would have seen a rise in evangelical strength immediately prior to the outbreak of hostilities, but this did not occur.

Instead, Christians behaved politically during the American Revolution in the same way that they have behaved during the centuries before and since. That is to say, those who were predisposed to a conservative outlook, to condemn rebellion, and to maintain the tie with the British Crown, found biblical and religious reasons to do so (Paul's instruction in Romans 13, the deference due from subjects, rebellion being "as the sin of witchcraft," etc.), while those disposed to support the Revolution found religious grounds for their own stance (resistance to tyrants, the corruption of monarchs condemned in Scripture, God's desire for the liberty of his people, etc.). If early-twenty-first-century Christians—supporters of Labour, Liberal, or Conservative parties, Democrats and Republicans—avoid such selective and question-begging uses and abuses of Scripture and of the Christian doctrinal tradition, then the present writer has entirely failed to register the fact.

Religion and the Founders

The founding fathers were predominantly deists: Washington, Madison, Franklin, Jefferson. Yet none was overly dismissive of traditional religion. Indeed, religious concepts (worded, to be sure, with deliberate vagueness) kept creeping into their pronouncements, from the Declaration of Independence to the American Constitution: the "laws of nature and of nature's God"; "are endowed by their Creator"; "supreme judge of the world"; "divine Providence." But the phrases are largely rhetorical and keep themselves at a distinct distance from the minutiae of the biblical revelation. The thing with which men were "endowed by their Creator" turned out to be "unalienable rights"—a concept that owed everything to the secular philosophers of the Enlightenment and nothing at all (except by eisegesis) to Scripture, even if popes since Vatican II and the 1960s (and evangelicals rather earlier) have come to adopt the new argot.[8] The other claims, too, were less biblical than newfangled. It was simply that religious and quasi-religious rhetoric was irresistible as a backup for them—both for its own sake (since it trumps all other considerations in pitching for the moral high ground), and because biblicist religion was so widespread among the population as a whole as to make self-justificatory reference to it a natural recourse.

To reiterate: The founding fathers were not by any means inimical to religion and considered it a necessary underpinning for a free society. They merely insisted that no particular brand of religion be imposed upon the public by government—an insistence that implied a permission for infidelity also, presumably on the same calculated gamble whereby democracy implies freedom for fascists and communists to bid for power at the polls: that the actual electoral support for such deviance will, in practice, be very limited. If either gamble is lost, then a free society is at an end—as the twentieth century demonstrated in respect of the latter gamble and the twenty-first century is beginning to demonstrate in respect of the former.

Thomas Jefferson, himself a deist, asked whether the liberties of a nation can "be thought secure when we have removed their only firm basis, a conviction in the minds of the people that these liberties are the gift of God? That they are not violated but with his wrath?" Franklin, another skeptic, proposed that each day of the Constitutional Convention's proceedings begin with prayer. John Adams opined in 1798, "Our constitution was made only for a moral and religious people. It is wholly inadequate to the government of any other." George Washington urged his fellow Americans not to "indulge the supposition that morality can be sustained without religion. . . . Reason and experience both forbid us to expect that national morality can prevail in exclusion of religious principle." And the physician Benjamin Rush—who actually *was* an orthodox Christian believer—concurred: "The only foundation for a useful education in a republic is to be laid in religion. Without it there can be no virtue, and without virtue there can be no liberty, and liberty is the object and life of all republican governments." The historian Gertrude Himmelfarb adds the comment that, in addition to the republic's separation of church and state, "It is noteworthy that the Constitution says nothing about education either, leaving that, like virtue and religion, to individuals and the states."[9] It was not that religion, virtue, and education did not matter but that, on the contrary, they mattered so very much that the government should not dare to interfere in them.

The Power of Pluralism

The historian Mark Noll has recently observed that American republicanism was embraced by "deists and Unitarians" and by supporters of "the older British churches, . . . new-breed evangelicalism, . . . traditional Protestant faiths from the Continent" as well as by Roman Catholics and members of the then-tiny Jewish community.[10] If the coalition was that eclectic—as indeed it was—then we are safe in concluding that evangelicalism was not, in any direct sense, the trigger for the American Revolution. Almost all of the Christian churches, with the exception of baptistic groups, inclined, historically speaking, in favor of monarchy and against republics. And the whole point of baptistic groups was that they had no religio-political inclinations at all.[11] So how did all of these religious believers contrive to support a republic that would separate church and state?

It was the simple fact of overwhelming variety in religion that made a separation of church and state both necessary and desirable. So many different groups of Christians had come to America to find a "refuge in the wilderness" (thereby swamping the Puritans' "city on a hill") that colonial governments had long since had to accommodate themselves to the facts on the ground. And the fact that no church commanded anything like a majority, except at the most local of levels, caused even the most socially conservative of them, such as the Catholics, Anglicans, and Presbyterians, to conduct themselves according to sectarian rules: strength and support were gained by winsomeness, not by attempted resort to power.

The state of Massachusetts, to be sure, included a clause in its own Declaration of Rights of 1780 that upheld "the public worship of God" and "public instructions in piety, religion and morality"—but this is perhaps best understood as a sop to the nearly broken power of the Congregationalist establishment there. Massachusetts's proposed constitution of two years earlier had attempted to maintain laws disadvantaging Baptists and other sectarians, but it had come under furious attack from Isaac Backus, the Separate Baptist leader, who insisted that if Baptists were forced to pay for state churches they never attended and religiously repudiated, then they were being "taxed without representation"—the very principle against which the American Revolution had broken out in the first place. This ingenious (but hardly unreasonable) line of argument enabled him to claim that religious freedom was "the matter [that] kindled this bloody war." Though Massachusetts succeeded in maintaining an established church within its boundaries until 1833, it did not succeed in suppressing sectarians.[12]

Other states attempted to uphold at least some religious specifics in public life. Both Delaware and North Carolina, for example, resolved in 1776 that public appointments be made conditional upon acknowledgment of the divine inspiration of Scripture and a trinitarian declaration of faith. Even Pennsylvania imposed only a slightly broader test for members of its legislature. Tennessee, more liberal yet, excluded from public office only atheists or deniers of a future state. The following year Georgia resolved that elected representatives must be "of the Protestant religion," and in 1776 New Jersey extended religious toleration only to Protestants. New Hampshire in 1784 allowed for local authorities to "make adequate provision at their own expense, for the support and maintenance of public protestant teachers of piety, religion and morality"—though it added that no supporters of one denomination should be required to pay the maintenance of teachers of another. How these two stipulations were to be squared in the case of inhabitants who were not Protestants was left unstated. Yet even these restrictions eroded with time. In 1790 Delaware anulled its previous stipulation by declaring that "no religious test shall be required as a qualification to any office, or public trust."[13] America became yet more pluralist after the Revolution, not less.

Pluralism, then, made for voluntarism. And what could be more voluntarist than the evangelical gospel? Evangelicalism gained support, in part, by being in tune with the times and with the country in which it found itself. It has done so ever since.

But the absence of compulsion did not push even nonevangelicals toward skepticism or irreligion. The winsomeness of churches was matched by the need of countless immigrants and by most of their descendants for continuing communal identity. To be alone in a vast continent of multiple languages, churches, and cultures was bewildering, alienating, and isolating. To be a Swedish Lutheran was immediately to have a home-away-from-home. And even the days of thicker settlement of the country from the mid-eighteenth century onward found religion, of any kind, an all but indispensable aid to social restraint.

Loyalism

It should be remembered, though, that by no means all churches or all Christians were supportive of the Revolutionary War. Like their more worldly minded neighbors, Christians differed about the rights and wrongs of the issues involved. Indeed, the rebellion itself took on

something of the nature of a civil war because possibly as few as 20 percent but perhaps more than 30 percent of the population of the thirteen
colonies were Loyalist in sympathy. About 35,000 Loyalists, justly fearful
of Republican reprisals, moved north of the new border with Canada
after the war into still-British Nova Scotia; thousands more moved into
Upper Canada, in the regions immediately north of lakes Ontario and
Erie.

Even in the decades before the war, Anglicans had been viewed
as an unwelcome Trojan horse for growing royal power in the colonies. Missionaries sent by the Church of England's Society for the
Propagation of the Gospel were sent to areas of Congregationalist and
Presbyterian strength, a move that caused these latter to explore, from
1766 onward, "A Plan of Union" between themselves in order to resist
Anglican encroachments. The Anglicans' intention to appoint a bishop
for America was also much feared as an implicit claim to Anglican jurisdiction in the colonies on a par with that back in England. And indeed,
when the fighting started, it was the Anglicans who most frequently
took the side of the British and of the king. Most Congregationalists and
Presbyterians, by contrast, lined up on the revolutionary side. On the
sound principle that "my enemy's enemy is my friend," Congregational
and Presbyterian support for the rebels weighed heavily enough with
at least a few Baptists, fed up with the heavy-handedness of the New
England religious establishment, to fight for the king—even if the wider
principles of Baptist thought pushed more of them either toward neutral-
ity (there is no "Christian polity" for a state) or toward the revolutionary side (freedom of religion implies universal participation in public
life). Some Catholics favored monarchy—even a heretical, Protestant
one—to a republic, while others saw a pluralist democracy as their best
protection from oppression by the majority in what was clearly fated
to be a Protestant continent.

Miles Cooper, an Anglican of New York and president of King's College
(better known today as Columbia University), articulated the familiar
argument that once the people "conceive the governed to be superior to
the Governors," then they would come to "despise dominion and speak
evil of dignities and . . . open a door for Anarchy, confusion, and every
evil work to enter." Other Anglicans made the same point; Isaac Wilkens,
a New York layman, sailed back to England rather than be forced to
fight the Crown or to subsist in the anarchic revolutionary state that
he was sure would ensue upon any successful rebellion. But even the
occasional Congregationalist or Presbyterian could be found singing the
same tune, as John Smalley of New Britain, Connecticut, did in 1775,

when he condemned the "downright rebellion against Majesty itself." "What!" he asked (rhetorically, as he thought), "Will you fight against your king?"[14] The late seventeenth and early eighteenth centuries had viewed the regicide of Charles I in 1649 as the ultimate political and social horror; even in the 1770s, many could still do nothing but recoil from the prospect of rebellion against the Crown.

More typical of Congregationalism, however, was the attitude of the General Association of Ministers of Connecticut, which urged the "sad necessity of defending by Force and Arms those precious Privileges which our fathers fled into this Wilderness quietly to enjoy." The blunders, the insensitivities, the burdensome taxation, and, above all, the meddling of British rule in the colonies threatened to undo the very thing the Puritans of the previous century had sought to establish. Less convincingly, Nathaniel Whitaker, Presbyterian minister of Salem, Massachusetts, found in Judges 5:23 ("Curse ye Meroz, said the angel of the LORD, curse ye bitterly the inhabitants thereof; because they came not to the help of the LORD . . . against the mighty," KJV) a justification for his parishioners to curse all of their neighbors who would not join in the revolutionary struggle.[15]

The Strength of Christianity

But Christians had this much in common: whichever side they were on, they resorted to scriptural or generally Christian-sounding justifications of their position. This, of course, is exactly what Americans did again, just over three quarters of a century later, during the American Civil War: both sides appealed to the Bible and the Christian tradition. The propensity to act this way reflects the strength of religion generally, and perhaps of evangelicalism specifically, in American society; it tells us much less about what the "correct" political orientation of faith should be than it does about the willingness of Christians to identify their own political opinion with Christian orthodoxy.

Perhaps the most important thing to be noted about the relationship between the American Revolution and religious belief is the entire absence of that antipathy to Christianity that was to be so characteristic of the French Revolution little more than a decade later. British rule in North America had neither legitimized nor justified itself in religious terms. Its early attempts to establish a particular church had been feeble, had differed from one colony to the next, and—most important of all—had been utterly unavailing. Indeed, in Britain itself religious pluralism had taken deep root; the limited toleration granted in 1689 to trinitarian Protestants had been broadening itself in practice during the course of the eighteenth century. To overthrow British rule had no immediate implications for the place of religion in American life.

To be sure, there were implications for individual church bodies. The Anglicans found themselves bound by practical, institutional, and political ties and by inevitable loyalties to the British Crown; the Methodists remained formally part of the Anglican communion, and John Wesley's royalism and opposition to the Revolution were generally known. The Quakers and Mennonites refused to fight the British or anyone else. These derogations from revolutionary fervor brought disadvantages for the groups concerned. The pacifist churches, in particular, often suffered reprisals from one side for helping escaping prisoners or wounded soldiers of the other. But even these difficulties were temporary; by the mid-1780s the Episcopalians (Anglicans), though much reduced in numbers of parishes (259 in 1789, down from 318 in 1774), were able to appoint three bishops, who set to work to Americanize and republicanize the church's ethos and to rebuild its structure. Above all, the difficulties of particular churches did not generate a lasting hostility even to those churches, let alone to religion in general.

We commenced this section by labeling the founding fathers as principally deists—an identification that will have exasperated some readers. And it is true that several of the founders were indeed possessed of a warmer piety, or made more concessions to traditional Christianity, than this categorization implies. Yet when all of the arguments are weighed and all of the concessions made, this remains the safest *general* assessment to make of their religious outlooks.

And perhaps a modern comparison is in order here: millions of ordinary Americans today hold views which are mostly shaped by the pop-philosophy of the day, especially New Age spiritualities and relativist moral judgments—yet they simultaneously cling to biblical or quasi-biblical ideas concerning piety, or "brotherhood," or a reverence for Jesus, or a vague belief in life beyond the grave. And they do so because millions of other Americans around them hold to these biblical notions, many of them more consistently, or at least somewhat more so. But will the equivalents of right-wing academics two hundred years hence try to claim that Bill Clinton was "really" an evangelical, because he was a Southern Baptist who sometimes preached? Washington, John Adams, Madison, and the others were no less sincere than Bill Clinton. But they were no more consistent. The fact that they appreciated the importance of religion, and that their deviations from secular thought, and in particular from deism, toward orthodox Christianity were sometimes noticeable, was because Christianity was so very important to so many people around them. And this in itself tells us much of what we need to know about the level of American religiosity.

14

THE GREAT AWAKENING

▼

The Great Awakening of the eighteenth century, and in particular the birth of Methodism, shook to the foundations the religious life of the various countries of Britain and also of its American colonies and reshaped them decisively for the future. These events are by common consent considered to be the birth of "evangelicalism" in its modern sense. And where a common understanding is quite evidently correct, no purpose is served by challenging it; there are other ways to demonstrate agility of mind.

This happy unanimity on the point stems from the conjunction, from the mid-1730s onward, of what Professor David Bebbington has recently taught us to identify as the four cardinal characteristics, or descriptors, that are essential to a definition of "evangelicalism." These have been so frequently quoted and described that it is tempting to omit them here. However, the patient and generous reader will ascribe the stunning lack of originality in the next few paragraphs to a touching concern by the present author that some may not have encountered the "descriptors" elsewhere and will abstain from eye-rolling on account of their inclusion now.

The first characteristic is *conversionism*. Agony under conviction of sin, guilt, faith, relief of guilt: the experience of these marks the difference, in evangelical eyes, between a Christian and a non-Christian, and so it is more important than any denominational distinctions or differences about secondary theological matters. In this, the continuity with Pietism is clearly seen. It also makes faith very personal—with both the advantages and disadvantages that flow from that emphasis (the "own personal Savior" mentality being seldom far away).

Second, we note *activism*. Evangelicals seek the conversion of others; they attend meetings for prayer, mutual edification, worship, etc. They participate in charity, good works, projects for social amelioration, and moral campaigns. They are, in short, busy people.

Third, evangelicalism is *biblicist*. Like the Pietism from which it emerged, it strongly promotes the private study and practical application of Scripture. But biblical authority is also much more highly esteemed than that of ecclesiastical leadership, tradition, reason, or appeals to "the Holy Spirit." Different evangelicals may accept the importance, in varying measures, of any or all these other things, but they are secondary; the litmus test to which every doctrine and practice must be subject is always that of Scripture.

Of course, the Bible, as many have noticed, is a large book, and many bizarre interpretations may be extracted from it by artistically creative exegetes. But evangelicals are, in practice, creedally orthodox—though the historic creeds function as a tacitly agreed parameter within which teaching takes place, not as a formally canonical authority on a par with Scripture itself. (The Nicene and Chalcedonian Creeds, for instance, are silent about some matters that evangelicals consider to be absolutely vital.) To stray outside the bounds of the creeds is to risk expulsion—not by ecclesiastical fiat but by gradual exclusion from the network of informal, mutual recognition—from the body evangelical.

Finally, evangelicalism is *crucicentric*. All theology, preaching, and devotional life return incessantly to the theme of the cross. The apostle Paul is never more appropriately claimed by evangelicals as one of themselves than when he wrote, "We preach Christ crucified" (1 Cor. 1:23). The cross is central because it is the location of salvation and justification; it highlights human lostness and divine love; it is the focal point of conversion, the motivation for activism, and the hermeneutical key through which the Bible is interpreted.

The Key Conversions

The Great Awakening had multiple beginnings in multiple locations: England, Wales, and North America. We shall have cause to notice each of these in turn.

The beginnings in England relate to an extraordinary pious society among Oxford students in the 1730s. Certainly no one could have accused the Holy Club of frivolousness of purpose. In their efforts to capture heaven by storm, its members (who included John and Charles Wesley) committed themselves to a rigid regime of devotions, good works, and extreme austerities, from which one student went mad and later died. Another of the group, George Whitefield (1714–1770), was seriously ill as a result of these excesses and was driving himself into bizarre behavior in his efforts to find peace with God. In April 1735, however, he was given assurance of salvation: the *Wiedergeburt* (or "re-birth") of which the Pietists spoke.

That same early spring, across the border in Wales, another conversion was taking place under not entirely dissimilar circumstances. Hywel Harris (1714–1773) was a young schoolmaster from Trefeca, near Brecon. In the weeks prior to Easter, he attended Talgarth parish church, where the reluctance of the parishioners to attend communion was evidently taxing the minister's patience. From the pulpit, the vicar fulminated: "You say that you are not fit to come to the Table. Well, then, I say that you are not fit to pray; yea, you are not fit to live and neither are you fit to die."[1]

It was an age when few had the secularized confidence to shrug off such clerical preachments completely. Certainly the young Harris had not. The minister's words ringing in his ears, he was convicted of his sins and strove for five weeks to live a perfect life, giving away his money and his best clothes, eating bread and water four days a week, and fasting altogether for the other three. On Whitsunday he went tremblingly to communion but "fully expecting that I should lose my burden." He later recorded that, even during the service itself, he was tempted by inner voices to yield to rationalist objections to basic Christian belief. The Enlightenment may not have penetrated as far as the peasants on the benches next to him, but it was starting to tug at the young schoolmaster. The Pietistic nature of his response to those temptations is therefore interesting: "I was wholly passive," he records, "without power to do anything, or to bring any argument to defend [my Christian beliefs]; that was just as well, otherwise I should have been fighting Satan with his own weapons, and should have been overcome."[2] Whether this was Harris's later gloss, as a Methodist preacher, on that initial struggle, or whether he had already been affected by Pietism makes little essential difference; the battle between Enlightenment rationalism and Pietist fideism was what counted.

Instead of batting off his doubts with "reason," Harris simply asked, "If there is no God, how was the Communion ever invented, and why are so many wise people deceived?"[3] It was an argument that would impress few demons nowadays. In 1735, though, it still sent them scuttling for cover. The social solidity of outward Christian observance was a circumstance that predisposed only very few people to challenge its basic premise. The fundamental ideas of a society change slowly, but those prevailing at a given moment, so that they are adhered to unreflectively, provide a sort of mental, emotional, and social safety; to reject them consciously is to step into the void. Surely, not all could be deceived about the reality of what happened at communion. It was easier to believe that the majority treated their salvation too lightly than to believe that there *was* no salvation.

Finally, Harris's conversion was crucicentric: "At the Table, Christ bleeding on the cross was kept before my eyes constantly; and strength was given me to believe that I was receiving pardon on account of that blood." He went home "leaping for joy" and immediately became an activist: "I said to a neighbour who was sad, 'Why are you sad? I know my sins have been forgiven.'"[4]

These events transpired in Harris's life within a few months from the conversion, under the preaching of Griffith Jones, of the man who was to be the other leading light of the Great Awakening in Wales. Daniel Rowland (1711–1790) was born in Llangeitho, Ceredigion, where his father was parish minister. The young Rowland was ordained in 1734 and made curate at his father's parish; he was married that same year.

Griffith Jones had been a nonconformist in his youth, but he had joined the Church of England and become rector of Llanddowror. More importantly, he was the founder of about 3,000 circulating schools, teaching people to read the Bible in Welsh. This was a development opposed by the ecclesiastical authorities. Jones's evangelistic preaching drew large crowds (which also got him into trouble), and it was at one of these meetings that Rowland, already a clergyman, was converted. Rowland's parish of Llangeitho was to become a center for the revival that was on the cusp of breaking out, which would lead Wales into the most glorious episode of its Christian history since the days of the saints in the fifth and sixth centuries.

As calendar years go, 1735 was a busy one; on the far side of the Atlantic, the first major drama in the American Great Awakening was taking place that same year. Quickenings from dead orthodoxy had begun fifteen years earlier among the Dutch Reformed in New Jersey. Their German-born leader, Theodor Jacob Freylinghuysen (1691–1748), had also convinced Gilbert Tennent (1703–1764), a Scottish Presbyterian, to adopt the same methods with his congregation as he had done himself, calling for conversion and deep personal commitment to Christ. Tennent did so, and the same increase and spiritual growth resulted. But it was 1734–1735 that saw the first decisive rise to prominence of Jonathan Edwards (1703–1758), who was to epitomize the revival in America, when his preaching brought about the conversion of three hundred people in the town of Northampton, Massachusetts, where he was the parish minister.

Like Rowland in Wales, Edwards came from a clerical caste. Congregationalism was the established, government-supported church in New England, and for generation after generation clergymen's daughters had married other clergymen and had then, in their turn, spawned fresh waves of the same. So after being converted as a student at Yale in his teens, when the young Edwards went on to become minister of the church at Northampton in 1724, it was a duty he shared with his grandfather, Solomon Stoddard, until the old man's death five years later. The excitement of 1734–1735 was just the first episode in a career of preaching and writing that was to make Edwards the most influential single figure (in a veritable galaxy of bright stars) in American Christianity until the twentieth century—and arguably down to the present.

Although 1735 was a significant year for the Wesley brothers also, it was not marked by their conversions, which still lay in the future, but because that was the year in which they went to the British colony of Georgia as missionaries. John (1703–1791) had already been ordained in 1728. Both he and Charles had been deeply involved in the Oxford Holy Club, called "Methodists" by their scornful student detractors because of their methodical way of using every minute of the day to best advantage, certain as they were of having to give an account to God for it. Every minute had for long been used to the best advantage in the household of their parents, Samuel and Susannah Wesley, in Epworth, Lincolnshire, where Samuel had been the High Church rector; John and Charles were their fifteenth and eighteenth children respectively. Both boys were sent to study at Oxford, and it was there that they became the moving spirits in the Holy Club. This, in turn, led them to consider undertaking ministry in the New World. The mission to Georgia was a disaster, and John alienated almost everyone. On his return in 1738, he wrote sorrowfully: "I went to America to convert the Indians; but, oh, who shall convert me?"[5]

Yet the circumstances that would lead to John Wesley's renewal were already in motion. On the outward voyage to America, the Wesley brothers had been deeply impressed by a group of Moravian Pietists who had been on the same ship and who, when it looked to be in danger of sinking at one point, had been remarkably calm and prayerful amid the general panic all around them. Back in London, John and Charles encountered another of the same tribe, Peter Boehler, who in April convinced John of his need for saving faith.

Wesley, chastened, asked Boehler whether he should cease preaching until he had attained assurance of faith for himself. Rather surprisingly, Boehler replied, "By no means." But what, countered Wesley, should he—a yet unsaved man—preach? "Preach faith till you have it. And then, because you have it, you will preach faith." Nearly three centuries later, it still appears that there is a logical flaw somewhere in that recommendation. But it is entirely beside the point, for it bore the desired fruit. Finally, on 24 May 1738, Wesley attended a devout society in Aldersgate Street, London, where Luther's preface to the Epistle to the Romans was being read aloud. As the speaker "was describing the change which God works in the heart through faith in Christ, I felt my heart strangely warmed. I felt I did trust in Christ, Christ alone, for salvation; and an assurance was given me, that he had taken away *my* sins."[6]

Finally, we should mention the extraordinary conversion of John Cennick (1718–1754), who was to have such a glowing career as an evangelist during his short lifetime. Born in Reading, England, he came under a period of agonizing conviction of sin from 1735, when he was just seventeen years old. He records: "Though all my days had been bitter through the fear of going to hell, yet I knew not any weight before, like this." Cennick spent the following two years as a wandering hermit on Salisbury plain, "eating acorns, leaves, crabs and grass" and "sweating, groaning, and crying aloud for mercy" for his sins. He came to assurance of salvation in 1737 and became one of the first of Wesley's lay preachers.[7]

What can we conclude from the above accounts? That there were in England many people who, notwithstanding the rationalism of high society, the immorality of the age, and the spiritual torpor of the official church, had nevertheless imbibed enough of orthodox faith to be very, very fearful for their souls. The Church of England was creating a spiritual hunger that was often left unsatisfied and a sense of guilt, which it did too little to assuage. A high proportion, at the least, of those who felt this hunger and guilt were young men.

As for the unconnected, virtual simultaneity of the conversions and opening acts in the drama, mere historical explanations start to break down or become unconvincing. Like the arguments about "Who moved the stone?" when all of the rationalistic explanations peter out into implausibility, one is left with that of miracle.

Whitefield and Wesley

George Whitefield was ordained by the bishop of Gloucester in June 1736, and he preached his first sermon the following Sunday. It was a triumph, and several complained to the bishop that he'd driven fifteen people mad! Those of us who have been trying for decades to drive our audiences over the brink of insanity might envy the young minister his success at first flush. But it did not stop there. Whitefield preached in London with resounding success and then went to Georgia for most of 1737–1741, promoting revival where the Wesleys had harvested only acrimony.

On a brief visit home to Britain, Whitefield preached in the open air for the first time outside Bristol. Hywel Harris was already doing this in Wales, and a clergyman named Morgan had done the same to the miners at Kingswood, Bristol, on the basis that no church had been built there. It was still a very novel idea and considered extremely controversial.

The reasons for adopting this new practice were several. In the first place, the numbers of hearers who flocked to listen to the new-style preachers were sometimes too great for the parish churches to contain. In the second place, the clergy and bishops often refused permission for the churches to be used for such "enthusiastic" purposes. Furthermore, there was the problem of access; some parishes were very large, with the parish church sited some way from the new industrial settlements, to which the Church of England had not adapted itself—and would not adapt itself until well into the following century. The nascent Industrial Revolution, which was to provide the motor for Methodist growth, meant a mushrooming population and changing patterns in its distribution. The national church failed to take account of this by redrawing its parish boundaries or erecting new churches. The new industrial settlements were strongly prone to Methodism, which went where the people were.

In April 1739, after a brief struggle with his conscience over such improprieties, John Wesley "consented to be more foul" (as he quaintly described the move in his diary) and joined Whitefield in preaching to the miners at Kingswood, Bristol, in the open air. The previous July, shortly after his conversion, Wesley had traveled to Germany, where he had met Zinzendorf at Herrnhut. Inspired, he had returned home determined to evangelize Britain.

The period of cooperation between Wesley and Whitefield was brief but fruitful. Both men were powerful preachers—the latter having perhaps the greater ability to affect his hearers. Indeed, many of their

John Wesley preaching
at Bolton Cross.
Illustration from *John Wesley
the Methodist*, 1903.

meetings witnessed tumul-
tuous outpourings of emo-
tion. Thousands flocked to
hear them, and, for precisely
this reason, their gatherings
caused alarm to polite society. Selina Hastings, Countess
of Huntingdon (1707–1791),
was almost alone among
aristocrats in her support for
the evangelists, and in 1737
she received a letter from
the Duchess of Buckingham
reproving her for her poor
taste: "It is monstrous to be
told, that you have a heart as
sinful as the common wretches
that crawl on the earth. This is
highly offensive and insulting;
and I cannot but wonder that your Ladyship should relish any sentiments
so much at variance with high rank and good breeding."[8]

Even at a distance of almost three centuries, it is a delight to see the
operating assumptions of the wielders of power brought into the public
gaze. Sinfulness, it seemed, was a monopoly of the lower orders; that
was why the national church's primary function was to keep them in
their place. When Wesley preached in the open air at Bath in June 1739,
fashionable society saw its chance to be revenged upon him. A whisper
went around the town that Beau Nash, the famous (or notorious) dandy,
was to give Wesley his comeuppance, and perhaps a thousand members
of the upper classes added themselves to the throng, not so much to be
saved as to be amused. Partway through Wesley's sermon, Nash barged
his way through the crowd and demanded Wesley desist because the
meeting was an illegal conventicle. When Wesley replied that the act
covered only seditious meetings and that this meeting was not at all seditious, Nash replied that it was, because Wesley was scaring people out
of their wits. "I asked if he had ever heard me preach. If not, how could
he judge of what he had never heard? He said, 'By common report, for

he knew my character.' . . . I went on: 'Give me leave, sir, to ask, Is not your name Nash?' Answer: 'Sir, my name is Nash.' 'Why then, sir, I trust common report is no good evidence of truth.' Here the laugh turned full against him, so that he looked about and could scarce recover."[9]

It is devoutly to be wished that presence of mind and repartee had been enough to rescue Wesley and Whitefield from the consequences, from 1741, of their mutual disagreement. They contrived to fall out so seriously over the subject of predestination that they ceased to cooperate. This bone of contention has been a cause of recurrent dispute since Augustine created Christian predestinarianism *ex nihilo* in the early fifth century; in other historical contexts, the argument has been an issue of some real moment, but in the situation of Wesley and Whitefield it was a matter of the merest pedantry, for both men wanted the same things. Both were evangelical members of the Church of England, creating a Methodist church-within-the-church via their preaching. In this case, it was Whitefield who had deliberately chosen, voluntarily and unconstrainedly, to be a Calvinist, while Wesley was one of those foredoomed from before the foundations of the earth to be a free-willer. And on this difference the movement sundered.

Of the two, one would have to judge that Whitefield was being the more consistent. Calvinism had always fitted far better with the combination of state church and evangelical soteriology (which was why all of the Protestant Reformers had adopted it and their Anabaptist rivals had uniformly rejected it), by making the identity of the true believers a secret known only to God, thereby undercutting the argument for a believers' church. The true source of Wesley's free-will doctrine was emphatically not the Anabaptism of the "left," however, but his parents' Arminianism of the "right": his father had been a High Churchman, and Wesley strove both before and after his conversion to reconcile biblicism with elements of High-Churchmanship. Indeed, his hapless hearers in Georgia had been unable to make out what religion he was preaching, and even after his conversion his early followers were dogged by incongruous accusations of popery.

Nor was this the end of Wesley's theological eclecticism. He taught a belief in entire sanctification that was to have enduring consequences for vast swathes of later evangelicalism. "Every one that hath Christ in him the hope of glory" (Col. 1:27), he later preached, "purifieth himself, even as he is pure" (1 John 3:3). The implication was that a Christian can, in principle (however seldom in practice), live like Christ. The apostle John, he pointed out, had said that "'Herein is our love made perfect, that we may have boldness in the day of judgment. Because as he is, so are we in this world.' The Apostle here, beyond all contradiction, speaks about himself and other living Christians, of whom . . . he flatly affirms, that not only at or after death but in *this world*, they are as their Master (1 John 4:17)."[10]

Truly, the argument is biblically formidable, and if it finds little favor among evangelicals today, it nevertheless became standard Methodist doctrine until well into the twentieth century. It was also to spawn the massive Holiness movement in the nineteenth century and proved a stepping-stone (via some important shifts from the 1870s onward) to Pentecostalism and, in our own times, the charismatic movement.

Concerning charismata, Wesley himself concluded that they had disappeared in the later years of the early church, not because they were intended solely for the apostolic period, but only because "faith and holiness were well-nigh lost." This loss was neither irretrievable nor intended by God, for Wesley did not "recollect any Scripture wherein we are taught that miracles were to be confined within the limits either of the apostolic or the Cyprianic age, or any period of time, longer or shorter, even till the restitution of all things."[11] However, although one of his young preachers, Thomas Walsh, recorded an experience of speaking in tongues in 1750, there is no indication that Wesley did so, either then or later, nor any justification for the frequently heard claim today that the Methodists were a "charismatic movement" in the sense of exhibiting the charismata.

In response to the quarrels about predestination and entire sanctification, Whitefield wrote reprovingly to Wesley in September 1740, before the final break, pointing out the inconsistency of believing in "sinless perfection" while at the same time denying the Calvinist doctrine of perseverance (that one cannot lose one's salvation). If people could be perfect, then they could not fall. He continued: "But this and many other absurdities you will run into, because you will not own election. And you will not own election because you cannot own it without believing the doctrine of reprobation."[12] Wesley had to reject perseverance because he wished to reject individual predestination to salvation—and he had to reject the latter because it entailed its necessary counterpart, predestination to damnation.

This was a little unfair. Wesley did not hold to a belief in *non posse peccare* (the impossibility of sinning) but only in *posse non peccare* (the ability not to sin). The latter, he might have argued, included by definition the contrary possibility of sinning—and also of falling away entirely. Still, Whitefield had identified a real tension, and the later part of his analysis, at least, is probably correct: Calvinist doctrines stood or fell together. But it was all of little relevance to the evangelization of Britain within the confines of the national church.

The disagreement also bore little relevance to other practical problems on the ground. Methodism was provoking fierce opposition and mob violence, often stirred up by gentry and parish clergy. Preachers and their hearers were attacked and sometimes killed. Houses and chapels were smashed up. Cennick's successes as an evangelist in Wiltshire, for example, were marred by many violent attacks upon himself and his followers. In mockery of his preaching "the blood of Christ," a mob at Stratton "got a butcher to save all the blood he could, in order to fill the engine, and so 'give us blood enough,' as they said." But it could get much worse: the windows of one convert's home were stoned and his family injured. Cennick recorded one particularly vicious incident in 1741: "Before I had said much the mob came again from Swindon, with swords, staves and poles, and without respect to age or sex they knocked down all that stood in their way. Some had the blood streaming down their faces, and others were almost beaten or trampled to death. . . . At last they came to a part of the road with many gates, where they posted themselves, and beat each of us inhumanly as we rode by; this continued for two miles."

The work of Wesley and Whitefield continued, despite the rift between the two men. Wesley spent most of the rest of his life traveling to every part of Britain, preaching several times a day (a lifestyle which, in addition to his own natural cantankerousness, put an intolerable strain upon his eventual, unhappy marriage). There is now scarcely a pre-nineteenth-century brick in England unadorned with a plaque bearing the legend "Wesley stayed at this house" (or some such) and a date. He invariably traveled on horseback and, anxious as he was to use every minute to the best possible advantage, caught up on his reading and correspondence as he rode along.

Wesley was a much better organizer than Whitefield: from 1742 he organized his converts into classes, which met for mutual confession, encouragement, Bible study, and prayer. Apart from the distinctively Methodist element of regimentation, these bore the hallmark of their origins in Pietism. The classes were arranged in circuits (another distinctive Methodist innovation) from 1746. By contrast, Whitefield's people were, in his own words, "a rope of sand."

This difference had a decisive effect on the future of the two men's work. Whitefield preached, made converts, and moved on. Certainly he received financial assistance and support from the Countess of Huntingdon, who had several chapels built in which services were conducted according to the rites of the Church of England but with evangelical preaching. (A legal decision in 1779 forced her to register them as dissenting meetinghouses.) But these, the so-called Countess of Huntingdon's Connexion, were virtually all that remained in institutional form of Whitefield's work after his death in 1770.

He had spent much time in North America, where his evangelism had a remarkable effect and where he cooperated freely with Congregationalists, Presbyterians, and even Baptists—a noteworthy broad-mindedness in that era, and symptomatic of the new evangelical mentality that was coming into existence (characterized by the descriptors mentioned at the start of this chapter).

Charles Wesley, John's brother, was also involved in evangelism and was the great hymn writer of Methodism. He is estimated to have produced 7,270 hymns of widely varying quality, many of them very long (a dozen or more verses being not uncommon). Many of the greatest are still mainstays of church worship everywhere;[13] many more have lapsed into well-earned obscurity. Some were used quite self-consciously to convey distinctively Wesleyan doctrine—a feature later editions have often seen fit to tone down.

In 1787 Wesleyan chapels were registered, like those of the Countess of Huntingdon before them, as dissenting meetinghouses, but actual separation from the Church of England was fiercely resisted by both John and Charles Wesley during their lifetimes. After John's death in 1791, however, the break with the national church was made explicit in the 1795 Plan of Pacification, which allowed for the administration of sacraments and the holding of weddings and funerals by Methodist ministers. A new denomination had been created.

Jonathan Edwards and North America

The revival in Northampton, Massachusetts, that had attended the preaching of Jonathan Edwards in 1734–1735 spread in the years that followed. The visits of George Whitefield from England encouraged this and, in the autumn of 1740, he addressed crowds of upward of 8,000 daily for more than a month. Two factors need to be borne in mind when assessing how impressive such events were and what a mark they made upon the minds of those who attended. In the first place, this was an era before microphones and sound systems; to address an audience of even a fraction of this size required a strong voice and powers of endurance from the speaker and utter silence from the listeners. In the second place, the population of most areas in the British colonies was very thinly scattered, especially in those districts more recently settled by Europeans; a crowd of 8,000 might represent virtually the entire population from many miles about in all directions.

One man, Nathan Cole, recorded the events of the day he was converted through Whitefield's preaching. The news of the time and location had reached him while he was plowing. He rushed indoors, told his wife to get ready, and, sharing the horse by the "ride a mile, walk a mile" system, they traveled twelve miles briskly to the riverbank, where they found the entire neighborhood making their way to the preaching station.[14] Brutally stated, the visit of a famous preacher might be the only event of public interest to have occurred in years. Certainly the revivals created their own momentum as rumor hardened into news and generated strong curiosity and a disposition to give the revivalists a favorable hearing.

In 1741 there was a further renewal in Jonathan Edwards's parish of Northampton. That July there occurred the most famous incident of his career, when he preached, as a mere visiting speaker, his sermon *Sinners in the Hands of an Angry God* at Enfield, Connecticut, on Deuteronomy 32:35, "Their foot shall slide in due time" (KJV). He had preached the sermon several times before, but on this occasion the fire fell and strong men clutched the pillars of the meetinghouse, crying aloud for mercy. Vainglorious emulators and would-be pulpit demagogues have fantasized about repeating the phenomenon ever since. Perhaps the magic of that day owed something to Edwards's suggestion, partway through the sermon, that "some of you will remember this discourse in hell." Certainly Nehemiah Strong confided to his diary that "without one thought to the contrary" the sermon had led him to expect the "awful judgment to be unfolded on that day and in that place."[15]

Whatever the source of Edwards's impact upon his listeners (and the Enfield incident shows that, lamentably, he was not above psychological manipulation), he was emphatically not guilty of the declamatory, shouting style of preaching used by some of the less sophisticated practitioners of the Great Awakening, and which continues to curse many quarters of evangelicalism down to the present. On the contrary, he tended to read his sermons aloud from a little notebook, and the emphasis was upon content. His preaching was all the more powerful for it.

The principal criticisms of the Great Awakening by the clerical establishment in New England, however, were that it lent itself to emotionalism and a loss of control by the learned clergy. Leadership would tend to pass into the hands of unlearned enthusiasts, thereby rendering the original Puritan vision of a godly, orderly "city on a hill" obsolete.

The Presbyterians grasped this painful nettle even before the Congregationalists did. In 1738 the Philadelphia Synod decreed that no minister would be recognized without a degree from a university in the Old World or from Yale or Harvard. It sounded reasonable enough for a church of the old, confessionalist type, if a little mysterious as to why such a decision should be formalized only several generations after arrival in the western hemisphere. The Presbyterians' new evangelical faction saw no mystery at all, however; it was a blatant attempt to exclude those students who had studied at the one-room "Log College" founded eight years before by William Tennent. The learning imbibed at this establishment seems to have been considerable; several of its erstwhile students went on to found colleges of their own and one to become president of Princeton (founded in 1746). But the principal objection to Tennent's institution was that he was training up a future generation of young evangelicals whose enthusiasm came as a sharp challenge to the dry, decorous Calvinist orthodoxy of the established clerical class.

The triumphant preaching tour of George Whitefield in Pennsylvania and New Jersey during 1739–1740—a tour which took in a visit to the Log College—boosted the morale of the evangelical firebrands even as it outraged the establishment. By 1740 Gilbert Tennent (one of four sons, all of them ministers, of William Tennent Sr.) preached a sermon on *The Danger of an Unconverted Ministry*, full of implications about his low opinion of his father's opponents. (It was also, of course, a rather un-Calvinistic insinuation that one could discern who "the converted" actually were.) In it, he chided those who

> are contented under a dead Ministry. . . . If they can get one, that has the Name of a Minister . . .; if he is free from gross Crimes in Practice, and takes good care to keep at a due Distance from their Consciences. . . . O! think the poor Fools, that is a fine Man indeed; our Minister is a prudent charitable Man, he is not always harping upon Terror, and sounding Damnation in our Ears, like some rash-headed Preachers, who by their uncharitable Methods, are ready to put poor People out of their Wits.[16]

The younger Tennent did not disdain to employ anti-intellectual rhetoric. Worst of all from the standpoint of Puritan clericalism, his airing of these differences in public was an unconscionable display of contempt for the tradition of professional solidarity.

By the following year, the schism was complete. The evangelicals withdrew from the synod just in time to save themselves from being kicked out. They then established a rival, New York Synod, founded in 1745, which proceeded to prosper more than the body it had abandoned. Every local manifestation of the dispute gave the "New Sides" (evangelicals) the opportunity to appeal for populist support on the basis of lay participation and experiential faith. And mostly, they got it.

The split was a clash of cultures as much as of theology or spirituality. The "Old Sides" clergy were on average a decade older than the evangelical upstarts. They had also, for the most part, immigrated to the New World as adults; the evangelical Presbyterian leaders were mostly either American-born or had arrived as children. The educational differences reflected those of origin: Scottish universities, on the one side; Yale, Harvard, and the Log College on the other. The rebellion of the evangelicals was, in a sense, the repudiation by the New World of the formalities and hierarchies of the Old World.

And the troubles spread soon afterward to the New England Congregationalists, who divided between "Old Lights" and "New Lights," along exactly the same set of issues as their Presbyterian brethren. Indeed, they were encouraged in that direction by the publication of the selfsame sermon that had aroused the Philadelphia Synod to such fury. For if those Presbyterian clergy who shook their heads doubtfully about the revival and its exponents were not truly converted, surely the same thing must be true of the Congregationalist "Old Lights."

If there were any doubt on the subject, the twenty-six-year-old minister James Davenport did his best to dispel it. Preaching outside Boston, he named a dozen of the city's ministers as being unconverted. Not only did such claims to spiritual discernment place him outside of his denomination's Calvinist orthodoxy, but his embarrassed fellow evangelicals thought it placed him literally out of his wits also. Indeed, it seems from a range of accounts that he was. But the damage was done.

The initial revival was at full tide only for a few years, between 1739 and 1745. By the latter date, opposition was becoming manifest. Yale and Harvard warned their students against "enthusiasm." Some of Edwards's own later writings, though phrased as defenses and explanations of the revival, are partial retractions—or at least qualifications—concerning some of the wilder manifestations that accompanied it. New England Congregationalism was too wedded to the establishment and too deeply embroiled in cultivating stability and a settled way of life, to look entirely favorably upon a movement that lived by exciting the emotions to fever pitch.

The influence of revivalism, however, affected almost all Protestant denominations, including non-English-speaking groups, whose Pietism was confirmed and renewed and who were drawn closer to the English-speaking mainstream by these events. The numbers of blacks, young people, and servants—all groups underrepresented in church attendance, proportionate to their numbers—affected by the revival was particularly marked during these years. The revival's emphasis upon oral transmission of ideas, rather than upon exacting standards of literacy, made it particularly appealing to such groups. The average age upon admission to full membership in Congregational churches fell, for a while, by six years; the revival was short-circuiting the follies of youth and bringing about early decisions for a life of sobriety and responsibility.

In addition, revivalism nudged the colonies toward democratization. The assumption that only conversion counted and that (the frequent Calvinism of its advocates notwithstanding) a person's convertedness could be discerned by others—at least on a rough-and-ready basis—tended to undermine the clericalist paternalism of the Puritan founders. The traditionalist clergy were forced to appeal to their own status as learned founts of knowledge to buttress their position and minimize the standing of the enthusiastic preachers and exhorters who vied for a popular following. That was the meaning of Charles Chauncy, the revivalists' nemesis among the Congregationalist hierarchy, when he complained of the "young persons, sometimes lads, or rather boys; nay, women and girls, yea, Negroes" who "have taken upon them to do the business of preachers." Dismissing their exhortations as "a mere passionate Religion," he rhetorically asked what device "the Devil himself ever made Use of, to more fatal Purposes, in all Ages, than the Passions of the Vulgar heightened to such a Degree?"[17]

The Great Awakening in Wales

Back in Wales, Hywel Harris went, after his conversion, to friends and neighbors and then further afield, reading aloud from Scripture and religious books to whomsoever would listen to him, in order to awaken his hearers from sin. Mindful of the prohibition on conventicles and of his own unordained status, he claimed not to be preaching but merely "exhorting." Even so, people who admitted him into their houses were fined a ruinous £20 by unappreciative magistrates.

Harris was turned down for ordination in the Church of England because of his activities. He was tempted to join the dissenters, who made him welcome, but a possibly misplaced loyalty made him stick with the establishment. His loyalty was not repaid to him; even some previously sympathetic Anglicans deserted him when they discovered that he'd been fraternizing with dissenters.

In 1737 Daniel Rowland and Hywel Harris made contact with one another. Both began to found "societies" for their converts along lines later to be followed by the English Methodists. They also cooperated with Whitefield to form a Calvinistic Methodist movement in Wales, which contrasted with the Wesleyan-Arminian model prevailing in England. Rowland's preaching ministry, based on Llangeitho, where he was curate to his brother, was both very powerful and successful.

In 1752, however, Rowland and Harris fell out over Christology, and their organizations split for a decade before the breach was healed. It was during this difficult period that Harris founded a commune at Trefeca, where the Countess of Huntingdon later added a college for training ministers.

One of Harris's early converts was William Williams of Pantycelyn (1717–1791). Williams was the son of a Congregationalist elder and had been educated at a dissenting academy. But he turned churchman and was ordained deacon in 1740, though he was refused full ordination as a priest in 1743 because of his evangelical activities.

Williams was a great organizer of societies, had a gift for helping people with spiritual or psychological difficulties, and had wide intellectual interests. A prolific author, his works include an account of the world's religions and, exhibiting a spirit quite at variance with later evangelical prudery, a book on sexual ethics. Williams has won most lasting fame, however, as a hymn writer. One volume of his hymns appeared with the striking title, *Ganeuon y rhai sydd ar a Môr o Wydr* ("Songs of those Standing on the Sea of Glass"), evoking Revelation 4:6. By now most of his greatest songs (e.g., "Guide Me, O Thou Great Jehovah") have long been translated into English from the Welsh in which all his works were written. One poem defended the widely criticized practice of dancing in the revival meetings.

Daniel Rowland, a figure who was stern enough to judge by his surviving portrait, also wrote in defense of the emotionalism that characterized many of the services, and which had led the Methodists of his country to be stigmatized as "Welsh jumpers": "You English blame us, the Welsh, and speak against us and say 'Jumpers! Jumpers!' But we, the Welsh, have something also to allege against you, and we most justly say of you, 'Sleepers! Sleepers!'"[18]

In 1760 Rowland's brother died, but Rowland himself was nevertheless again passed over for the rectorship of Llangeitho, and it was given to his own son. In 1763 he was finally thrown out altogether by the episcopal authorities. Separation of Welsh Methodism from the Church of England would have happened then and there but for the continuing loyalty to the establishment on the part of Hywel Harris—who was never ordained at all! As a result, separation did not formally take place until 1795, and the Calvinistic Methodists were formally organized with a procedure for ordination in 1811. They were about to embark upon a golden century of revivals, evangelism, and the sending of missionaries.

Scotland

Scotland was not to be left entirely untouched by the Great Awakening, but the dour seriousness of its predominant Presbyterianism ensured that any awakening there would be, at the very least, strongly imbued with Calvinist concerns. Though the Presbyterian settlement of the Kirk had been secure enough since the end of the seventeenth century, sufficient bitterness had been generated by the disputes of the previous fifty years to bequeath little ease in Zion to adherents of the Westminster Confession. Supporters of episcopacy still held firm to some parishes; Catholic clansmen continued to hold out for the Old Faith; the system of patronage to parish appointments smacked to tender consciences of ungodly Erastianism (and to almost everyone, godly or otherwise, of unwelcome English interference); rationalism was making its unbelieving hand felt through the the University of Glasgow in the training of ministers. Such nagging worries—which must have seemed vindicated by the 1715 and 1745 Risings—left any amount of constitutional assurances from London seeming hollow and beside the point.

It is possible, therefore, to read some aspects of the revival of the 1740s as incidents in the internal tensions of the Presbyterian Church that were producing the Secession by people disaffected with the influences of patronage and rationalism. Ebenezer and Ralph Erskine had been, since the late 1730s, in the process of encouraging such believers to secede from the Church of Scotland. By the mid-1740s, the Secession Church had the support of about forty congregations.

Whitefield, having received a bizarre series of mixed messages about whether he was or was not invited to come to Scotland to help things along, was unable to restrain his curiosity and, in the summer of 1741, made the journey north. On his arrival he found himself caught between the Seceders, led by Ebenezer and Ralph Erskine, and the evangelical party that remained within the Church of Scotland. Though he preached for both sets, the former were of two minds about whether to continue the relationship with him; the fact that Whitefield served in the prelatical Church of England, had sworn the oath of supremacy, and abjured the Solemn League and Covenant played ceaselessly on the Seceders' minds and overshadowed any work he might do among them in the mere directing of people to Christ.

Whitefield's preaching for the evangelical party within the Church of Scotland bore happier results. After one sermon in Edinburgh, he was approached by a Quaker who had insinuated himself into the throng, who shook him by the hand and greeted him with, "Friend George, I am as thou art; I am for bringing all to the life and power of the everliving God: and therefore, if thou wilt not quarrel with me about my hat, I will not quarrel with thee about thy gown." In reporting the incident to one of his correspondents, Whitefield commented: "I wish all of every denomination were thus minded." Amen, and amen.

But in 1742 a revival broke out in Cambuslang, on Clydeside, under a new minister, William McCulloch, in one of the churches that remained in the Church of Scotland. Whitefield returned that summer to Scotland and preached in both Edinburgh and Cambuslang to tumultuous receptions. Whether or not it was out of jealousy, the Seceders repudiated the revival; the emotionalism that attended the meetings, including outcries and tremblings, were, they insisted, proof positive that it was the work of the devil. This much, at least, can be said for the Seceders in making such judgments: they correctly perceived that evangelical revivalism was out of tune with the more sedate Presbyterian tradition of intense, but one-at-a-time, conversions.

Such insight did not, perhaps, quite justify their publication of *The Declaration, Protestation, and Testimony of the Suffering Remnant of the anti-Popish, anti-Lutheran, anti-Prelatic, anti-Whitefieldian, anti-Erastian, anti-Sectarian, true Presbyterian Church of Christ in Scotland*. Whitefield, this modest pamphlet averred, was "a limb of Anti-Christ," "a scandalous idolater" whose "foul, prelatic, sectarian hands" had dared to administer communion to Presbyterians. It was no surprise to the godly for he was (and this was doubtless the most telling point) "from the anti-Christian field of England." No reply is possible to diatribes of this sort, either then or now, and Whitefield wisely refrained from attempting one.

Whoever's work it was, the revival lasted only a few months. But Wesley, whose Arminianism must have made him a thousand times worse than Whitefield in the swiveling eyes of the Seceders, also made some limited inroads into Scotland during the following decades. But even with non-Seceders, his failure to attribute every last raindrop to the ineluctable and eternal decree of Providence gave him even higher diplomatic hurdles to leap over than those that had faced Whitefield. Nevertheless, starting in 1751, Wesley visited the country twenty-two times, and a Methodist work was well established north of the border by the end of the century.

Evangelicalism and the Development of North America

The democratizing effects of the revival have already been noticed in this chapter. But the British colonies in North America were to prove profusely fertile soil for the new form of evangelicalism, not just during the Awakening, but after it. The colonists had arrived in countless varieties, religiously speaking, and once in the New World, their creativity and energy, their divisions from one another, and the simple vastness of the continent's geography all lent themselves to a fecundity of denominations and movements that would have left the Protestant Reformers of the Old World, two centuries before, and even the Pilgrim Fathers themselves, utterly aghast.

The Great Awakening had fractured the unity of the Presbyterians— though that breach would be repaired by the late 1750s. But the Congregationalists remained divided between Edwards's supporters and those who feared "enthusiasm" more than they longed for conversions. The middle colonies were already home to a bewildering mixture of (among others) Anglicans, Baptists, Quakers, Scottish Presbyterians, Dutch Reformed, Lutherans, German Reformed, Dunkers, and Mennonites. Each was prone to splits as a result of the absence of Old World constraints. Many had a shortage of ministers or preachers, with the consequent tendency of congregations to make do with enterprising laypeople. These often took their churches in new—or, at any rate, less formal, more biblicist, and experiential—directions than was the pattern of their denominations hitherto. The denominations could try to interfere—and provoke a split. Or they could leave well enough alone. Either way, the same result: large swathes of church life in the colonies fell into the hands of pragmatic, populist, biblicist leaders.

The future of evangelicalism in North America lay largely with the exclusively revivalist groups, mainly Methodists and Baptists, which thrived among the new settlers living away from the coast. Methodists and Baptists provided a flexible form of religion, in terms of congregational organization, which the established churches had been less quick to provide. These aggressively evangelical churches required no parish structures, elaborate buildings, or formally trained clergy, and so they could move immediately wherever the people were. Indeed, at its most basic institutional level, evangelicalism was a do-it-yourself religion that did not even need, in every circumstance, to be *brought to* the settlers at all but moved naturally *with* them. In consequence, the frontier was to remain permanently revivalist and, thereby embedded in the American psyche, it became part of the American way of life, with results that remain with us.

The Baptists grew sharply in the southern colonies (Georgia and the Carolinas) from the 1750s onward, providing an exciting alternative to the Church of England, which had hitherto predominated there. They were followed in the 1770s by the Methodists.

Growth by the first of these, the Baptists, stemmed largely from the work of the Sandy Creek Association of Separate Baptist churches. Nine churches established the organization in 1758; their leading spirits were Shubal Stearns (1706–1771) and his brother-in-law Daniel Marshall (1706–1784), Bostonians who had moved to North Carolina from New England three years beforehand for the purpose. Stearns was possessed of an authoritarian manner in private and a magnetic preaching style in public, able to evoke either tears or terror in his listeners more or less at will. A contemporary noted, "All the Separate ministers copy after him in tones of voice and actions of body; and some few exceed him."[19] Utilizing converted laymen as pastors and preachers and (controversially) permitting women to pray aloud in their meetings, the movement grew rapidly in areas where the population was often thinly scattered. The poorer sort of settlers who were persuadable by such lowly preachers and emotional styles of delivery were often despised by their betters, and when the evangelists came into contact with wealthy landowners and the upholders of official religion, then there was frequently conflict. Thus it was that when a Baptist by the name of Waller attempted to preach in Tidewater, Virginia, in 1771, he was horsewhipped by the combined forces of parson and sheriff.

But Waller kept at it. So too did dozens more like him. By then the Sandy Creek Association's members numbered in the thousands across Virginia and the Carolinas. In 1787 they made their peace with the more staid Regular Baptists upon a platform of moderate Calvinism, a theological stance that owed as much to the origins of many of the Baptist leaders (who were frequently defectors from New England Congregationalism) as it did to any historic preponderance of Reformed theology among North America's Baptists. But it was not their theology that caused the Sandy Creek Separates to flourish so much; it was their fundamental good sense and their optimal

The ordination of Francis Asbury in 1784 (as imagined in 1882).

combination of firebrand evangelism with moderation, pragmatism, and spiritual warmth.

This combination was shared by the Methodists—that other evangelical grouping to whom belonged the American future. In the early years, however, they bore a burden that the Baptists did not: strong historical and organizational connections with the colonial power—an authority that, during the 1770s, was in the process of being overthrown. Connections of this sort proved nearly fatal to the Anglicans, whose numbers were decimated during the Revolutionary War and continued to decline for generations afterward. Yet the Methodists thrived, notwithstanding Wesley's well-publicized opposition to the "rebels" against the Crown.

For a while after 1775, Francis Asbury remained Methodism's only missionary in what was about to become the United States of America. Yet Methodist numbers grew from a mere 3,000 at that date to 60,000 in 1790.

It should be remembered, of course, that the Methodist movement remained formally within the Church of England until 1795. Yet friend and foe alike could see that it was an unwelcome guest within that body— and, in revolutionary America, that could do it no harm. Furthermore, the embarrassing handicap of Wesley's unhelpful political stance was outweighed by his other legacies: pragmatism and "the common touch."

The Baltimore Conference of 1784 was faithfully reflecting the latter when it sternly instructed its itinerant evangelists: "Do not affect the gentleman. A preacher of the gospel is the servant of all." Few admonitions could have been better calculated to accord with the American temper, both in that age and for long afterward.

Like the Baptists, the Methodists' organization was flexible, their preaching simple and direct, and their spirituality fervent. In neither movement was lack of formal scholarship a necessary barrier to participation in active ministry. They were to prove key ingredients in the participatory, fluid, and energetic society of the young United States.

Evangelicalism, Modernity, and the Industrial Revolution

The relationship between evangelicalism and modernity is a topic about which debate is currently raging. Postmoderns wish to dismiss evangelical biblicism as the product of a text-bound culture and evangelical dogmatism as stemming from modernist ideas of absolute truth. There is, of course, something to be said for such accusations, though they are half-truths at best. But it can escape the notice of few that evangelicalism makes its inroads today among the newly literate but rootless urbanites of the Third World and wins its converts in eastern Europe from the most Westernized sections of the population. To that extent, it is indeed modernist.

In the Great Awakening and afterward, evangelicalism focused upon personal "decisions" to follow Christ. It also encouraged popular, spontaneous, every-member participation in church life and worship. In doing so, it both assumed and fostered a degree of personal autonomy in decision making that has not been true of the vast majority of human experience. Peasants can rarely make decisions for themselves; they are too greatly constrained by the demands and expectations placed upon them by others, whether landlords and social superiors, family members, or neighbors—none of whom would be inclined to view a tenant's, son's, or neighbor's change of religious allegiance as "a private matter." It is no accident that evangelicalism came to birth during the Industrial Revolution and made the greatest headway in those societies most affected by the social fluidity of modernization. It also saw its greatest advances in the most modern sectors of those societies: industrial artisans, factory and mine workers, the newly urbanized, the immigrants, those whom economic circumstances had recently relocated. In England it was strongest in London, Newcastle, Bristol, and Cornwall, the last three all associated with mining.

Evangelicalism was modern in other related ways. By focusing upon Scripture and insisting that all could and should read it for themselves, it both assumed and encouraged literacy. Learning to read was a religious duty of the believer and a channel of faith to the unbeliever. This much had been true of the sixteenth-century Reformation; eighteenth-century evangelicalism widened and accentuated the same impulse. It was no accident that Griffith Jones, the trailblazer of Welsh evangelicalism, won his most enduring fame as the founder of thousands of circulating schools. The Industrial Revolution required even many of the poor to be able to read, as well as swelling the proportion of the population that was urbanized, and so the pool of potential recruits for the new evangelicalism was growing apace.

Evangelical activism also both relied upon and promoted a capacity for individual initiative and responsibility that most cultures lacked before the modern era. The nineteenth century was to be the age of "societies" in Britain, as individuals came together on the basis of personal interests, obsessions, and ideas to collect postage stamps or convert the heathen, to study kingfishers or to free the slaves. This was a stark contrast to the "given-ness" of relationships in the premodern world—and the rise of evangelicalism was a precursor of the newfound ability of individuals to take action with likeminded others in a given cause. Evangelicals were themselves, of course, among the most prolific founders of societies—whether for missions, philanthropy, or the promotion of some political or social campaign.

The new evangelical churches also provided emotional refuges for those who, in more than one sense, were lost souls. The Industrial Revolution pitchforked millions from the security of rural life into the anonymity and insecurity of the new towns. Severed from the parishes where their ancestors had lived for generations and where they had been surrounded by known faces, many people suffered acutely from the dislocation and uncertainty of their new existence. The Methodists and the other new churches provided replacement communities and a rescue from anonymity and from the heartlessness of the stark industrial world. Precisely this phenomenon, and precisely these people, are among the best responders to evangelicalism in the mushrooming cities of South America, Africa, and Asia today.

Evangelical beliefs invested with dignity those who felt that their dignity had been torn from them, whose lowly but secure place in a village had been lost and who were now worth only what they could earn in cash wages—which was usually little and sometimes nothing. The evangelical gospel told them that they were worth a divine Savior's blood. It also provided avenues for meaningful religious activity to make good the profound loss of meaning experienced by those who felt themselves adrift in the new, harsh landscape. All surveys show that dissent was strongest, and the established church weakest, in the industrial towns.

Despite the Toryism and royalism of Wesley and the conservatism of the Methodist denominational leaders, it was the participatory nature of Methodist and evangelical church life that fostered democratic attitudes. In 1741, the year of the break with Whitefield, Wesley finally, though very unwillingly at first, allowed laymen to preach. Once this step was made, however, he later advanced to a permission for women to preach too. Sometimes women were also class leaders in early Methodism. Example and experience won out over precept. To that extent, the reactionaries who decried Methodism as a threat to the established order were proved correct by events.

The Myths of the Great Awakening

Like many historical developments that possess a continuing legacy in the present, there has been a marked tendency for the latter to create a sort of historical propaganda for itself concerning the former. This has generally taken the form of myth-creation about the heroism of the past. Some modern nation-states produce such mythologies concerning their own history and in the process create a projected past that never was. And evangelicals have not been immune to the same kind of temptation.

It would be no caricature to say that, insofar as evangelicals today have an image of the Great Awakening in Britain, it has mainly been picked up by anecdotes in sermons they have heard or, among the more serious-minded, from popular biographies of Wesley, Whitefield, or Rowland. The resultant popular-evangelical image consists, broadly, of three crucial elements:

   an utterly wretched, spiritually bankrupt national church *before* the Awakening (because of the absence of godly ministers);
   vast numbers of converts *during* the Awakening (all converted by heroic preachers during meetings of cataclysmic spiritual power and emotional fervor);
   a transformed country *afterward*, as a direct result of the ministries of Wesley, Whitefield, and their fellow-workers.

That this vision is, for the most part, perpetuated by the instruction available in colleges that train evangelical preachers is, no doubt, a mere accident.

It is no diminution of the importance of the Great Awakening to point out that all three elements represent gross exaggerations of the eighteenth-century reality—that they are, in fact, myths. The myth-making was undertaken (doubtless in all good faith) by nineteenth-century Methodist historians who, unsurprisingly, wished to emphasize the magnitude of the change wrought by the advent of Methodism. This they did, in part, by painting the picture of the religious state of Britain beforehand in the darkest hues possible.

Now it is certainly true that biblicist faith was, relative to the periods that preceded and followed it, at a low ebb during the three-quarters of a century between the Restoration of the monarchy in 1660 and the conversions of the Great Awakening's principal evangelists in 1735. But this does not amount to a landscape of universal misery, ecclesiastical corruption, and spiritual bankruptcy. Some recent historians have found the early-eighteenth-century church to be in surprisingly good health—however defective it may have been from an evangelical point of view. Neither were the Wesleys the only Britons to have been affected by Germanic Pietism; religious societies and pious fraternities abounded in the capital and elsewhere—even if the general tenor of the times was running against them. The ravages of the new rationalism had affected the upper classes and the learned more profoundly than ordinary people, whose sensibilities on most things had (and still have) a time lag of a generation or two. So there was plenty of religious susceptibility for the evangelists to pick up on from the late 1730s. Furthermore, although the legacy of the Puritan period had been suppressed and its exponents ejected from the seats of power, it had not entirely disappeared. Nor had all of the Dissenters succumbed to death or Unitarianism; several of the key participants in the Great Awakening had some background in Old Dissent.[20]

Regarding the second point, the numbers of converts during the Great Awakening were substantial, but they were not numbered in the millions, nor did their impact amount to a transformation of national mood. Late-eighteenth-century Britain remained a deeply unattractive society, prone to riot and violence, and with a harsh penal code. Though the novels of Henry Fielding, such as *Pamela* and *Tom Jones*, and the paintings of Hogarth were contemporary with the early decades of the Awakening itself, their depictions of both the gin craze and the general seediness and debauchery that characterized the age were hardly unrecognizable to the era of

King George III that followed. And even as late as the early nineteenth century, the clergyman Charles Simeon could still be counted as an irritating idiosyncrasy for insinuating himself into a Cambridge parish and preaching his evangelical doctrines to generations of undergraduates.

But by then, evangelical influence was starting to count in the country as a whole. Indeed, Simeon was a trailblazer for the real transformation that still lay ahead. In 1800, membership of all Methodist groups (who had, after Wesley's death, separated from the national church) ran to just under 94,000. Even allowing for the undoubted fact that many of the converts of the revivalists had chosen to remain within the Church of England, thereby nurturing an incipient evangelical movement there, that is not a lot to show for all of the sound and fury of the Great Awakening. Yet by 1850 there were just shy of half a million Methodists: a truly impressive growth in fifty years. For the Congregationalists and Baptists, the story is the same: a fivefold increase (from 35,000 and 27,000 respectively to 165,000 and 140,000 respectively) over the same period. The really big numbers of converts, then, did not come about from the huge rallies and exciting preaching of the big-name evangelists of the Great Awakening—exciting and important though those were. The real transformation was produced only later by the smaller, more undramatic witness, preaching, and moral and spiritual influence of individual congregations and individual believers.

Concerning the third point—the idea that the Great Awakening left a transformed country—our conclusion should by now be obvious. It did not tip the country upside down. But it did lay the essential groundwork for what would follow. By the mid-nineteenth century, evangelicals held a position of cultural and moral near-dominance within Britain that saw crime rates falling and moral expectations of each individual rising, along with a whole raft of social improvements and reforms—from the abolition of slavery to Factory Acts—of which evangelicals were the principal protagonists. The Great Awakening had laid the foundation for the attainment of that distant zenith; it had not witnessed its creation.

15

REASON AND POWER

RATIONALIST THEOLOGY
AND THE DIVINE RIGHT OF KINGS

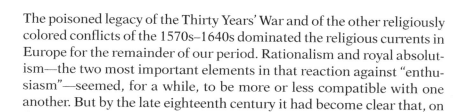

The poisoned legacy of the Thirty Years' War and of the other religiously colored conflicts of the 1570s–1640s dominated the religious currents in Europe for the remainder of our period. Rationalism and royal absolutism—the two most important elements in that reaction against "enthusiasm"—seemed, for a while, to be more or less compatible with one another. But by the late eighteenth century it had become clear that, on the contrary, their differences portended new, dangerous conflicts.

The Rationalist Challenge to Religion

Modernist rationalism tended to suppress religious enthusiasm and to call into question the certainties upon which such zeal was based, at least insofar as these touched the distinctions between one variety of Christianity and another. Absolutist monarchy, on the other hand, sought to make the support of a political order the chief purpose of religion, and thereby to domesticate its concerns. Only during the course of the eighteenth century did rationalism turn into new directions that questioned the very basis of divine support for monarchy.

Rationalism had developed as the quest for knowledge about humanity and the world that did not depend upon faith or revelation. It was also a quest for the basis for a public polity that would be similarly free of any need for religious sanction. At least, that was one side of the story. The other side is that it was a continuation of the same impulses that had produced Protestantism itself: the critique of established institutions in the name of abstract "truth"; the primacy of principle over persons; the elevation of the printed text above the visual spectacle; a preference for the results of investigation over the authority of tradition; and the delusion that impartiality and objectivity were attainable goals.

Calvin, for example, had criticized the Catholic Church for arrogating to itself the right to interpret Scripture; instead, he maintained, it was "a depository of doctrine" that described the character of God "by the standard of eternal truth" rather than by any human standards. "If the doctrine of the apostles and prophets is the foundation of the Church," he reasoned, then "the former must have had its certainty before the latter began to exist."[1] In matters of authority, then, truth trumped institutions.

Concerning the elevation of the printed text, John Foxe, the English martyrologist, had prophesied: "'Either the Pope must abolish Knowledge and Printing, or Printing at length will root him out.' Popes and priests are ever the enemies of printing, for their power depends upon 'lack of knowledge and ignorance of simple Christians.'"[2] It was a perspective that endured over centuries, supported by the observable social reality that, in areas with religiously mixed populations, Protestant literacy rates far outstripped those of their Catholic neighbors. The idea that Catholicism was obscurantist and thrived on ignorance became a stock Protestant jibe that long outlived the renewed educational drive of the Jesuits and the new seminaries founded in the wake of the Tridentine reforms.

However, the advantages were not entirely one way; the fact that elements of rationalism were present within Protestantism itself made it more prone to theological erosion and creeping liberalism. When rationalism and even deism began to infect some Protestant church bodies, as they did during the late seventeenth and eighteenth centuries, then it could be said that they had become partially, at least, heretical—and that not merely from the standpoint of Catholic polemicizing, but in actual fact. One of the corollaries of this was that in Protestant countries the rationalist thinkers and philosophers of the eighteenth century were seldom explicitly antireligious. In the more constrained atmosphere of France, they often were. In the yet more constrained atmosphere of Spain and Portugal, they seldom appeared at all.

It is at least arguable, of course, that the rise of rationalism, and most especially its relationship with religion, has been grotesquely distorted in nineteenth- and twentieth-century (so by now, traditional) accounts. Rationalism has been portrayed in unabashedly secular terms; religion has been portrayed as obscurantist—the great impediment to the progress of knowledge and the advancement of human flourishing. In short, the intellectual history of the early-modern period as it has traditionally been taught represents a triumph of spurious, secularist propaganda. As one writer has recently put the matter,

> The identification of the era beginning in about 1600 as the "Enlightenment" is as inappropriate as the identification of the millennium before it as the "Dark Ages." And both imputations were made by the same people—intellectuals who wished to discredit religion and especially the Roman Catholic Church, and who therefore associated faith with darkness and secular humanism with light. To these ends they sought credit for the "Scientific Revolution" (another of their concepts), even though none of them played any significant part in the scientific enterprise.[3]

Harsh, but fair. There is a good deal to be said in favor of this assessment of the matter. For one thing, most of the major scientists were religious, and in more than a merely formal sense. Newton and Galileo—both idols of later, secular protagonists of science—are prime cases in point. The former wrote more about religious and even mystical-esoteric matters than about the themes that have made him so celebrated by later scientists. Nineteenth- and twentieth-century historians, where they have deigned to notice Newton's religiosity at all, have expressed astonishment at this supposed paradox. How could a man of such amazing perspicuity have bothered himself with complex calculations about the date of the second coming? Yet, as so often with moderns observing the past, the misunderstanding is all ours. In Newton's own mind there was no conflict at all between observing the universe and seeking to understand its Maker. As John Maynard Keynes, the twentieth-century economist who collected Newton's papers, concluded, "He regarded the universe as a cryptogram set by the Almighty."[4]

Newton was interested, like many other intellectuals of that age, in astrology and even alchemy, as well as theology and eschatology. Though his calculation of the date of the second coming of Christ—1948—has proved incorrect, his prediction that this date would be four years after the "end of the great tribulation of the Jews" seems eerily close to the mark in the light of actual twentieth-century events.[5]

Galileo (1564–1642), likewise, is far from being the cut-and-dried case of "man of reason" martyred to the irrationalist demands of an obscurantist church. For most of his life Galileo was the friend of Cardinal Matteo Barberini, who became Pope Urban VIII in 1623 (until his death in1644). It was the manner in which Galileo chose to publish his 1632 book, *Dialogue Concerning the Two Chief World Systems*, that turned the two men's friendship to enmity for the final decade of their lives. It had been made clear to Galileo all along that if he wished to support Copernican arguments, he could do so, but that he must express himself in hypothetical language (i.e., he should point out that this was the conclusion to which purely mathematical arguments, taken on their own, *would* point).[6]

Not only did Galileo fail to meet this stipulation, but he expressed himself, in his *Dialogue*, in needlessly insulting terms. Yet the demand that he express himself with restraint, though irksome, was hardly unique to the "age of faith." Its necessary hypocrisies are with us still: statisticians, accountants, and politicians, for example, speak every day about the impending pensions crisis, but they confine themselves to the abstract language of finance, management, and increasing longevity; to point to the actual causes of Western demographic collapse would be an intolerable affront to the central platitudes of post-1960s society. As now, so then: in the seventeenth century, Galileo could have done better. As it was, he was forced to recant his heliocentric view and was kept under house arrest for the rest of his life.

But leaving aside the rights and wrongs of Galileo's case, the central fact remains that he considered himself a good Catholic even after the church itself started to account him a bad one. His basic Christian certainties remained undisturbed by his scientific endeavors. As Galileo himself said, "The book of nature is a book written by the hand of God in the language of mathematics."[7]

In this respect, Newton and Galileo were at one with Christian apologists such as William Paley (1743–1805), the clergyman and fellow of Christ's College, Cambridge, whose books and teachings argued that the new scientific discoveries pointed conclusively to the existence of a benign God. He coined the now-famous analogy of the watch and the watchmaker. The watch is so complex, with each part serving a particular essential function, that, if we did not already know it, we would be forced to infer the existence of a watchmaker. Living creatures, observed

Paley, are more complex than watches "in a degree which exceeds all computation"; a Creator is unavoidably inferred by the sheer fact of our existence. "The marks of design are too strong to be got over. Design must have had a designer. That designer must have been a person. That person is God." Paley's *View of the Evidence of Christianity* (1794) remained influential at Cambridge for more than a century after its publication. His *Natural Theology: or, Evidences of the Existence and Attributes of the Deity, Collected from the Appearances of Nature,* did not appear until 1802. Both works remained staples of Protestant apologetics on both sides of the Atlantic throughout the nineteenth century.

Yet the received story of the Enlightenment is that secularist philosophy and the rise of modern science went hand-in-hand. It was a propaganda that originated with the eighteenth-century secularists themselves: "Never mind that the actual discoveries had been made by 'serious and often devout Christians.' What mattered was that, in the words of Peter Gay, 'science could give the deists what they wanted—Newton's physics without Newton's God.'"[8]

Yet once all of the secularist propaganda about the Enlightenment has been debunked, the undoubted fact remains that the intellectual tide was turning against orthodox Christian doctrines and that it was doing so on account of rationalism. While Newton's theology was far from the mere philosophical deism that later propaganda has claimed it to be (his *Principia* insisted that "the true God is a living, intelligent, powerful Being [who] . . . governs all things, and knows all things that are done or can be done"), his adoptionist view of Christ's deity means that he nevertheless is considered heretical by the canons of received Christian orthodoxy—and heretical because of his *rationalist* approach to the incarnation. And many of the other leading intellectual luminaries of the age—Hume, Gibbon, Adam Smith, Diderot, Voltaire, Rousseau— repudiated Christian orthodoxy to a much greater extent.

But leading intellectual luminaries are, by their nature, atypical of the society in which they live. They are more typical (if their work endures and their ideas spread) of the ages that follow them, who feel more at home with them. Their thought, generally in debased and simplified form, becomes the common stock of those succeeding eras. "Human rights" counted as radical in the age of Tom Paine but merely platitudinous in ours; "nations" defined as "the people" threatened monarchies and empires during the *ancien régime* but seemed axiomatic by the twentieth century. It is possible, therefore, to misread the past by counting the atypical thinker (in this case, the atypical secularist and rationalist) as somehow representative of "the way people were thinking"—especially when

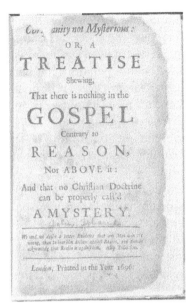

The attempt to square faith and reason.
Illustration from *Christianity not Mysterious*,
John Toland, 1696.

their (debased, simplified) thoughts *are* typical among ourselves. When this fact is added to the normal tendency of popular history to misread our ancestors as moderns (only in poor housing and different clothes), then the preconditions for misinterpreting the Age of Enlightenment as a popular tide of secularism sweeping away the old, imposed religiosity are complete.

In reality, the rationalism and skepticism of the age between the Peace of Westphalia and the French Revolution was confined, for the most part, to the upper classes and the fashionably educated—and only to an important minority even of them. In 1737, for example, when Queen Caroline, wife of King George II of England, was on her deathbed, various courtiers suggested that prayers might be in order. The prime minister of the day, Robert Walpole, suggested to Princess Emily that John Potter, archbishop of Canterbury, be called for, adding, "Pray, Madam, let this farce be played; the Archbishop will act it very well. You may bid him be as short as you will. It will do the Queen no hurt, no more than any good; and it will satisfy all the good and wise fools, who will call us atheists if we don't profess to be as great fools as they are."[9] A better instance of the prevailing mentality among the upper classes would be hard to find: an awareness that ordinary people did not share—and perhaps were not even aware of—the skeptical sentiments of their rulers; the traditional instincts (prayer on a deathbed) among some within the palace itself; a willingness to assuage popular feeling even while being contemptuous of it; a clear drawing short of any admission that "we" are actual atheists (indeed, mostly they were not; in most cases, deism was as far as it went).

Frederick the Great of Prussia (reigned 1740–1786) was similarly skeptical about Christianity. His policy of religious toleration was founded, at least in part, on the belief that all religions were equally deluded. Yet, like his English counterparts, his repudiation was private; churches and their ministers were responsible to himself as chief magistrate, and open attacks upon them were not tolerated, for they kept social order and were thus too useful to be dispensed with. But the appointive power he held to about one third of clerical positions was used to promote modernizers and rationalists within the church itself. This power was strengthened during the course of the eighteenth century by the capture of the University of Halle by teachers who espoused the new rationalist critiques.

Johann Salomo Semler (1725–1791) was the most prominent—though not the most radical—of the new teachers at Halle. At a young age, he rejected his father's Pietism and sought the roots of Christian faith in the lived experience of the early church. His four-volume *Treatise on a Free Enquiry into the Canon* (1771–1776) pointed out that Christianity had been spread orally both before the New Testament itself was composed and for long afterward, since different churches had varying canonical lists and no agreement had been reached until late in the fourth century. Every stage of the process, he argued, from the teaching of Jesus through to agreement on the canon, had shown accommodations to previously existing ideas, leaving the faith deeply marked by both Judaism and Hellenism. This being so, theologians in the present need not make rigid adherence to formulas (which were, after all, historically conditioned) an essential test of orthodoxy.

Even so, Semler remained conservative by the standards of some of his peers. He at least upheld the crucifixion, resurrection, and atonement and the work of the Holy Spirit. Even so, the thrust of his argument that the contents and canon of Scripture were historical products seemed dangerous to many. As one of the greatest modern commentators on historical theology has sagely observed,

> There is a sense in which the very notion of tradition seems inconsistent with the idea of history as movement and change. For tradition is thought . . . not [to] have a history since history implies the appearance at a certain point in time, of that which had not been there before. According to the *Ecclesiastical History* of Eusebius, orthodox Christian doctrine did not really have a history, having been true eternally and taught primitively; only heresy had a history, having arisen at particular times and through the innovations of particular teachers. . . . It seems that theologians have been willing to trace the history of doctrines and doctrinal systems which they found to be in error, but that the normative tradition had to be protected from the relativity of having a history or of being, in any decisive sense, the product of a history.[10]

By implication, then, to find the orthodox tradition guilty of "having a history" was to find it "in error." Freedom from the taint of historical contingency was to be found only in the truths attainable by unfettered reason. The *Natural Theology* of Christian Wolff (1679–1754), who taught at Marburg and Halle, tended in the same direction. Whether Wolff and Semler intended it or not, the groundwork was being laid for that nineteenth-century flowering of modernist liberal theology and biblical criticism that would find its epicenter in Germany.

The Prussian church was not the only one to be contaminated by deviations from historic orthodoxy. Benjamin Hoadly, successively bishop of Bangor, Hereford, Salisbury, and Winchester during the 1710s to 1740s, was accused, not without cause, with actual deism by his enemies. Hoadly was an extreme case, but John Tillotson, archbishop of Canterbury (1691–1694), was nearly as pleasing to deists and religious skeptics such as Hume, Voltaire, and Anthony Collins, and he was constantly cited by them as vindication for their own attacks upon hitherto accepted orthodoxy as mere "enthusiasm" or "superstition."[11]

"Enthusiasm" and "superstition": these were the two things over against which state-church Protestants defined themselves during the age of the *ancien régime*. "Enthusiasm" was the error of the sectarians—and, indeed, of the Puritans who had rebelled against the king. Radical applications of biblical texts, claims to personal spiritual enlightenment or revelation, demands for religious experience in the self or others: all of these could be—and were—stigmatized as "enthusiastic," fanatical, and therefore dangerous. "Superstition," on the other hand, was the error of the Roman Catholics: doctrinaire understandings of the Christian tradition among Protestants—whether of the Trinity, of the sacraments, or of the normative interpretations of Scripture—could be lumped together with indulgences and the Donation of Constantine as so much papist hokum, thereby allowing the rationalists to claim good Protestant credentials for themselves even as they debunked Protestantism as it had been understood since the Reformation. For Christianity was being redefined as mere reasonableness. As Tillotson, archbishop of Canterbury, put the matter, God had commanded nothing "either unsuitable to our reason or prejudicial to our interest; nay, nothing that is severe and against the grain of our nature."[12]

John Locke's book, *The Reasonableness of Christianity* (1695), summed up the desire of many to demonstrate that reason and Christianity were one and the same. But in the process, the distinctively Christian aspects of Christianity—especially the miraculous and those didactic elements that depend upon revelation—were sidelined. What was left was morality. And even this, as Tillotson had observed, was to be understood as something entirely in accordance with reason. The chief purpose of God was reduced to that of underwriter of the moral—and so of the social—order. And though this fitted admirably with the actual, observable function of official churches in the late seventeenth and eighteenth centuries, it left them highly vulnerable to the later critiques of Marx.

In point of fact, however, there was no need to wait until Marx. The critics—those who would deride Christianity and its morality as a trick played upon the common people to keep them in order—were already at the door.

> The chief thing, therefore, which lawgivers and other wise men that have laboured for the establishment of society have endeavoured, has been to make the people they were to govern believe that it was more beneficial for everybody to conquer than indulge his appetites, and much better to mind the public than what seemed his private interest. . . . Those that have undertaken to civilise mankind, . . . being unable to give so many real rewards as would satisfy all persons for every individual action, they were forced to contrive an imaginary one, that as a general equivalent for the trouble of self-denial should serve on all occasions, and without costing anything, either to themselves or others, be yet a most acceptable recompense to the receivers.[13]

Thus did Bernard Mandeville launch his sly attack upon the doctrine of the afterlife in his 1714 book, *The Fable of the Bees; or, Private Vices, Publick Benefits*. Historian Edward Gibbon's famous *Decline and Fall of the Roman Empire* laid the blame for that event (in genteel language diffused over thousands of pages, to be sure) squarely at the door of Christianity. He "thought that the assent by people of his own age to 'supernatural truths is much less an active consent than a cold and passive acquiescence.'"[14]

In Catholic France, the thinkers of the Enlightenment were often more obsessively antireligious than their counterparts in Protestant Europe. Even David Hume was said to have found them irritating and presumptuous in their atheism. Voltaire (1694–1778), though not himself an atheist, spent much of his literary energies in attacking the church and fundamental religious ideas, such as providence and miracles. These he considered to have been made redundant by the mechanistic universe posited by Newton—a view with which Newton would hardly have agreed. The Lisbon earthquake of All Saints' Day 1755, which had killed well over 100,000 people and had destroyed 85 percent of all buildings in the city, including nearly all of the churches, was cited as evidence that the world was not governed by a good God. Christian beliefs such as the resurrection sprang, not from the teaching of Jesus, but from the concoctions of his disciples; the Church had grown from these early untruths by perpetrating fresh inventions and dogmas.Voltaire's famous *Encyclopédie*, published in thirty-five volumes between 1751 and 1780 with the collaboration of Denis Diderot (1713–1783) and others, was to act as a skeptic's and materialist's bible.

The other unavoidable French thinker of the age was Jean-Jacques Rousseau (1712–1778). Born to a Calvinist family in Geneva, converting for pecuniary advantage to Catholicism at the age of sixteen—and back again at the age of forty-two—he managed to fall out with all faiths and with all of his rich, doting patrons, whom he treated almost as abominably and ungratefully as he did his common-law wife. This woman, an illiterate servant girl, bore him five children, all of whom he gave away to likely death at the foundling hospital—a fact which in no way daunted Rousseau from expatiating, in his novel *Émile*, on the correct way to bring up children. His central idea on this point, flatly contradictory to Christianity, was that people are essentially good; what corrupts them is society. Almost the whole of modern, "child-centered" education is founded upon convictions deriving ultimately from what one commentator has called "the most influential educational tract ever written."[15] So too is the quest for a perfect social model; for it followed that, if there are problems in the world, it cannot be the fault of human sinfulness of the kind posited by Christian teaching or of the inevitable shortcomings of a fallen world, but it must be of social and political structures, which can be, and should be, altered until perfection is attained.

Rousseau, then, is the patron saint, not only of the modern mis-educator, but of the modern technocrat. His idea, expressed in *The Social Contract*, is that men can be "forced to be free"—a delusion that has been and is shared by almost all moderns, from Communists, to interfering legislators styling themselves "liberals," right through to American neoconservatives. Rousseau stands as the principal progenitor of an aspect of eighteenth-century thought, which, though it counts as part of the Enlightenment, is nevertheless in profound conflict with its rationalism: romanticism. His idealizations of human nature, of childhood innocence, of the "noble savage"—these are irrational elements that, irrationally cojoined with eighteenth-century rationalism and sharing with it only its repudiation of the Christian past, have become the dominant legacy of that age to the present.

To reiterate, however: the rationalists, deists, and outright unbelievers of the century before 1789 were confined, for the most part, to the intellectuals and a proportion of the ruling classes. Their full impact would be felt only later. In the meantime, most ordinary people remained at least formally religious—as they were to do, by and large, down to the twentieth century. The slyness of Mandeville's attack, the willingness of Walpole to placate popular opinion, the concern even of Frederick the Great to uphold religion in general—all indicate quite clearly that the critics knew themselves to be in a tiny minority. The eighteenth century was an age in which Methodists, Pietists, and devout Catholics could speak their minds plainly; the rationalists took refuge in guarded or high-flown language, designed to shoot over the heads of the uneducated.

The Divine Right of Kings

Like rationalism in thought, so absolutism in politics was not itself a simple product of the post-1648 world; it had been gestating since at least 1500. The sixteenth century had been dominated by power struggles between central and local government in almost all states, and these continued into the seventeenth century. They were an early episode in the grand narrative that has continued down to our own times: the rising power of central government vis-à-vis the people who live under it. Both the size and the sphere of control of government have been growing steadily since the Middle Ages, and they show no signs of retreating. Even those developed economies today that are given over to what we laughingly call "the free market" are, in actual practice, dominated by government, whose meddling subsumes between a quarter and a half of GNP and in which no product or service (including the book you now hold in your hands) is saleable without coming under the strict regulation of standards and procedures by official bureaucracies. The only exceptions to this stranglehold are to be found in the developing world—which are closest to the premodern state. As states have modernized, so the tax collector has taken more and more to fund the spiraling concerns of government.

The early-modern world was at one of the lower rungs on this particular ladder of central government control. Queen Elizabeth I was one of the earliest monarchs of England who could give instructions in London with a fair chance that they would be obeyed, sometime in the not-too-distant future, in Newcastle and Carlisle. Other rulers reached this exalted position rather later. And once they had attained such rudimentary control, most of them found that they liked it. Furthermore, traditional power holders at the local level—knights of the shires, justices of the peace, junior and senior nobility, town councils—rather resented the fact that their traditional jurisdictions were slipping away from them and that power was moving toward the center. Much of the history of the world over the past five hundred years could be written through the grid of this perspective.

The point that concerns us here, however, is that in the early-modern period kings were that "center." The strong central powers that today are vested in presidents and Parliaments resided first in monarchs. Those monarchs strongly favored the churches that supported their growing powers and could provide a religious legitimation for them. That legitimation was generally found in the doctrine of the Divine Right of Kings: God had chosen that monarchs should rule absolutely and without restraint. Charles I of England had put the matter eloquently in the face of those who were about to execute him: "A subject and a sovereign are clear different things."[16]

Protestantism and Roman Catholicism each had, from the point of view of centralizing monarchs, one advantage and one drawback—though the balance seemed to be tilted, for absolutist princes, in favor of the latter. A Protestant state church had the benefit of locating ecclesiastical control firmly within the kingdom, principality, or other polity itself. Luther had taught this principle, and in Lutheran principalities the church of the seventeenth through the nineteenth centuries proved a compliant tool of the monarchs. The Reformed tradition was more ambivalent, expecting the ruler to uphold and enforce the church upon his subjects without being able actually to control it. For this reason Lutheranism was more conducive to absolutist princes than was Reformed Protestantism. The downside of any form of Protestantism, from the point of view of centralizing monarchs, was the relative lack of hierarchy in Protestant churches and the tendency to address the mind in sermons and Bible-reading rather than overawe the spirit with artistic splendor and ceremony. The churches of the Reformation, therefore, had a bothersome potential for doctrinal disputes that might extend into the very political factionalism that absolutist monarchs wished to suppress in the name of unity.

The advantage of Catholicism was its traditionalism, its ecclesiastical hierarchy suggestive of a secular equivalent whose summit was the king, and its emphasis upon sacred mystery from which ordinary people were held at a respectful distance. The disadvantage was the fact that, being universal in scope and intention, its summit of authority lay in Rome, outside the jurisdiction of any monarch; its interests and policies might at any moment conflict with the purposes of a Catholic prince; its enemies may be his friends, and its presently favored sons his enemies.

After 1648 this disadvantage was largely hypothetical, however. As we suggested in chapter 6, the fact that the Reformation had succeeded in entrenching itself in a significant number of states had the effect of making the pope a de facto client of each and every sovereign who chose to remain Catholic (or to revert to Catholicism), not vice versa. This reality was evident in the relationship between monarchs and the Catholic Church in every major Catholic country. The situation after the Peace of Westphalia witnessed a general recognition of the reality: in return for upholding and enforcing Catholicism, the church would support the Divine Right of Kings.

The irresistible strength of the modern monarchies is nowhere more clearly seen than in the suppression of the Jesuits, on the instruction *Dominus ac Redemptor* of Pope Clement XIV in 1773. The Society of Jesus, the glory of the Counter-Reformation, had made itself almost universally detested by monarchs during the course of the seventeenth and eighteenth centuries. Impeding the depredations of the South American Indians at the hands of the colonists, while nevertheless suspected of growing rich from their *reducciones* (settlements) and heavily implicated in the bitter church disputes within France, the Jesuits were rich and powerful everywhere. And their personal oaths of obedience to the pope made them, in the final analysis, less compliant tools of monarchy than the rest of the church had become by the late eighteenth century. Machinating by an array of Catholic monarchs and their ministers during the 1750s and 1760s finally produced concord on the point: the Society of Jesus should be suppressed. The very election of Clement, himself a Franciscan, as pope in 1769 was bound up with this dispute and, despite several years of prevarication, he finally complied for the sake of preserving Catholic unity.

In Russia the church by its very nature fitted in easily enough with monarchical autocracy. As the only Orthodox territory not under non-Orthodox rule, Russia was rapidly attaining to preeminence among the legatees of Byzantine culture and religion. Yet its rapid expansion during the seventeenth and eighteenth centuries threatened to make Orthodox Christians a minority even there, necessitating vigorous mission activity among the newly conquered animist and Muslim tribes. This was more successful, on the whole, among the former than among the latter, though even then Christianity remained, often enough, a thin veneer on the surface of shamanism and other traditional beliefs.

The increasing international status of the Russian church made it at once harder and more important for the tsars to control. The disruptive effects of the internal changes brought about in the mid-seventeenth century in order to effect greater alignment with Greek practice we have already noticed in chapter 5. Peter the Great (reigned 1694–1725) and his chief ministers had been greatly influenced by Western ideas of statehood, most notably from Hobbes's *Leviathan*. His modernization program, like that of Patriarch Nikon before him, angered traditionalists in Russia because he appointed German Protestants to ministerial positions in his government and forbade the boyars to wear beards. These affronts to conservatism outweighed Peter the Great's ostentatious displays of piety and his repudiation of Uniatism.

His conflict with Patriarch Adrian was ended by the latter's death in 1700, but Peter went on to defy tradition by preventing the election of a successor. He made do with ad hoc arrangements for most of the rest of his reign, but in 1721 he appointed a Holy Synod, which was to govern the church henceforth. This marked a significant break with the rest of the Orthodox world, which Russia was otherwise in a position to lead. Furthermore, the synod's responsibility for the affairs of non-Orthodox religious bodies—even those of non-Christians—made it effectively an almost secular body, like a modern "Department of Religious Affairs." Above all, it was a compliant body. As one historian has observed, "The Synod had no choice but to accept the government's directives concerning matters which nominally lay within its own jurisdiction. . . . Nor could it . . . rightfully claim to be the successor of the patriarchs in any but the strictly temporal sense of the word." Indeed, its own spokesmen confessed as much: "This ecclesiastical administration . . . is not like that of the patriarchs . . . it does not govern in its own name, but rather by decrees of His Majesty, who . . . has established Himself as Supreme Ruler and Judge of this Holy Synod."[17]

Russia, however, was a special case. For most monarchs of the era in western and central Europe, the relationship available with the Roman Catholic Church appeared the most appealing religious settlement. The political culture thereby created entailed plenty of political cutting and trimming—but the papacy was, and remains, a master of the art of the possible. It was an arrangement that eventually came to be so congenial to the church that it continued to support royal power during the nineteenth century, when absolute monarchies were palpably fading away, and did not finally reconcile itself to the new world of democracies, republics, Parliaments, and human rights until the Second Vatican Council of the 1960s.

The foremost Catholic monarchy of the age was the Austrian Empire. It is a fine example of the ultimate powerlessness of the papacy, under post-1648 conditions, to thwart royal wishes where those conflicted with the desires of the Holy See. Empire and papacy had been rivals since time out of mind, and the popes continued to tweak the imperial nose where they could, which was mostly in northern Italy. Yet Empress Maria Theresa and her son Joseph II, though both pious Catholics after their respective fashions, enacted a series of reforms that the popes were powerless to prevent. The sees of Salzburg and Passau, both subject to foreign prince-bishops, were curtailed within Austrian territory; parishes were drastically reorganized and rationalized; church finances (or some of them) were tapped off and redirected to state purposes; many monasteries were closed, their denizens pensioned off, and the property sold to fund compulsory schooling. Most radically of all, Emperor Joseph II, after he had become sole ruler following the death in 1780 of his widowed mother, issued the famous Patent of Toleration of 1781, whereby Protestants were tolerated so long as they each registered and declared themselves to the government. His motives were several: his personal commitment to Enlightenment principles was sufficient to persuade him of the rightness of this action; he wished to deprive an already aggressive Prussia of an excuse for meddling in Austrian affairs; persecution had proved fruitless and sometimes even counterproductive; and he wanted many of the industrious Protestant expellees back. He was rather shocked, however, at just how many of his subjects chose to take advantage of the toleration they were now proffered, and the mechanism for registering was made more arcane and difficult. The resultant dispensation was thus one which, as a recent historian has aptly described it, "combined toleration with a good deal of informal intolerance" at the point of grass-roots implementation by officialdom.[18] Such an arrangement remains entirely familiar to religious minorities across much of central and eastern Europe.

In Italy the church found itself living under a variety of regimes: the Papal States under the direct governance of the pontiff, but also the states of Venice, Lombardy, Modena, Tuscany, and the kingdoms of Sardinia and Naples. Italy as a whole had a huge concentration of bishoprics, with most sees being far smaller than their counterparts elsewhere; the kingdom of Naples alone had 131. The episcopal office there, as elsewhere in Italy, tended to be more open to men of humble birth than was the case north of the Alps or in Iberia. Many were local men who had risen through service in the pontifical administration—a phenomenon that was still observable in the twentieth century.

The religious confraternities of the late Middle Ages had involved many ordinary people in the devotional life of the church, and this institution had done much to save urban northern Italy (whose social and economic conditions were in other respects a good predictor of susceptibility to Protestantism) from the Reformation. That salvation was protected, not just by the Inquisition of Pope Paul IV, but more constructively by the preaching missions of Capuchins and Jesuits from the late sixteenth century onward. The Capuchins emphasized the very doctrines the Protestants attacked; their habit of exposing the communion bread and wine in churches for a period of forty hours (to commemorate the period between the death and resurrection of Jesus) compounded popular devotion to the transubstantiated elements as vehicles of salvation. Generations of Catholic revivalists were active during the seventeenth and eighteenth centuries, from the Jesuit Paul Segneri (1624–1694) to Pietro Ansalone (1633–1713), who employed a variety of theatrics while converting thousands to a devout life. Alfonso Liguori (1696–1787), whose preaching emphasized fear of hell, devotion to the Virgin, and contemplation, and who practiced self-flagellation, established the Redemptorist Order in 1732 for religious work among the rural poor.

In these figures it is possible to see Catholic parallels to the Methodist and Pietist revivalists of Protestant Europe. Not only was there at least some similarity in their methods, but their populism emphasized exactly those aspects of traditional religion that elite, intellectualist religion skirted, and they employed novel forms to do so. The analogy should not be pressed too far, for the long-term effects were very different. Methodism encouraged attitudes of personal independence and self-discipline of a kind that were consonant with the values required by the Industrial Revolution and a commercial society; Catholic traditionalism achieved almost the opposite.

Italy, in any case, remained largely subject to Spanish domination for most of our period. After 1648 Spain's links with the northern Netherlands were permanently severed and its military and supply link—the Spanish Road—no longer existed. Remaining Spanish energies in Europe were directed toward the Italian peninsula. The flavor of southern European Catholicism tended, as a result, to be somewhat insulated from the ongoing contact with Protestantism that so affected the Catholic faithful to the north and inclined them inch by painful inch toward rationalism and the values of commerce.

The Spanish church itself was organized as illogically as much else in that declining empire. There were 60,000 priests in the late eighteenth century (for a population of ten million), of whom only 22,000 were employed in parish work. The rest cluttered up the offices of cathedrals and pious foundations in the cities, while nearly 3,000 of the country's 19,000 parishes had no priest at all.[19] In consequence, the church was locked into a situation whereby it transferred large amounts of wealth from the countryside to the towns via tithes and rent upon land—thereby contributing to the grinding poverty of the former without promoting useful commerce in the latter. Revenues of bishoprics varied enormously and were not related to a see's size or importance; administration was poor and the various religious orders poorly integrated into the structure of the church. Relations between Crown and papacy were often bad, though this was one battle the Crown was in a position to win.

The Portuguese situation resembled that of Spain in many respects: a too-numerous and underemployed clergy, with nevertheless a great shortage of priests in the countryside. Yet the Portuguese church was wealthier than in Spain, and the second quarter of the eighteenth century saw a boom in the building of churches and convents. In Portugal the monasteries and convents continued to play the role they had done throughout medieval Europe as the semiuseful (occasionally very useful) receptacle for younger sons and unmarriageable daughters (unmarriageable, at any rate, to an heir) of noble houses. In both countries, bishoprics tended to be filled by the sons of the nobility.

But religious influence often enough follows political power (witness the influence of the British as disseminators of Christianity in the nineteenth century, and of the Americans in the twentieth), so perhaps it should be agreed that France was the most fertile soil for developments within Catholicism during the age of the *ancien régime*. The battle between Jansenists and Jesuits we have already noticed in chapter 5. But the Quietist movement, though it originated in the writings, especially the *Spiritual Guide*, of the Spaniard Miguel Molinos (1628–1717), found its greatest flourishing and its most famous exponent in the kingdom of Louis XIV. Madame Jeanne Marie Guyon (1648–1717) had been married at the age of fifteen to a man twenty-two years her senior. Having borne him three children, she declared at the age of twenty-four that she had entered into a spiritual marriage with the child Jesus, which required her to live the life of a religious. Her husband had not long to endure this, for four years later he died. His relatives were even less impressed by their widowed in-law's next action in abandoning her children and embracing a life of contemplative prayer. Though her writings on prayer were hugely influential, she later found herself a pawn in the battle between Bossuet and Fénelon, the two greatest churchmen of their day, and spent a stretch imprisoned in the Bastille.

From 1727 onward, French Catholicism was troubled from a new direction. The death of François de Pàris, a popular Jansenist in the poor Paris district of Saint-Médard, occasioned a chorus of claims that he had posthumously worked miracles of healing. The embarrassment came not so much from demands for his beatification as from the sheer excitement of crowds thronging the district, mobbing the grave, and hoping for healing. The fact that Jansenism had been officially condemned made matters many times worse. In early 1732 the authorities closed the cemetery. To no avail: the movement went underground and found ways of continuing without recourse to the shrine. The resentment caused among the Parisian poor appears to have been permanent; as one historian observes, "Two generations later, the Parisian districts where this kind of Jansenism was strong were stuffed with *sansculottes*."[20]

Indeed, the slippery slope whereby Catholic-backed absolutism led to revolution is perhaps the most important contribution of France to the religious history of the later part of our period. As we have seen, French intellectuals were alienated from Christianity to a far greater degree, and with more real animosity, than was the case in Protestant Europe. And it is sufficient to note the strong linkage of throne and altar, which necessitated those who would overthrow the one to bring down the other while they were about it. The Bourbons had not treated the popes well; it might, theoretically, have been possible for an antiroyal movement to have clothed itself in the religious garments of papal loyalism long before 1789. But in fact, and for reasons we have rehearsed, the popes made little enough resistance to being bossed about. Certainly they made no serious attempt to appeal beyond the French monarchs to elements within the populace in order to thwart growing royal authority within the church.

In point of fact, the fiscal disaster that afflicted government and monarchy in 1789 positively demanded that church property be drawn upon to square otherwise impossible financial circles. This at least some among the clergy were willing to concede, and the Constituent Assembly of 1789 at first seemed likely to achieve compromise. But as it became clear that all monasteries and convents would need to be sold to obtain the necessary sums, radicals pressed for the suppression of monastic vows, and many among the clergy—and outside of it—became wary. The die was irrevocably cast. But that is a story for a succeeding volume.

16

THE ARTS

▼

The Protestant Reformation had seen divergent attitudes toward art and music. Most of the Reformers had been at least somewhat suspicious, acutely aware of the ability of both to move human passions, and torn between the desire to utilize that ability and the wish to smother it. Protestantism was, after all, in part a new emphasis upon the word, with its preeminent address to the cognitive element in humanity. Furthermore, art in particular had been used by the Catholic Church to enhance its own status and to propagate its message, especially to the illiterate. One of the Reformers' central points was that the ideas conveyed by the written (and now printed) text had been sidelined for far too long. Worst of all, art had often been used in an idolatrous fashion, with veneration that amounted to worship being directed toward images. The Protestant leaders "saw that the Incarnation had *not* in fact divinized wood and paint and stone . . . The continued chasm between God and creation turns an image—any image—from an aid in worship into a misleading caricature."[1]

Both the strength and the weakness of such an assessment, of course, was its dualism. Material objects could not convey spiritual benefit. But did that mean that religious art was likely to be intrinsically harmful? Many Protestants thought so. Karlstadt, one of Luther's early co-workers, for example, argued for "probably the most complete divorce between matter and spirit this side of Gnosticism."[2] Most religious radicals, Anabaptists and the like, took the same view.

Music

Notwithstanding all of this, human attachment to the arts, particularly to music, was usually too deeply embedded and too hard to resist to allow them to be abandoned completely. Their potential for conveying the very thoughts and sentiments that the Reformers themselves wanted impressed upon the minds and hearts of the population could not be forgone in its entirety.

Luther had been easily the most pragmatic of the Reformers, happy to keep traditional religious art where it was not used idolatrously and keen to use the resources of music to encourage ordinary people to worship. Himself an enthusiastic singer and player of the lute, he composed a number of hymns and was eager to utilize a range of sources for church music, whether traditional Catholic songs, folk tunes, or new compositions. He was content that "Street songs, knightly and miners' songs, changed in a Christian, moral and ethical manner, in order that the evil, vexatious melodies, the useless and shameful songs to be sung in the streets, fields, houses, and elsewhere, may lose their bad effects if they can have good, useful Christian texts and words."[3]

In consequence, the Lutheran tradition was provided early on, and on principle, with a range of hymnbooks. Luther himself, and his successors, exhorted congregations to practice hymn singing, "not so that the liturgy might be accomplished but so that God's Word might be better internalized and bear fruit."[4] Most hymnals expected the singers to sing unaccompanied, but this was more from the common experience of poverty than from disapproval of instruments; organs and other instruments were freely used when they were available.

The Reformed tradition took, on the whole, a much harsher view of music's potential than did Luther. Singing and dancing were not viewed as harmless amusements but as frivolities that were the precursor and accompaniment to lewdness of all kinds. In answer to the obvious biblical objection, Calvin resorted to special pleading: "Instrumental music was only tolerated in the time of the Law [i.e., the Old Testament] because of the people's infancy."[5]

Eventually, however, the Genevans talked themselves round to the idea that psalms—and only psalms—might be sung. But there were to be no harmonies nor accompanying instruments of any sort. The Genevan Psalter appeared in 1562 with metrical psalms translated by Theodore Beza (Calvin's most important co-worker and destined to succeed him) and others, and music by Louis Bourgeois. The tunes were memorable. (Indeed, Bourgeois himself seems to have remembered them from all kinds of sources of which his mentors would have disapproved—Lutheran, folk, even Gregorian chant. By drastic amendment, however, he incorporated them into his Psalter.) And once in existence and translated into the variety of tongues spoken wherever the Reformed faith had spread, no censures could forever prevent their eventual embellishment with harmonies and adornment with instruments.

Bourgeois himself, along with other Reformed composers, produced many polyphonic settings of the Psalms. The first edition was published in Lyons in 1547, most likely because the authorities in Geneva disapproved of such departures from simplicity. Though the Genevans relented to the point of permitting the publication of this material within the city, Calvin himself "was clear that" such fancy stuff "did not belong in the liturgy, where only unison, unaccompanied psalms would suffice." The evidence seems strong that Reformed composers responded to such strictures by producing polyphonic settings for use in homes, while use of the bare melody was supposed to prevail in church liturgy.[6] Though the Genevan edition of the Psalter utilized over a hundred different meters, the English edition used just one. This is what one modern scholar refers to when he speaks of "the crippling musical restrictions" placed on the composers by their own ideology, which is the demand for almost brutal spareness and stark simplicity and which produced "the musical equivalent of bread and water."[7]

Anabaptists had begun, in the mid-1520s, with an absolute prohibition upon singing. One of their first leaders pitched in with a piece of the most crass literalism: "We find nothing taught in the New Testament about singing, no example of it. . . . Paul very clearly forbids singing in Ephesians 5:19 and Colossians 3:16 since he says and teaches that they are to speak to one another and teach one another with psalms and spiritual songs, and if anyone would sing, he should sing and give thanks in his heart." In fairness, though, the pragmatic observation with which he followed it up rings all too true across the centuries: "Whoever sings poorly gets vexation by it; whoever can sing well gets conceit."[8]

In any case, the prohibition did not endure more than a few months. One of that very circle of early leaders, Felix Manz, composed at least one hymn before his martyrdom in 1527. Its first line, *"Mit Lust so will ich singen"* ("I Will Sing Heartily"), betrays no impression that it was intended merely for voiceless rhapsodizing. Subsequent Anabaptists produced a steady stream of verses, many of them set to the tunes of secular songs already current in the wider society. The resultant *Ausbund*, a collection of Anabaptist hymnody, is the oldest Protestant hymnal still in use.

In the Elizabethan Church of England, Sternhold and Hopkins's metrical translations of the psalms appeared in 1562, the year after its Genevan model.[9] Psalm singing became extremely popular—and not just in church—during the late sixteenth century. "Sternhold and Hopkins" had appeared in sixty-five editions by 1599, and it was reprinted most years (sometimes more than once a year) for the next three centuries.

In the English cathedrals, however, spare metrical psalms gained less favor than more elaborate works. Singing of these latter was generally the prerogative of the choir during the late sixteenth and seventeenth centuries; congregations were mostly silent. Nor did such sophisticated Protestant pieces disdain to use the Latin—*Benedictus, Jubilate, Te Deum laudamus, Nunc dimittis*—that had dominated the liturgy before the Reformation, thereby doubtless confirming the Puritans in their mistrust of episcopacy and all its organs. Voluntaries by composers such as William Byrd were much in vogue also. Wind instruments of many kinds were preferred over stringed, because of the difficulty of keeping the latter in tune. At least this was the pattern until the civil war and republic, when all instruments were banned under parliamentary ordinances of 1644 "for the speedy demolishing of all organs, images and all matters of superstitious monuments" in cathedrals and parish churches. After the Restoration, the opposite extreme was in favor, with King Charles II introducing dozens of violins to the Chapel Royal, a French (and so Catholic) innovation, which the diarist John Evelyn tut-tutted was "better suited to a Tavern or Play-house than a church."[10] But the trend was not to be stopped, and Henry Purcell (1659–1695) became the greatest of the new style of composers, combining voice and instruments in anthems designed for performance rather than participation by congregations.

During the sixteenth century Protestants had not been the only ones to worry about the worldly potential of church music. The fathers of the Council of Trent had sternly instructed that music designed for masses should contain no intermingling of profane music and that the trend for complex vocal pieces be rejected: the words must be clearly intelligible to all (or at least to all who knew Latin).

Giovanni Pierluigi da Palestrina (ca. 1525–1594) is one of the most famous of those who sought to live within these new requirements, even though not personally persuaded by them. His masses have remained popular ever since. The Counter-Reformation produced a range of such composers, for example the Spaniard Tomás Luis de Victoria (1548–1611), who composed for the monastic choirs, both male and female, of the Discalced at the monastery of Santa Clara. And, in Spain, the best intentions of the Tridentine instructions were undone as folk songs, *villancicos*, were applied to new, religious uses by the church composers.

In Italy the early seventeenth-century origins of secular opera were quickly embraced by the Catholic Church; the powerful emotions to which the new style gave expression were seized upon as a vehicle for promoting the faith. Monteverdi's *Vespers* of 1610 is a notable example of the result, fully meeting churchmen's long-standing demand that mere musical and choral cleverness not be allowed to obscure clarity and meaning. Early seventeenth-century Italy also saw the rise of musical dramatic treatments of biblical—especially Old Testament—narratives, which were presented, not in the context of regular church services, but as special meetings in prayer halls, known as oratorios (from *orare*, to pray). Giacomo Carissimi and Alessandro Stradella were among the most successful composers.

Throughout the eighteenth century the Catholic Church, much more than its Protestant rivals, continued to pursue high art and modern music, accumulating in the process a rich store upon which Christians of all kinds—and even many cultured pagans—continue to draw. It was not possible, however, for ordinary, rural parishes to reproduce the performance music of the court and cathedral cities, and many parishes had to make do with much humbler fare.

During the seventeenth century the Russian Patriarch Nikon added the importation of Western musical styles and musical annotation to his other crimes against tradition. Unsurprisingly, the Old Believers rejected them along with his liturgical changes and continued to practice the ancient *znamenny* chant. But the Russian Orthodox Church as a whole moved toward Western, Catholic—particularly baroque harmonic—styles of church music. Toward the end of the eighteenth century, Italian operatic features began to appear.

One giant of the era who lived further west was, of course, Johann Sebastian Bach (1685–1750). He spent his entire life within the compass of Saxony, the last twenty-seven years in Leipzig, producing over two hundred cantatas, including music specifically designed for each part of the church's calendar. Like Handel, he had spent his earliest years training as a church organist.

Bach's compositions were complex, yet they had their roots in the experience of congregational worship. A number of his pieces built upon

Luther's chorales, which he revitalized with new harmonizations. His *St. John's Passion* and *St. Matthew's Passion* remain two of the most widely performed and remarkable larger works, using soloists and orchestra, arias and chorales.[11]

Georg Friederich Handel (1685–1759) is, perhaps, the only other musical figure of the era whose stature can be said to rival that of Bach. Indeed, Beethoven later described Handel as "the greatest composer who ever lived. I would bare my head and kneel at his grave."[12] Born in Halle, he was apprenticed at the age of seven to the organist of the Marienkirche, on the advice of the Duke of Saxony, who had been impressed by Handel's precocious musical ability. In 1707, during his three-year sojourn in Italy, his settings of two psalms and other pieces were commissioned by Cardinal Carlo Colonna and played during vespers in Rome for the feast day of Our Lady of Mount Carmel. At Easter of the following year his new oratorio, *La Resurrezione*, was performed, though the singer who took the part of Mary Magdalene was forced to withdraw for the second night following papal complaints about the propriety of women performing on the public stage. She was replaced by Pippo, a male castrato—one of a breed (though this is a term one uses with some misgivings) who had been placed in that condition because of the unfortunate beauty of their youthful voices. And the papal conscience was thereby satisfied.

Following a brief interlude in Hanover from 1710 to 1712, Handel moved to England where, apart from excursions, he spent the rest of his life. His output was prodigious, including anthem settings of the psalms and religious oratorios, the most famous of the latter being, of course, the *Messiah* of 1741.

In England and its North American colonies, the 1640s saw the advent among Puritan congregations of "lining out," a practice that was to endure well into the nineteenth century wherever literacy levels were low. In essence, a leader read or sang a line from the psalm (though the procedure was later transferred to hymns), which the congregation would then repeat. The same would then be inflicted upon the next line, and so on through to the end. The idea was to enable nonliterate people to participate and understand and congregants too poor to possess a songbook to sing along. (It's a consolation, early in the twenty-first century, to know that ignorantly misspelled and mispunctuated overhead projections and powerpoints represent an actual improvement upon something.) But what lining out saved in printed paper, it clearly lost several times over in musicality—a fact lost neither on the Westminster Assembly, who recommended it merely "for the present," nor on John Cotton, who stressed that the practice was needless where there were enough books to go round. In the early eighteenth century Isaac Watts (1674–1748) noted, with evident regret, that lining out "cannot presently be reformed," and so he wrote his hymns to accommodate the necessity, by ensuring that each line contained a completed thought, without anything hanging over to the next.[13] Singing schools became an established institution on both sides of the Atlantic for improving congregational singing and helping people to sing "by note" rather than "by rote."

Hymns had begun to appear among the Particular Baptists during the late seventeenth century—though only after fierce controversy. But it was Watts, who was a Congregationalist, who became the first of the really prolific hymn writers of the new era. The Great Awakening from the 1730s onward precipitated a rush of popular composers to express in words what God had done for them, or their adoration to him—and, in the process, to provide material for their fellow worshipers to do the same. The popularity of the productions of Watts prompted Charles Wesley, William Williams, and the other great hymn writers of the revival, whose work in turn precipitated a veritable avalanche that has continued ever since.

Then as now, and as the career of Handel illustrates, music and its practitioners often showed a certain contempt for theological enmities. We have already noted the musical borrowings, even of the Genevan Psalter. During the height of the Thirty Years' War, Heinrich Schütz (1585–1672), composer of church music for the court of Protestant Saxony, spent a couple of years among the papists of Venice, learning the new styles of Monteverdi, which influenced his own later compositions. In Restoration England, Anglicans found it almost impossible to extirpate the metrical psalms of the Puritans because they had become too popular. And the hymns of the dissenters, such as Watts (or even of the imprisoned Bunyan), became in due course the property of the very churchmen who disapproved of them. During the Great Awakening, Arminian leaders urged Charles Wesley's hymns upon their converts while Whitefield and the Calvinist leaders pleaded for the use of Watts and his ilk—but their followers ignored them and used songs of both theological flavors without distinction. The songs of the revivalists, Church of England clergymen as they were, were adopted in turn by the dissenters. And the story continues down to the present: the most popular mid-twentieth-century hymnal for British Pentecostals contained songs by the medieval Catholic abbot, Bernard of Clairvaux—while some of their own choruses have been detected in Catholic parish worship in traditionalist Croatia. Christians, it seems, are just suckers for a good song.

Painting, Sculpture, and Architecture

Just as the Council of Trent had enjoined plainness and clarity, with no intermingling of profane influences, upon musical composers, so it instructed painters and those who sponsored them that

> no images, (suggestive) of false doctrine, and furnishing occasion of dangerous error to the uneducated, be set up. . . . Moreover, in the invocation of saints, the veneration of relics, and the sacred use of images, every superstition shall be removed, . . . all lasciviousness be avoided; in such wise that figures shall not be painted or adorned with a beauty exciting to lust. . . . In fine, let so great care and diligence be used herein by bishops, as that there be nothing seen that is disorderly, or that is unbecomingly or confusedly arranged, nothing that is profane, nothing indecorous, seeing that holiness becometh the house of God.[14]

The Tridentine fathers' worries about artistic portrayals of "a beauty exciting to lust" were far from merely hypothetical. The artists of the Renaissance and, even more, of its later embellishment, mannerism, had for long proclaimed a desire to honor God for the beauty of his creation. The result had been an outpouring of art portraying the naked human form, stemming partly from a humanistic conviction of its nobility and from a new fascination with the material world and partly from a desire to emulate the painting and sculpture of ancient Greece and Rome. Statues of the naked King David, a Sistine Chapel adorned by a naked Adam, depictions of the naked infant Jesus suckling at the open breast of the Virgin Mary—all had resulted from the artistic fashions of the late fifteenth century and the first half of the sixteenth, which had sought to emulate the paintings of the Hellenistic world. Medieval art had seldom depicted nudity; when it had done so it had been generally in the context of death, putrefaction, plague, or sorcery and had been intentionally repellent. The sharply contrasting Renaissance glorification of the human body seemed, by the mid-sixteenth century, to add the accusation of indecency to the Protestants' central charge that religious art was idolatry. Furthermore, Renaissance fascination with the mythology of antiquity had resulted in some synthesis between Christian symbolism and that of pagan Greece and Rome, with nonbiblical characters and deities creeping onto painters' canvases and from thence onto the walls of churches. (In fairness, though, it should be added that even early Christian paintings from the catacombs had been guilty of this.)

By the 1550s artists were being commissioned to retouch the work of their predecessors (or even of living colleagues) by putting breeches—or at least strategically placed leaves or pieces of cloth—over the offending anatomical bits and pieces. And in their twenty-fifth, and final, session in 1563, the fathers of Trent made it clear that future religious art should be free of such embarrassments or derogations from faithfulness to the biblical accounts.

Almost a decade later, the sculptor Bartolomeo Ammanati wrote a public letter renouncing his own earlier depictions of the naked body. Perhaps the repudiation was the result of pressure, but there were so many changes of heart and such a pronounced change in tone among Catholic artists of the late sixteenth and early seventeenth centuries that only a credulous commitment to secularist dogmatism (a quality not entirely lacking among historical writers at the present time) could insist that it was all the result of mere duress and of some terror, peculiar to artists, of a call from the inquisitors.

It is not that the Inquisition was entirely inactive in such matters. Paolo Veroncse found himself dragged up before them in Venice in 1573 for allowing artistic license too free a rein in his depictions of biblical events. But such incidents were rare; the pressure of peers and official-dom was then—as now—far likelier to elicit social compliance with publicly accepted pieties than was the threat of a visit to (or from) the inquisitors. An even more compelling reason for toeing the line is to be found in the prevailing atmosphere among the sources of patronage. The foremost among these, the papacy itself, was transformed from the decadent, soft institution that it had been in the early decades of the sixteenth century. The new religious orders, great builders of churches, were similarly products of the Counter-Reformation and wanted no truck with the suave self-assurance of Renaissance or mannerist art. The Catholic aristocracy of central Europe, the third (though lesser) sponsors of religious painting and building, were anxious enough to halt the inroads of Protestantism and willing, especially after the Thirty Years' War, to subsidize work likely to promote the specifically Catholic glories of Holy Mother Church: dramatic portrayals of the Madonna, imposingly ornate churches, miracles of the saints (especially recent Catholic heroes, such as Ignatius Loyola), the wounds of the Savior. Indeed, gruesomely realistic portrayals of martyrdom in general, and that of Jesus in particular, were among the most important elements in the new baroque art. Like the Counter-Reformation generally, it betokened a new seriousness to match—or outmatch—that of the Protestants.

The baroque style excelled in inspiring the emotions with a sense of fervent thankfulness and humility. Apart from the sufferings of Christ and the saints, favored themes included the glory of heaven—and, by reflection, of the church that ushered its adherents thither. Drama, emotion, grandeur: these were the qualities that baroque painting and sculpture sought to portray, as saints prostrated themselves at the cross or as heaven burst open to reveal itself to a prayer-enraptured soul. It was not, perhaps, that art was more emphasized by the Counter-Reformation than it had been in earlier periods; rather, its function changed. Where the art of the Renaissance had made a display of its own skill, that of the baroque drew the attention to the thing portrayed; where the former sought to illuminate, the latter sought to persuade. Baroque art was, in that sense, part and parcel of the Counter-Reformation's proselytizing thrust: shoring up the faithful and appealing to the emotions and imagination of the doubting.

The enterprise was aided by the fact that a number, at least, of the rising generation of artists were themselves in holy orders. Particularly was this so among the Jesuits. Neither was the new wave of pious art merely an imposition of the powerful; it took deep root among the Catholic populace. Antwerp—positioned close to the frontier with Protestant heresy, and itself a major focus of activity of the Reformed until they were driven out in the 1570s—was one of the major centers of Counter-Reformation art during the early seventeenth century. Almost 750 masters were enrolled in that city's guild of painters between 1601 and 1650 producing works, not only for its two colleges and numerous churches, monasteries, and convents, but for patrons further afield. Woodcuts and engravings for printed matter were also intended for popular consumption. For humbler folk still, do-it-yourself art expressed the outpouring of Catholic devotion. As one recent historian records, "In pilgrimage sites, such as Altötting in Bavaria or in the Provence, hundreds of crudely painted votive pictures represented the ailments and bodily members cured by divine miracles," while "[s]haring a common theological grammar" with the high art of the great masters, such as Caravaggio or Rubens.[15]

Outside of Europe the Jesuits' ability to interact with the artistic traditions and cultures of the various societies to whom they directed their missions was little less than extraordinary. Even in the early phase of their mission to Japan (the late sixteenth century), the Jesuits "were already accommodating wholesale to indigenous styles" in the architecture of their church buildings.[16] The paintings produced by Japanese Christians were frequently copied from European styles, but often enough distinctively Japanese elements emerged, as in the *Madonna of the Snows*, painted in the late sixteenth century, hidden for years, and rediscovered only in the 1960s.[17] Much Christian art, and most church building, in China followed closely its European models. Indians proved more willing to experiment—but many who portrayed Christian subjects were themselves Hindus or, more risky, Muslims.[18] It was in South America that the indigenization of Christian art was most far-reaching. Guaraní artists, in particular, incorporated motifs and patterns—elements that appeared to Europeans as merely decorative embellishments—into the painting of Christian subjects in such a way as to interpret them as "incarnations of their own gods and spirits, such as God the Creator, Ñanderuvusú, and the sylvan devil Añá."[19] Not all Christian art in Latin America was syncretistic to quite this extent, but much of painting and architecture incorporated native elements.

Protestant religious art was largely hobbled by the Reformation's reaction against many of the features of Catholicism, which had dominated art during the Middle Ages and which the Counter-Reformation chose to emphasize: veneration of the Virgin Mary; the focus upon reverence for the saints; the use of art for devotional purposes, which, to a Protestant judgment, bordered on the idolatrous. The Reformed and the more puritanical among other Protestants tended to avoid religious art entirely; others used it cautiously and limited depictions to strictly biblical themes. But popular propaganda was not shy of depicting Catholic atrocities against the Protestants' coreligionists—martyrologies such as those of Foxe or of the Anabaptist *Martyrs Mirror* abounded in woodcuts of a kind which, to any rational analysis, amounted to a close equivalent of depictions by Catholics of St. Sebastian or of St. Ursula.

Protestant architecture reflected the same dichotomy: Presbyterian and Reformed churches tended to be spare and functional, owing whatever imposing characteristics they possessed to the Renaissance emphasis upon the Greek and Roman elements of the Western tradition; moderate or "high" Protestants were more relaxed about borrowing from Catholic traditions or even from recent developments within the Catholic world. A Reformed church such as that at Lug, in Baranja, is typical of the more austere in that its center of gravity is a raised pulpit, halfway along the longer side; the typical centrality of the sermon in Protestant worship is built into the architecture. In eastern Poland, many such places of worship took on elements of defensive fortification—a characteristic shared by some Orthodox churches. On the other hand, less sombre, more sedate forms of Protestantism tended to design their buildings, not so much in a conscious repudiation of their Catholic counterparts, but in dialogue with them: the new St. Paul's Cathedral in London, built in the aftermath of the catastrophic fire of London in 1666, borrowed freely from the inspiration of St. Peter's in Rome.

The English dissenters of the eighteenth century—Presbyterians, Congregationalists, Baptists, and Quakers—built along the most functional lines of all. Their square, galleried auditoriums, focusing upon a central pulpit and unembellished, for the most part, by painting or sculpture of any kind, continue to adorn the small towns and villages of England.

As in music, so in the visual arts: Protestants and Catholics sometimes chose separate paths but, as often as not, found themselves feeding off one another. It has to be said, though, that Catholic influence upon Protestant developments was somewhat greater than its converse, with Protestants often disagreeing among themselves as to how far it was proper to borrow from "the enemy"—or even, sometimes, to engage in such "vanities" at all.

CONCLUSION

Two centuries of folly and fury: the Age of Reason, which exalted dispassionate inquiry and shunned superstition, commenced with savage wars, supposedly sanctioned by religion and certainly sanctioned by religious leaders. The sequel had seen a series of slow divorces: between confessional adherence and foreign policy; between some states and some churches; and, increasingly, between faith and reason. The age closed with the French Revolution, which would justify fresh bloodbaths sanctified on the altar of enlightenment and the rights of man. The musings of the *philosophes* would come to stand in paternal relationship to the murderous ideologies of the modern age. The "enthusiasts" of Anabaptism and the sixteenth-century Catholic mystics and "beatas" had given way to the "Inspired," the Russian "spirit-wrestlers," the Jansenists of Saint-Médard, the Methodist lay preachers, and the revivalists of the American frontier. Meanwhile, the creative work was being achieved by pragmatists, such as the selfsame evangelical revivalists and the Jesuits, who had absorbed just enough rationalism to focus upon outcomes rather than theory but not enough to cut themselves loose from the fundamental articles of belief that had given meaning to Christian life—and would continue to give meaning long after the very phrase "Age of Reason" had become the trigger for ironic smiles.

Christians during the two centuries we have been considering were divided among themselves, and not only in the confessional sense that we have been considering. Some Protestants and some Catholics, even in the eighteenth century, viewed one another much as their ancestors had done during the heyday of the Reformation and Counter-Reformation. Even Jonathan Edwards, a modern man if ever there was one, took it as axiomatic that the pope was Antichrist and that Protestantism had come

395

to supplant the Church of Rome. For Irish Catholics of around 1700, the challenge within Protestantism to the old Puritan rigidities by the new Anglican rationalism ("latitudinarianism") meant nothing, and the Reformation can hardly have seemed to the Irish adherents of Rome like merely old news. Other Christians could see that both the world and the churches within it were changing, but they feared that the change was for the worse. No pope after 1648 could have failed to be aware that his leverage over Catholic monarchs was but a shadow of that wielded by his predecessors. And even after all due allowance has been made for the perennial tendency of preachers to denounce the evils of their own age as uniquely ungodly, it is hard not to sympathize with those who saw among the unchurched of the new industrial towns, the deists of the salons, and the principled godless of the *sansculottes* the passing of Christendom as it had been for more than a thousand years.

Finally there were those who saw the advent of the modern age as a doorway of opportunity. Rising literacy could make every man and woman a Bible reader; the moral was to print more tracts and New Testaments. In the economically and politically most advanced countries—Britain, the Netherlands, the United States—the churches had lost most, or all, of the powers of coercion; they needed to remake themselves by appealing to the loyalty and the understanding of ordinary people and by cultivating their informed enthusiasm. The expansion of European empires had offered huge opportunities for Catholic evangelism; the rise of the British Empire beckoned Protestants to do the same, and more.

Modernity offered huge challenges, not just for the Christian church, but for religion generally. In the first place, the French Revolution was the harbinger of a key strand of modernist dogmatism that would assert itself in harshly antireligious terms. It exalted the rights of government over private initiative, of the masses over the individual, of the abstracted nation over minorities, of the demands of the present moment over the legacy of the past, and of the center over the local. Although some twentieth-century nationalists would find ways of centering most of these emphases within a populist—but harsh and unpleasant—religious vision, the consequence was more frequently irreligious. The nationalists of the nineteenth century and the socialists of the nineteenth and twentieth centuries were, for the most part, strongly secular if not downright atheistic.

In the second place, it was becoming clear that modern modes of existence, irrespective of any modern philosophies or ideologies, were inherently secularizing. Industrial employment practices made a nonsense of inherited, sacralized bonds of care and esteem between landowner and tenant or between lord and serf. Urban living was unavoidably somewhat anonymous; the parish could no longer be the self-conscious focus of social, political, and religious life, nor could participation be coerced by a hundred petty sanctions and stigmas. Religious pluralism, as we have seen, was one of the best preconditions for a thriving commercial economy even before industrialization. After it, religion was bound to become more and more a private choice.

Yet the American Revolution offered hope for a happier cohabitation between modernity and the Christian churches. The deism of America's founders was not a mere cover for irreligion, for humoring the still-religious masses with Christian connotation words while robbing them of their strictly biblicist content or else deploying them for novel—and really rationalist—ends. That may have been the effect, but it was not, for the most part, their intention. Even Jefferson believed religion absolutely necessary for upholding morality, social order, and even patriotism. But to have its full social effect, it had to be a religion voluntarily subscribed to by each individual for himself or herself. And that demanded religious liberty. If the churches could adjust to the new terms—and, clearly, this was easier for some, such as the baptistic churches, than for others—then they might thrive. As shown in the United States, they have. American modernism was suspicious of government and supportive of private initiative—including in the religious realm. Though it exalted the idea of "the nation," in practice it was a diminished nation, which allowed minorities to carve out niches for themselves on easy terms. The fetish of the flag, the Constitution, and other symbols arose precisely because so little else—certainly not religion—held its people together.

American-style modernity was in fatal accord, however, with that of the French in attributing primacy to the demands of the present moment over the legacy of the past. Though this seemed to strike harder at the great, historic institutions of the Catholic Church and the weightier, more ponderous of its Protestant stepsisters and to give the short-term advantage to the lightweight, pragmatism-and-Bible-driven churches of the revivalists, the price has, in the end, been paid by all of them. All have had to redefine themselves and their mission in terms more consonant with "the spirit of the age"—only to be forced to repeat the exercise a few decades later when that spirit had expired and been replaced by another. All churches stood charged, potentially or actually, with repressive conservatism, with obscurantism, and with being impediments to progress. In their desperation to avoid such imputations, Christian doctrines were subtly recast—free will as humanistic "can-do"; predestination as the progress myth or manifest destiny; humanity in the image of God as human rights; repentance as self-improvement—until time had eroded eternity and the Judge of all the earth was reduced first to the deist's benign providence and then to an ever-diminishing god-of-the-gaps, filling in what science had not yet explained.

Few of these prospects were clear in 1789. But the advent of the French Revolution certainly served to concentrate minds. Yet even as antireligious fury was erupting in the heart of Catholic Europe, so another, quieter event was happening, that same year, on the other side of the Atlantic: John Carroll was taking up his appointment as the first Roman Catholic bishop in the United States. As the Old World alliance of throne and altar creaked at the seams and began to break up (a disintegration not finally complete until the carnage of World War I), so the See of Rome began coming to terms with the modern world of republicanism, religious pluralism, and incipient democracy. It is perhaps no accident—yet ironic, all the same—that the most imperious of churches found it easier to come to terms with the American, pragmatic-nationalist model of modernity than it did with the French, secular-nationalist model. The American principles took no notice of churches but were supportive of religion generally; those of the French model were deeply mired in rejectionism of the throne-and-altar period that had preceded the Revolution. (For the same reason, the papacy would be unwilling even to recognize the existence of the Italian national state from the 1860s until the Lateran Treaty with Mussolini.)

Protestants, too, found the American model more conducive, though for slightly different reasons. For one thing, it was based upon a Protestant consensus rooted in the Anglo-Saxon origins of its dominant ethnicity. And, though that dominance was already far eroded by the end of our period, its consensus would continue. Within Britain, the greatest world power by the close of our period and for more than a century after it, religion was for all practical purposes as free, and the Protestant consensus as strong, as in the United States.

By 1789 the leverage the Christian churches could exercise over states, governments, and polities had waned considerably from what it had been in 1570. And it was about to wane yet further: that was the meaning of the French Revolution. Yet the power of the historically Christian countries vis-à-vis non-Christian states had grown sharply, opening up opportunities for churches to enter and evangelize areas that had been closed to them for centuries, and raising the possibility, realized in our own day, of a truly global church. Yet whether the loss of formal power in historic Christendom could be compensated for by the maintenance of informal power, that is, influence and popular support—this would be left to the nineteenth and twentieth centuries to decide.

TIME LINE

Date	Major Developments in Church/Religion	Major Developments in Government/Society
1570	Pope Pius V's bull *Regnans in Excelsis* declares Elizabeth I of England deposed *Confession of Sandomiersz* reconciles Polish Protestant groups	
1571		Battle of Lepanto—Christian naval victory over the Turks
1572	St. Bartholomew's Day Massacre Death of Scottish Reformer, John Knox	Fourth War of Religion in France (1572–1573)
1575	*Confessio Bohemica* Death of Lutheran Reformer Matthias Flacius Illyricus (Matija Vlačić)	
1576	Spanish Fury: sack of Antwerp	Fifth War of Religion in France
1577	Formula of Concord attempts to heal rift within Lutheranism	Sixth War of Religion in France
1580		Seventh War of Religion in France
1581	First bishop of Manila appointed Jesuit Edmund Campion executed in London	
1584–1589		War of the Three Henries in France
1586	Death of Slovene Reformer Primož Trubar	
1587	Emperor Hideyoshi of Japan begins to reverse his pro-Christian policy	Mary Queen of Scots executed
1588		Spanish Armada

Date	Major Developments in Church/Religion	Major Developments in Government/Society
1590	First complete Hungarian Bible	
1593	Henry of Navarre converts to Catholicism	
1596	Union of Brest creates Ukrainian Uniate Church English Separatists' *True Confession*	
1598	Edict of Nantes gives limited toleration to French Huguenots	
1599	Synod of Diamper imposes Catholic domination on Indian Thomas Christians	
1604	Death of antitrinitarian Fausto Sozzini	
1605		Gunpowder Plot foiled in London
1606	Christianity outlawed in Japan	
1609	Death of Arminius John Smyth establishes first English Baptist church in exile in Netherlands	Truce between Spain and United Provinces
1610	Death of Jesuit Matteo Ricci in China	Henry IV of France assassinated
1611	Authorized (King James) Version of the English Bible published	
1618		Thirty Years' War begins
1619	Synod of Dort defends Calvinist orthodoxy	Execution of Oldenbarneveldt in Netherlands Frederick of the Palatinate accepts Bohemian crown
1620	*Mayflower* lands in America	
1621	Death of Cardinal Robert Bellarmine	Spanish-Dutch truce expires: war resumes
1625	Sigan-Fu stone discovered in China	Denmark enters Thirty Years' War
1630		Sweden enters Thirty Years' War
1631		Sack of Magdeburg Battle of Breitenfeld
1632	Galileo forced to recant	
1635		Tokugawa Edict closes Japan to outside world
1638	Anne Hutchinson expelled from Massachusetts Bay	
1640	Cornelius Jansen's *Augustinus* published	
1641		Irish revolt breaks out

Date	Major Developments in Church/Religion	Major Developments in Government/Society
1642		English Civil War begins
1644	Particular Baptist *London Confession*	Chinese Ming dynasty replaced by Manchu
1648	Westminster Confession	Peace of Westphalia ends Thirty Years' War
1649		Execution of King Charles I
1653	Indian Thomas Christians reconstitute their church Jansen's *Augustinus* condemned by Pope Innocent X	
1660		Restoration of Charles II as monarch following collapse of the Republic
1662	Death of Blaise Pascal Great Ejection of dissenting clergy in England	
1675	Spener's *Pia Desideria* published	
1678	Bunyan's *Pilgrim's Progress* published	
1682	Execution of Avvakum, leader of Russian Old Believers Pennsylvania founded on basis of religious toleration	
1683		Jan Sobieski lifts siege of Vienna by Turks
1685	Revocation of the Edict of Nantes by Louis XIV	
1689	Toleration Act passed by English Parliament	Temporary Austrian victory over Turks south of the Danube Arsenije III leads Serbian *Velika Seoba*
1690		Battle of the Boyne
1692	Chinese Emperor K'ang Hsi issues edict of toleration for Christianity Witch trials in Salem, Massachusetts	
1693	Amish break away from Mennonites	
1700		Great Northern War begins
1701		War of Spanish Succession begins
1714		War of Spanish Succession ends
1717	Virgin Mary crowned as "queen of Poland"	

Date	Major Developments in Church/Religion	Major Developments in Government/Society
1721	Emperor K'ang Hsi bans Christianity Peter the Great of Russia appoints Holy Synod	Great Northern War ends
1727	Awakening in Herrnhut Miracles reported in Saint-Médard, Paris	
1732	Protestants expelled from Salzburg	
1735	Conversions of Hywel Harris, Daniel Rowland, George Whitefield Revival in Jonathan Edwards's parish of Northampton, Massachusetts	
1738	Conversions of John and Charles Wesley	
1741	Split between Whitefield and Wesley	
1742	Revival in Cambuslang, Scotland	
1751		First volume of *Encyclopédie* published
1752	Split between Daniel Rowland and Hywel Harris	
1755		Lisbon earthquake
1756		Seven Years' War begins between Britain and France
1758	Sandy Creek Association of Separate Baptist churches established	
1759	Jesuits expelled from Brazil	
1767	Jesuits expelled from Spanish South America	
1772		First division of Poland
1773	Suppression of Jesuit Order	
1776		American Declaration of Independence
1778	First of Catholic Relief Acts in Ireland	
1781	Patent of Toleration in Austria	
1789	John Carroll first Catholic bishop in U.S.	French Revolution breaks out

SUGGESTIONS FOR FURTHER READING

Chapter 1

Atiya, A. S. *A History of Eastern Christianity*. London: Methuen, 1968. This work was published over three decades ago, but it provides a good outline of important churches with which Western readers are usually unfamiliar.

Black, C. F. *Italian Confraternities in the Sixteenth Century*. Cambridge: Cambridge University Press, 1989. Examines the distinctive phenomenon that undoubtedly contributed toward resisting Protestant inroads in Italy.

Chadwick, O. *The Reformation*. London: Penguin, 1990. This book has been in print for several decades but continues to provide a useful and lively introduction to this subject area.

Courbage, Y., and P. Fargues. *Christians and Jews under Islam*. New York: I. B. Tauris, 1998. The tables and charts in this book make it indispensable for those who wish to quantify trends and analyze statistics in the area of Eastern Christianity and Islam.

Dickens, A. G. *The Counter Reformation*. London: Thames and Hudson, 1968. Gives an excellent, illustrated introductory account of the Counter-Reformation.

George, Timothy. *Theology of the Reformers*. Nashville: Broadman, 1988. To describe this book as "accessible" sounds dangerously like an insult. He provides excellent thumbnail biographies and introductions to the theologies of Luther, Zwingli, Calvin—and also of Menno Simons.

McGrath, A. E. *A Life of John Calvin*. Oxford: Blackwell, 1990. Calvin is, like Luther, well served by biographers. McGrath skips over one decade of his subject's career a little fast, but he is sympathetic to his subject, considered, and clear.

Moffett, S. H. *A History of Christianity in Asia: 1500–1900*. Vol. 2. Maryknoll, NY: Orbis, 2005. Maddeningly, Moffett's book was published a little too late for the present writer to give it the attention it deserves. But it is clearly a work of the utmost importance and will be a prime source of reference on its subject for a long time to come.

Mullett, M. A. *The Catholic Reformation*. London: Routledge, 1999.

Oberman, H. O. *Luther: Man between God and the Devil*. London: HarperCollins, 1993. An ocean of material about Luther continues to pour forth from the presses. This book is one of the more popular biographies of recent years.

Pearse, M. T. *The Great Restoration*. Carlisle, England: Paternoster, 1998. Concerning the religious radicals of the era, those readers who don't like the present book will find this work similarly irritating.

Potter, G. R. *Zwingli*. Cambridge: Cambridge University Press, 1984. This biography is an excellent, detailed study of the Swiss Reformer.

Williams, G. H. *The Radical Reformation*. Kirksville, MO: Sixteenth Century Journal Publishers, 1992. Readers who have deep pockets, plenty of time, and a limitless fascination for the foibles of the radicals will find the oceanic scale of Williams's book a dizzying and massively informing experience.

Ye'or, Bat. *The Decline of Eastern Christianity under Islam: From Jihad to Dhimmitude*. Cranbury, NJ: Fairleigh Dickinson University Press, 1996. Gives a masterly survey of this huge subject.

Zernov, N. *Eastern Christendom*. London: Weidenfeld and Nicolson, 1961. Zernov and Atiya's works are elderly by now and general in scope (chapter 5 of the Zernov is the only part relevant to our period), but nevertheless they provide good outlines of important churches with which Western readers are usually unfamiliar.

Chapter 2

The Netherlands

Duke, A. *Reformation and Revolt in the Low Countries*. London: Hambledon Press, 1990.

Limm, P. *Dutch Revolt 1559–1648*. Harlow, England: Longman, 1999.

Parker, G. *The Dutch Revolt*. London: Penguin, 1990.

France and the Wars of Religion

Diefendorf, B. B. *Catholics and Huguenots in Sixteenth-Century Paris*. Oxford: Oxford University Press, 1991.

Holt, M. P. *The French Wars of Religion, 1562–1629*. Cambridge: Cambridge University Press, 1995.

Knecht, R. J. *The French Religious Wars 1562–1598*. Oxford: Osprey, 2002.

Labrousse, É. "Calvinism in France, 1598–1685." In *International Calvinism 1541–1715*. Edited by M. Prestwich. Oxford: Oxford University Press, 1985.

Mentzer, R. A., and A. Spicer, eds. *Society and Culture in the Huguenot World 1559–1685*. Cambridge: Cambridge University Press, 2002.

Prestwich, M. "Calvinism in France." In *International Calvinism 1541–1715*. Edited by M. Prestwich. Oxford: Oxford University Press, 1985.

Sutherland, N. M. *The Huguenot Struggle for Recognition*. New Haven: Yale University Press, 1980.

Germany and Central Europe (Bohemia / Moravia; Poland; Hungary / Transylvania)

Crăciun, Maria, Ovidiu Ghitta, and Graeme Murdock, eds. *Confessional Identity in East Central Europe*. Aldershot, England: Ashgate, 2002. A collection of specialist essays on a variety of themes, especially of Hungarian and Transylvanian interest.

Kloczowski, J. *A History of Polish Christianity*. Cambridge: Cambridge University Press, 2000, chaps. 4 and 5. This is a very "correct" and cumbersome work, as well as a little uncomprehending in handling of anything or anyone non-Catholic.

Maag, K., ed. *The Reformation in Eastern and Central Europe*. Aldershot, England: Scolar Press, 1997. Another collection of specialist essays on a variety of themes, especially of Hungarian and Transylvanian interest.

Pörtner, R. *The Counter-Reformation in Central Europe: Styria 1580–1630*. Oxford: Oxford University Press, 2001.

Teter, M. *Jews and Heretics in Catholic Poland: A Beleaguered Church in the Post-Reformation Era*. Cambridge: Cambridge University Press, 2005.

Říčan, R. *The History of the Unity of Brethren*. Bethlehem, PA: Moravian Church in America, 1992.

Chapter 3

Hastings, A., ed. *A World History of Christianity*. London: Cassell, 1999. Hastings provides many useful introductory or overview articles on all regions and periods.

The Union of Brest and Its Causes

Fedoriw, G. *History of the Church in Ukraine*. Toronto, Canada: St. Sophia Religious Association of Ukrainian Catholics in Canada, 1983. A useful account, but it is seen very much through the lens of modern, nationalist consciousness and concerns.

Gudziak, B. A. *Crisis and Reform: The Kyivan Metropolitanate/the Patriarchate of Constantinople/the Genesis of the Union of Brest*. Cambridge: Harvard University Press, 2001.

The Christianization of the Americas

Bradford, William. *Of Plymouth Plantation 1620–1647*. Edited by S. E. Morison. New York: A. A. Knopf, 1997. The classic edition of a classic original source, compared with G. F. Willison's more modern, narrative account.

Burkholder, M. A., and L. L. Johnson. *Colonial Latin America*. 3rd ed. New York: Oxford University Press, 1998.

Grahn, L. R. "Guajiro Culture and Capuchin Evangelization." In *The New Latin American Mission History*. Edited by E. Langner and R. H. Jackson. Lincoln, NE: University of Nebraska Press, 1995.

Willison, G. F. *Saints and Strangers: The Story of the Mayflower and the Plymouth Colony*. London: Heinemann, 1966. Gives a modern, narrative account.

Catholic Missions in Africa

Caraman, P. *The Lost Empire: The Story of the Jesuits in Ethiopia*. Notre Dame, IN: University of Notre Dame Press, 1985.

Hastings, A. *The Church in Africa 1450–1950*. Oxford: Oxford University Press, 1996.

Isichei, E. *A History of Christianity in Africa*. London: SPCK, 1995. Of the three surveys of African church history by Hastings, Isichei, and Sundkler and Steed, this one by Isichei is the least enormous—and most digestible.

Sundkler, B. and C. Steed. *A History of the Church in Africa*. Cambridge: Cambridge University Press, 2000.

Catholic Missions in Asia

Cummins, J. S. *A Question of Rites: Friar Domingo Navarrete and the Jesuits in China*. Aldershot, England: Scolar Press, 1993.

Drummond, R. H. *A History of Christianity in Japan*. Grand Rapids: Eerdmans, 1971.

Elison, G. *Deus Destroyed: The Image of Christianity in Early Modern Japan*. Cambridge: Harvard University Press, 1988.

Ross, A. C. *A Vision Betrayed: The Jesuits in Japan and China 1542–1742*. Maryknoll, NY: Orbis, 1994.

Whyte, Bob. *Unfinished Encounter: China and Christianity*. London: Collins, 1988.

The Eastern Churches

Hudson, D. D. *Protestant Origins in India: Tamil Evangelical Christians, 1706–1835*. Grand Rapids: Eerdmans, 2000.

Magocsi, P. R. *A History of Ukraine*. Toronto, Canada: University of Toronto Press, 1996. A massive, secular history of the Ukraine, which provides much useful material on the religious aspects, especially during our period.

Waterfield, R. E. *Christians in Persia*. London: George Allen & Unwin, 1973.

Werner, R., W. Anderson, and A. Wheeler. *Day of Devastation, Day of Contentment: The History of the Sudanese Church across 2000 Years*. Nairobi, Kenya: Paulines Publications Africa, 2000. A fascinating account of one of the least well-known aspects of Christian history—although little of it applies to our period, which was the nadir of Christian life in the Sudan.

Chapter 4

The German Lutherans and the Formula of Concord (1580)

Jungkuntz, T. R. *Formulators of the Formula of Concord*. St. Louis: Concordia, 1977. Jungkuntz and Kolb give the background story.

Kolb, R. *Andreae and the Formula of Concord*. St. Louis: Concordia, 1977.

———. *Sources and Contexts of the Formula of Concord*. Minneapolis: Fortress, 2001. Gives original documents and commentary upon them.

The English Church (1570–1625)

Collinson, P. *The Elizabethan Puritan Movement*. Oxford: Oxford University Press, 1967. This is probably still the definitive study of this subject.

Kendall, R. T. *Calvin and English Calvinism to 1649*. Oxford: Oxford University Press, 1981. Originally an Oxford doctoral thesis, when it was first published it started a spat among earnest Calvinists over Kendall's charge that the doctrine of limited atonement was not taught by Calvin and that, when his successor Beza insisted upon it, it led to disastrous pastoral consequences among English Puritans.

Lamont, W. M. *Godly Rule: Politics and Religion 1603–1660*. London: Macmillan, 1969. Without being heavyweight, this short, insightful book is nevertheless intellectually and analytically formidable. Highly recommended.

Trinterud, L. J., ed. *Elizabethan Puritanism*. Oxford: Oxford University Press, 1971. Provides key documents with excellent commentary upon them, their context, and their significance.

Tyacke, N. *Anti-Calvinists: The Rise of English Arminianism c.1590–1640.* Oxford: Oxford University Press, 1990. Less exciting than its title suggests, but this monograph nevertheless provides good coverage of early-seventeenth-century High-Churchmanship in England.

The Dutch Reformed Church (1570–1619)

Bangs, C. *Arminius: A Study in the Dutch Reformation.* Eugene, OR: Wipf & Stock, 1998. Remains the standard work on the temporizing Dutchman.

Hsia, R. Po-Chia, ed. *Calvinism and Religious Toleration in the Dutch Golden Age.* Cambridge: Cambridge University Press, 2002.

Chapter 5

The Roman Catholic Church

Bossy, J. *The English Catholic Community 1570–1850.* London: Darton, Longman & Todd, 1975. A full treatment of Catholicism in England.

Dures, A. *English Catholicism 1558–1642.* Harlow, England: Longman, 1983. Like much of the series of which the book is a part, this is a good, introductory account: easy to read but reliable and solid.

Headley, J. M., and J. B. Tomaro, eds. *San Carlo Borromeo: Catholic Reform and Ecclesiastical Politics in the Second Half of the Sixteenth Century.* Cranbury, NJ: Folger Books, 1988.

Holmes, P. *Resistance & Compromise: The Political Thought of the Elizabethan Catholics.* Cambridge: Cambridge University Press, 1982.

Hsia, R. Po-chia. *The World of Catholic Renewal 1540–1770.* Cambridge: Cambridge University Press, 1998.

Sedgwick, A. *Jansenism in Seventeenth-Century France.* Charlottesville, VA: University Press of Virginia, 1977.

Waugh, E. *Edmund Campion: Scholar, Priest, Hero, and Martyr.* Oxford: Oxford University Press, 1980. This is a piece of Catholic polemicizing by the English novelist Waugh—but perhaps little the worse for all that. This book is an easy read, and it raises—or resurrects—important issues from the period.

The Russian Orthodox Church

Hosking, G. *Russia: People & Empire 1552–1917.* London: HarperCollins, 1998. Though primarily a secular history, this gives good coverage of church affairs and religious issues.

Michels, G. B. *At War with the Church: Religious Dissent in Seventeenth-Century Russia.* Stanford, CA: Stanford University Press, 1999.

Chapter 6

The Thirty Years' War

Asch, R. G. *The Thirty Years War: The Holy Roman Empire and Europe, 1618–1648.* London: Palgrave Macmillan, 1997.

Bonney, R. *The Thirty Years' War 1618–1648.* Oxford: Osprey, 2002.

Parker, G. *The Thirty Years' War.* London: Routledge, 1997.

The English Civil Wars

Aylmer, G. E. *Rebellion or Revolution?* Oxford: Oxford University Press, 1986. Gives a good, entry-level account, along with some discussion of the historical debates, but religious issues are not Aylmer's central concern.

Fincham, K., ed. *The Early Stuart Church 1603–1642*. Stanford, CA: Stanford University Press, 1993. Gives the religious background to the war.

Foster, W. R. *The Church before the Covenants: The Church of Scotland 1596–1638*. Edinburgh: Scottish Academic Press, 1975.

Hill, C. *Puritanism and Revolution*. London: Mercury, 1962. Hill's work is concerned with the religious aspect of the war but views it—and everything else—in Marxist materialist terms. The same is inevitably true of his fascinating but perhaps misleading *The World Turned Upside Down* (Harmondsworth, England: Penguin, 1975), which looks at the turbulent world of Civil War–era sectarianism.

Manning, B., ed. *Politics, Religion and the English Civil War*. London: Edward Arnold, 1973. A useful collection of essays, though emanating from a period when it was professionally unwise to challenge fundamentally the prevailing "wisdom" of Marxists like Christopher Hill.

Mullan, D. G. *Scottish Puritanism 1590–1638*. Oxford: Oxford University Press, 2000.

Woodhouse, A. S. P., ed. *Puritanism and Liberty*. London: Everyman, 1986. Provides key documents from the period with minimal editorial comment.

Chapter 7

Ingle, H. L. *First among Friends: George Fox and the Creation of Quakerism*. New York: Oxford University Press, 1994.

Nolt, S. M. *A History of the Amish*. Intercourse, PA: Good Books, 1992.

Pearse, M. T. *The Great Restoration*. Carlisle, England: Paternoster, 2003.

Reay, B. *The Quakers and the English Revolution*. New York: St. Martin's Press, 1985. Reay's work inclines to the Marxist, materialist-reductionist school that blighted Western historiography during the Cold War, but he makes a lot of telling points along the way.

Tolmie, M. *The Triumph of the Saints: The Separate Churches of London 1616–1649*. Cambridge: Cambridge University Press, 1977.

White, B. R. *The English Baptists of the Seventeenth Century*. London: Baptist Historical Society, 1983.

———. *The English Separatist Tradition*. Oxford: Oxford University Press, 1971.

Williams, G. H. *The Radical Reformation*. Kirksville, MO: Sixteenth Century Journal Publishers, 1992, chapters 27–28, 30–31.

Chapter 8

Campbell, T. A. *The Religion of the Heart*. Columbia, SC: University of South Carolina Press, 1991, chapter 4.

Hamilton, J. T., and K. G. Hamilton. *History of the Moravian Church: The Renewed Unitas Fratrum 1722–1957*. Bethlehem, PA: Moravian Church in America, 1983, parts 1 and 2.

Lewis, A. J. *Zinzendorf the Ecumenical Pioneer*. London: SCM Press, 1962.

Stoeffler, F. E. *German Pietism during the Eighteenth Century*. Leiden, the Netherlands: E. J. Brill, 1973. The classic work on the subject.

Stoeffler, F. E., ed. *Continental Pietism and Early American Christianity*. Grand Rapids: Eerdmans, 1976.

Ward, W. R. *The Protestant Evangelical Awakening*. Cambridge: Cambridge University Press, 1992. A brilliant volume that experiments with the thesis that Anglo-American evangelicalism is not merely derived from continental Pietism but is all of a piece with it, in that most of continental Europe underwent an evangelical awakening during the first half of the eighteenth century. The argument doesn't quite work, but the material brought into play is so interesting that perhaps that shortcoming doesn't matter.

Weinlick, J. R. *Count Zinzendorf*. Bethlehem, PA: Moravian Church in America, 1984.

Chapter 9

Malcolm, N. *Bosnia: A Short History*. London: Macmillan, 1994.

———. *Kosovo: A Short History*. London: Macmillan, 1998. These two books by Malcolm and the following book by Mazower are among the very best of recent secular historical writing on the Balkans, in the process of which, all three discuss much material pertinent to church history in our period.

Mazower, M. *Salonica: City of Ghosts*. London: HarperCollins, 2004.

Runciman, S. *The Great Church in Captivity*. Cambridge: Cambridge University Press, 1968. This is a long-venerated work in this area.

Chapter 10

Dissent in Restoration England

Brown, R. *The English Baptists of the Eighteenth Century*. London: Baptist Historical Society, 1986.

Hill, C. *A Turbulent, Seditious, and Factious People: John Bunyan and His Church*. Oxford: Oxford University Press, 1989. A fascinating work, partly for its ostensible subject matter but also as a study in the part retraction, part stubborn defense of a Marxist historian in the evening of his life, writing as the collapse of Marxism around him is whipping the intellectual rug out from underneath him. The constant "translation" of spiritual and religious ideas into their "real" (so for a Marxist, social and economic) significance is interesting and illuminating by way of an alternative view of its topic.

Watts, M. *The Dissenters*. Oxford: Oxford University Press, 1978. Volume 1 is a brilliant, scholarly, and eminently readable survey of its subject, covering a period almost exactly coinciding with our own.

The Revocation of the Edict of Nantes and Its Aftermath

Joutard, P. "The Revocation of the Edict of Nantes: End or Renewal of French Calvinism?" In *International Calvinism 1541–1715*. Edited by M. Prestwich. Oxford: Oxford University Press, 1985.

The Tribulations of Scotland, 1660–1745

Drummond, A. L., and J. Bulloch. *The Scottish Church 1688–1843*. Edinburgh: Saint Andrew Press, 1973.

McIntosh, J. R. *Church and Theology in Enlightenment Scotland*. East Linton, Scotland: Tuckwell Press, 1998.

British Rule in Ireland

Clarke, A. "The Colonisation of Ulster and the Rebellion of 1641." In *The Course of Irish History*. Edited by T. W. Moody and F. X. Martin. Cork, Ireland: Mercier Press, 1994.

Greaves, R. L. *God's Other Children: Protestant Nonconformists and the Emergence of Denominational Churches in Ireland, 1660–1700*. Stanford, CA: Stanford University Press, 1997.

Rafferty, O. P. *Catholicism in Ulster 1603–1983*. London: C. Hurst, 1994.

Chapter 11

Bailey, G. A. *Art on the Jesuit Missions in Asia and Latin America 1542–1773*. Toronto, Canada: University of Toronto Press, 1999.

Burkholder, M. A., and L. L. Johnson. *Colonial Latin America*. 3rd ed. New York: Oxford University Press, 1998.

Goodpasture, H. McKennie, ed. *Cross and Sword: An Eyewitness History of Christianity in Latin America*. Maryknoll, NY: Orbis, 1989.

Greenleaf, R. E., ed. *The Roman Catholic Church in Colonial Latin America*. New York: Alfred A. Knopf, 1971.

Ruiz de Montoya, A. *The Spiritual Conquest Accomplished by the Religious of the Society of Jesus in the Provinces of Paraguay, Paraná, Uruguay and Tape*. Translated by C. J. McNaspy et al. St. Louis: Institute of Jesuit Sources, 1993.

Saeger, J. S. "Eighteenth-Century Guaycuruan Missions in Paraguay." In *Indian-Religious Relations in Colonial Spanish America*. Edited by S. E. Ramírez. Syracuse, NY: Syracuse University, 1989.

Schwaller, J. F., ed. *The Church in Colonial Latin America*. Wilmington, DE: Scholarly Resources, 2000.

Chapter 12

G. M. Marsden, Mark Noll, and Nathan Hatch are the premier exponents of American church history. Marsden's *Religion and American Culture*, Noll's *A History of Christianity in the United States and Canada*, and *Christianity in America*, edited by Noll, Hatch, G. M. Marsden, D. F. Wells, and J. D. Woodbridge are superbly competent, assured, well-crafted, and well-researched overviews. (See entries below.)

Bremer, F. J. *The Puritan Experiment: New England Society from Bradford to Edwards*. New York: St. Martin's Press, 1976.

Delbanco, A. *The Puritan Ordeal*. Cambridge: Harvard University Press, 1989.

Gaustad, E. S., ed. *A Documentary History of Religion in America to the Civil War*. 2 volumes. Grand Rapids: Eerdmans, 1982.

Hall, D. D. *Worlds of Wonder, Days of Judgment: Popular Religious Belief in Early New England*. Cambridge: Harvard University Press, 1990. This book looks at the more exciting aspects of spiritual life in the New World.

Jones, R. M. *The Quakers in the American Colonies*. London: Macmillan, 1911. Still one of the more useful starting points for its subject matter.

LaPlante, E. *American Jezebel*. New York: HarperCollins, 2004. A refreshing example of a study whose undoubted feminist concerns do not have the effect of grotesquely distorting the past or its characters. LaPlante gets it right: she understands Anne Hutchinson and her contemporaries very well and does not allow her own lack of sympathy for their faith to get in the way of her explication of it. In consequence, her comments about the role of gender are well-founded and would probably have been assented to by the principals themselves. An excellent read.

Lovelace, R. F. *The American Pietism of Cotton Mather: Origins of American Evangelicalism*. Grand Rapids: Christian University Press, 1979. This work presents the other side of the story told by LaPlante.

Marsden, G. M. *Religion and American Culture*. New York: Harcourt Brace Jovanovich, 1990.

McBeth, H. L. *The Baptist Heritage*. Nashville: Broadman, 1987.

McBeth, H. L. *A Sourcebook for Baptist Heritage*. Nashville: Broadman, 1990. Junior scholars should not be intimidated by the formidable size of McBeth's two companion volumes. They are very easy to read and not at all dry. The former provides a massive overview of Baptist history around the world, weighted—though not exaggeratedly so—toward American concerns. The latter provides an extremely useful compendium of documents and excerpts from documents, illustrative of that history, including the most important statements of faith.

Noll, M. *A History of Christianity in the United States and Canada*. Grand Rapids: Eerdmans, 1992.

Noll, M. A., N. O. Hatch, G. M. Marsden, D. F. Wells, and J. D. Woodbridge, eds. *Christianity in America*. Grand Rapids: Eerdmans, 1983.

Reinitz, R., ed. *Tensions in American Puritanism*. New York: John Wiley & Sons, 1970.

Speck, W. A., and L. Billington. "Calvinism in Colonial North America, 1630–1715." In *International Calvinism 1541–1715*. Edited by M. Prestwich. Oxford: Clarendon, 1986.

Staloff, D. *The Making of an American Thinking Class: Intellectuals and Intelligentsia in Puritan Massachusetts*. New York: Oxford University Press, 1998.

Chapter 13

Bonomi, P. U. *Under the Cope of Heaven: Religion, Society and Politics in Colonial America*. New York: Oxford University Press, 1986.

Gaustad, E. S. *Neither King nor Prelate: Religion and the New Nation 1776–1826*. Grand Rapids: Eerdmans, 1993.

Himmelfarb, G. *The Roads to Modernity*. New York: Alfred A. Knopf, 2004. This book looks at the wider picture. Gertrude Himmelfarb is a massively erudite and persuasive social historian, though of the neoconservative persuasion. This book, like her others, wears its learning lightly.

Marsden, G. M. *Religion and American Culture*. New York: Harcourt Brace Jovanovich, 1990.

Murphy, T. and R. Perin, eds. *A Concise History of Christianity in Canada*. Toronto: Oxford University Press, 1996.

Noll, M. *America's God: from Jonathan Edwards to Abraham Lincoln*. Oxford: Oxford University Press, 2002.

Westerkamp, M. J. *Women and Religion in Early America 1600–1850*. London: Routledge, 1999.

Chapter 14

Baker, F. *John Wesley and the Church of England*. London: Epworth Press, 1970. Deals with the difficult relationship between Wesley and his mother church (see also Brown-Lawson).

Bebbington, D. *Evangelicalism in Modern Britain: A History from the 1730s to the 1980s*. London: Unwin Hyman, 1989. Hailed upon its publication as a classic, and nothing has happened since to change or dent that assessment. If you read only one book in this area, read this one.

Bennett, R. *Howell Harris and the Dawn of Revival*. Bridgend, Wales: Evangelical Press of Wales, 1987. A reprinting of an early twentieth-century, hagiographical treatment.

Brown-Lawson, A. *Wesley and the Anglican Evangelicals*. Durham, England: Pentland Press, 1994. Deals with the difficult relationship between Wesley and his mother church (see also Baker).

Clarkson, G. E. *George Whitefield and Welsh Calvinistic Methodism*. Lampeter, Wales: Edwin Mellen Press, 1996.

Dallimore, A. *George Whitefield*. 2 volumes. Edinburgh: Banner of Truth Trust, 1970, 1980. Though somewhat hagiographical, this probably remains the standard work on the great evangelist.

Evans, E. *Daniel Rowland and the Great Evangelical Awakening in Wales*. Edinburgh: Banner of Truth Trust, 1985. This work suffers badly from the fact that, as the author admits from the outset, Rowland's papers were lost within a few years of his death. In consequence, the central character of this work remains somewhat remote throughout. These shortcomings being intrinsic to any possible study of Rowland, Evans's book is probably the best we have. But the reader should be wary, nonetheless.

Fawcett, A. *The Cambuslang Revival*. Edinburgh: The Banner of Truth Trust, 1971. There is little written on the Scottish aspect, but this work is one exception.

Hattersley, R. *A Brand from the Burning: A Life of John Wesley*. London: Little, Brown, 2003. This work can hardly fail to catch the eye because of the celebrity of its retired British politician, media-savvy author.

Heitzenrater, R. P. *Wesley and the People Called Methodists*. Nashville: Abingdon Press, 1995. Looks at the movement as a whole.

Jenkins, G. H. *Literature, Religion and Society in Wales, 1660–1730*. Cardiff: University of Wales Press, 1978. A useful and highly scholarly treatment of the background situation.

Marsden, G. M. *Jonathan Edwards: A Life*. New Haven: Yale University Press, 2003. This is likely to become the standard work on the great American revivalist.

Morgan, D. L. *The Great Awakening in Wales*. London: Epworth Press, 1988. One of the most scholarly treatments of the Welsh side of the story.

Rack, H. *Reasonable Enthusiast*. London: Epworth, 1989. If Methodism ever dies out, it will not be for lack of biographies of Wesley. Perhaps the best of recent years would include those by Rack and Tomkins. *Reasonable Enthusiast* is perhaps one of the most solid treatments.

Rohrer, J. R. *Keepers of the Covenant: Frontier Missions and the Decline of Congregationalism 1774–1818*. New York: Oxford University Press, 1995. This work covers the further consequences of the Great Awakening in America during our period.

Tomkins, S. *John Wesley*. Grand Rapids: Eerdmans, 2003. Of the Wesley biographies, this is a lot more fun than its rivals, being brief, rigorous, and not a little mischievous into the bargain.

Vickers, J. *Thomas Coke: Apostle of Methodism*. London: Epworth Press, 1969. Gives a biography of one of the chief protagonists of the Great Awakening in America.

Wigger, J. H. *Taking Heaven by Storm: Methodism and the Rise of Popular Christianity in America*. New York: Oxford University Press, 1998. As do Rohrer and Vickers, Wigger considers the consequences of the Great Awakening in America during our period and in particular deals with the meteoric rise of the Wesleyan movement in the decades after the American Revolution.

Chapter 15

Chadwick, O. *The Popes and European Revolution*. Oxford: Oxford University Press, 1981. Like everything by Owen Chadwick, this is superb, witty, and erudite. But it is voluminous.

Châtellier, L. *The Religion of the Poor: Rural Missions in Europe and the Formation of Modern Catholicism, c.1500–1800*. Cambridge: Cambridge University Press, 1997.

Cracraft, P. *The Church Reform of Peter the Great*. Stanford, CA: Stanford University Press, 1971.

Delumeau, J. *Catholicism between Luther and Voltaire*. London: Burns & Oates, 1977.

Gay, P. *The Enlightenment: A Comprehensive Anthology*. New York: Simon and Schuster, 1973.

———. *The Enlightenment: The Rise of Modern Paganism*. New York: W. W. Norton, 1966. Both books by Gay are authoritative and highly illuminating studies.

Heyer, F. *The Catholic Church from 1648 to 1870*. London: Adam and Charles Black, 1969. Provides a more compact discussion of the same topic covered at length by Chadwick in *The Popes and European Revolution*.

Martin, A. L. *The Jesuit Mind: The Mentality of an Elite in Early Modern France*. Ithaca, NY: Cornell University Press, 1988.

McManners, J. *French Ecclesiastical Society under the Ancien Régime*. Manchester, England: Manchester University Press, 1960.

Spellman, W. M. *The Latitudinarians and the Church of England, 1660–1700*. Athens, GA: University of Georgia Press, 1993.

Stark, R. *For the Glory of God: How Monotheism Led to Reformations, Science, Witch-Hunts and the End of Slavery*. Princeton, NJ: Princeton University Press, 2003. Sets out to slaughter the secularists' sacred cows. On the whole, Stark succeeds—though not without some major glitches in his own book.

Ward, W. R. *Christianity under the Ancien Régime*. Cambridge: Cambridge University Press, 1999.

NOTES

Preface

1. P. Jenkins, *The Next Christendom* (New York: Oxford University Press, 2002).

Chapter 1: Christendom Unraveling: The Scene in 1570 and a Glance Backward

1. Owen Chadwick, *The Reformation* (London: Penguin, 1990), 144.

2. The *filioque* was an addendum to the creed, which was adopted by the West but not by the East. According to it, the Holy Spirit proceeds not from the Father only but "from the Father and the Son." To this day, Eastern theologians, and others of both geographical persuasions whose livelihoods consist in expounding philosophically driven theologies, affect to find profound implications in this distinction. Whether these implications are utterly heretical or essential bastions of trinitarian doctrine seems to depend almost entirely, now as then, on the ethnic identity of the expositor's parents.

3. Chadwick, *The Reformation*, continues to provide a useful and lively introduction to this subject.

4. One of the more popular biographies of Luther is that of H. O. Oberman, *Luther: Man between God and the Devil* (London: HarperCollins, 1993).

5. The biography by G. R. Potter, *Zwingli* (Cambridge: Cambridge University Press, 1984), is excellent.

6. Calvin is, like Luther, well served by biographers. A. E. McGrath, *A Life of John Calvin* (Oxford: Blackwell, 1990), is sympathetic to its subject, considered, and clear. T. George, *Theology of the Reformers* (Nashville: Broadman, 1988), is accessible and provides excellent thumbnail biographies and introductions to the theology of Luther, Zwingli, Calvin—and also of Menno Simons.

7. M. T. Pearse, *The Great Restoration* (Carlisle: Paternoster, 1998), and in much greater detail and length, G. H. Williams, *The Radical Reformation* (Kirksville, MO: Sixteenth Century Journal Publishers, 1992), a massively informing work.

8. A. G. Dickens, *The Counter Reformation* (London: Thames and Hudson, 1968), 45–133, gives an excellent, illustrated introductory account of this period.

9. H. Troyat, *Ivan the Terrible* (London: Phoenix Press, 1984), 65–78, 85–86; G. Hosking, *Russia: People & Empire 1552–1917* (London: HarperCollins, 1997), 3–4, 9–11.

10. Bat Ye'or, *The Decline of Eastern Christianity under Islam: From Jihad to Dhimmitude* (Cranbury, NJ: Fairleigh Dickinson University Press, 1996), gives a masterly survey of this huge subject.

11. Y. Courbage and P. Fargues, *Christians and Jews under Islam* (New York: I. B. Tauris, 1998), 64.

12. Ibid., 57–90.

13. A. S. Atiya, *A History of Eastern Christianity* (London: Methuen, 1968), 365–67.

Chapter 2: Contested Territory: The Areas of Conflict between Protestantism and Catholicism (1570–1609)

1. Martin Luther, *Gesammelte Werke*, Weimarer Ausgabe, 127 vols., (Weimar, Germany: Hermann Böhlaus Nachfolger Weimar GmbH, 1883): 37.317.

2. *The European Reformations Sourcebook*, ed. C. Lindberg (Oxford: Blackwell, 2000), 270, http://info.abdn.ac.uk/history/documents/hi2510_frenchwars_religion.doc.

3. For a survey of this topic, see G. Parker, *The Dutch Revolt* (London: Penguin, 1990).

4. See M. P. Holt, *The French Wars of Religion, 1562–1629* (Cambridge: Cambridge University Press, 1995), for a survey of the conflict. M. Prestwich, "Calvinism in France," in *International Calvinism 1541–1715*, edited by M. Prestwich (Oxford: Oxford University Press, 1985), 71–108, gives a briefer introduction, while É. Labrousse, "Calvinism in France, 1598–1685," in the same book edited by Prestwich, 339–68, examines the aftermath of the wars.

5. For more details on Matija Vlačić, see chapter 4.

6. J. Gow and C. Carmichael, *Slovenia and the Slovenes* (London: Hurst, 2000), 63–64.

7. A. Zamoyski, *The Polish Way* (London: John Murray, 1987), 81–90.

8. Ibid., 83.

9. *The Catholic Encyclopedia*, s.v., "Mary Queen of Scots," http://www.newadvent.org/cathen/09764a.htm.

10. Ibid.

Chapter 3: Life on the Frontiers (1570–ca. 1610)

1. P. R. Magocsi, *A History of Ukraine* (Toronto: University of Toronto Press, 1996), 163–64.

2. Ibid.

3. Ibid., 166.

4. S. Huntington, *The Clash of Civilizations and the Remaking of World Order* (New York: Simon & Schuster, 1997).

5. Magocsi, *History of Ukraine*, 177.

6. R. Hakluyt, *Voyages and Discoveries* (London: Penguin, 1985), 164–70.

7. Ibid., 243–49.

8. M. Tanner, *Croatia: A Nation Forged in War* (New Haven: Yale University Press, 1997), 40.

9. The term "Indian"—rather than the frigid (though continentally more exact) "native American"—is used in these pages to describe the inhabitants of the Americas whom the European explorers found already in residence.

10. L. R. Grahn, "Guajiro Culture and Capuchin Evangelization," in *The New Latin American Mission History*, ed. E. Langner and R. H. Jackson (Lincoln, NE: University of Nebraska Press, 1995), 132.

11. A. Hastings, ed., *A World History of Christianity* (London: Cassell, 1999), 336.

12. M. A. Burkholder and L. L. Johnson, *Colonial Latin America*, 3rd ed. (New York: Oxford University Press, 1998), 97.

13. E. Isichei, *A History of Christianity in Africa* (London: SPCK, 1995), 64–65.

14. B. Sundkler and C. Steed, *A History of the Church in Africa* (Cambridge: Cambridge University Press, 2000), 48–49.

15. Ibid., 74–77.

16. Ibid., 71–72.

17. C. R. Boxer, *The Christian Century in Japan 1549–1650* (Berkeley: University of California Press, 1951), 58.

18. A. C. Ross, *A Vision Betrayed: The Jesuits in Japan and China 1542–1742* (Maryknoll, NY: Orbis, 1994), 2.

19. Bob Whyte, *Unfinished Encounter: China and Christianity* (London: Collins, 1988), 65.

20. Ibid., 63.

21. W. H. Clark, *The Church in China* (Philadelphia: Macrae Smith, 1973), 28.

22. Ross, *A Vision Betrayed*, 163.

23. Whyte, *Unfinished Encounter*, 49.

24. Ibid., 79–83.

25. Gregory the Great, *Letters*, XI.76.

26. J. G. Aragón, O. P., "The Controversy over Spanish Rule," in *Studies in Philippine Church History*, ed. G. H. Anderson (Ithaca, NY: Cornell University Press, 1969), 11.

27. R. E. Frykenberg, in *A History of Christianity*, ed. A. Hastings, 157–72, gives a good introductory account of this period.

28. R. E. Waterfield, *Christians in Persia* (London: George Allen & Unwin, 1973), 63.

29. R. Werner, W. Anderson, and A. Wheeler, *Day of Devastation, Day of Contentment: The History of the Sudanese Church across 2000 Years* (Nairobi, Kenya: Paulines Publications Africa), chapter 5 covers this ground well.

Chapter 4: The Conflicts within Churches: Protestants

1. Luther, *Gesammelte Werke*, Weimarer Ausgabe, vol. 26, 462.

2. See the whole text in L. J. Trinterud, ed., *Elizabethan Puritanism* (Oxford: Oxford University Press, 1971).

3. P. Collinson, *The Elizabethan Puritan Movement* (Oxford: Oxford University Press, 1967), 112–13.

4. This point should be stressed. We need to forget that the Presbyterians are now a separate denomination; during *this* period they were a brand of Puritan within the Church of England who wanted that church to be governed along presbyterian lines.

5. See W. M. Lamont, *Godly Rule: Politics and Religion 1603–1660* (London: Macmillan, 1969), 23–25.

6. N. Tyacke, *Anti-Calvinists: The Rise of English Arminianism c.1590–1640* (Oxford: Oxford University Press, 1990), remains one of the definitive studies of this development.

7. C. Bangs, *Arminius: A Study in the Dutch Reformation* (Eugene, OR: Wipf & Stock, 1998), is the standard overview of Arminius's life and thought.

8. The classic exchange in this particular debate is perhaps that between R. T. Kendall, *Calvin and English Calvinism to 1649* (Oxford: Oxford University Press, 1981), and P. Helm, *Calvin and the Calvinists* (Edinburgh: Banner of Truth, 1982).

Chapter 5: The Conflicts within Churches: Catholics and Orthodox

1. Dickens, *The Counter Reformation*, 161.

2. Ibid., 164.

3. R. Po-Chia Hsia, *The World of Catholic Renewal 1540–1770* (Cambridge: Cambridge University Press, 1998), 146.

4. Ibid., 148.

5. Cited in A. J. Freddoso, "Molina, Luis de," in E. Craig, ed., *Routledge Encyclopedia of Philosophy* (London: Routledge, 1998), http://www.nd.edu/~afreddos/papers/molina. htm.

6. J. M. Houston, ed., *The Mind on Fire: an Anthology of the Writings of Blaise Pascal* (Portland: Multnomah Press, 1989), 41.

7. "Pope Pius V's Bull against Elizabeth (1570)," Tudorhistory.org, http://tudorhistory. org/primary/papalbull.html.

8. In G. Cavendish and W. Roper, *Two Early Tudor Lives: The Life and Death of Cardinal Wolsey and the Life of Sir Thomas More*, ed. R. S. Sylvester and D. P. Harding (New Haven: Yale University Press, 1968).

9. *Encyclopedia Britannica*, 11th ed., *Online Encyclopedia*, s.v. "Sanders, Nicholas," http://encyclopedia.jrank.org/SAC_SAR/SANDERS_NICHOLAS_c_1530_1581_.html.

10. E. Waugh, *Edmund Campion: Scholar, Priest, Hero, and Martyr* (Oxford: Oxford University Press, 1980), 190–91.

11. A. Dures, *English Catholicism 1558–1642* (Harlow, England: Longman, 1983), 36.

12. Ivan's nickname *Grozny* (the Terrible) is often explained as referring to the archaic meaning of that term: awesome, or perhaps awe-full. A brief acquaintance with the details of his career, however, confirms that, in his case, the applicability of the title has survived the vicissitudes of linguistic drift with some ease.

13. Hosking, *Russia*, 64–74.

Chapter 6: Meltdown: The Cataclysm of 1618–1648

1. H. J. C. Von Grimmelshausen, *The Adventurous Simplicissimus. Being the description of the life of a strange vagabond named Melchior Sternfels von Fuchshaim*, A. T. S. Goodrick, trans. (New York, 1912), chap. 4.

2. Ibid.

3. Ibid.

4. Ibid.

Chapter 7: Fractions of Fractions: The Progress of Sectarianism

1. Thieleman J. van Braght, *Martyrs Mirror* (Scottdale, PA: Herald Press, 1950), 12.

2. Cited in B. R.White, *The English Separatist Tradition* (Oxford: Oxford University Press, 1971), 24.

3. C. Burrage, *Early English Dissenters*, vol. 2 (Cambridge: Cambridge University Press), 15–18.

4. A. Peel and L. H. Carlson, eds., *The Writings of Robert Harrison and Robert Browne* (London: George Allen and Unwin Ltd., 1953), 162.

5. Ibid., 169.

6. *True Confession*, cited in W. L. Lumpkin, ed., *Baptist Confessions of Faith* (Valley Forge, PA: Judson Press, 1969), 82–97.

7. Ibid.

8. Pearse, *The Great Restoration*, 134–38.

9. Williams, *The Radical Reformation*, 1094–95.

10. Ibid., 1119.

Chapter 8: The Rise of Pietism

1. J. Boehme, *Of Heaven and Hell* (1624), http://kingsgarden.org/English/Organizations/OM.GB/Boehme/HeavenAndHell.html.
2. Ibid.
3. P. C. Erb, ed., *Pietists: Selected Writings* (London: SPCK, 1983), 57.
4. Ibid.
5. Ibid., 56.
6. Ibid., 105–106.

Chapter 9: The Cross, the Crescent, and the Star: Christians and Jews under Ottoman Rule in the Balkans

1. S. Runciman, *The Great Church in Captivity* (Cambridge: Cambridge University Press, 1968), 189–91.
2. N. Malcolm, *Bosnia: A Short History* (London: Macmillan, 1994), 53–54.
3. M. Mazower, *Salonica: City of Ghosts* (London: HarperCollins, 2004), 46–65.
4. A. Matkovski, *A History of the Jews in Macedonia* (Skopje, Macedonia: Macedonian Review Editions, 1982), 37–67.
5. Runciman, *The Great Church in Captivity*, 201.
6. N. Malcolm, *Kosovo: A Short History* (London: Macmillan, 1998), 133–34.
7. Runciman, *The Great Church in Captivity*, 208–12.
8. Ibid., 215–18.
9. Malcolm, *Kosovo*, 129–30.
10. Ibid., 131–32.
11. C. A. Frazee, *The Orthodox Church and Independent Greece 1821–1852*, 9.
12. Runciman, *The Great Church in Captivity*, 364–66.

Chapter 10: Misruling One Another

1. H. L. McBeth, The Baptist Heritage (Nashville: Broadman, 1987), 175.
2. Ibid., 162–63.
3. Cited in M. Watts, *The Dissenters*, vol. 1 (Oxford: Oxford University Press, 1978), 388.
4. J. H. S. Burleigh, *A Church History of Scotland* (Oxford: Oxford University Press, 1960), 236–37.
5. A. Clarke, "The Colonisation of Ulster and the Rebellion of 1641," in *The Course of Irish History*, ed. T. W. Moody and F. X. Martin (Cork, Ireland: Mercier Press, 1994), 198.
6. *The Catholic Encyclopedia*, s.v. "Peter Talbot," http://www.newadvent.org/cathen/14432c.htm.

Chapter 11: Latin America

1. Burkholder and Johnson, *Colonial Latin America*, 204.
2. R. E. Greenleaf, ed., *The Roman Catholic Church in Colonial Latin America* (New York: Alfred A. Knopf, 1971), 140–47.
3. A. Ruiz de Montoya, *The Spiritual Conquest Accomplished by the Religious of the Society of Jesus in the Provinces of Paraguay, Paraná, Uruguay and Tape*, trans. C. J. McNaspy et al. (St. Louis: Institute of Jesuit Sources, 1993), 85–86.
4. K. Mills, "The Limits of Religious Coercion in Midcolonial Peru," in *The Church in Colonial Latin America*, ed. J. F. Schwaller (Wilmington, DE: Scholarly Resources, 2000), 150.

5. H. McKennie Goodpasture, ed., *Cross and Sword: An Eyewitness History of Christianity in Latin America* (Maryknoll, NY: Orbis, 1989), 63-66.

6. Ibid., 83-85.

7. Ibid.

8. For more on las Casas, see chapter 3.

9. José de Anchieta, cited in Goodpasture, *Cross and Sword*, 51-52.

10. Ibid.

11. About 8 million slaves were imported into the Americas as a whole during the same period. Compare that with about 350,000 slaves who were imported into British North America up to the time of the American Revolution. (U.S. numbers rose sharply after the 1790s until the Civil War.) See Burkholder and Johnson, *Colonial Latin America*, 127.

12. Goodpasture, *Cross and Sword*, 58-59.

13. Burkholder and Johnson, *Colonial Latin America*, 261.

14. Goodpasture, *Cross and Sword*, 102.

15. Hastings, *A World History of Christianity*, 337.

16. Cited in G. A. Bailey, *Art on the Jesuit Missions in Asia and Latin America 1542-1773* (Toronto, Canada: University of Toronto Press, 1999), 42.

17. Goodpasture, *Cross and Sword*, 48.

18. Hastings, *A World History of Christianity*, 337-38.

19. G. Pendle, *A History of Latin America* (Harmondsworth, England: Penguin, 1976), 62.

20. Goodpasture, *Cross and Sword*, 48.

21. Bailey, *Art on the Jesuit Missions*, 147.

22. Ibid., 242.

23. J. S. Saeger, "Eighteenth-Century Guaycuruan Missions in Paraguay," in *Indian-Religious Relations in Colonial Spanish America*, ed. S. E. Ramírez, (Syracuse, NY: Syracuse University, 1989), 55-86.

Chapter 12: North America: Toleration and Nontoleration

1. Cited in M. T. Pearse, *The Great Restoration*, 281.

2. E. S. Gaustad, ed., *A Documentary History of Religion in America to the Civil War*, vol. 1, 2nd ed. (Grand Rapids: Eerdmans, 1982), 133-34.

3. Ibid.

4. W. A. Speck and L. Billington, "Calvinism in Colonial North America, 1630-1715," in Prestwich, *International Calvinism*, 265.

5. E. LaPlante, *American Jezebel* (New York: HarperCollins, 2004), 130.

6. I. Mather, *The Order of the Gospel* (1701), cited in Speck and Billington, "Calvinism in Colonial North America," in Prestwich, *International Calvinism*, 265-66.

7. M. A. Noll, *A History of Christianity in the United States and Canada* (Grand Rapids: Eerdmans, 1992), 49-50.

8. A. S. P. Woodhouse, ed., *Puritanism and Liberty* (London: Everyman, 1986), 266.

9. Roger Williams, *The Bloudy Tenent of Persecution, for the Cause of Conscience, Discussed in a Conference Between Truth and Peace* (London: 1848), 375.

10. Woodhouse, *Puritanism and Liberty*, 266.

11. Cited in R. Reinitz, ed., *Tensions in American Puritanism* (New York: John Wiley & Sons, 1970), 109.

12. Ibid., 111.

13. Peel and Carlson, *The Writings of Robert Harrison and Robert Browne*, 162.

14. W. Penn, *No Cross, No Crown* (London, 1669), 4.22, 23.

15. W. Penn, *Select Works* (London, 1825), i.163-65.

16. A. B. Benson, ed., *Peter Kalm's Travels in North America* (New York: Dover Publications, 1966), ii. 649–50. I am grateful to my former student Austin Stevenson for unearthing this gorgeous quotation.

17. McBeth, *The Baptist Heritage*, 147.

Chapter 13: North America: Coming to Terms with Pluralism

1. J. P. Dolan, *In Search of an American Catholicism* (New York: Oxford University Press, 2002), 14.

2. Cited in M. Noll et al., *Christianity in America*, 54.

3. Cited in Noll, *History of Christianity in the United States and Canada*, 126.

4. Answers.com, http://www.answers.com/topic/list-of-united-states-presidential-religious-affiliations?method=22, provides a full list.

5. P. U. Bonomi, *Under the Cope of Heaven: Religion, Society and Politics in Colonial America* (New York: Oxford University Press, 1986), 203–5.

6. See chapter 11.

7. G. M. Marsden, *Religion and American Culture* (New York: Harcourt Brace Jovanovich, 1990), 30.

8. For a discussion of this topic, readers who prefer their blood pressure ratcheted nice and high should consult my *Why the Rest Hates the West* (London: SPCK, 2003; Downers Grove, IL: IVP, 2004), chap. 3.

9. G. Himmelfarb, *The Roads to Modernity* (New York: Alfred A. Knopf, 2004), 204–5, 208, 210–11.

10. M. Noll, *America's God: from Jonathan Edwards to Abraham Lincoln* (Oxford: Oxford University Press, 2002), 64.

11. Admittedly, their persecution by Christian monarchies tended to make Baptists at least latent supporters of secular—and so presumably nonmonarchical—states.

12. See McBeth, *The Baptist Heritage*, 260–62.

13. E. S. Gaustad, *Neither King nor Prelate: Religion and the New Nation 1776–1826* (Grand Rapids: Eerdmans, 1993), 161–74.

14. Quotations given in M. A. Noll et al., eds., *Christianity in America*, 140.

15. Ibid., 138–39.

Chapter 14: The Great Awakening

1. Cited in R. Bennett, *Howell Harris and the Dawn of Revival* (Bridgend, Wales: Evangelical Press of Wales, 1987), 20.

2. Ibid., 25.

3. Ibid.

4. Ibid., 26.

5. J. Wesley, *Journal*, 24 January 1738.

6. Ibid., 24 May 1738.

7. Cited in A. Dallimore, *George Whitefield*, vol. 1 (Edinburgh: Banner of Truth, 1970), 301.

8. Ibid., 132.

9. John Wesley to James Hutton, Bristol, June 7, 1739, in *The Letters of John Wesley*, vol. 1, ed. J. Telford (London: Epworth Press, 1931), http://wesley.nnu.edu/john_wesley/letters/1739.htm.

10. J. Wesley, *Sermons*, 40.26–27.

11. John Wesley, journal entry, August 15, 1750, http://www.godrules.net/library/wesley/274wesley_b5.htm and John Wesley to The Lord Bishop of Gloucester, November 26, 1762, "A Letter to the Right Reverend," http://www.godrules.net/library/wesley/274wesley_i8.htm.

12. G. Whitefield, *Letters of George Whitefield 1734–1742* (Edinburgh: Banner of Truth, 1976), 211–12.

13. Charles Wesley's better-known hymns include: "And Can It Be That I Should Gain," "Christ the Lord Is Risen Today," "Come, Thou Long Expected Jesus," "Hark! the Herald Angels Sing," "Jesus, Lover of My Soul," "Love Divine, All Loves Excelling," "O For a Thousand Tongues to Sing," "Rejoice, the Lord Is King," and "Soldiers of Christ, Arise."

14. M. Noll et al., *Christianity in America*, 112–13.

15. O. E. Winslow, ed., *Jonathan Edwards: Basic Writings* (New York: New American Library, 1966), xx.

16. Noll, *History of Christianity in the United States and Canada*, 120.

17. Ibid., 140.

18. Cited in E. Roberts and R. G. Gruffydd, *Revival and Its Fruit* (Bridgend, Wales: Evangelical Library of Wales, 1981), 35.

19. Cited in McBeth, *The Baptist Heritage*, 228.

20. This case has been ably made by Geraint H. Jenkins in respect to Wales but, *mutatits mutandis*, it holds good for England too. See, e.g., G. H. Jenkins, *Literature, Religion and Society in Wales, 1660–1730* (Cardiff: University of Wales Press, 1978), 305–9; G. H. Jenkins, *Protestant Dissenters in Wales 1639–1689* (Cardiff: University of Wales Press, 1992), 1–8.

Chapter 15: Reason and Power: Rationalist Theology and the Divine Right of Kings

1. J. Calvin, *Institutes of the Christian Religion*, book 1, chapter 6, sections/chapters 3, 4; book 1, chapter 7, sections/chapters 1, 2.

2. K. L. Sprunger, *Trumpets from the Tower: English Puritan Printing in the Netherlands 1600–1640* (Leiden, Netherlands: E. J. Brill, 1994), 8–9.

3. R. Stark, *For the Glory of God: How Monotheism Led to Reformations, Science, Witch-Hunts and the End of Slavery* (Princeton, NJ: Princeton University Press, 2003), 166.

4. Cited in ibid., 172.

5. Ibid., 171.

6. This is not so absurd as modern Westerners might assume. Even in the former U.S.S.R., debate was possible if the right form of words were used. Readers in many societies have shown greater mental agility at "reading between the lines" than is exhibited by some current Westerners in reading the lines themselves.

7. Cited in ibid., 165.

8. Ibid., 167, citing Peter Gay, *The Enlightenment: The Rise of Modern Paganism* (New York: W. W. Norton, 1966), 23.

9. A. Plummer, *The Church of England in the Eighteenth Century* (London: Methuen, 1910), 109.

10. J. Pelikan, *The Christian Tradition*, vol. 1 (Chicago: University of Chicago Press, 1971), 7.

11. Gay, *The Enlightenment*, 326, 344.

12. Cited in ibid., 345.

13. Bernard Mandeville, *The Fable of the Bees; or, Private Vices, Publick Benefits* (1714), cited in D. Wootton, ed., *Divine Right and Democracy* (Harmondsworth, England: Penguin, 1986), 494–95.

14. Cited in L. Damrosch, *Fictions of Reality in the Age of Hume and Johnson* (Madison, WI: University of Wisconsin Press, 1989), 148.

15. P. Gay, *The Enlightenment: A Comprehensive Anthology* (New York: Simon and Schuster, 1973), 304. "Never show a child what he cannot see. . . . Talk to him of what he knows he can use now. . . . Let there be no comparison with other children, no rivalry, no competition, not even in running races. I would far rather he did not learn anything than

have him learn it through jealousy or self-conceit. . . . I hate books; they only teach us to talk about things we know nothing about" (ibid., 313). Of such teachings have several hundred million principled ignoramuses been made.

16. Cited in C. V. Wedgwood, *The Trial of Charles I* (London: Fontana, 1970), 217.

17. P. Cracraft, *The Church Reform of Peter the Great* (Stanford, CA: Stanford University Press, 1971), 209.

18. W. R. Ward, *Christianity under the Ancien Régime* (Cambridge: Cambridge University Press, 1999), 198.

19. Ibid., 35–36.

20. Ibid., 32.

Chapter 16: The Arts

1. T. C. Work, "'Iconomy': A Rule Theory for Images in the Church," TelfordWork.net, 1999, http://www.westmont.edu/~work/articles/iconomy.html.

2. Ibid.

3. Cited in A. Wilson-Dickson, *A Brief History of Christian Music* (Oxford: Lion, 1992), 96.

4. J. Herl, *Worship Wars in Early Lutheranism* (New York: Oxford University Press, 2004), 67.

5. Cited in Wilson-Dickson, *A Brief History of Christian Music*, 101.

6. J. D. Witvliet, *Worship Seeking Understanding: Windows into Christian Practice* (Grand Rapids: Baker, 2003), 224–25.

7. Wilson-Dickson, *A Brief History of Christian Music*, 101–2.

8. G. H. Williams and A. M. Mergal, eds., *Spiritual and Anabaptist Writers* (Philadelphia: Westminster Press, 1957), 75–76.

9. An earlier version of their work had appeared in 1549, during the reign of King Edward VI. P. Westermeyer, *Te Deum: The Church and Music* (Minneapolis: Augsburg Fortress, 1998), 170–71.

10. Cited in A. Wilson-Dickson, *A Brief History of Christian Music*, 120.

11. Westermeyer, *Te Deum*, 239–41.

12. Ludwig van Beethoven quoted by Edward Schulz, "A Day with Beethoven," *The Harmonicum* (1824), cited in "Handelian Anecdotes," G. F. Handel, http://gfhandel.org.

13. Westermeyer, *Te Deum*, 188, 205.

14. J. Waterworth, ed. and trans., *The canons and decrees of the sacred and oecumenical Council of Trent* (London: Dolman, 1848), 235–36.

15. Hsia, *The World of Catholic Renewal 1540–1770*, 159.

16. Bailey, *Art on the Jesuit Missions*, 59.

17. Ibid., 75.

18. Ibid., 105–9, 137–41.

19. Ibid., 145.

GLOSSARY

alumbrados. Spanish term meaning people who are "enlightened" or "illuminated," in a spiritual sense.

beatas. Spanish term meaning women who were "blessed": in particular it refers to women living separated, devout lives in their own homes.

boyars. Russian aristocrats.

Bruderhof. German term, referring to the place where "brethren," i.e. Hutterite Anabaptists, lived in community.

catholicos. A primate in the Eastern churches.

Consensus Sandomiriensis. A synod of 1570, uniting Polish Protestants.

conversos. Spanish Muslims who had been converted—either actually or merely outwardly—to Catholicism after the expulsion of the Moors from Spain in the late Middle Ages.

Discalced. "Without shoes": the name given to particularly rigorous orders of sixteenth-century monks and nuns.

Donation of Constantine. An eighth-century forgery, which purported to be written by the Roman Emperor Constantine, giving absolute secular authority to the pope. It was generally accepted as authentic until the fifteenth-century scholar Lorenzo Valla exposed it as spurious.

Essenes. A Jewish ascetic movement around the time of Christ. The Dead Sea scrolls were produced by members of this community.

ex opere operato. Latin term meaning "working by virtue of the work wrought"; in particular, a sacrament has its spiritual effect by virtue of having been performed correctly and is not affected by the state of grace (or absence thereof) of the person—especially the priest—performing it.

forensic justification. The name for the Protestant Reformers' doctrine of the process whereby a person is justified: righteousness is imputed to him or her, in a legal sense, by virtue of the merits of Christ's death.

Glagolitic. The alphabet designed by Cyril and Methodius in the ninth century, in order to write down the liturgy and Scriptures in the speech of the Slavs. Cyrillic script (named for Cyril) was later developed out of Glagolitic. The original script itself continued to be used for some purposes, especially in Croatia, until the nineteenth century.

landgrave. German nobleman, roughly the equivalent of a count.

Mar. In the Indian church, saint—hence Mar Thoma, after the apostle Thomas—or title adopted by patriarch.

Padroado. Powers of religious patronage given by the pope to the King of Portugal over episcopal sees in India.

philosophes. The French philosophical-political writers of the eighteenth century.

rederijkerkamers. Chambers of Rhetoric, which put on plays and acted as venues for the exchange of ideas, especially in the promotion of biblicist doctrines during the period of the Reformation.

Ritterakademie. A college for the sons of the German nobility to study sciences, statecraft, and languages. The institution of this type mentioned here is that of Brandenburg.

Rus'. A term that denotes the early Slavic peoples, and their Scandinavian rulers, who lived in what is now Ukraine during the early and central Middle Ages. They and their kingdom were scattered by the Mongol invasions. Modern Russians and Ukrainians both claim direct descent of their nations from the Rus'.

sansculottes. French term meaning "without knee breeches"—the ragged-trousered poor (or often, those who merely presented themselves as such) who formed the most truculent backbone of the French Revolution.

secular clergy. Ordinary clergy who do not live according to a monastic or other rule. (Those who do live by such a rule are "regulars".)

Sigan-Fu Stone. Sometimes called also the Nestorian Stone; this eighth-century monument, rediscovered in 1625, has extensive inscriptions, giving information about the bringing of Christianity to China in the seventh century.

Stauropegial. Also, Stavropegial, literally means "fixture of a cross": in Eastern Orthodoxy, it is a term used of a monastery that is directly under the authority of the primate of a church—and especially those that owed canonical allegiance to the Patriarch of Constantinople—rather than under the local diocesan bishop.

szlachta. Polish nobility.

Untermenschen. Nazi term for "subhumans." Used in the preface to this book sarcastically, to pillory overheated nationalisms; its nearest equivalent might be more like "scarcely human ethnics."

Vlach/Vlachs. A Balkan language and the people who speak it. The Vlachs are thought to be descended from the Romanized inhabitants of the Balkans; their speech is generally considered to be related to Romanian. The Vlachs were pastoral people who maintained their life and culture by staying away from heavily settled areas. Unsurprisingly, their language has been seriously eroded in recent centuries, and many have been absorbed into Slavic and other larger population groups. A number remain in Macedonia and elsewhere.

INDEX

Page number in italics refer to maps and illustrations.

Printed and bound by CPI Group (UK) Ltd, Croydon, CR0 4YY

13/04/2025

14656477-0003